**Political
Campaign
Management**

Political Campaign Management

A Systems Approach

Arnold Steinberg

Lexington Books
D.C. Heath and Company
Lexington, Massachusetts
Toronto   London

Library of Congress Cataloging in Publication Data

Steinberg, Arnold.
  Political campaign management.

  Includes bibliographical references and index.
  1. Campaign management.   2. Campaign management—
United States.   I. Title.
JF2112.C3S74   658'.91'32901   75-36014
ISBN 0-669-00374-3

Copyright © 1976 by D.C. Heath and Company

Published simultaneously in Canada

Printed in the United States of America

International Standard Book Number: 0-669-00374-3

Library of Congress Catalog Card Number: 75-36014

Contents

List of Figures

List of Tables

Foreword

The art and practice of politics is as old as time itself. The practitioners of politics and public affairs have frequently written about their own experiences and campaigns. Many have been the subjects of biographical research. Large number of "How to Do It Books" have been written. The precinct is rediscovered about every five years. The processes of political campaigns have been written about from almost everybody's perspective. The campaigning process has been reformed, re-reformed and re-re-reformed, and today it has been legislated almost to total confusion. However, to the best of my knowledge, no one before has approached a campaign with the application of management theory. Therefore, Mr. Steinberg is to be congratulated on undertaking this task. It is an exceedingly valuable contribution to the literature of political science as well as management application. All serious practitioners of the art, as well as students of politics, will find this book an important part of their library. Those who desire to try to understand the political campaign in a sensible and rational manner must read this book. I am sure that it will be discussed and evaluated in many different ways by both practitioners and academia, but its contribution is clearly present in its systematic approach.

F. Clifton White

Mr. White, co-founder and former president of the American Association of Political Consultants, has counselled candidates for nearly every elective office, including the Presidency.

Foreword

Arnold Steinberg has performed a useful service for every person involved in politics.

Too often we approach campaigns purely on the basis of emotion; he injects an element of logic that all too often is lacking.

In today's complex political systems, both prior to and after the election has taken place, management skills are required—and frequently missing.

In this book, Arnold Steinberg has reduced these political complexities to terms which combine the best elements of common sense and managerial technology. Everyone who tries to run a political campaign, or a government, will benefit from the knowledge compressed in these pages.

Joseph Napolitan

Mr. Napolitan is an international public affairs consultant. He has managed campaigns and provided counsel for Democratic Party candidates for President, Senator, Governor, Congress, and other offices.

Preface

In the last of the free-wheeling, big-spending elections, candidates for House and Senate seats used almost $74 million in their campaigns last year. . . .

—Associated Press
April 16, 1975

Political campaigns not only exert a major impact on American life by providing the means by which elected officials are chosen. They are also big business. Regardless of the recent trends in reform legislation, political campaigns are likely to remain big business for campaign managers and management firms, survey researchers and pollsters, advertising agencies, television producers, direct mail fund raisers, etc. This book examines the management of the political campaign organization, the structure devised to elect the candidate, and its components.

This is not a political science book. It is not a business or finance text. It is an examination of the relevance of management principles to the operation of a political campaign. It is a theoretical treatment with practical application, but it is not a "how to" manual of methodology. Although there is no single authoritative "how to" text, the major political parties produce a variety of manuals on the *mechanics* of a political campaign. None of these manuals, however precise and methodical their treatment of a particular facet of political campaigning, provides a unified overview of the organization. This study seeks to provide a consistent, systematic view of the political campaign organization.

Examples and illustrations are frequently cited throughout the text. Their purpose is to illustrate the relevance of principles or theories. In many cases, subjects are treated superficially, e.g., fund raising, press, advertising, direct mail, scheduling. Each of these fields and others discussed in the text could be the subject of a large volume. Such a volume would likely include lengthy discussions of methodology, "nuts-and-bolts" details, logistics and alternative means of accomplishing particular ends. This study is principally concerned with the broader questions:

1. Why do we need political campaigns? (chapter 1)
2. What is the nature of the political environment? (chapter 2)
3. What kind of organizational theories are relevant to the political campaign organization? (chapter 3)

4. What is the meaning of a systems view of political campaigns? (chapter 4)
5. What are the behavioral implications of a political campaign? (chapter 5)
6. How should a political campaign approach its finance problems? (chapter 6)
7. Why is the political campaign a marketing organization? (chapter 7)
8. How should the political campaign manager make decisions? (chapter 8)

In answering these questions many examples are drawn from past Presidential elections, including the recent campaigns reported so well by Theodore F. White. Because Presidential campaigns are dramatic and visible, and the organizational unit is larger, they are more interesting and easier to study. Many references to statewide, Congressional, and local contests are also included. Generally, they reflect my own experiences since 1963 as a volunteer, staff member, or consultant involved in many types of campaigns in different states. The assumptions and selection of topics in this book reflect the biases of those years.

Although this text is most applicable to Presidential and statewide campaigns rather than lower level campaigns limited by modest budgets and the inappropriateness of large scale television, media, and scheduling plans, *any* political campaign requires a systematic view. This unified perspective does not treat actions or decisions in a void but as part of the entire organization, its activities, and its relationship to the environment. The principles outlined here are identical for any campaign, but they must be adapted to different circumstances.

There are several important limitations to this text. First, federal, state, and local legislation relevant to campaigns and their adjudication in the courts is altering the legal aspects of the political environment. No text can possibly keep pace with the latest court decisions. Second, the two-party political environment is accepted as given, although the strength of the Democratic and Republican parties is generally declining. The present turbulent environment cannot guarantee the indefinite existence of these two parties as the major parties, despite both traditional and legal biases favoring them.

The third limitation is simply that the systems approach is a way of looking at things as much as it is a way of doing things. Precisely because open systems campaigns are flexible and not intransigent, they are innovative and adaptive. Hence as the political environment continues to change in the years ahead, methods will change, requiring new illustrations and examples and even modifications of theories. Thus readers' reactions and ideas are welcome and will be appreciated.

Many campaign managers have been and will be eminently successful without reading this text. Many readers of this text may never win a campaign. Many reasons account for this. First, many managers approach their tasks systematically, i.e., always conscious of the whole campaign and the environment, without being conscious of systems theory *per se*. Second, many readers who understand systems theory may lack the personal qualities and managerial ability to lead a campaign. Third, there is no way to teach creativity, inspiration, or strategy.

Fourth, there is no substitute for a minimum amount of practical experience in each phase of campaigning.

The questions analyzed here pertain to structure and organizational theory, behavioral theory, and quantitative theory. The order of topics chosen emphasizes the environmental context in which the political campaign exists. Special attention is given to behavioral theory because my experience has convinced me that managers are deficient in this area.

Finally, I acknowledge the charge that undue emphasis on marketing, media, surveys, and quantitative theory "dehumanize" the campaign. As will hopefully become apparent, especially in the behavioral sections, this book seeks to make the political campaign organization more efficient so it can better do its job of electing the candidate. Within that context, it seeks to realize human potential and volunteer assistance, not supplant the human element with mechanization.

**Political
Campaign
Management**

1

Government, Politics, and the Political Campaign

Ever since Aristotle's time, the notion has been widely shared that a political relationship in some way involves authority, ruling or power.

—Robert A. Dahl

Modern Political Analysis

The modern political campaign is the method by which citizens in a democracy decide who shall govern them. Politics is "the practice or profession of conducting political affairs," i.e., "exercising or seeking power in the governmental or public affairs of a state, municipality, etc." It is also the "use of intrigue or strategy in obtaining any position of power or control, as in a business, university, etc."[1] No one would condemn the *idea* of planning or formulating a strategy to achieve a goal, without some reference to the goal itself. Strategy is one thing; intrigue is quite another. In politics, the motive of power is suspect; the means of attaining power is also political, and also suspect. Americans are even more suspicious than most people of the motivation for power.[2] The legacy of Watergate is the escalation of natural skepticism and innate suspicion of "politicians" to a profound distrust. Watergate has become a code word for government secrecy, favoritism, and privilege, big money and bribery, corruption and kickbacks, and the lust for power.

Besides the historical roots of the American Revolution, there is another, fundamental reason for suspicion of political leaders or public officials. It is the universal reason for awe, suspicion, and even fear of political leaders: they are more powerful than even the most powerful leaders in business or the university. The dictionary can define "politics" to include the means of attaining power in private institutions; but in government, "politics" is also the end. It includes the legal monopoly over the use of force.[3] No private citizen, no leader of any corporation, educational institution or any other private organization, is legally entitled to use force, except under carefully defined circumstances, precisely, the classic case of self-defense. Individuals may fear their peers who seek power in any organization, but they have special cause to fear those who seek *political* power, within which resides the exclusive, monopoly power of coercion.

The dictionary definition of politics is noteworthy for its applications beyond government, political campaigns, and public affairs. Any use of strategy or intrigue to gain ascendancy, control or, to use the more emotive term, power, is necessarily political. Business, labor, agriculture, foundations, the media, the

1

academy, religion—no sector is immune from the political impulse.[a] The political campaign is the formal and explicit effort, as well organized as possible, to secure power. But it is hardly the only example that could be cited; it is simply the most visible. For purposes of this book, the political campaign refers to a managed, organized effort to be *nominated, elected,* or *re-elected* to public office. This definition is not concerned with a political campaign to secure a position within the private sector.

The universal application of politics, meaning political skills, is illustrated by considering its fundamental elements. (a) There is a strategy, an appeal to issues, means of communication and persuasion, and a constituency. The professor seeking tenure and the religious leader seeking a more prestigious pulpit each define a constituency to which they must appeal. (b) The strategist must discern and discriminate among seemingly conflicting priorities to accomplish the overall goal. There is no unique path to achieve the political objective. The intangible human quality of judgment is critical. (c) Sometimes, only experience can teach the practical lessons of politics. Yet certain individuals can succeed with little experience, while other individuals can never succeed, regardless of the breadth and depth of experience. (d) Superior interpersonal skills are required. These include the ability to get along with people, to recruit and motivate followers, to inspire loyalty, to select and place people in positions best suited to their aptitude, interests, and talents—in short, the ability to lead others.

Needless to say, good judgment and keen interpersonal skills are recognized as valuable in any profession or employment, although some professions place a premium on certain attributes over others. The major difference between political campaigns for public office and political campaigns for objectives within the private sector is visibility. The most vehement detractors of politicians may themselves, within their own spheres of influence, practice politics in the most deceitful way. In the case of political campaigns for public office, the candidate is on display. He also appoints a manager who is in overall charge of this visible, public effort to acquire power.

The political environment, which is more fully discussed in chapter 2, must be understood in terms of the inextricable relationship between government and politics. The relationship does not concern the general definition of politics (which includes business, labor, education, and other fields) but the narrow focus of choosing who shall govern. Perhaps the word "government" has a more favorable connotation than the word "politics." Nevertheless, under the present system of democracy, leaders are chosen, for better or worse, by the electoral process, which requires political campaigns to inform the electorate of the

---

[a]During my experience on Capitol Hill I often addressed visiting groups. Professors questioned the value of seniority in Congress but defended the value of tenure in the academy; clergymen raised the issue of abuse of power, but they sought federal grants for their own pet projects.

choices.[b] Politicians may wish to be perceived as public servants or as statesmen, but they must act politically to get elected to office. Once elected, they may endeavor to be perceived as "above politics," and they may, to some extent, succeed; but they inevitably act politically or they are unlikely to be re-elected.

Political campaigns are now big business. The President, the Vice President, one hundred United States Senators, 435 United States Congressmen: there are usually two candidates (or more) for each office, not counting the primary elections. There are fifty states—each with Governors and each with one or two houses in the legislature. State senators, assemblymen, county supervisors, county executives, mayors, councilmen, aldermen; in some states and localities, there are elections for judges, sheriffs, members of local and state boards of education. There are ballot propositions, referenda, recalls, initiatives. These campaigns are numerous, they cost money, and they intrude into our lives. Only a hermit can dare hope to escape the mailings, door-to-door canvassing, newspaper, radio and television advertising, billboards, even skywriting. Political advertising intrudes into the privacy of one's home by hiding surreptitiously in the middle of a citizen's favorite television show. Perhaps the hermit can escape all this, but he lives in a world whose destiny is increasingly controlled by politicians. Even if he escapes taxation, even if he somehow ingeniously manages to avoid being assigned a social security number, the decisions made in Washington and other seats of government control much of his life. If government had little influence over the life of this mythical individual, it would still have branded him a criminal, because he failed to pay taxes, or, if a male, failed to register for the draft. Someone else may have appended his signature to a "social contract," or some other compact which allegedly links him to society and to the institution of government, but no court exists which will decide in his favor. Courts, after all, are designed to legitimize government.

Government and Politics

Citizens perceive differently the need for order within society. They may seek self-discipline, social order, religious order to define order for their lives. Limited government may be preferable to the welfare state, and no government may be preferable to government. But anarchy does not exist. Its closest alternative, autarchy or "self-rule," which presumes that all transactions and exchanges are voluntary, does not exist and has never been tried.[4] (Its proponents argue that laissez-faire capitalism can succeed without the existence of the state to guarantee liberty; that if it failed, the worst that could happen would be a return

---

[b]Visible, public campaigns, especially media-oriented campaigns, are present in democracies. In the Soviet Union, leaders utilize less visible campaigns pitched to smaller constituencies (e.g., the Politburu) to secure power.

to the status quo.) The libertarian approach suggests that the best government governs least.[5]

Whether government is necessary, or whether it is evil, or whether it is a necessary evil, it exists. There is no evidence that the institution is on the way out.[c]

Thomas Hobbes concluded that only government could mitigate the terrible conditions inherent in man's normal state. He took the worst view of man: every man was against every other man. How could industry or culture survive, let alone thrive, in an environment of distrust and rapacious power-seeking? "The life of man," in his famous words, would be "solitary, poor, nasty, brutish, and short." Hobbes, because he rejected theology as a basis for political theory and instead based politics on the methodology of seventeenth-century natural science, was a precursor of modern political science.[6]

John Locke insisted that although men are free and equal by the law of nature, some men do not operate under the "common law of reason," and they attempt to deprive other men of their natural rights. Locke, who emphasized reason, suggested that the infringement of one man's rights by another was unreasonable. Such infringement was an act of war; if government were the infringer, it provided the justification for revolution. Rousseau pointed out that reason may not always prevail; emotions and sentiments are also important. The existence of government was accepted.[7]

Government is necessary, one argument proceeds, because man is evil, and he requires government to restrain him. Government must secure the peace and provide public order; it must, in short, protect man against himself. The argument is paradoxical: if man is so wicked that government is required, why presume that the rulers of the government, who, after all, are human, are benevolent and not wicked? If man is good and capable of ruling others, then the others, since they are also human, must be inherently good. Why do good men require government?[8]

Within the democratic ideal, citizens choose their leaders. If dissatisfied, they will have a second chance—another election. Presumably, it would be self-contradictory for citizens to vote in communism or any other system that permanently forecloses the opportunity for change. Some theorists have questioned whether the democratic *process* conflicts with the democratic *ideal,* whether manipulation of opinion is consistent with free choice.[9]

There is no way to prove the unprovable—that citizens prudently and wisely select those who govern. They make what they believe to be a rational choice. Despite its imperfections, democracy is still defended by its supporters as the best form of government. Although there is no guarantee that the "best person" will be selected by the democratic process, idealistic democrats display a zeal

-----

[c]For the record, my own bias favors little or no government.

and self-righteousness about their crusade, though, as Jacques Ellul has pointed out, the lessons of history show "that in certain periods the lie is all-powerful."[10]

Partisan supporters of Lyndon Johnson might have proclaimed that the resounding defeat of Barry Goldwater showed that democracy works. They might argue that the good sense and wisdom of the common people was demonstrated by the electoral results. When Ronald Reagan was elected Governor of California two years later, they might have chosen to argue that (a) the people were uninformed or misinformed; or (b) democracy does not work. Since they were unlikely to argue the latter, they would have resorted to a variant of Ellul's theme.

Democratic theory cannot be tied to a value judgment about a particular candidate. When someone says democracy does not work, he may be saying that he disagrees with the democratic verdict of the people. During the late sixties, campus rebels proclaimed that "the system was not working . . . democracy was not working." In fact, the rebels who took over an administration building on a university campus to protest ROTC recruiting acted precisely because democracy was working very well. The majority of students supported "open recruiting"— including representatives of the government and military. Force was the alternative left to the student protestors.[d]

In a democratic society, people accept some rationale for the existence of government; at the minimum, they assume it is here to stay. In early education, the egalitarian mentality is inscribed in youngsters, and they are predisposed as adults to democracy. This democratic mentality is encased in an idealistic, optimistic outlook. Yet, cynicism is directed toward politics, although it pervades the entire culture—school, church, business, union, club, PTA, civic association.[11]

Many citizens do more than vote for a candidate. Options range from part-time or full-time volunteer work to paid staff positions. Not all candidates are career politicians: many citizens choose to run for office. Why do people choose *any* activist roles? They may believe in a candidate, a party or a cause; they may earn their livelihood from politics; or it may be just a game or sport. Perhaps they just enjoy being where the action is. Some people may thrive on the stress and tension of campaigning; perhaps they are on a "power trip." People may be active in politics for one or more of these reasons. Motivation is not the issue, nor do we sit in judgment to suggest which ones have noble, selfless motives versus those "in it for themselves." People are active in politics for the same reason they do anything—because they voluntarily choose to do so. They receive

---

[d]At Columbia University in May, 1968 and at universities throughout the nation, students resorted to violence. During 1967–1969 I visited many campuses and observed the discrepancy between majority opinion on a campus and the goals of the protestors. See John C. Meyer, "What Happened at Columbia (and why)," *The New Guard,* Vol. VIII, No. 7 (Sept., 1968).

some degree of satisfaction. Even the most "altruistic" volunteer has selfish reasons, in the sense that he is active because he wants to get satisfaction.

Political Campaigns in the United States

For the nation's founding fathers, government was a necessary evil. It followed that political parties were also an evil, and it was hoped that elections could be accomplished without them. ("If I could not go to heaven but with a party," Thomas Jefferson exclaimed, "I would not go there at all."[12]) The United States Constitution, which did establish elections, did not establish parties. The development of political campaigns in the United States is largely the development of political parties, whose existence facilitated organized campaigning between prescribed elections. Like-minded citizens organized local groups, which were convenient mechanisms to communicate viewpoints, maintain rapport, and instill a feeling of cohesion and unity. Candidates achieved a kind of economy of scale: they were able to communicate more effectively than on an individual basis. The political party, as a whole, was greater than all of its candidates put together, the sum of its parts. It was a permanent, structured organization with an indefinite life span.

Parties made it easier to stress themes and issues, because the party label was a standard of identification. Once a party label achieved recognition, it became a symbol, a kind of rough index of where someone stood. It may not have been entirely reliable or accurate, but it signified something. Party identification formed a base of support among the constituency that identified favorably with the party. It was upon that relatively secure base that a candidate could build a coalition. As early as the election of 1800, a clear relationship emerged between candidates, parties, themes and issues, and targeting to an electoral constituency. Without demographic analysis and surveys, parties constituted the fundamental unit of analysis: citizens with certain characteristics (now categorized statistically by geography, age, income level, education, etc.) tended to affiliate with a particular party. Others with similar characteristics but unaffiliated with the political party might be persuaded to support the party's candidate, if the appeal to their views was skillfully pitched. By 1800 Jefferson's policies provided identification for the Republican Party; additionally, he modified his rhetoric to reach into the cities.[13]

The existence of political parties, barring complications, is a stabilizing factor in the strategic planning and forecasting of political campaigns. A candidate may be a relatively untested commodity, but the drawing power of his party in the prior election furnishes some *indication* of his base of strength. If the predecessor candidate had much more appeal than only to the party's constituency, his vote tally would represent an overestimation of the party's base. Nevertheless, there is some minimum figure of support for a party's candidate, almost without regard to the physical attractiveness or unattractiveness of the candidate, his honesty or corruption. In earlier years, when census data was less precise, demographic analysis was undeveloped, and statistical tools were not used, the party was the one central, stabilizing element of each campaign. Once a party was perceived as representing something, or some collection of ideas or positions, or some groupings within society, people identified with that party—until the perception changed.

Throughout American political history, precedents for modern day political activity abound, illustrated by the election of 1800.[14] Planning and image have always been important in political campaigns. Candidates have often tried to conceal and disclaim political ambitions while simultaneously presiding over minutely detailed campaigns. Lyndon B. Johnson and Richard Nixon were both masters at utilizing the benefits of incumbency to convey an image at odds with reality. President Nixon's campaign assiduously sought to convey to the electorate that he was too occupied with the responsibilities of the Presidency to campaign. His trips to the Soviet Union and Communist China were part of this plan. In 1964, Lyndon Johnson's staff found seemingly "nonpolitical" events and forums related to his responsibilities as President to dramatize the burdens of his office. In both cases, each President was intimately involved in the carefully choreographed effort to make it appear that the President was not campaigning.[15]

Andrew Jackson's 1828 campaign provided a model for future "non-campaigns." The well-organized, heavily structured, goal oriented Jackson campaign also was notable for its coordinated committee structure and carefully planned fund raising. Its managers compensated for fund raising deficiencies by raiding the public treasury "to shift the main burden of their campaign costs to the federal government."[16]

Grover Cleveland's early political record was distinguished by his determined planning to run for higher office. Despite his alliance with machine politics, Cleveland carefully cultivated an independent image. He sought to be honest and political at the same time. His formula was to "impress the voters with his independence of machine politics" while quietly accepting machine aid—to "be a politician without seeming to be one."[17]

It is apparent that past campaigns are like novels: there are few new plots, only adaptations of old ones. Issues change, technology changes, the political environment changes; basic strategy remains much the same. For example, Eugene McCarthy was a single-issue (Vietnam) candidate in 1968, when he opposed President Johnson. Nearly three quarters of a century earlier, William McKinley rose to prominence on a single issue—the McKinley tariff.[18] Yet, single-issue campaigns are the exception, not the rule. Rarely does a single issue so capture the interest and imagination of the electorate; rarely can such an issue symbolize the many concerns of the electorate.

The McKinley campaign illustrated the importance of powerful external forces, in this case, the economy, in the resolution of an election. The campaign also was an example of what determined and affluent financial backers can do for a candidate. Mark Hanna was the prototype "fat cat" who made an early decision to support McKinley. He had been won over to McKinley in 1888, and he became determined to use his considerable wealth to insure McKinley's election to the Presidency. Hanna was McKinley's personal benefactor, just as Bebe Rebozo was to Richard Nixon. Although the depression had provided McKinley with the winning political issue, it also led to $17,000 of credit losses. Hanna set up a fund, comprised of contributions from his wealthy friends. The purpose was to bail out the financially hard pressed politician, William McKinley.[19]

Political machines are rare today. Patronage has been dissipated by civil service, and the level of government that is consuming the most private resources is the federal government—the level farthest from the people. Graft and corruption exist, but the line between the political contribution and the awarding of a contract is not readily apparent. The governmental bureaucracy is so vast, and so many bureaucrats are involved in the decision making process, that a machine finds it difficult to function. The importance of the news and advertising media, especially television, makes the machine's traditional get-out-the-vote effort less important. Ward bosses and their soldiers are not essential to communicating with the voters and bringing them to the polls.

The machine was a business operation designed to earn a profit for its entrepreneurs. Although criticized for corruption, the machine performed one valuable service: it made *someone* accountable for public services. If you wanted your trash collected on time, and the municipal trash collectors were not doing the job, you did not have to try and find a bureaucrat who might take an interest in the problem. You went to the local political representative. Because he valued your vote and the support of your fellow residents, *he* corrected the problem. Tammany "was a center of community life, a benevolent big brother" for immigrants who received advice, help, loans and jobs in exchange for their votes.[20]

Every political campaign is a public relations effort. The task in the nineteenth century was essentially the same—persuade a certain number of registered voters to support your candidate. That task has become progressively more involved and challenging. The printed word was dominant, through improved printing technology, the growth of newspapers, the telegraph and wire services, and the inauguration of magazines. Radio did not become important until well into the twentieth century, and it was succeeded by television as the medium with the most "reach"—the capacity to reach more people, and more kinds of people, than other media. The message of the campaign still appears on buttons, signs, billboards, bumperstrips, and in literature and in direct mail campaigns. The small campaign, which cannot generate news suitable for television, and which cannot afford to pay for advertising priced to reach a market much larger than the political subdivision involved (Congressional, State Senate or Assembly District), must rely on traditional media.

Public relations oriented political campaigns sought to stimulate interest in the candidate. They tried to increase the candidate's identification and recognition among voters; to publicize the candidate's views on several critical issues; and to motivate voters to go to the polls to vote for the candidate. They also sought to persuade the undecided, and sometimes even to convert those inclined to support the opposing candidate. The PR approach contrasted with the machine oriented campaign, which relied on personal contact, patronage, and direct feedback to assure the desired electoral result. The PR approach relied both on the news that the campaign could generate and on the time and space that the campaign could purchase (advertising). The PR approach, as exemplified by the pioneer political PR firm of Whitaker and Baxter, emphasized "issue control" to help *persuade* voters rather than simply *deliver* voters—the function of a political machine.[21]

It would be wrong to dismiss campaigns of the nineteenth and early twentieth century as inept because they were less developed in modern day public relations techniques. Those campaigns confronted the basic problems common to any campaign:

1. Each campaign has three elements—the candidate, the organization, the funding. The candidate is not only the physical presence, but his utterances, positions, attitudes also have their effect. The organization is the structure, the volunteers, the loyalists and supporters. The funding is what pays for the whole operation.

2. Each campaign must confront the same questions. Who is the candidate and what does he stand for? What issues concern the electorate? What is the constituency, within the broad electorate, to which the candidate can and must appeal?

3. How does the campaign go about communicating with its defined constituency? The problem is identical for any candidate for any office—high or low. The means employed are necessarily different. The candidate for local office can and should go door-to-door; an election can be won this way. The candidate for higher office could go door-to-door constantly, and the number of people reached would still be statistically insignificant. The candidate for statewide or national office must use television to reach the masses; the candidate for minor office generally cannot use television, because the boundaries of the television media market are much wider than the boundaries of his district. Such a candidate is paying to reach a large audience, nearly all of whom cannot vote for him, because they live outside the district.

The manager does not have to be a graphics artist, a printer, or a television producer or director, to understand the principles of communication. Technical expertise can always be hired, but it cannot supplant the seasoned judgment of a professional manager who has keen political antennae. He has an *instinct* for what the message to the voters should be. How the message is transmitted is largely a function of the size of the campaign: the larger campaign is more media

intensive, the smaller campaign is more personal. Between the extremes of television campaigning and the candidate going door-to-door, there are alternative
combinations. The manager must decide what communications strategy is
appropriate. Even in the age of media, the candidate for a local office can
actually win by going door-to-door, perhaps with some assistance by a direct
mailing to eligible voters. The contacts made by the door-to-door travels of the
candidate and volunteers may be statistically insignificant if he were running for
President or Senator; for lesser offices, such "grassroots" work can make the
difference.

Management skills do not guarantee competence as a political manager.
Political intuition and judgment do not guarantee competence as a political
manager. Both managerial skills and political "savvy" are necessary ingredients in
making a good political campaign manager. Management skills usually connote
administrative ability, and the kind of judgment and peculiar intuition required
may be associated with a more creative person. If the two are together, so much
the better. If the two are separate, the campaign may require the politically
astute person to head it, and the administrator to run it.

The trade-off between political astuteness and administrative competence
has probably always been a consideration in selecting individuals to manage
political campaigns. In contemporary campaigns, media plays the dominant role;
since the politically astute person is more closely associated with the creative
personality, this person is likely to be the chief executive in such an organization,
with the administrator second in command.

Contemporary Political Campaigns

The Kennedy-Nixon television debates of 1960 symbolized the television
era in American politics. Television debates currently enjoy only nominal ratings
(in contrast to the segments lifted out of the debates for use in the evening and
late evening television news). The Kennedy-Nixon debates received phenomenal
ratings, because (a) they were a novelty; (b) the election concerned the Presidency; (c) there was great curiosity about Kennedy; (d) Americans were not as
apathetic as they are today. The audience of nearly 70,000,000 per debate also
reflected the new television era: in 1950, 11 percent of America's families had
a television set; by 1960, 88 percent. During the "stampede" years 10,000
American homes were installing a new set daily.[22]

The debates not only increased Kennedy's identification, but they placed
Kennedy, previously perceived as an inexperienced challenger, on the same plat-
form as the Vice President. Nixon did not come across well with his pedantic
debater's style; it was apparent that a special kind of candidate, coached by television specialists, was best able to appeal to voters on the new medium.[23]

Television demonstrated its power to reach masses of people, and to reach them quickly. They could be reached with a visual impression—and the combined impact of sight, sound, and motion. Television also showed that it could, if properly used, overcome the historic advantage of incumbency. Since the 1960 Presidential campaign, television has become the most pervasive political instrument for achieving name identification and visual recognition. It is difficult to find a national or state election in which the incumbent was unseated without the benefit of television—both in terms of news programs and paid spot advertising.

Television cannot be useful if it is utilized in a vacuum. Just as public relations firms were not and are not a panacea for a political campaign, television cannot do what a campaign cannot; it can only do more quickly and effectively and visually what a campaign does at a local level. If the campaign strategy is ill-advised, the television spots which implement that strategy may achieve name recognition, but the candidate's image will not be enhanced, the most significant issues will not be effectively discussed, and voters will not be persuaded to support him. It is possible that a television campaign emphasizing the wrong issues could conceivably hurt the candidate. Television, both in terms of news coverage of the candidate and in terms of paid spot advertising, must be understood in traditional terms. Television is the most technologically relevant and effective means of communicating with *large* numbers of voters. As a tool, television must reflect the strategy formulated by the campaign management, just as door-to-door canvassing, brochures, billboards, the candidate's speeches, and other means of communication reflect the campaign's strategy.

In 1966, Ronald Reagan's campaign for Governor of California represented an integrated, systematic effort to elect a candidate. Reagan was an accomplished television performer and actor, but television was still not treated as something apart from the campaign. Reagan won not because he was more television oriented, or because Brown was seeking an unprecedented third term as Governor and his popularity had declined. Nor was money the factor, since Brown had a respectable campaign budget, and his television spending was quite adequate. Television was *integrated* into the overall Reagan campaign, managed adeptly by the firm of Spencer-Roberts, in contrast to the disorganized Brown campaign. Spencer-Roberts emphasized tight managerial control over the campaign, which utilized simple television spots—lacking the staging, gimmicks, and special effects associated with Hollywood (Reagan's background). Reagan's consistent campaign contrasted with Gov. Brown's erratic shifts in position.[24] Overall, the Reagan campaign was probably closer to an integrated, systematic approach than any campaign in the 1960s.

Any political campaign requires management to mobilize the resources, staff and citizen-volunteers to elect the candidate. The management must help organize and activate key committees of volunteer supporters and fund raisers. It must also guide and counsel the candidate, analyze issues and devise strategy.[25] Many campaigns employ consultants, usually hired part-time for a fee to provide *strategic* counsel for the candidate and the full-time, salaried manager. It is important to understand (a) consultants can never *manage* the campaign; (b) some managers require the expertise provided by certain consultants, and other managers do not.

Regardless of the consultant/managerial mix in a given campaign, particular strategic and tactical functions must be performed. As the role of parties is diminished, the political campaign becomes more crucial to electoral outcomes. The ad hoc organization, constituted solely for the relatively short-term purpose of electing a candidate to office, operates in a turbulent political environment. Events at home and abroad affect voter perceptions and attitudes; mobility, income level, schooling, changing mores—all may affect voter behavior. (See chapter 2.) How does this ad hoc organization survive in such an environment, and how does it cope with change? In short, how does it elect a candidate?

Like any other organization, the campaign functions most efficiently when its membership agrees on the organization's goals and understands them. The overall goal of electing the candidate can only be accomplished if other, intermediate objectives are fulfilled. The organization must be broken down into spheres of responsibility or specialization; e.g., scheduling the candidate, research, press relations, fund raising, volunteer coordination, get-out-the-vote drives, etc. In a major campaign, each component is divided again, e.g., the fund-raising component may be divided into direct mail for mass solicitation of contributions, a finance committee to solicit large contributions, a dinner committee for a fund-raising banquet, etc. In contrast, the small campaign may combine several responsibilities in a single division or even with the same individual. For example, in an assembly campaign, the candidate's press secretary may also be in charge of research and advertising.

Anyone who hopes to manage a political campaign must first understand how the parts of a campaign work, before he can understand how they work together. The best way to understand the parts of a political campaign is by practical political experience at electing candidates for various offices, and as a volunteer and staff member.

Strategy is the plan for action. The formulation and implementation of strategy affects the ultimate success or failure of the strategy. The strategy that is formulated impetuously or based on inaccurate data or wrong perceptions of reality is likely to fail, just as the shrewd and resourceful strategy that is ineptly implemented is likely to fail. Strategy requires nuts-and-bolts, detailed work to become reality. Unless the campaign is technically able to make use of a strategy, the strategy is irrelevant. For example, scheduling strategy dictates the priorities of using the candidate's time. Invitations must be screened, solicited, rejected or accepted; sometimes events have to be invented. The logistic work of arranging transportation, airplanes, automobiles, hotel reservations, must be done, and crowds must be turned out. Publicity must be secured to turn out crowds, and the press division is actively involved. The schedule is formulated to encourage press coverage. In a larger campaign, advance men are used to check all logistic details, to stimulate crowd attendance, and to insure that the event is successful—should the press turn out to cover it. The local organization (whether the state chairman for a national campaign, or the local neighborhood coordinator for a very small campaign) is recruited to help plan local events and make them a success. No strategy, however thoughtful or even brilliant, is worth very much unless all the parts of a campaign are working together and in harmony to achieve common objectives.

Earlier, the need to translate the overall goal of electing the candidate to intermediate goals was mentioned. Each part or division of the campaign must have its own goals or objectives. Staff and volunteers need to relate to more specific, identifiable objectives than the common goal of electing the candidate. When these goals are not defined, or they are unfulfilled, lack of harmony and lack of coordination result. The use of certain issues, the scheduling of particular appearances, the cultivation of specific reporters and success in achieving media coverage that is plentiful and favorable, the detailed advance work preceding a candidate's appearance—these and other components of the campaign all interact with each other. Unless each division is technically proficient, it cannot do its part in implementing the strategy. If each division is technically proficient, it cannot perform in a void; there must be a strategy, a plan, directions, a theme—*consistency* emanating from the very top to the very bottom. In the campaign for city council or for President, consistent leadership begins with the candidate and the campaign manager. Even the lowest level volunteer envelope stuffer may be able to discern that the campaign lacks direction—that it does not know where it is going.

The way in which the political campaign, as an ad hoc organization operating in a fast-moving environment, survives and succeeds is by emphasizing and practicing *precision*. No word is more important in any campaign for any office. The campaigns for high office may be large-scale, well-financed efforts, including statewide and national travel, with heavy emphasis on advance men, large staffs, and substantial media advertising, especially television. The campaign for local office may emphasize personal appearances of the candidate. Each meeting he addresses, every shopping center he visits, each hand he shakes, has a statistically greater impact on the election day results than in the larger campaign. In the large campaign the schedule is more *media oriented* (i.e., constructed to generate news and feature stories, especially visual stories for television); in the smaller campaign, the schedule is more authentic, and its value lies mainly in its content, since media coverage is far less extensive.

In the smaller campaign, more use has been made of direct mail communication, usually relying on data processing for list production and maintenance, and even personalized computer letters. Door-to-door work and telephone campaigns have been systematized to permit canvassers to find out "where the votes are" and later to make sure voters favoring the candidate turn out to vote. The media emphasis is on the use of weekly newspapers and local radio stations, and limited use of daily newspapers, larger radio stations, and television stations. Advertising dollars are also spent in the localized, cost effective media that reach into the small district, rather than into a much larger (more costly to reach) universe of voters. Scheduling has more modest goals: the smaller the campaign, the smaller the crowd required for a candidate to accept an invitation.

Efficiency requires precision in all phases of the campaign. The people involved in the political campaign can be high achievers or low achievers, highly motivated or less motivated workers. They may be honest and moral, or dishonest and immoral. Precision is more likely when staff and volunteers are spirited and enthusiastic; competent, professional, and high achievers. Although the emphasis on winning can bring out the worst in people, it can also bring out the best in people. Tight organization, methodical precision, and an emphasis on efficiency have characterized some forms of tyranny; they also characterize well-run organizations that may have laudable purposes.

The campaign of the Committee to Re-Elect the President probably spent much more than was required to re-elect Richard Nixon, even by a comfortable margin. Despite its well-known ethical shortcomings, the campaign management succeeded in organizing a precision operation, which masterfully pinpointed Nixon's 1972 constituency. What the Nixon campaign did on a national level in precisely identifying probable Nixon supporters, reaching them, and encouraging them to vote on election day is what even the most modest local campaign should do on a more limited scale. It is too bad that the campaign's technical aspects were overshadowed by what turned out to be a criminal and illegal operation and cover-up.[26]

The campaign chiefs lacked an ethical compass. Even if one were prepared to ignore moral considerations, the blurring of the lines of authority in permitting the Watergate burglary and other excesses, the squandering of campaign funds, the lack of accountability, and the failure to relate these morally questionable actions to goals more directly related to the campaign are considerations that were hardly efficient from a management point of view.

Organization and precision in political campaigns will, for general reasons and because of Watergate, be associated in the minds of some with authoritarian rule. Professionalism will be depicted as a repudiation of citizen-volunteers, although the true professional utilizes volunteers to the fullest. Whenever volunteers disagree with the goals or standards of a campaign, some will be tempted to characterize the differences as attempts by authoritarian professionals to dominate "grassroots" volunteers. The chaotic campaign may pretend to be grassroots, but its lack of structure and organization prevent it from maximizing volunteer involvement.[e]

---

[e]When I served as a consultant during a 1974 Senate campaign, one volunteer refused to accept advice in preparing for the visit of an out-of-state Senator helping in the candidate's campaign. The volunteer characterized the conflict as between grassroots volunteers familiar with local conditions and an outside consultant who was unable to work with volunteers. The fund-raising reception in question raised virtually no funds.

When a candidate (or a supporter) is on the losing side against a well-organized political campaign, the temptation to overstate the case against professionalism may be overpowering. Hubert Humphrey, addressing a Jewish group in Milwaukee during the 1960 Wisconsin primary, reacted to the steamroller campaign organization of his opponent, John F. Kennedy in this way:

> To elect a President it's more important that he be good of heart, good of spirit, than that he be slick, or clever, or statesmanlike-looking. . . . Has the leader given you something directly from his heart?—or has it all been planned in advance, all been scheduled? Is it efficient? If you want efficiency in politics, you can go to the communist or totalitarians. I believe politics is simply to deal with people and to be human. Every now and then I read in the paper how disorderly Hubert Humphrey's campaign is and I say, THANK GOD.[27]

2 The Political Environment

Don't even attempt, at this point, to take into account what the key issues and broad public opinion trends may be 18 months from now: Whether the economy is booming back or still depressed; whether the public has become bitter over the loss of Vietnam or preoccupied with a Mideast war or other foreign crisis; whether crime, abortion, busing or some other social issue has become compelling; whether citizens remain disillusioned with current political leaders and are anxiously searching for a new "non-political" face.

... With the situation so monumentally uncertain, the politician or pundit wishing to appear in the know must resort to gypsy-like reading of tea leaves.

—Alan L. Otten
The Wall Street Journal

Most graduate schools of business or management have at least one course, or block of courses, concerned with the role of the business firm in society, and the effect of society or the environment on the firm or organization. Subjects discussed usually include, regardless of the terminology employed: (a) the "public" or "social" responsibility of business or corporate managers; (b) the effect of public policy, especially regulations at the federal, state, and local governmental level, on the operations of the firm or organization; (c) the attitudes, ideas, and expectations of the organization's constituency, i.e., its suppliers, consumers, employees, etc.; (d) the relationship between major trends in population, income, consumption habits, etc. and the welfare of the organization; (e) the state of science and technology.

The business firm does not operate in a void. The wise and prudent manager seeks to understand the increasingly complex environment in which the modern firm operates. Precisely because the environment is changing at such a rapid rate,[1] strategic planning must encompass the many variables subject to change. The manager can control certain variables; he can partially control other variables; by planning ahead and preparing for the future, he may be able to increase his span of control to include more variables. If the manager is a captive of events and relies on an inadequate research and development budget, if he fails to develop new markets for his products and fails to innovate, the changing world may leave him and his organization behind.

The political campaign organization, like the business firm, operates in an environment. In systems theory, the political environment is termed the *suprasystem*. The political campaign organization is a system that operates within the broader environmental suprasystem. Just as the business firm cannot operate in a void, but operates within a changing real world, so the political campaign is not independent of reality, but part of and subject to what is going on in the nation and in the world. The campaign for President of the United States is more vulnerable to what happens thousands of miles away than the campaign for school board member. Each campaign is more or less likely to be influenced by particular environmental factors, although the factors vary with the level of the campaign. Even the school board race is subject to the influence of the nine appointees of the U.S. Supreme Court, who could rule a certain way on the explosive issue of school bussing for racial balance.

It is the task of any manager to define the relevant environment, to assess what impact and weight different elements of the environment have on the organization, and to measure specific effects on the organization's strategy. In the political campaign organization, the manager must be aware of the environment that determines the parameters within which the organization operates. Once *that* environment and its implications are understood, the manager can develop a strategy best able to cope with it.

What is the Political Environment?

The elements that comprise the political environment can be viewed as constraints that restrict the freedom of action of the manager. For example, a manager who respects an ethical code will not pursue activities that conflict with it, although such activities might increase the likelihood of electing the candidate. The law is merely a formalized ethical consensus. It too acts as a constraint on actions which, when considered alone, might be optimal. The manager may not agree with legislation restricting the campaign's activities; yet, he may feel a duty to obey it, he may be pledged to obey it, or he may be unwilling to accept the consequences of disobeying it—the probability of apprehension, trial, and punishment.

What some regard as constraints, others look upon as opportunities. The candidate who explicitly embraces a higher code of ethics than that which prevails in political life can exploit his adherence to a higher moral standard. The law itself, although a constraint, has within it "loopholes," or opportunities for initiative. Incumbent legislators who originate and write the laws can be partial to their own interests.[a] Laws change, and their evolution partly reflects changing mores. Sometimes laws that have been on the books for years are never enforced;

---

[a]The 1974 federal campaign legislation was an excellent example. The constitutional challenge to the law (U.S. Dist. Court, District of Columbia, Civil Action No. 75-0001) summarized the law's favorable treatment of incumbents and the two major parties. The law had also established a Federal Election Commission—at a time when federal regulatory commissions in general were under increasing criticism. It was not surprising that during 1975 the FEC's rulings repeatedly favored incumbents and the two major parties.

then they are enforced rigidly. It seems as if the rules of the game have changed; in fact, they are only being applied. The post-Watergate era has included the enforcement of laws previously unenforced, as well as a new standard of morality much less tolerant of political machinations.[b] Ethics and laws, like domestic and foreign policy, impose parameters on political debate and political action; within those parameters, opportunities should be discerned by the thoughtful strategist.

The environment can never be judged retrospectively, for decisions are made in the "here and now." An individual may or may not adhere to a constant moral standard, but what society views as ethically and morally acceptable or unacceptable is not constant. For example, when Nelson Rockefeller campaigned for President in 1964, his divorce and subsequent remarriage were major political liabilities, because of the public's beliefs *at that time*.[2]

The economic and social climate of the nation is part of the political environment. The economic and social climate of the world is relevant for candidates for national office. Local candidates are affected more by domestic developments. Incumbents at every level can, to a degree, influence economic and social developments. What can be influenced can be exploited. Ethical limitations may prevent exploiting certain issues, especially foreign policy and national security. Moreover, as Lyndon Johnson learned from the Vietnam war, foreign policy can prove more of a constraint than opportunity.

The general economic and social climate, coupled with the domestic and foreign policies of government, are macro-factors. When the economy is bad, when the nation suffers a foreign policy defeat, the incumbent is likely to be blamed, rightly or wrongly. A "throw the rascals out" feeling may result in the defeat of officials simply because they are incumbents. Voters do not always accept the fact that economic developments, especially over the very short term, are not totally controllable. In domestic and foreign policy, events may have been set in motion by a prior administration, or even by Congress, but the incumbent administration is likely to be blamed. A new assemblyman or a freshman city councilman deals with problems he did not create. He may face a budget deficit caused by the taxing and spending policies of his predecessors. For incumbents, macro-factors may be an albatross around their neck; for the challengers, macro-factors may represent opportunities to be exploited.

When the nation enjoys economic prosperity and prestige abroad, macro-factors favor the incumbent. When economic problems abound, the challenger is generally favored. Foreign affairs have ambiguous effects, since voters may prefer to stay with an incumbent during a crisis.

Another set of environmental factors is *macro-political.* A partial list would

---

[b]The Corrupt Practices Act was succeeded by both the 1971 and 1974 federal campaign legislation. Although the CPA had prohibited corporate and labor contributions, these prohibitions were not taken seriously. (See, for example, Michael C. Jensen, "How 3M Got Tangled Up in Politics" (*New York Times,* March 9, 1975); also Douglas Caddy, *The Hundred Million Dollar Payoff* (New Rochelle, N.Y.: Arlington House, 1974).

include the changing role of the party in the American political system, the ascendancy of the independent voter, the "coattails" effect (or lack of it) of a President or another head of a ticket, party registration, voter turnout, apathy, etc. There are the demographic factors: the changing complexion of the electorate—expressed in terms of age distribution, geography (residence), profession or occupation, union membership, education, income level, religion, national origin, etc. *Macro-factors,* i.e., the social and economic climate, partly attributable to government policy, are manifested in *macro-political trends:* attitudes, perceptions, opinions, and ultimately, voting behavior.

Macro-political factors can be severe constraints. For example, party registration limits the number of people in each party eligible to vote. The universe only includes registered voters; it does not include people too young to vote, those who are not citizens, or those with felony records. More importantly, the universe does not include people who would be eligible to vote but who *fail* to register. It does not matter what the nonregistered voter thinks, or how he views the candidate; he will not affect the outcome on election day (except for the statistically insignificant factor of how much he talks to or influences his friends or relatives who are registered voters).

Macro-political factors are best analyzed by discovering and interpreting trends of attitudinal formation and public opinion. Survey research is the most scientific way of discerning trends, but well-read, well-informed analysts can judge what concerns dominate public consciousness, and what kinds of people are most concerned about different problems. Before survey research was developed, political strategists relied on their own informal soundings, experience and seasoned judgment. If a small campaign cannot afford survey research, its strategists must use their own judgment—based on limited data and survey information. Keen observers of people have some idea of what troubles them. What they lack, which survey research offers, is the quantifiable measurement of public opinion. Survey research indicates precisely (with a margin of error) what people think, and which kinds of people (in terms of geographical location, party registration, race, religion, income level, etc.) share a particular attitude or opinion.

Macro-political factors do not have to be constraints; they can be opportunities that can be seized upon by a shrewd strategist. Using his own judgment and survey research, he can discover *how* to reach segments of the electorate. The macro-political factors, once the constraints are understood and evaluated, suggest opportunities *within* the constraints. Which strategy offers the greatest likelihood of winning, given the macro-political environment? Which strategy can anticipate change and cope with it? Essentially, the interpretation of survey research or other data suggests the effect on attitudes and opinion (and ultimately voting behavior) of different events.

In other words, how do macro-factors affect politics? How do they affect what people believe and how they might vote? Only a limited number of political analysts understand the demographic forces at work and their implications. A smaller number can interpret the data and apply it to a political campaign.

The final environmental factor considered is an institutional variable: *the news and advertising media.* The political campaign utilizes the media by generating news and paying for advertising to reach its universe. There are two different sets of factors relating to the importance of the media.

1. The increasing population, the number of registered voters, their interest (or lack of it) in government and the political process, etc. are *demographic* factors. How do these people get their news? How are they influenced by advertising? To what degree are television, daily newspapers, weekly newspapers, radio, billboards relevant to a particular campaign? What are the quantitative implications for a political campaign? For a national or even statewide campaign, the numbers and types of people who must receive the candidate's message cannot be reached without media. In-person campaigning—speeches, door-to-door visits, receptions, dinners—can only reach a limited number of voters. Moreover, and this is critically important, the voters reached may be qualitatively inferior, e.g., they may be partisans already committed to the candidate. Campaign dinners and rallies have a how proportion of voters who attend to be persuaded or who can be persuaded. There is some value in securing one's base of support and stimulating additional volunteer work; but there is a point of diminishing returns, especially when compared with the large numbers of potential supporters who need only to be reached with a specific thematic appeal.

2. The *structure* of the news and advertising media is the second set of factors relating to the importance of the media. There are different kinds of media—subway, bus, and outdoor (billboard) advertising; newspapers—daily and weekly; magazines of all types; special publications for groups, organizations, and ethnic constituencies; radio; television; wire services; correspondents; bureaus and bureau chiefs; television networks; political writers; managing editors, reporters, assignment editors, etc. The components of the media, its rules and practices, customs, traditions and habits, attitudes and biases provide both opportunities and limitations for the campaign. Each type of media and each individual within the media require appropriate servicing from the campaign.[3]

The first set of factors explains why the news and advertising media are important, and which media, including specific newspapers or television stations, are more or less important in reaching the campaign's constituency. The second set of factors is much more specific: they explain the technical reasons why the news-gathering organizations and advertising media function the way they do. News-gathering budgets, the difference between "hard" news and features, a "visual" story for television versus a less visual print media story—are a few examples.

The campaign manager can do little or nothing to affect population trends, the number of citizens old enough and registered to vote, the number of people who get their news from television, compared to daily newspapers, etc. He must understand this *media* environment, and he must hire staff people who can relate to it. The campaign requires a liaison, usually called a press secretary, to play interference between the campaign/candidate and the news media to over-see the servicing of the news media. The campaign also requires a liaison, includ-ing staff or an advertising agency, to supply finished advertising material to the media.

The campaign manager cannot change the fact that the media, through news and paid advertising, is the primary means of communicating with the electorate. The larger the campaign, the more important is the role of the media, especially television. This is not to say that television would not be very important in a race for state senate: a single television story could help immensely; however, smaller races are usually not covered by television for many reasons, including the large number of such races going on within a single media market. The cam-paign manager needs to understand *why* and *how* the news media and adver-tising media can affect the electoral outcome, and the campaign must act on that information. The media is so important that it is singled out as a separate ele-ment of the political environment.

The political campaign manager must understand the environment: the ethical and legal framework, the macro- and macro-political factors, and the media. The political campaign manager must understand the environment to manage an organization that, in electing a candidate, copes with that environ-ment. The political campaign manager requires a variety of experience and skills. He should be adept at management, organization and finance; he will draw upon political science, history, psychology; he must understand communications and public relations, including journalism and advertising. He must be able to interact with lawyers, accountants, pollsters.

Ethical and Legal Factors

No one has ever conducted a scientific study to determine if people in politics—elected officials, candidates, campaign managers, staff and volunteers—have moral standards that are different than those of the rest of society. Morality, ethics, standards, a code of conduct are all different ways of expressing the same thing. Barbers, doctors, advertising copy writers, teachers, salesmen, cooks, lawyers, automobile assembly plant workers, and just about any other profession or occupation cannot be catalogued by reference to morality, ethics, standards, or a code of conduct. Some professions like lawyers have formal codes of ethics, but lawyers are not necessarily more ethical. Is advertising by lawyers unethical, as the bar associations have maintained for many years?

The political world is under microscopic observation by the news media. Common abuses in society are brought to light when they occur in politics, although they may hardly be unique to political life. If specialized reporters covered people engaged in other careers, one can only speculate on the results.

The Ervin Committee's investigation of political wrongdoing, corruption, and illegality was limited by a committee vote along partisan lines to an investigation only of the 1972 election. The committee did not investigate similar abuses in the Presidential elections of 1960, 1964, and 1968. Recent revelations confirm what Washington political observers have long known: many practices uncovered by Watergate occurred in prior administrations. What was especially odd about the abuses of Watergate was that they occurred in an administration that preached law-and-order in its pronouncements and in its legislative program, and that crusaded for decentralization of power.

Machiavelli postulated that morality, or "what should be," is to be excluded from the consideration of politics, which concerns itself with "what is." Machiavelli, considered more "scientific" about politics than any previous thinker, said that human nature is a constant throughout time, and its characteristics might be good or bad, but must be treated, for the purposes of politics, as bad. "Men are wicked and will not keep faith with you," he wrote in *The Prince.* "Unless men are compelled to be good, they will inevitably turn out bad." When people contemptuously decry the evil motivation of politicians, they often impute "Machiavellian tendencies" to them.[4]

American political history is replete with instances of misdeeds and character assassination. A colorful example was the Presidential election of 1884, in which Republican supporters of James G. Blaine were put on the defensive. They retaliated by conducting a personal attack on Grover Cleveland. One article in a Buffalo newspaper, entitled "A Terrible Tale," told of his relations with "the comely widow Halpin." Cleveland, the story went, fathered her illegitimate son, encouraged her to believe he would marry her, and then proceeded to commit the son to an orphan asylum.[5]

Despite the furor over President Nixon's claims of executive privilege to justify his refusal to release documents and tapes pertaining to Presidential conversations and actions, the doctrine of executive privilege was not new. A Democratic President, Grover Cleveland, threatened with the use of the Tenure of Office Act by Republicans, invoked executive privilege to deny Congress access to information. Cleveland considered the information requested by the Senate to be private and confidential; the Senators claimed they required access to the information in order to perform their constitutional duties. They reasoned that Cleveland would appear to have something to hide if he did not accede to the request.[6] Cleveland, like Nixon, insisted that he had a constitutional right to withhold information of a private or confidential nature, and that *he* had the prerogative to decide which material was private and confidential. Cleveland, who won the fight, has been praised for his defense of the doctrine. Had people perceived his defense of executive privilege to be a transparent dodge, a method to prevent improprieties from being uncovered, he would have been perceived as a man afraid of the truth. Without denying that absolute ethical standards exist, that there is a difference between right and wrong, it can be seen that in politics, what appears to be, and not necessarily what is, also applies to perceptions of morality and ethics.

Perception, and not reality, determines public opinion—what people think, not what is. Perception may coincide with reality, but not necessarily. In the ethical realm, appearances are very important in politics. An action may be unquestionably legal; it may even be justifiable morally. But if it presents a bad picture in appearance, then all of the facts and data may not change the public's impression. If the public changes its perception after election day, there is no way to undo the damage done by an impression created of immorality or unethical behavior.

Few acts are ethical when measured against high, absolute standards. How many acts are ethical when, to be considered ethical, the motives, means, ends, and effects of the act must all be considered? Some behavioral theorists state that an ethical decision is one that "enhances self-respect, develops personal integrity in relationships, dissolves unreal barriers between people, builds a core of genuine confidence in self and others, and facilitates the actualizing of human potentials without bringing harm to others."[7]

The ethics of politicians and campaign managers are most often called into question when evaluating how they appeal to the electorate. What will they do to win? They may say one thing during a campaign and do something else when elected. The recent classic example was the 1964 Johnson-Goldwater contest, in which Johnson's antiwar campaign contrasted with his escalation of American military involvement in Southeast Asia. It seems unethical to make promises that one does not intend to keep, but politicians do it all the time. In some cases, they may even deceive themselves into believing that they will keep the promises. There is also the ethical issue of what a candidate and his campaign can say about his opponent and his campaign. Today, the television spots that depicted Goldwater as a nuclear madman might be condemned because of changed standards.

More prevalent than specific attacks against an opponent is the use of loose, imprecise language that conceals the candidate's real positions, makes them less offensive, or avoids taking positions. Another tactic is making statements that, although they promise nothing specific, use "code words" and emotive terms from which certain voters infer something that is unsaid. Appeals to racism by skillful use of "law-and-order" rhetoric could fall in this classification. People hear what they want to hear—with some assistance from the candidate and campaign. George Orwell, in his famous essay on the use of the English language in politics, contended that a "mixture of vagueness and sheer incompetence" helped politicians to avoid meaningful communication. Sometimes, political language ". . . is designed to make lies sound truthful and murder respectable, and to give an appearance of solidity to pure wind."[8] The use of language in American political campaigns usually has more modest goals of misrepresentation, perhaps to make a tax increase sound like "tax reform," or an inflationary budget deficit into "stimulating the economy."

The political campaign manager and his staff have ethical standards that exert constraints on the organization. The candidate exerts the most important constraint. Just as his nature, personality, and temperament are reflected throughout the campaign, so his ethical standards are likely (but not always) to be reflected throughout the organization. The "win at any cost" candidate will likely retain a campaign manager and staff of similar disposition. In any campaign a basic, implicit understanding or consensus among candidate, campaign manager, and key staff members exists regarding ethical questions. Conflicts arise if such a consensus does not exist or is violated. Any condition of optimality must fully consider the ethical consensus. For example, staff members may perform less efficiently, or not at all, if asked to do something they perceive as unethical. A campaign manager whose tactics violate the candidate's moral code might be dismissed. In contrast, the candidate who describes his campaign manager as "too soft" may really mean that their ethics differ; in replacing the manager with a more aggressive "hard-liner" he may be opting for an individual with lower ethical standards.

Voters will choose a candidate they perceive as ethical in preference to one they perceive as unethical or less ethical. Even voters who assert that "all politicians are crooks" will still vote for the "lesser of evils." Considerations of self-interest are important; voters may support candidates they perceive as unethical because they believe they will be, or that they have been, effective elected officials. ("He's running a vicious campaign, and he's in politics for the money, but he really gets federal contracts for our area.") One should not be misled by partisans who say they prefer the clearly immoral enemy, because he is easier to confront and defeat. These ideologues associate morality with positions on issues. In sum, (a) the voter who says "all politicians are crooks" seeks to rationalize his choice; (b) the electorate's perception of a candidate as honest and moral is a net plus; (c) it is preferable for the electorate to have a neutral perception or no perception of a candidate than to perceive him as unethical; (d) strategy and tactics acceptable ethically to the candidate and his campaign manager may so violate the ethical standards of the electorate that votes are lost.

When politicians speak of morality and campaign on "moral" issues, they do not necessarily have a high ethical code. In terms of public perception, the moral pronouncements of the politician *may* be controlling. It is the politician's behavior that is the real standard. It may be possible to hide the discrepancy between image and reality during a campaign, but such deception is difficult over the long term. Although perception and not reality is important in reaching the electorate, it is asserted here that the most efficient way to be perceived as ethical is to be ethical.

The law, ethics codified on a basis presumably applicable equally to everyone, is less ambiguous than ethics. For political campaigns, laws vary from mundane, routine requirements (e.g., identifying campaign material) to complex rules governing fund raising and spending. Sometimes one level of government may have sole jurisdiction (the federal government has authority over elections to federal offices); other times, several levels of government have jurisdiction (a headquarters supporting candidates for federal and state office may be subject to several layers of government).

Legislation need not be titled "campaign" to apply to political campaigns. Sections of corporate law, internal revenue law, and labor legislation may pertain to campaigns. For example, although labor unions are under the jurisdiction of the National Labor Relations Board (NLRB), the AFL-CIO operates a national political organization that is a virtual adjunct of the Democratic Party.[9] It has avoided prosecution for engaging in illegal political activity by asserting that only funds collected on a voluntary basis are used in political operations.

The protected legal status accorded the AFL-CIO's Committee on Political Education and the AFL-CIO has enabled organized labor also to allocate political funds from compulsory dues. Labor expert Douglas Caddy has pointed out that most of labor's political contributions are not on-the-record *dollar* contributions, but *in kind* contributions in goods and services. For example, unions loan talented and well-paid staff people to work in campaigns, but these people are paid out of union treasuries. Labor facilities are used—meeting halls, automobiles, sound equipment, telephones, expense accounts—for the benefit of ongoing political campaigns. Registration drives are conducted—but the new registrants are overwhelmingly Democrats. These "in kind" contributions are not publicly reported and are illegal. Until the law is enforced or more rigidly defined, these contributions will continue, and they will exert tremendous influence on political campaigns—especially for the races involving the United States Senate and House of Representatives.[10]

The Internal Revenue Service is another agency concerned with issues which, like those before the National Labor Relations Board, generally do not involve campaigns. IRS regulations *do* apply to campaigns, especially in terms of possible tax liability if certain conditions are not met. The tax laws also influence contributors, who may now take advantage of limited tax deductions or tax credits for contributions to candidates for federal office. One example of the complex legal/tax environment facing the campaign was an ambiguous interpretation of the laws governing the relationship between the campaign and its heavy benefactors. In the past, multiple committees have been formed primarily to receive large contributions, which were divided into $3,000 (or less) units, to avoid incurring a gift tax. The campaign might form ten separate committees to receive a total of $30,000 from a single individual, who would write ten $3,000 checks—one to each committee. The committees were merely "paper" organizations and, based on a long-standing practice, were set up exclusively to maintain the fiction that the donor was giving separate "gifts" and not a single gift. In the early part of 1975, there was speculation that the IRS would change its prior ruling allowing multiple committees and might do so *retroactively.*[11]

The most recent federal campaign legislation, the Federal Election Campaign Act Amendments of 1974 (Public Law 93-443), was so complex that even its framers could not interpret its provisions.[c] On January 2, 1975, Sen. James L. Buckley (Cons.-R., N.Y.) and a diverse group of co-plaintiffs, including Eugene McCarthy and the American Civil Liberties Union, filed suit to challenge the constitutionality of the new law.[12] The legal battle and Supreme Court decision, as well as the rulings of the Federal Elections Commission during 1975, illustrated several effects common to most campaign reform proposals.

1. Limiting campaign expenditures—at the federal, state or local level of candidacy—favors the incumbent; he normally has a higher identification and recognition among the electorate and therefore requires a smaller campaign budget to support media spending.

2. Legislation enacted by incumbents will never allow sufficiently for the built-in advantages of incumbency. An incumbent is always running for re-election, not just in campaign years, or during the formal election campaign. A United States Senator, for example, has a large payroll, the franking privilege, free office space, telephones, a travel allowance, subsidized use of television and radio facilities in the Capitol, free data processing use for mailings, etc.[d] A City Councilman has a budget, an office, telephones, and other privileges. He also can use his office constantly to improve his recognition, service constituents, do favors for possible voters. Incumbents do not give up such privileges, nor do they

---

[c]In early 1975 I queried experts who helped draft the 1974 legislation and received ambiguous and confusing replies. During 1975, rulings of the Federal Elections Commission often contradicted Congressional intent. For example, the FEC ruled, in effect, that funds raised through dinners and cocktail parties could count only partially toward receiving matching federal funds, in contrast to funds raised through direct mail appeals (*New York Times,* Aug. 31, 1975). Weeks later the FEC totally reversed itself (*Los Angeles Times,* Oct. 9, 1975).

[d]Americans for Democratic Action studied the perquisites of incumbency and calculated a Congressman has a $488,505 advantage over a challenger (*Los Angeles Times,* Aug. 26, 1975); my calculations indicate this estimate is quite conservative. For example, just two political mailings promoting Sen. John V. Tunney (D.-Cal.) cost the taxpayers at least $125,000 in 1975 (*Los Angeles Times,* Sept. 9, 1975). The figures often underrate or do not include related services: my Congressman, Henry Waxman, sent a mailing to constituents in October 1975 offering a wide variety of free government pamphlets whose cost is borne by various government agencies. When the Federal Elections Commission, which had been created by the 1974 campaign legislation, ruled that incumbent "slush funds"—monies raised to pay for political expenses not covered by government allowances—must be deducted from applicable campaign spending limits, incumbents indicated they might invoke the clause in the "reform" legislation permitting them to reject any commision rule within 30 days. Finally, the commission modified its ruling to consider only a portion of the "slush funds" against the incumbent's campaign spending limit. The Senate found even this modification unacceptable and in October 1975 overruled the FEC (*Washington Post,* Sept. 17, 26, 1975; *New York Times,* Sept. 15, 18, 25, 29, 1975; *Los Angeles Times,* Oct. 9, 1975).

allow, within campaign reform legislation, for offsetting advantages to their
challenger.

3. Uncertainty benefits incumbents. Incumbents have the position, facilities,
and staff to secure superior information, more rapidly, than possible challengers.
When the interpretation or effect of a new law is in doubt, whether it is a
national campaign law or Proposition Nine in California, or a city ordinance, the
possible challenger and his supporters must speculate on what they can and what
they cannot do. Legal and accounting questions, the status of a possible campaign committee, and a variety of prudential considerations paralyze the possible
challenge to the incumbent. The time element favors the incumbent, who continues to enjoy the benefits and perquisites of his office.

4. Limitations on contributions can help challenger or incumbent but are
more likely to favor the incumbent. Since large contributions have traditionally
provided the "seed money" to finance the initial phase of a campaign, limitations
may prevent a recognition/identification media intensive effort to stimulate
public interest. Until public interest in the candidate reaches some minimum
level of consciousness, more modest contributors are difficult to find. The net
effect of such a law is ostensibly to encourage the solicitation of small contributions (such solicitation requires much more overhead); in fact, to deny to the
prospective candidate the revenue sources to reach the stage at which small
donors can be effectively solicited. In addition, any direct mail campaign to
reach the masses of small donors requires start-up or "up front" money to pay
for list rentals, postage, printing, and fund raising assistance.

5. Disclosure can hurt the challenger. When everyone must be on public
record when they give, the trend-setting contributor may shy away. He may be
wary of offending an incumbent who *is* in power and who may *continue* to be in
power. People are more reluctant to support a challenger, especially one who is
not considered to have a very good chance.

6. Detailed accounting provisions may be too cumbersome for challengers.
The more volunteer and grassroots oriented the campaign, the less likely it will
be able to cope with the more detailed accounting provisions of laws. The small
campaign is unable to understand and interpret some provisions; it may be unable to afford the bookkeeping assistance or to conform to rigid reporting
deadlines.

7. Allocation formulas or limitations on certain kinds of spending will
probably hurt challengers more than incumbents. For example, if candidates for
county supervisor are restricted to only a certain amount of spending on media
advertising, the challenger, who has less public recognition, cannot compete with
the incumbent. If a federal candidate is restricted to certain kinds of media,
within an overall media limitation, as was the case with the 1971 federal law (succeeded by the 1974 federal law), the challenger can be prevented from utilizing
his most effective medium. Billboards may be effective because of the residential
and travel patterns in an area; television may be effective because the candidate

is television oriented, or because of the audience it reaches. But the choice is circumscribed.

The rationale behind formula limitations is that someone else, other than the candidate or campaign manager, can prescribe budget allocation. It should be apparent that Government intervention in the political process, especially in detailed expenditure controls, has ominous implications. The assortment of other federal regulatory commissions clearly indicates the special interest character which all regulation assumes. The inevitable relationship between elected officials and regulatory authorities would also apply to so called "electoral reform."

8. Restricting the composition or types of contributions or expenditures results in a less efficient management of the campaign than if the law did not exist. Because the campaign for each level of office (local, state, federal) must appeal to a different size constituency, certain methods are more suited for each level campaign. Even if a restrictive law applies equally to all candidates running for the same office, each candidate is different, and his campaign manager formulates a unique strategy. The particular mix may call for a certain percentage of campaign revenue to be raised through direct mail fund raising, or through dinners, or for a certain portion of funds to be spent in television spot commercials. The restrictive law distorts the optimum mix of fund raising or expenditure; the alternative method results in a higher cost of funds raised, or less return (in votes) per dollar spent.

Consider a specific example. If $10,000 is required for a project or phase of a campaign, assume the campaign manager can find two individuals to give $5,000 each. In fact, each individual offers to underwrite the entire $10,000 project. Assume a state law limits contributions to a maximum of $1,000 per individual, and that neither individual has yet contributed any funds, so each is still entitled to give up to $1,000. The manager accepts $1,000 from each individual, and he now must raise the additional $8,000. The cost of raising the funds from the two individuals is nil; not even a dinner or cocktail party is required. The cost of raising money by direct mail, if it can be done, is estimated by the manager to be 2/3 of every dollar raised.

Table 2-1, a simplified version in which no overhead is charged to raising money from the "fat cats," shows the cost of the "reform" legislation to the campaign. In the first case, the campaign nets the entire amount; in the second case, the campaign nets 38¢ for every dollar collected. It might be argued these figures are irrelevant if the direct mail sources are there. However, the example assumes (a) certainty, (b) no effect on aggregate fund raising and (c) no opportunity cost. In fact, the probability of raising money through direct mail is not assured. The expenses of printing, postage, list rental, etc. may exceed the revenue derived from the mailing. Also, funds raised through direct mail may exhaust the capacity or willingness of small contributors. In contrast, the larger contributors able and willing to give more are turned away. Finally, time is worth

Table 2–1
Effect of Campaign Law on Fund Raising

Without Law		With Law	
One or both individuals contribute funds for the project. Each is still willing and able to fund additional projects.		From two individuals: Campaign must use direct mail for remaining $8,000.	$ 2,000
Gross Funds Raised to Net $10,000:	$10,000	*Gross Funds Raised to Net $8,000:*	$24,000
Net for Project:	$10,000	*Net for Project:* $2,000 + $8,000	$10,000
Ratio: Net/Gross $10,000/$10,000 = 1.00		$10,000/$26,000 = 0.38	

something to the campaign. The direct mail method is not only riskier, it consumes time that could more profitably be devoted to other fund-raising means or other campaign projects, and its receipts take longer to arrive.

The trend in recent years is toward public financing of campaigns.[e] Aside from the ethical question (diverting public, taxpayer-supplied funds involuntarily collected to political campaigns), public financing is a crude special interest device. For example, assume a large state grants $1,500,000 to any major party candidate running for Governor in the general election, with no restrictions on spending; however, *no* private funds can be raised. Candidate A is a charismatic figure who relates well to the concerns of the middle class. Without the scheme, his campaign manager could raise about $1,750,000, nearly half in small contributions solicited by direct mail. Candidate B won the primary by utilizing many student volunteers and the get-out-the-vote machinery of several major unions. Apathy was high and voter turnout low, and he narrowly won. His manager, who is also less competent than the manager for Candidate A, could raise about $1,250,000 for the general election campaign.

The public financing scheme ignores the public appeal either candidate may have; both candidates receive exactly the same funding, with no private fund raising allowed. The first candidate is unable to exploit his relatively greater opportunity to raise funds. Nor can he utilize the professionalism and skills of his campaign manager, who is adept at direct mail fund raising, as well as an innovative producer of luncheons and dinners, which can raise substantial sums at $50 and $100 a person. The public financing scheme thus has one additional effect: it renders irrelevant the professionalism and skill which the campaign

[e]For example, public financing has been proposed for city elections in Los Angeles (*Los Angeles Times,* Nov. 18, 1974). Local campaign limits, such as those applied to the 1975 mayor's race in San Francisco (*New York Times,* Sept. 11, 1975) seem to be the precursors of partial or total public financing. A recent Michigan statute provided public funding for that state's 1976 gubernatorial races and established a "Political Ethics Commission" with police powers (*Los Angeles Times,* Aug. 31, 1975).

manager for Candidate A can bring to the campaign. His fund-raising skills are *irrelevant.*

We have not addressed the question of equity. First, why should only the major party candidates, and not minor party candidates, receive financial support from taxpayer funds? Second, doesn't automatic support encourage candidates to run just to get a free ride? For example, in a primary in which any declared candidate receives a minimum level of taxpayer assistance, the field would be flooded with aspirants for public office; not to mention the campaign managers who will be running candidates in order to make a living. All the sub-contractors—advertising agencies, printers, mailing houses, sign makers, bumper-strip manufacturers—will find an assured, stable and permanent market, since the demand curve is guaranteed by the taxpayers.

Reform legislation has untold effects on the way in which campaigns are administered, their priorities set, the timetable followed, etc. Consider George Wallace who, in 1974 and early 1975, again prepared to run for President. His strategists examined the 1974 federal law and discovered they were entitled to a federal subsidy of as much as $5 million. In order to qualify for the matching federal funds, the candidate (Wallace) must raise at least $100,000; the total raised must be distributed in at least twenty states: at least $5,000 in under-$250 contributions raised in each state. Once this condition was met, the candidate (Wallace) became eligible for matching federal money for each dollar raised (in under $250 contributions). Wallace retained veteran campaign fund raiser Richard A. Viguerie, a direct mail specialist, who designed a program not simply to raise aggregate dollars, but to raise the dollars in such a way that the Wallace campaign would qualify for the federal subsidy.[13]

The purpose here is not to catalogue the applicable laws, which are subject to constant revision and court interpretation. One compilation of federal legislation alone consumed 88 pages of small print.[14] The examples cited illustrate that the legal framework is a critical element of the political environment facing the campaign manager. The manager must seek legal counsel (a) to be aware of the relevance of laws at each governmental level; (b) to understand the implications for the campaign; (c) to understand the nature of the constraints *and* the opportunities. Generally, legislation impairs efficiency and prevents the campaign manager from formulating an optimum strategy. His strategy, when adjusted for conformity to all applicable legislation, is suboptimal. Optimality is therefore defined to mean optimum performance when *all relevant laws and legislation are considered.*[f]

---

[f]Artificial constraints reduce the efficiency of campaign management. Suppose that 30- or 60-second spot commercials for political candidates are banned; only political programs of five minutes or longer duration are permitted. Proponents of such a law evade the real problem—public apathy makes the short spots the most efficient way to reach the public. The effect of the law is to force campaigns to spend scarce dollars on blocs of television time with substantially fewer viewers than the spots. In fact, programs are a much better buy, in terms of cost per minute, than the spots; but spots are more *efficient.*

Ethical and legal considerations are important because (a) the campaign reflects the interaction of the ethics of the candidate, campaign manager, staff, volunteers, other candidates, voters, etc.; (b) explicit and implicit campaign legislation also provides limitations on the campaign. Hopefully, ethical and legal considerations will not unduly discourage aspiring candidates.[g]

Macro-Factors

The isolated campaign manager who does not keep abreast of what is happening outside his narrow circle of friends cannot hope to relate to public opinion. For such a manager survey research is simply a collection of numbers. On the other hand, the alert manager who is conscious of the world around him knows that the numbers can come alive with meaning and stand for something. Interpretation of survey research can be taught and mastered only up to a point. Other elements include natural intelligence and the intangible ingredients of wisdom, judgment, and shrewdness. Yet, these intangibles are partially based on knowledge of people and society.

The manager need not be a historian, but he does require a general working knowledge of current events. Any manager who isolates himself from observing the developments and trends that could ultimately affect politics can never aspire to be more than a mere technician. The manager must be especially attentive to macro-factors that affect the particular election and constituency. For example, the manager of a Presidential or Senatorial candidate is sensitive to foreign policy developments; the manager of a local campaign is more sensitive to macro-factors at the local level. Both managers are concerned with the "big picture"—the broad landscape, within which the election campaign occurs. Both managers must recognize the importance of research assistance, briefings, and expert counsel, for both the candidate and senior staff, on macro-issues which concern the election. They need to know where, how, and to whom to go for information.

The incumbent must determine which events he can influence or control. Both the incumbent and challenger need to know what kind of macro-environment will confront them days, weeks, months ahead or, in the case of a Presidential candidate, even a year or two ahead. The shape of the economy or the state of detente may profoundly affect the strategy to be adopted. Any incumbent affects events to the extent that his actions change the macro-environment.

---

[g]Current trends favor candidates with access to shrewd attorneys and accountants. Even reform-minded volunteer activists have found post-Watergate state and local legislation oppressive. One supporter of California's Fair Political Practices Commission cited numerous instances of technicalities and trivia. For example, the Commission after considerable discussion decided that the female dog of an assemblyman could mate with the male dog of a lobbyist and produce profitable pups without the lobbyist being required to report a political contribution. Concluded the disenchanted reformer, "Dogs are going to do it no matter what we do." (*Los Angeles Times,* Oct. 10, 1975)

Ultimately, the issues that concern voters at any level mirror what is happening in their daily lives, and what is important to their welfare—*as they perceive it.* Campaign issues are not in a vacuum, and the manager who discerns macro-trends before they are apparent to others can predict issues which are likely to emerge in a campaign.

Catastrophic events—and the reaction of government leaders to them—can influence an entire election. The candidate should select a manager who can intelligently assess conditions, and who can present alternative strategies to optimize each possible state of nature. Although it would be silly to formulate contingency plans for events with virtually no probability of occurring, some attempt must be made to assess the probability of events and government policies with a reasonable chance of occurrence. Too often political campaign managers formulate a strategy to deal with the most likely state of nature and are unprepared for other macro-factors. In other words, a strategy formulated to dramatize the Vietnam war may collapse if peace negotiations begin. How likely that something will happen or that a trend will materialize determines how much time should be devoted to formulating *that* strategy or contingency plan.

Any campaign issue is related to macro-factors—the state of the economy, inflation, unemployment, national defense, the Middle East, detente. The difference between macro-factors and *micro*-factors is simply one of degree: micro-factors describe more specific, categorized causes of problems or manifestations of problems. For example, consider the candidate who makes a campaign issue of drugs. In the inner city, the issue might mean "hard" drugs; in turn, heroin addiction is related to urban crime. Suburban voters may be worried about their children using amphetamines. Only by understanding differing sociological environments, can the strategist relate the issue to different constituencies. The issue itself represents a convergence of a multitude of causes and effects—opium cultivation in Turkey, heroin refinement in France, international drug smuggling rings, American crime syndicates, treatment centers for addicts, youth alienation, unregulated distribution of amphetamines, etc.

The electorate is composed of citizens who see things in simple terms—not economists or foreign policy experts. Hence even complex issues must be explained in simple, easy-to-understand terms. Any campaign must find ways to transform the raw research data and background material into dramatic issues that relate to the personal life of the voter. Obviously, some issues, notably war and peace and boom and bust, are so overbearing that little dramatization is required. Given the economic conditions in 1932, it is difficult to see how Franklin D. Roosevelt could have lost the 1932 election.[15] The macro-factor of the economy was so dominant that Roosevelt's rhetoric was almost irrelevant. Ironically, Roosevelt criticized the Hoover administration because it was "committed to the idea that we ought to center control of everything in Washington as rapidly as possible." He even promised a 25 percent aggregate cut in the federal budget. "I accuse the present Administration of being the greatest spending

Administration in peace times in all our history," Roosevelt said in a campaign appearance in Sioux City, Iowa, in September, 1932. "It is an Administration that has piled bureau on bureau, commission on commission, and has failed to anticipate the dire needs and the reduced earning power of the people." Later, he told a Pittsburgh audience that he regarded "reduction in federal spending as one of the most important issues of the campaign." One historian suggested that even more striking than his pronouncements and his vacillation on some issues was his failure to mention deficit spending, massive federal public works, federal housing, increased income taxes, and other New Deal policies he would pursue. He did not mention these proposals "in part because they had not yet crystallized, but even more because his primary task was to get himself elected, and, as the front-runner, he saw little point in jeopardizing his chances by engaging in controversies that might cost him more than they would win."[16]

The focus on the Presidency should not obscure the pervasive effect of macro-variables on lesser offices. Republicans at all levels of public office were facing difficult times in the thirties. Macro-forces may be so powerful that a candidate who does "everything right" is still destined to lose an election. Adequate funding, professional staff, and competent management cannot overcome the political cross-currents. Defeated candidates and their managers may be correct in blaming their defeat on powerful trends or developments (e.g., Watergate). However, the trend may explain the defeat, but not its magnitude, which is due to inept campaign management. In other cases, negative macro-factors make the political environment less favorable for a candidate, but the competent manager able to discern an appropriate strategy may still win the election.

The interaction between events at home and abroad and the policies of the national government and subsidiary levels of government help mold the political environment. The macro-events affect public perceptions, ideas, attitudes; the resulting tendencies toward certain kinds of voting behavior (discussed in the next section) directly affect the political environment. The campaign manager wants to optimize the performance of the campaign given the total political environment, i.e., given the macro-events and policies and the macro-political trends they influence and affect.

Macro-Political Factors

Macro-political factors or trends are of two types. (1) *Autonomous* trends seem to be self-generating, or at least no clear cause-and-effect relationship can be found. At the very least, there are complex, multiple, and perhaps long-term causes. Autonomous trends and variables might include the current relationship between Presidential popularity and the prospects for electoral success of candidates of the same party as the President; the relationship of parties to candidates and to political campaigns, especially the strength of party identification and loyalty among the electorate; etc. The relationships here concern elected officials, parties, Congress and lesser legislative bodies, campaign committees, etc. The various structures may affect fund-raising capabilities and the degree to which funds are available for individual political campaigns. Demographic variables describe the American electorate in terms of age, sex, religion, national origin, income level, party affiliation, voting history, etc. (2) *Dependent* trends or reactions can be more closely related to causes. For example, a shift in American public opinion favoring increased defense spending might be partially due to an attack against a United States ship. On a broader level, probable voting behavior may be correlated to urban/suburban population shifts, family income, education, etc.

Dependent trends or reactions are important because if a correlation holds true during a given time period, shifts in public opinion and ultimately voting behavior may ensue. Autonomous trends sometimes just seem to be present: the causes are complex or ambiguous or debatable. If the analyst cannot draw a convincing cause-and-effect relationship, it may save time to treat the macro-political factor or trend as autonomous—and then proceed to gauge the probable effects on the specific campaign.

The most important macro-political factor is the nature, structure, and influence of political parties. Following a brief discussion of political parties, we shall treat the principal measuring tool relating macro-factors to macro-political factors: the use of demographics to measure population and related shifts, correlated to attitudinal shifts and voting preference.

Political Parties

As James MacGregor Burns has pointed out, the founding fathers were reluctant to form political parties. James Madison, George Washington, Thomas Jefferson, and Alexander Hamilton feared the pernicious effects of parties, and Madison was especially fearful of democracy. Yet, Madison's successor, James Monroe, presided over the completion of a political cycle common even today in the early stages of political development. The United States under Washington inaugurated a one-party system; under Adams and Jefferson, two national, competitive parties emerged. Under Madison and then Monroe, one party, the Republicans, achieved wide electoral support, and the one-party spirit reappeared. One party meant no strong opposition, hence many smaller parties might appear.[17] Andrew Jackson expressed at this time an interest in eliminating political parties altogether, although his election of 1828, as previously indicated, was a model of political organization. During the early period the nation tested a two-party model. Despite the occasional dominance of one party over another, the two-party model has persisted.

It may be that the *equilibrium* of the American political system is a two-party model. There is really no way to prove this, but if it is true, third party movements are inherently doomed to failure.

During the post–Civil War period, the Republican Party is considered to have been in the ascendancy.[18] Although the party won three of the five Presidential elections from 1876 to 1892, it never carried a majority of the popular vote. Republicans controlled the presidency and Congress at the same time for only four years (1881–1883 and 1887–1889). Nevertheless, the period reflected the favorable position which the party had inherited from "the magic tradition of Lincoln." The political environment facing candidates in the late nineteenth century was influenced by the Lincoln legacy, the public's perception of the Republican Party, and the odd nature of the party's coalition.[19]

The bias in political science courses favors a *two* party system. It is asserted that such a system helps form intelligent public opinion, defines issues, presents the voters with choices and makes the winning party responsible for operating the government.[20] In reality, political parties are partisan, not educational organizations. The choice presented to the voters may be one of personality, not viewpoint. The winning party may represent a coalition of *repudiation,* not a mandate; in 1964 and 1972 voters repudiated the caricature of Goldwater and McGovern, respectively. David Broder, perhaps the dean of American political reporters and a "true believer" in the two-party system, has chronicled its decline in both his book and columns. The election of independent candidates, like Maine's James B. Longley, who was elected Governor in 1974, illustrates that an independent candidate can even win statewide office. Significantly, Broder, unlike other advocates of two-party politics, has opposed special interest legislation, like the 1974 federal campaign law, giving preferential treatment to the Republican and Democratic parties and to their national committees.[21]

Parties have provided a guide to voting behavior in the past, but how reliable a guide will they be in the future? Historically, analysts generalized reasonably safely about the voting behavior of blacks, Jews, Catholics, Irish, Italians, . . . who voted overwhelmingly Democratic; upper-income, professional people who were WASPs tended to vote Republican. Racial, religious, and other characteristics of people provide only an *indication,* not an infallible yardstick, of voting behavior. The variance *within* groupings suggests that generalities have to be highly qualified or perhaps eventually disregarded. For example, in New York State, Senatorial candidate James Buckley in 1970 and Presidential candidate Richard Nixon in 1972 both failed to carry the Jewish vote; Buckley received about 18 percent and Nixon about 38 percent. In each case, Buckley and Nixon, the showing was significantly better among Jews who tended to be older, more orthodox, more traditional, less affluent, and, most importantly, residents of areas directly affected by high crime, drug abuse, poor public schooling.[22]

A party with demonstrated weakness among a portion of the electorate (a historically poor showing among Catholics or Jews, among blue-collar workers, or even within a certain Congressional district) may tend to write off the weak groups or weak areas or districts. Inroads can be made because macro-factors radically alter the political environment, which then must be *exploited*. The inroad may be temporary, or it may be a base upon which to make further in-roads. Past voting history may be a valuable guide that suggests how priorities should be set in going after certain groups and areas; it can also merely reflect the failures of the past while concealing the opportunities of the present. Reli-ance on past voting behavior and historical statistics can provide a very mislead-ing assessment of the *current* political environment.

The burden of proof, however, must rest with those who advance a new hypothesis and who suggest the existence of a new trend. The political novice or the overconfident strategist with limited experience may see a nonexistent trend. Since the data suggest that his hypothesis is very questionable and his strategy risky, he may suggest that *only* the electoral outcome can validate his theory. He is suggesting a win/lose situation; once the strategy is pursued, there is no way to see its worth until it is too late. However, survey research will always support a hypothesis in accord with reality; hence, many visionaries reject surveys. A national or statewide campaign can afford survey research to see what people are thinking about, and which groups within the electorate can be reached by the candidate. The smaller campaign can at least rely on public surveys (Gallup, Harris, et. al.) to discern general trends, within which they project a local out-come. Even if survey research or other data suggest that blacks, Jews, Southern-ers, or the voters in a given council district *can* or *may* shift, *will* they shift to the other party or candidate?

The lower the level of the election, i.e., the more local the contest, the more difficult it is to apply a national trend. Media is less relevant in a local election in which the candidate must rely principally on less effective media than television, and on personal appearances. The campaign must always consider: (a) the num-ber of eligible voters reached in person and by other methods; (b) the impression made and the retention factor, and the *actual* impact on their voting behavior; (c) the statistical significance of the numbers: can the election be affected by the number of people so reached? The "magic" newspaper advertisement, the bril-liant brochure, the "army" of door-to-door volunteer canvassers—the all-purpose, super strategies generally do not overcome the built-in party loyalty of a voter.

The political party that enjoys widespread support can provide a secure base of support for its candidates; the political party with declining support can be a liability. Surveys in late 1974 and early 1975 indicated that although the Repub-lican Party was in trouble, both parties had problems.[h] George Gallup concluded:

---

[h]Lance Tarrance Jr., author with Walter DeVries of *The Ticket Splitter* (Grand Rapids, Michigan: William B. Eerdmans, 1972), found that 69 percent of a national sample agreed that "for the most part, the government serves the interest of a few organized groups such as business or labor, and isn't very concerned about the needs of people like yourself"; 43 per-cent concurred that government as now organized and operated "is hopelessly incapable of dealing with all the crucial problems facing the country today"; 73 percent said "the gov-

"Combined with the impact of the media, which weakens party loyalty by allowing candidates to bypass the organizations and appeal directly to the voters, this rise in the appeal of independence threatens the hold that Democrats and Republicans alike may have on their traditional voters."[23]

The Republican National Committee's private surveys in late 1974 and early 1975 showed that 18 percent of Americans considered themselves Republicans, 42 percent Democrats, 40 percent Independents; 27 percent thought Republicans competent, 30 percent thought them incompetent, 43 percent had no opinion, compared to 44, 13 and 43 percent, respectively, for the Democrats; 25 percent thought Republicans trustworthy, 13 percent thought them untrustworthy, compared to 45–13 percent for the Democrats. In a national survey in late 1975 pollster George Gallup confirmed the earlier surveys performed for the RNC by pollster Robert Teeter. Gallup found only 21 percent of adult Americans considered themselves Republicans.[24]

In recent years much speculation has centered on the direction of a new third party. George Gallup has suggested the Republican Party might consider changing its name to the Conservative Party.[i] Conservative publisher William Rusher has suggested that a new conservative party would be a second party, taking the place of the Republican Party, rather than a third party.[25] Projections for a new conservative party overlook two important factors:

1. There is a divergence between economic conservatives who advocate free market economics and social conservatives preoccupied with personal social behavior. The latter support government intervention in social areas but do not necessarily oppose economic intervention.

2. Many self-professed conservatives will vote for a Democratic candidate if he is perceived as conservative. Gary Hart, George McGovern's campaign manager in 1972, was successfully elected to the Senate in 1974. He said that liberal and conservative labels were obsolete; he urged less waste in federal spending; less bureaucracy; he campaigned against inflation; he came out against across-the-board gun controls and blanket amnesty for draft evaders.[26]

Despite the bias among political scientists and in election laws favoring the two party system, it can no longer be passively accepted. Regardless of his party, the candidate must consider its image and drawing power. Generally, the lower the level of office, the more important is the party label. The primary reason is

---

ernment often fails to take necessary actions on important matters, even when most people favor such action." McGovern pollster Pat Caddell found that voting declined as concern over the direction of the country increased, because "the expectation no longer exists as much that the vote is linked to a policy result. There's the feeling that it doesn't make much difference." (*Wall Street Journal,* Jan. 30, 1975). Four out of five Americans between the ages of 18 and 21 stayed away from the polls in the 1974 midterm elections; overall, only 45 percent of eligible voters went to the polls (*L.A. Herald Examiner,* Jan. 27, 1975).

[i]Gallup said, "Americans like the conservative name. If we ask people what their ideology is, we usually find that a majority describe themselves as conservatives. The word 'liberal' has never been very popular except among academics and intellectuals who pride themselves on being liberals" (*Battle Line,* Nov. 1974).

the relatively lesser role of the media (news and advertising) in local elections, and the tendency among even discriminating voters to support candidates of the two major parties at the local level. As the stability of the major parties is called into question and the independent vote rises, the base provided by the normal party vote becomes a less reliable indicator of the innate strength of the local candidate.

Demographics

The political environment is influenced by demographic trends and measured by *demographics,* which must be understood, interpreted, and applied to the election at hand. The primary source of data is the U.S. Census Bureau, which provides information to determine the composition of survey research samples. Secondary sources of data are based on census information and election statistics. The electorate is segregated by voter registration, age distribution, income, race, nationality or ethnic background, religion, education, etc.; data processing provides cross-tabulations between these demographic factors and attitudes and voter preference.

In a classic study Scammon and Wattenberg used census and electoral data to demonstrate that the electorate was "unyoung, unpoor and unblack."[j] They theorized that voters will move massively if they are confronted with a major issue or personality who unambiguously and emotionally represents their concerns. They emphasized the "social issue"—crime, drug abuse, student unrest, bussing, civil turmoil, pornography. Each component of the social issue is a potential "Voting Issue," i.e., one capable of moving an election. It is difficult for any candidate to articulate the concerns of the middle-class electorate, but it is apparent that Americans no longer vote simply on the basis of economic issues.

The assumption that the electorate was middle-American underscored many campaigns in the 1970s, notably the Senate campaign of James L. Buckley in New York (1970), Richard Nixon's campaign (1972), and Jesse Helms's Senate campaign in North Carolina (1974). Using demographic data interpreted by Arthur J. Finkelstein, all three candidates did indeed shift massive numbers of Democratic voters to their allegiance. Finkelstein has stressed the need for a voter to perceive the candidate in his image. Richard Nixon came closest to

---

[j]Based on the 1968 vote, 17 percent of the electorate was from the under-30 age group, 68 percent from the 30–64 age group, 15 percent from the 65-and-over group; in terms of income level, 9 percent of the electorate had a family income under $3,000, 13 percent had $3,000–$5,000; 66 percent had $5,000–$15,000; 12 percent had $15,000+; the percent of eligibles who voted was, respectively, 54, 58, 72 and 84 percent. White voters comprised 91 percent of the electorate; non-white, 9 percent; their voter turnout was 69 and 56 percent, respectively. Richard M. Scammon and Ben J. Wattenberg, *The Real Majority: An Extraordinary Examination of the American Electorate* (New York: Coward, McCann & Georghegan, 1970), pp. 20, 46–48.

achieving this ideal in 1972: most conservatives perceived him as a conservative, most moderates perceived him as a moderate, although most liberals did not perceive him as a liberal. Finkelstein analyzed the middle-class from another vantage point: the peripheral urban ethnic. This voter tended to be (but was not always) ethnic—especially Catholic, Irish, Italian, Eastern European and lived around the fringe of the inner city.

In a more recent volume Wattenberg utilized census and survey research data (including Field, Gallup, Harris, Roper, Yankelovich, Opinion Research of Princeton, and the Institute for Social Research of the University of Michigan) to evaluate how much the United States had changed during the 1960s. Wattenberg found that newer voters were younger and better educated, more suburban and more affluent, "but politically and attitudinally they were earthy 'middle class.'" Wattenberg related what we have termed macro-factors to attitude formation in tracing the effects of the Arab oil boycott and energy crisis: "Americans remembered that while a clean environment is good, materialism is also good, and sensible environmentalists and sensible materialists tried to figure out ways to have both." The author noted these salient data from the 1972 Presidential election: in October 1972, 8 percent of the American electorate perceived George McGovern as conservative; 12 percent, moderate; 31 percent, liberal; 31 percent, radical; 18 percent, not sure. It was axiomatic that if voters indeed opt for a candidate they perceive in their own image, George McGovern was destined for a major defeat.[27]

William Watts and Lloyd A. Free have formulated an interesting measurement of how Americans perceive the state of their personal lives and the state of the nation. Using an imaginary "ladder of life" with a scale ranging from 0.0 to 10.0, Americans are asked to rate their personal lives. In 1974, the average ratings of Americans as a whole were 5.5 for the *past,* 6.6 for their *present,* and 7.4 for their *future.* The authors interpreted these figures to indicate "a significant sense of personal progress" (the present rating was 1.1 higher than the past) and "considerable optimism" (the future rating was 0.8 higher than the present). There has also been remarkable stability in the past, present, and future ratings Americans as a whole gave their lives. In terms of the National Ladder Ratings, it was reported that people feel they are doing reasonably well but that the nation is doing poorly.[28]

The Watts-Free data, as well as other compilations of survey research,[29] explain "the big picture." Political forecasting is analogous to economic forecasting (Table 2-2). Just as a firm supplying parts to an automobile manufacturer must understand the macroeconomic variables before it can forecast demand for its particular product, the political campaign manager realizes that voter preference for his candidate reflects macro- and macro-political factors. Similarly, past market research for a product may have limited application to current forecasts; survey research is merely historical unless it is current. Older surveys *may* explain what is happening, but their reliability is questionable. Only very

Table 2-2
Forecasting[a]

For a Business Firm: *Auto Parts Supplier to* *Automobile Manufacturer*		*For a Candidate* *for Public Office*
	The Big Picture	
Macroeconomic Gross national product Disposable income Consumption etc.		*Macro* Economy, Foreign Policy Government Actions Social & Economic Trends Long-term demographic shifts
	Industry Demand Curve	

Industry
Auto sales
Types of vehicles
etc.
		Macro-Political
		Effects of above and long-term
		  shifts in population, age
		  distribution
		Picture of electorate

	Localized Demand (Area)	

Auto Firm (Mfg.)
Specific sales forecast
		Macro-Political (Specific)
		Current public/electorate
		  perceptions, attitudes,
		  positions on issues

	Specific Demand Curve	

Parts Supplier Firm
Expected sales for parts
  supplier firm
		Election
		Voter preference in specific
		  election for candidate

[a]The demand curve needs to be forecast for a business firm and for a candidate/political campaign.

current surveys explain what is happening *now*. Demographic data assists the campaign manager in formulating strategy, but the only important datum on election day is voter preference.

Media

During the nation's early history the party organizations used quasi-house organs to reach the electorate. In 1850 only five percent of the newspapers were neutral or independent. By the 1870s party propaganda gave way to authentic news reporting. Daily newspaper circulation reached 16 million by 1900 and grew to 54 million by 1950. By the 1930s radio was a factor, but it was succeeded by television, now the preeminent media tool for reaching voters in national and statewide races.[30]

Television rarely covers local elections, unless (a) the election is a special election being held to fill a vacancy; (b) an election for an office that roughly includes a major portion of the media market (e.g., county supervisor or executive or mayor); (c) a sparsely populated media market that has one or two television stations and includes only a few Congressional districts. In larger media markets there are far too many candidates to cover, and most viewers are uninterested in candidates in a neighboring district. Advertising is wasteful, since the rates are based on reaching many more people than are eligible by residence to vote for the candidate.

Television's advantages, which are most relevant to candidates for national and statewide office who can utilize this medium, include the following:

1. Television spot advertising intrudes into the living room of even the most apathetic viewers.
2. Television has the combined impact of sight, sound, and motion.
3. Television news reaches voters who receive most of their news from television, or who rely on television as their sole source of news, 60+ percent and 30+ percent, respectively.[k]
4. Television spot advertising reaches some viewers who cannot be reached *any other way* over the short term.
5. Television advertising is pervasive. It is more difficult to mentally "tune out" the TV spot than to simply turn the page of a newspaper.
6. Television can reach a mass audience in a short time.
7. Television is best able to stir enthusiasm and arouse interest in a campaign. It tells voters who the candidate is *visually*.

Television and radio rarely provide the in-depth coverage provided by the daily newspaper, but they do provide more current and timely coverage. The electronic media attract listeners and viewers who want *immediacy*, as well as those too lazy, busy, or apathetic to read newspapers. In tracing the ascendancy of television news, Theodore H. White found that the dominance of the *magazine* reached its peak in 1940 when *Time, Life, Look,* and the *Saturday Evening Post* created Wendell Willkie as the Republican nominee and imposed him on the Republican Party. By 1940 magazines were threatened by radio, symbolized by FDR's fireside chats. For FDR, radio was "the simplest direct appeal over a hostile printed press to the ears of the American people." By 1972, 50,000,000 adult Americans watched one of the network news shows each evening![31] The larger prime time viewing audience suggests the importance of television spot advertising for political candidates.

Daily newspapers supplement their local coverage and political reporters with services (e.g., Associated Press, United Press International, Reuters) and with bureaus and correspondents affiliated with various newspaper chains— Newhouse, Cox, Scripps-Howard, Knight, Gannett, Copley and Hearst. Several

---

[k]These are minimum figures; for example, the Roper survey found that 64 percent of all Americans receive most of their news from television.

newspapers syndicate news articles and correspondent reports, notably the *New York Times, Washington Post,* and *Los Angeles Times.* As the number of newspapers declines, those remaining become more efficient and rely on fewer news sources. Most cities currently have only one or two daily newspapers; the same chain may own both of the city's daily newspapers.[1]

The importance of television does not imply the irrelevance of newspapers. As television news directors and station executives compete more fiercely for ratings, they tend to de-emphasize political news. In the print media the trend is toward more intensive and thorough coverage of politics. The television audience may dwarf newspaper readership, but there are *qualitative* differences. It seems logical to expect that voters who read more reflect their interest in current events and politics and are more likely to vote. These citizens may also be more influential among their peers. The *joiner* or *activist* is a member of one or more civic, community, or religious organizations and is active in service groups, charitable causes, patriotic organizations, perhaps the local union or PTA. These citizens can be expected to read newspapers more regularly than their more apathetic counterparts; some activists may be in that small minority with irregular television viewing habits. Finally, most of the nation's top political reporters are in the print media, not the electronic media. Many newspapers have full-time political editors and reporters who specialize in year-around coverage of politics. Their stories can set the mood for future campaigns.

Partisan campaigners read newspaper articles for reinforcement. The campaign staff member and the volunteer worker, as well as the citizen newly converted to the candidate's cause, may read the newspaper coverage of the campaign to reaffirm their commitment. Print media can be very important to the morale of these people, especially those who are not regular television news viewers. Newspaper coverage helps set the tone for the campaign: articles that are "upbeat" and optimistic encourage optimism among campaign staff and volunteers; gloomy, pessimistic news accounts of the campaign produce an atmosphere of doom and gloom.

News articles and features, syndicated columns, editorials, wire service reports, analysis or "think" pieces, magazine articles, background discussion pieces, interviews, all contribute to setting the tone of the campaign. News directors and assignment editors in television stations read the newspapers and are influenced by them. Thus, the positive or negative tone of coverage of a campaign in the print media may also affect the tone of coverage in the electronic media. At any given news conference, the questions asked by television reporters may be influenced by what they read on the wire service tickers, or by an article in the morning newspaper.

---

[1]As daily newspapers become more technologically advanced, they tend to indirectly pool their news resources by greater reliance on expanded wire and news service coverage. Thus, a Copley News Service or Gannett News Service story, like an AP or UPI story, can penetrate many media markets.

Advertising in the print media can be more detailed than in the electronic media. In some cases, it can be more specialized, inserted in a particular section of the newspaper. Such advertising can provide the detail and background to supplement a television advertising campaign; it can more easily solicit funds than a television advertising spot; it is often more conducive to negative campaigning in the event that such a strategy is appropriate.[m] Some newspaper advertising, such as targeted appeals in weekly newspapers, may have specific objectives in reaching particular kinds of readers.

Advertising is inferior to news because it costs money and news does not; advertising, perceived as a paid, contrived package offered by the campaign, lacks the credibility of news. But the content of news, unlike advertising, cannot be totally controlled; news is difficult to generate, especially for television. As incumbent, by virtue of his position, can find "official" reasons to generate news, before and during the campaign. The candidate is more often a supplicant seeking coverage. An excellent example of an incumbent's exploitation of the news media was President John F. Kennedy during his tenure in office.[32]

For challenger candidate, as well as incumbent candidate, *accessibility* is important; first, because an accessible candidate can provide news when it is needed by the media (a slow news day; a fast-breaking development that requires comment; the need to meet a deadline, etc.); second, accessibility generally gives the candidate credibility, because it shows he wants an open relationship with the media. Accessibility can hurt if the candidate speaks impetuously, is inarticulate or not fluent, or if he otherwise "puts his foot in his mouth." As a goal accessibility requires knowledge of the media, including an understanding of and willingness to be governed by deadlines, and technical proficiency in generating a media oriented schedule, i.e., newsworthy, topical statements and visuals at appropriate locations and time of day.

To deal with the media component of the political environment, the campaign manager and appropriate members of the campaign staff must understand the structure, practices, traditions, habits, biases, and needs of the news and advertising media. In dealing with the news media, professional judgment is required to judge questions like how long a news conference should last, how it can be concluded gracefully, when the candidate should be "available" rather than hold a formal news conference, when a "one-on-one" interview with a key reporter is preferable to a news conference open to everyone, whether the news conference should be at a motel or airport, and at what time of day, etc.

These "how to" questions are beyond the scope of this discussion. They are part of education and training in public relations, press relations, editing, writing, television work, etc. No technical competence among the staff in a campaign can

---

[m]In the Helms Senate campaign (1972) the print media advertising campaign was heavily negative, linking Helms' Democratic opponent to George McGovern. Helm's television advertising was affirmative (entirely pro-Helms); hence, the negative campaigning did not upset the positive image of Helms.

compensate for a candidate who does not understand the media, refuses to cooperate with it, or is offensive to news people. When a candidate understands the crucial importance of media, he is willing to expend time and effort to generate favorable news coverage. The media is the principal means for both elected official and challenger to communicate with constituents and electorate, respectively. *Momentum*—a central concept in later chapters—is largely a function of the amount and tenor of media coverage. The narrow point of view only perceives the morale boost given by favorable coverage of a campaign rally, or the disheartening effects of a negative news story. The systems view suggests that if media is the main determinant of momentum, the campaign must adapt itself to the media environment.

3 The Political Campaign Organization

. . . but each office had its own plan, its own approach. There were five, six, seven or more major plans for winning the election, which is natural in any national headquarters. Only no two of them fitted together.

The flaw fissured from the top down. "George McGovern," said Gary Hart, "just doesn't understand organization. . . ."

—Theodore H. White
The Making of the President 1972

The political campaign organization is not permanent. It exists to elect a candidate and it ceases to exist on election day or shortly thereafter. It may take several days or weeks for a losing candidate and his campaign to settle affairs. For the winning candidate, the campaign organization may perform a liaison function in the interim between election and assumption of office. The staff is trimmed, the campaign organization is phased out, and financial affairs are put in order. For winner or loser, reports required by various laws must be filed with the appropriate authorities. A lingering deficit may require a shell of an organization to fund the debt and eventually extinguish it. For winning candidate or losing candidate, the campaign organization as a dynamic force ceases to exist after election day.[a]

Staff members of a political campaign are usually compensated, but sometimes an individual is able and willing to *contribute* his labor on a full-time basis. The individual who volunteers a considerable amount of time, even 40 hours a week, is not necessarily a staff person. For someone who is not paid to be considered a staff person, (a) the time contributed must be on a regular basis, a given number of hours per day, or days per week; (b) the person must have established responsibilities; (c) the person must be treated as if he is a paid staff person, subject to the same demands and discipline as a paid (staff) employee; (d) the person must have a position or slot on a campaign organization chart or, if such a chart does not exist (and it should), he would have a position or slot if the chart did exist.

Volunteers who meet the conditions and definition of being staff are considered and treated as staff—regardless of the fact that they receive no com-

---

[a]A notable exception was the Committee to Re-Elect the President (Richard Nixon). The Committee existed long after the 1972 election—using a surplus for legal fees to defend itself and its staff members accused of Watergate crimes.

pensation. The term *staff* will be used to mean full-time paid personnel, and it will include any volunteers who are formally accepted as staff. The term *volunteer* includes the many citizens who donate their time to help in the campaign, but who are not considered staff. Almost everyone who contributes their time is a volunteer; few who contribute their time assume staff slots.

Volunteers dominate a campaign numerically, but they cannot be permitted to "run away" with the campaign, which requires *professional* management. The campaign that is both professionally managed and volunteer oriented is best able to utilize the commitment of time and energy given by enthusiastic and dedicated volunteers.

The modern political campaign may be "ad hoc," i.e., a temporary organization, but it cannot be hastily put together. Its management may act quickly and decisively, but not impetuously. In order to mount a well-defined, precise effort to achieve a clear goal, the election of a candidate, within a known and short-term time frame, the campaign must be carefully structured and organized to encourage maximum volunteer participation, and to make the best use of the experience, skills, and talent of each individual volunteer. At the same time, the elements of management must be applied by the campaign manager, who selects professional staff, in contrast to the volunteers who are engaged full-time in activities other than the campaign, and who are *amateurs* in political campaigns. It should be emphasized that some volunteers in campaigns have been involved in several campaigns, even many campaigns over a period of ten or twenty years; they may still have amateur status, because they do not have the detached professionalism of the staff member. They lack the discipline and purpose of the full-time, paid employee of the campaign.

The campaign manager must consider the people shown in Table 3-1.

The Management Problem

Ernest Dale has described seven elements of management: planning, organizing, staffing, direction, control, innovation, and representation.[1] These ele-

Table 3-1
People in a Campaign[a]

---

1. The candidate; his family; friends, relatives, very close supporters.
2. Constituency or base of support, and their volunteer representation in the leadership of the campaign (campaign chairman, local campaign chairmen).
3. Campaign staff. (Almost all staff receive monetary compensation.)
4. Volunteers. (These people receive no monetary compensation.)
5. Ad hoc or adjunct groups. (Seemingly outside the campaign organization, these groups, such as "Lawyers for . . . (the candidate)" "Doctors for . . . ," etc. are controlled by it.)
6. Financial supporters. (The finance committee partially reflects this constituency.)

---

[a]These are the people in a campaign organization.

ments of managing a business firm can be applied to the management of a political campaign organization.

Planning

The manager must first decide what he wants done. He must set short- and long-run objectives for the organization and decide on the means to accomplish them. Hence, he must forecast. He must plan, and planning involves setting up a budget, which is merely a plan to spend a certain amount of money to accomplish goals.

In the political campaign, the manager must decide if winning is the objective. It usually is and, for this analysis, will be considered to be the objective. Candidates have run for office for other reasons: to dramatize an issue (Eugene McCarthy on the Vietnam War in 1968), to represent a particular point of view (George Wallace numerous times), to increase name identification (to prepare for a future race, to stimulate clients if the candidate is a local attorney, or just for prominence). If winning is the objective, the manager must decide the question of the desired margin. It is insufficient to say that maximizing the vote is the objective, since successive efforts to increase the possible victory margin on election day may involve risks to the outcome itself.

For example, consider the objective of Richard Nixon in 1972. He wanted to achieve a *record* popular vote, and to do so he was willing to wage an independent campaign. The Committee to Re-Elect the President did not cooperate with other Republican candidates because it feared compromising Mr. Nixon's victory margin.[b]

The ultimate objective may be victory on election day, but its achievement depends on the outcome of relatively shorter- and longer-run efforts. Consider, for example, the campaign to secure the nomination of Barry Goldwater. The Draft-Goldwater Committee, and, before the formal organization of the committee, the movement, was designed to achieve a series of successive objectives, without which the ultimate goal of the Goldwater nomination would be impossible. First, political strategist F. Clifton White and his colleagues sought to enlist Senator Goldwater's assistance; if not his assistance, his tacit cooperation. Next, they prepared plans to organize rallies at which Goldwater might appear, in order to demonstrate popular support. They formed a viable, embryonic organization to serve as a base. Subsequently, when Goldwater became an announced candidate, they had as their objectives victories in various primary states.[2]

Even the short-run campaign requires the delineation of interim objectives,

---

[b]Arthur J. Finkelstein, chief demographics consultant to the Nixon re-election committee, recommended a closer tie-in with Senate and Congressional candidates. The President's victory margin would have been cut, but more Republicans would have been elected to the Senate and House of Representatives.

as illustrated by the Buckley Senate campaign in New York (1970); objectives were set July 3—precisely five months before election day (Table 3–2). Each objective had a deadline, and each required subobjectives with their own deadlines.

Objectives are ends, but the means to achieve objectives can become ends. For example, a fund-raising goal, as an objective or end, requires a finance committee as a means to the end. For the person charged with organizing the committee or recruiting the finance chairman, these tasks are ends. The manager must understand the interaction of the political campaign and the political environment in order to set interim objectives intelligently.

Table 3–2
Interim Objectives of a Campaign[a]

Interim Objectives (Buckley Campaign)

Date: May 3, 1970
Survey had been taken.
Management and press secretary had been hired.

To Do:

1. Borrow "seed money" for start-up expenses of campaign (by June 3).
2. Establish Buckley for Senator Committee of prominent citizens (by Sept. 1).
3. Establish Buckley for Senator Finance Committee to raise funds (by Sept. 1).
4. Decide on strategy (by June 3).
5. Decide on advertising agency (by June 15).
6. Travel throughout state to recruit local chairmen, finance chairmen, and meet with editors (all during parts of July and August).
7. Produce graphics material, brochures, etc. for approval (by July 15).
8. Go into production and ship out initial campaign materials (by August 1).
9. Recruit key staff people to head divisions of campaign (by July 15).
10. Recruit most additional staff (by Sept. 1).
11. Formulate media mailing list (by Aug. 1).
12. Mail complete press information kits throughout state (by Aug. 15).
    .
    .
    .

Each interim objective could be subdivided into other objectives. *For example,*
Interim objective No. 12 could be subdivided as follows:
a. Complete all photo-taking of candidate for use in promotional literature (by July 20).
b. Select all official photos of candidate and family (by July 25).
c. Compile and complete official campaign biography of candidate (by Aug. 5).
d. Print and obtain one of each campaign brochure, button, bumperstrip, etc. for inclusion in kit (by Aug. 10).
e. Arrange for volunteers, workloads, and volunteer supervisors to coordinate all inserting, folding, etc. for kits (by Aug. 10).
    .
    .
    .

[a]On May 3, the campaign management laid out its first assessment of objectives to achieve victory on election day.

Forecasting is critical, since erroneous forecasting may result in uncorrectable errors—once the election is over. Forecasts predict more than election day vote totals; they predict the components of those totals—voting preference tabulated by geography, age, ethnic background, etc. They predict changes in voter attitudes, reactions of the opposing candidate to the campaign, reactions of journalists to issues that will be raised, etc.

Budgeting is both monetary planning and monetary forecasting: what will revenues (fund raising) be, and what will expenditures (the cost of the campaign) be? To forecast revenues, one must forecast components of the revenues. What will direct mail raise? What will dinners raise? Receptions? Newspaper ads? and so forth. To forecast expenditures, one must predict the impact of expenditures: how much television time will have to be purchased to increase the candidate's identification factor? In a local race in which television cannot be used, and with few issues, identification may elect the candidate: the candidate whose name gets around the most wins. How many billboards will have to be purchased (i.e., space rented) to achieve enough recognition and identification to win the election for school board member?

In any campaign, quantitative tools are required for forecasting. The larger the campaign, the more money involved, the greater the need for quantifying variables, and using probability to predict possible outcomes. Guesswork may do in a campaign whose outcome is really not in doubt, but it will not suffice in a competitive contest.

In conclusion, it should be emphasized that forecasting requires an understanding and evaluation of the effects of interdependent variables. For example, in forecasting fund raising, one cannot forecast direct mail receipts without predicting the response of those solicited; that is, what percentage will respond? What will be the average per capita response? How these people respond will depend on other variables; e.g., the publicity the campaign is receiving; to what extent it is perceived in the press as an efficient campaign with a chance to win; whether the issues raised by the candidate in the campaign are perceived by those solicited as important; whether events in the political environment favor the campaign—thus, if the candidate is raising student unrest as an issue, his direct mail appeals may bring in more funds if campus problems persist during the time the direct mail solicitations are being received.

Organizing

The objectives and the work necessary to attain the objectives dictate the skills that will be needed. In organizing, the manager decides on the positions to be filled and on the duties and responsibilities attached to each position. Coordination is an essential part of organization.

The time span of a political campaign is so short that organization must be appropriate for the goal; it must be precise and methodical. A uniform structure throughout the organization is inappropriate, since different needs must be served. To some extent, the structure reflects the nature and personality of the candidate, just as every other aspect of the campaign reflects the candidate. The way in which work is organized also reflects the style of the manager and the staff. The manager who is not given a wide charter by the candidate and campaign committee may not delegate much responsibility and authority to the staff.

Compensation is a factor in motivating staff, which can receive salary hikes or cuts; employees can be promoted or demoted, even fired. In contrast, volunteers need not tolerate undesirable working conditions or unpleasant rigidities, although volunteers with limited skills may require and accept considerable coordination as they perform simple, repetitive tasks (e.g., stuffing envelopes). *Volunteers can always quit without any loss in pay.* Their assistance should be valued and appreciated, and they should be treated well.

Generally, the more creative the task, the less rigid the structure. Staff members in press and media, research, writing, editing, and advertising require a creative environment. Given the campaign's short time duration, there must be inflexible deadlines, beyond which creativity cannot be invoked as an excuse for delay. Creative staff positions should only be filled by individuals who can work as part of a team, accept direction and meet deadlines.

Staffing

In organizing, the manager establishes positions and decides which duties and responsibilities properly belong to each one. In staffing, he attempts to find the right person for each job.

Critical positions, such as scheduling director, cannot be filled by an employment agency or by examination. Similarly, the press secretary must be able to articulate the candidate's views. Such key staff members must be able to relate well to the candidate, take direction from the manager and work easily with other staff. Even at the campaign's lower levels coordination and teamwork are essential, although the candidate may not be directly affected by problems. It is easier to identify specific skills that can be readily tested when dealing with clerical positions.

In the large campaign, the campaign manager may hire only the major staff members who, in turn, hire subordinates. There may even be a personnel operation to fill the large number of support positions. In the campaign with less than two or three dozen staff members, the manager should try to hire, or confirm the hiring of, each new staff member. The smaller the effort, the more important each staff member is to the operation, and the greater the interest the campaign manager should take in each individual hired.

The campaign manager must decide how important various factors are in staffing. These factors include interest in politics and in the campaign, political philosophy and beliefs, and loyalty to the candidate. These factors should not be applied uniformly, nor can they ever replace competence. Philosophical commitment may not be as important in the mailroom as in research or the press office, but it is helpful in both places. Unfortunately, the cost in time and money to recruit ideal individuals for each slot is prohibitive; however, competent individuals philosophically compatible with the candidate can be found, if the desire on the manager's part is evident, and a real effort is made.

The temporary nature of the campaign makes it difficult to recruit competent people. For example, a highly skilled secretary may already have a well-paying and secure position; why should she sacrifice it for an insecure campaign position with less pay and lacking typical fringe benefits? Campaigns generally do not have overtime, medical insurance, and other customary fringe benefits found in the private sector.

The political campaign manager must attract individuals by offering them a challenging, fast-moving work environment with an adequate, and hopefully, comparable, salary. If they are philosophically motivated, the candidate can be a plus factor. The manager is looking for philosophical commitment, interest in politics, positive feelings about the candidate. He is also looking for a variety of personal attributes: good character, honesty, loyalty; superior work habits, dedication, dependability, perseverance; intelligence and ability; human relations skills; amiability, even temperament, ability to work under stress. These personal factors must be balanced against the individual's experience, education, and professional competence at a given task. Experience can be very overrated, because it may be experience at doing a *poor* job. The campaign stressing innovation can be compromised by too many experienced employees, whose prior and extensive campaign experience consisted of mediocre work, bureaucratic-oriented work, or performance to meet standards lower than the excellence sought by the innovative campaign.

Bright, aggressive novices can learn quickly; less intelligent, apathetic employees or those with character defects may have problems the campaign cannot overcome. Novices can work under the direction of more experienced staff members, including the manager. The attributes sought in the staff member are summarized in Table 3-3.

Direction

Since no one can predict with certainty just what problems and opportunities will arise in the day-to-day work, lists of duties must naturally be couched in rather general terms. The manager must, therefore, provide the day-to-day direction for his subordinates.

Direction, like any other aspect of campaign management, reflects the

Table 3–3

Personal and Professional Attributes Sought in Staff Members by the Manager in Recruiting and Selecting Staff Members

1. Good character
   a. honesty
   b. loyalty

2. Superior work habits
   a. dedication
   b. dependability
   d. perserverance
   d. attentive to detail
   e. takes pride in work; wants to win

3. Innate ability
   a. intelligence level
   b. verbal, mathematical aptitudes

4. Acquired skills (quick learner?)
   a. specific work skills
   b. knowledge, vocabulary, ability
      to communicate in office
      environment

5. Human relations skills
   a. amiability
   b. even temperament
   c. ability to work long hours
      under stress
   d. sensitivity to others

6. Philosophical orientation
   (one or more of the following)
   a. interest in public affairs and
      government
   b. philosophically motivated
      (i.e., interested in ideas)
   c. favorably inclined toward
      candidate's party
   d. favorably inclined toward
      candidate
   3. motivated by campaign

7. Specific campaign
   a. loyalty to campaign manager
   b. interested in challenge of
      this campaign
   c. motivated by campaign issues

8. Experience:
   The applicant's experience in prior
   campaigns may have to be balanced
   against much of what is involved in
   items 1 thru 7.

personality of the candidate *and* the leadership style of the manager. Staff members and volunteers require different kinds of direction; different kinds of staff members or volunteers also require varied direction. Creative people will be stifled if direction is too cumbersome and overbearing. The resulting morale problem can impair the efficiency of the campaign. Less creative people, and volunteers at low levels, may require more direction, or they will do a poor job, which also impairs morale. If each staff person hired is motivated by the *idea* of working in the campaign, this motivation may reduce the need for direction. Staff members who are motivated *and* competent do not need to be told what to do, and they may often originate their own ideas.

Control

In directing, the manager explains to his people what they are to do and helps them do it to the best of their ability. In control, he determines how well the jobs have been done and what progress is being made toward the goals. Reporting is a means of control.

The measure of a political campaign is the outcome on election day. As a measure of control, this outcome is useless; it is too late to remedy what has been done inefficiently or poorly. The campaign manager requires control mechanisms that continuously monitor the progress of the campaign toward its ultimate goal of victory on election day. These mechanisms must measure what can be effected or altered by the manager, not those aspects of the environment over which he has no control.

Control is impossible unless there is clarity in staff roles and responsibilities. Staff members should not be permitted to fail because they did not know what was expected of them. Also, they must receive the support and backup to accomplish the task; otherwise, the staff member's own ability will not be fully utilized. Control requires that responsibilities and tasks be broken down into units so that activities can be controlled and individuals held accountable. Consider the problem of a press secretary who is responsible, among many other things, for several news releases a day going out, including the candidate's schedule, which is mailed twice a week. Table 3-4 breaks down a few elements of control.

Innovation

If the manager merely attempts to continue doing what he has been doing in the past, making the best possible showing in view of external circumstances and the resources available to him, his organization will be a static one at best. Further, it is more likely to decline than to stay in the same place if the environment is competitive.

Innovation is overlooked as an element of managing political campaigns for several reasons. Many campaign managers are influenced by the comfortable

Table 3-4
Control Mechanisms for Mailing News Releases[a]

Area to Be Controlled	Staff Member Responsible
Final approval of copy	Press secretary
Typing and format	Press secretary or (name
Proofreading, OK for duplication	Press secretary or (name)
Duplicating, choice of paper, folding	Mailroom (name)
Preparation and posting of data processing address labels; running thru postage meter	Mailroom (name)
Volunteers for stuffing envelopes	Volunteer coordinator
Delivery to post office by messenger	Headquarters manager

[a]*Assumption:* Research division, campaign manager, press, scheduling, etc. working harmoniously with each other and candidate. Delivery mechanisms—by-hand, by telecopier, by telephone, by audio feed—are working well. However, news releases are not being mailed promptly.

environment of the past: in certain areas a candidate of a given party was virtually assured of election or reelection. Other campaign managers are influenced by
their political party organizations, which are stable, sometimes bureaucratic, and
rarely innovative. Finally, innovation involves more thinking and more work
than doing things as they always have been done. The campaign manager who
uses past political campaigns as a guide and who refuses to recognize the unique
nature of each election and each candidate can only succeed if the environment
is unchanging and the opposing candidate's campaign manager is also a captive
of the past.

The environment is not static; what is innovative in one election may be
outdated two years later. The "old South," in which the Democratic Party sur-
vived with *non*-campaigns, typified stability; most political races now reflect the
uncertainties of the environment. Candidates wage *competitive* races; competition means the candidate skillfully exploits issues and effectively utilizes the
media. In a competitive race, the leading candidate can lose on election day if he
"stands still" while the opponent runs an innovative campaign.[c]

Representation

The manager's job includes representing his organization in dealing with
outside groups.

The political campaign manager is a very "public" figure. The candidate
and his family may be more visible; the press secretary may deal more directly
with the press; but the campaign manager meets with the most important reporters, he confers with substantial financial contributors or solicits prospective
backers, he may meet with leaders of business, unions, veterans or patriotic
groups, ethnic blocs or religious groups, women's organizations. . . . He will often
represent the candidate in negotiations with these *outside* groups, i.e., outside
the regular campaign organization.

In a large campaign, the representation function may be assigned to a senior
manager, equivalent to the chairman of the board of a corporation, and the
actual direction of the campaign assigned to a manager equivalent to the corporation president. The managers, regardless of how they apportion the management
functions (Table 3–5), operate within an external environment beyond their
control. In contrast, lower level managers and subordinates can persuade their
superiors to change their minds. Thus, the framework of the top managers, who

---

[c]For example, in the 1970 Senate race in New York Democrat Richard Ottinger won
the primary with an expensive television spot campaign. Faced with three Democratic rivals
with similar positions on the issues, Ottinger won on the basis of positive identification. His
strategists pursued the identical strategy in the general election campaign, but Ottinger's
lead evaporated as Buckley achieved *issue* identification and rose from about 25 percent to
39 percent to win the three way race.

Table 3–5
Management Functions

1. *Planning* (includes *Forecasting* and *Budgeting*)
2. *Organizing* (includes *Slotting Positions* and *Coordinating*)
3. *Staffing* (includes *Recruiting* and *Selecting Staff*)
4. *Direction* (includes *Day-to-Day Direction*)
5. *Control* (includes *Reporting*)
6. *Innovation* (includes *Competing*)
7. *Representation* (includes *Negotiating outside the Campaign*)

represent the campaign to the outside and who make the major strategic decisions, is far wider than the framework that circumscribes their subordinates *but it may be more rigid.*[3]

Four basic limitations apply to the campaign manager: the environment, the candidate, the nature of the ad hoc organizational structure, and the campaign's short time span. This treatment has emphasized the environment and the influence of the candidate's personality, temperament, and style and the temporary nature of the campaign.

The candidate can at any time exercise his prerogatives to further circumscribe his manager. The candidate can modify his schedule or refuse to keep a scheduled commitment. He can change his position on an issue or, without any advance warning to the manager, stake out a new position. He can demand that a staff member be dismissed or that a volunteer local chairman be removed. He can repudiate the manager; in the extreme case he can cease to be a candidate. Although the candidate can be counselled and pampered, prompted and cajoled, motivated, orchestrated, and scheduled, he cannot be *controlled.*

The candidate may personally be unable to cope with detail; ordinarily, he may be late and unreliable. Yet, his campaign is methodically scheduled. How can a candidate be unorganized and his campaign organized? The manager overcomes the candidate's personal liabilities. He relates to and is trusted by the candidate, who gives him broad authority. The manager has precisely what the candidate lacks—a flair for detail and a quest for precision.

It is said that a lawyer who defends himself has a fool for a client. The candidate who manages his own campaign has a fool for a campaign manager. The candidate is often in the least likely position to manage the effort. His time should be devoted to the actual work of campaigning: travel, hand-shaking, media interviews, speechmaking, even the planned, programmed rest intervals, which are an indispensable part of the routine. The candidate's perspective is not conducive to decision making. He is most involved in the campaign's excitement and hence most immune to the hard realities of survey research. He spends more time with his supporters than with the uncommitted. He goes from emotional highs to emotional lows and resolves his insecurity by surrounding himself with partisans.

In George McGovern's 1972 Presidential campaign, the rejection of a hierarchical structure, which reflected the candidate's rejection of organization, was
a major factor in the lack of integration (i.e., coordination). In contrast the
Committee to Re-Elect the President, with its hierarchy and careful strategic
planning, reflected Richard Nixon's lawyer-like, detailed approach (except for
Watergate). The planning began early as the President and his top lieutenants
exploited the incumbency. The hierarchy extended from the campaign organization to the White House itself.[4]

There are incumbents who have been in office so long that the campaign
organizations are mere formal recognitions of their machines. Mayor Richard J.
Daley of Chicago ran the city in a businesslike way. His organization was not
limited just to campaign years; it was a full-time service organization that provided
civic services through its political operatives, including many who were on the
city payroll. When someone had a complaint about police protection or garbage
collection, he could route his complaint through the political organization, or
the local political operative. During election years, the machine became the formal re-election apparatus of Mayor Daley, and it performed admirably the get-
out-the-vote function.[5]

Machine politics is the exception, not the rule in the United States. As the
media becomes more and more important, it permits candidates to bypass both
party and machine. The party, the machine, the incumbency—all these can, to a
degree, circumvent the time frame of the campaign and its consequences. The
party, with its full-time, year-around staff; the machine, with its patronage and
funding; the incumbent, with the perquisites of his office; these are the elements
for organization outside the campaign period—ways of funding rent, telephones,
office equipment, staff. These benefits of party, patronage, or incumbency partially overcome the inherent obstacles of a short-term, ad hoc campaign that
must move quickly against time.

Any campaign must resolve ten seemingly conflicting demands.

Staff versus volunteers.   A hierarchical structure with full-time, paid staff is
essential; yet, volunteers must be recruited. Their lack of compensation creates a
barrier to the enforcement of a hierarchical structure that distributes responsibility and *authority*. Volunteers highly motivated by philosophical considerations or by the candidate are naturally suspicious of paid staff; they do not
always recognize that only the staff can provide the professionalism needed for
the campaign, although some volunteers can be exceptionally able and talented
professionals.[d] Volunteers provide the massive manpower that could only be
duplicated at probably prohibitive cost to the campaign.

-----

[d]Prominent advertising executives may serve on a campaign's media advisory committee. Sales executives may act as volunteer advance men.

Generalists versus specialists. Each component of the campaign requires skilled specialists—experts in scheduling, advertising, logistics; bookkeepers and accountants; researchers, speechwriters, etc. The questions of strategy and judgment cannot be resolved by the specialist. The generalist (who may be and should be familiar with the specialties required in the political campaign) is in a superior position to make decisions that reconcile the demands and needs of all the specialists within the campaign. The generalist may have received his initial political experience as a specialist, perhaps as a press secretary, or an advance man, or get-out-the-vote technician. The campaign manager who has, at various times, served as a press secretary, a finance director, scheduling director, advance man, etc. will have a superior understanding of each specialty. As a generalist, his decisions will reflect the influence of those specialties he has practiced.

Candidate versus campaign manager. The candidate is the ultimate source of authority in the campaign. He symbolizes for many volunteers the reason for their activism: what he says and what he stands for represent their constituency. Whether he chooses to exercise his authority and prerogatives or not, he is responsible for what happens in the campaign. Regardless of the broad charter of the campaign manager or of the influence of substantial financial contributors, the candidate is more closely identified with the campaign than anyone else, and he will retain that identification—win or lose. Regardless of the closeness between the candidate and manager, their friendliness, mutual respect and confidence, there is inevitable friction, because the manager is a taskmaster. He pushes the candidate on, orders him to rest, persuades him to do something he does not want to do. The candidate must understand that in overruling his manager, he may undermine, not reassert, his own authority. He may be perceived as indecisive, or may implicitly suggest his own bad judgment in selecting the manager initially.

Routine versus creative. Many staff members work at relatively routine tasks—the receptionist, mail clerk, switchboard operator. The campaign cannot function without these staff members. It also requires creative people in media and press relations, research and speechwriting, advertising, scheduling and advance work. They must act on their own initiative, not react to circumstances, if they are to cope with the political environment. The campaign must be a place both for the people involved in routine, mundane chores and those involved in creative, challenging tasks. All must work together harmoniously.

Formal versus informal. The organizational chart is the formal organization. It is needed to legitimize the hierarchy and authority. The campaign requires clear lines of authority to facilitate decision making and rapid responses throughout the organization to decisions made at the highest level. The hierarchy is more than a structural element that delineates authority; it can be a valuable means of communicating. The informal organization arises spontaneously; although it is not shown on the organizational chart and may be in conflict with it, the campaign would be impotent without an informal organization. No campaign manager, at the time he formulates an organizational chart, can anticipate the need for each slot and the degree of authority to go with it. The organization must adapt, and the campaign itself is an adaptive process, extending even until election day. The dynamic organization is constantly adapting.

Some individuals rise to a given challenge and become more influential than envisioned. In a properly run campaign, competence is so highly regarded that competent people rise rapidly. They are given recognition and added responsibility; sometimes, more responsibility and authority than might be indicated by an organization chart that is unchanged. Indeed, some organizational positions may be preserved to protect individual pride and preserve harmony. The determining factor really is not what authority someone *formally* has, but what authority someone *has*. Thus, the press secretary with a flair for scheduling may so impress the candidate and campaign manager that he does more than sit in on schedule/strategy meetings; he emerges as the key decision maker in plotting a media oriented schedule. On the formal organizational chart, he remains the press secretary; in fact, he is also a deputy campaign manager, in charge of press and scheduling.

One final example of the informal organization might be the secretary to the campaign manager. On the chart, this person is only a secretary, presumably without authority. However, because it is a key position, with constant access to the manager—often involving the screening of many telephone calls and visitors; opening of correspondence, typing memos, filing material, and calling attention to matters for the campaign manager; the secretary becomes a very knowledgeable person. The secretary can provide helpful information to another staff member or supplicant, or be evasive. The secretary can prod the campaign manager to reply to a memo, or can conveniently file it. The examples are legion; the point is that the secretary's informal position is very important, just as the informal position of other people within the campaign is also important.

Free media versus paid media.   The free media space and time provided by news and feature coverage cannot be easily separated from advertising. The efficient campaign maximizes media coverage generated by a creative campaign schedule; such coverage has greater credibility with the electorate than advertising. Both free and paid media exposure should reflect the same theme and emphasize identical issues. The value of any advertising is thereby enhanced; the free media and paid media are said to be *complementary*.

An advertising agency eager to generate commissions may advocate excessive advertising when the campaign would be better advised to deploy its scarce resources aggressively seeking and exploiting free media coverage—especially television. The press secretary should not dominate advertising; he should lead the effort to obtain free coverage. Sometimes free and paid media are inseparable; for example, a small town radio station or weekly newspaper may provide coverage only if time or space is purchased. From an advertising stand-point the dollars could be more effectively spent elsewhere; from a news point of view, the dollars represent an investment to assure minimum news coverage.

Manager versus consultants. An outside consultant may be retained to counsel the campaign on strategy, tactics, media, demographics, or other areas. Perhaps he is retained to work directly with the candidate for television appear-ances. Problems arise over jurisdictional disputes between manager and con-sultants. For example, can a media consultant bypass the press secretary and work directly with the advertising agency? Can a consultant ignore the manager and appeal to the candidate?

It is usually advisable to restrict the consultant's role to *consulting*, i.e., counselling and advising, not managing. For example, a finance consultant may structure a fund raising plan; if he is to have line authority to implement it, the consulting arrangement should be clearly spelled out at the outset, or explicitly changed. It is sometimes advisable to set a deliberate policy of ambiguity governing the consultant's relationship; e.g., a manager retains a consultant to improve some aspect of the organization, but he does not want to undermine staff by giving the consultant authority, yet he wants the consultant to have *some* authority, enough provided by the ambiguity, so that staff members take him seriously.

Challenger versus incumbent. It makes a difference whether a candidate is the challenger or the incumbent. The incumbent has a record, with both strengths and weaknesses; his office provides perquisites (staff, travel allowance, tele-phone, perhaps franking privilege, etc.); the office also provides drawbacks (e.g., the need to break a scheduled commitment, leave campaigning, and return to Washington or to the statehouse for a vote). All things being equal, the challenger is in a superior position to go on the offensive. The incumbent's record is known or can be made known; it is somehow vulnerable to attack. The challenger, un-less an incumbent seeking higher office, has a less visible record and is therefore less vulnerable (not invulnerable). The challenger lacks the legitimacy, prestige, and prominence of the incumbent and often encounters more difficulty securing media coverage. If apathy and disillusionment with politics continue to grow, incumbents will forfeit their cherished advantage of citing "experience"–which will be a liability.

Ideology versus pragmatism. Some staff members and volunteers are motivated by ideology, i.e., by resorting to a fixed set of principles and ideas to which they believe the candidate subscribes. Others reject ideology as self-defeating and masochistic "purism." The campaign may be composed of staff members and volunteers who do not fit easily into ideologue or pragmatist category. Ideology suggests that winning is unimportant or less important than adherence to principle; pragmatism suggests that ideology is unimportant or less important than winning.

The ideologue suggests that victory is meaningless if one must so modify his views to win that they are no different than the opposition viewpoint. The pragmatist suggests that principles can never be implemented unless the candidate or party is in power. The term ideologue suggests rigidity; the term pragmatist suggests flexibility. Between the two extreme characterizations, there is room for adherence to basic principles, yet exploitation of issues at hand. Often, the problem is one of emphasis, choice of phrases of words, priorities in choosing issues, rather than outright rejection of principle.

Differentiation and integration.   This is the basic problem that the organization of the campaign must confront: how to have each person on the staff, each county organization or local activist group, each subsidiary support group in the community (such as veterans, lawyers, youth, etc.) "do their own thing" most efficiently, yet with unity of purpose. Specialization must not be permitted to compromise the overall goal of victory.

The manager must possess seasoned judgment and decisiveness, especially under stress, to resolve these conflicts. He requires high native intelligence and should be able to apply that intelligence to analyze and solve new problems—quickly evaluating alternatives and selecting the optimum course. His self-confidence and self-assurance must withstand criticism and second-guessing; his humility must permit flexibility to reconsider decisions in light of new data. He is an administrator and organizer who can judge the ability and character of others to make difficult personnel decisions.

As a finance executive and accountant, the manager formulates the budget, makes revisions, recruits a finance chairman and oversees a control system. As a salesman, he must persuade contributors to support the campaign, journalists to take it seriously, the leaders of business, labor, special, and ethnic interests to favor the candidate, and the candidate, staff, and volunteers to persevere. As a technician, the manager is intimately familiar with a myriad of details. As a skilled practitioner of communications, he runs interference between candidate and campaign, staff and volunteers, and between factions within the organization.

The manager is a motivator—often a surrogate for the candidate, who is rarely present in the headquarters. He is professional, yet charismatic. As he arbitrates and inspires, he relies on both the authority of his image and competence and the authority given him by the candidate.

The campaign manager's primary responsibilities may be split into two areas. A senior manager, perhaps designated campaign manager, is the chairman

Table 3-6
The Campaign Manager and the Campaign Director[a]

The Campaign Manager	The Campaign Director
1. Most authoritative; closest to candidate; authority derived from candidate.	1. Authority derived from candidate and campaign manager; probably (not always) second closest to candidate.
2. Chairman of strategy committee; oversees issues strategy.	2. Helps formulate strategy; oversees implementation of strategy.
3. Sets basic policy; appoints and oversees volunteer chairmen.	3. Helps set and implement basic policy; offers support to volunteer chairmen.
4. Chief ambassador to media (with assistance of press secretary), to large contributors (with assistance of finance chairman), business, labor, special interests, ethnic and other constituencies.	4. Helps arrange political alliances and meetings; attends instead of or in addition to manager; implements decisions reached and helps service special constituencies; relays special instructions to press, finance, other divisions within campaign; oversees all operating divisions within campaign.

[a]In a national campaign or statewide effort deputy campaign managers and assistant campaign directors would also play a role.

of the board who sets policy and oversees strategy. He is the campaign's chief representative to outside organizations. The second in command, perhaps called the campaign director, is more concerned with day-to-day administration (Table 3-6).[e]

Survey of Organization Theories

What organizational theories apply to the political campaign? No single theory is entirely applicable. The bureaucratic model is, in its entirety, too stultifying; the participatory model, without any qualifications or adjustment, undermines the authority and guidance needed from the top levels of the campaign. An eclectic approach, which selects relevant portions of different theories, is most in accord with reality.

Wilfred Brown has summarized four concepts of organization. The *manifest* organization is the one seen on the organizational chart. The *assumed* organization is the one perceived by individuals. The *extant* organization is the one revealed through systematic investigation. The *requisite* organization is the one in accord with reality. Brown notes that in the ideal situation, all four organizations would be the same.[6] In the political campaign, the organizational chart should be reasonably as close to reality as possible, so that the organization is

---

[e]The campaign manager/campaign director team approach was conceived by political consultant David R. Jones.

credible to its participants. People should perceive the organization as it is, so they are more likely to accept decisions of its middle level managers. The authority of its managers is less likely to be questioned if it is perceived as authentic. The campaign not in accord with reality will fail; unless the opposition is even more isolated from reality or the political environment proves to be fortuitously favorable.

Just as an individual must master his environment, so the campaign manager must master the political environment. Only then, can he effectively manage the campaign organization. Just as the individual must be flexible, so the organization must also have the freedom to learn through experience, to change with circumstances. The individual has a "certain unit of personality"; the organization, collectively, must know who it is and what it is to do in order to develop adaptability. To have this clearly defined identity, the organization's goals must be understood and accepted by its members, and the organization must be perceived realistically by its members. In the political organization, the participants must understand that victory at the polls is the overall goal; not educating the electorate, not dramatizing a particular issue, not criticizing the opponent, not attacking the incumbent President or Vice President. They must understand the subgoals: aggressive scheduling for the candidate, media exposure, a certain level of television advertising, etc. If the manager understands the political environment and the organization's participants understand the campaign's goals, then the campaign "is able to perceive the world and (itself) correctly," i.e., it can act in accord with reality.[7]

In one respect the campaign is superior to the business organization. Its participants more likely have a common denominator—commitment to the candidate. In campaigns that are impersonal or that lack philosophical motivation and interest in ideas, this commitment may not be present. Staff members are little more than paid employees—as in many business organizations.

The campaign collectively represents the mental health of its participants; its mental health reflects the strength of the commitment uniting its participants. This commitment, a base upon which to build spirit, enthusiasm, and higher motivation, does not guarantee organizational mental health. Each participant must believe that he or she is part of a unique campaign that has mastered the political environment. Participants must believe that the manager and the "people on top" are not captives of events. The overall confidence of participants in the success of the campaign affects motivation and morale. No campaign can be mentally healthy without the active participation of staff and volunteers who *identify* with it.

The manager and his immediate subordinates must explain the campaign's goals to staff and volunteers. Participants should feel they have a voice in the formulation of goals. Informed participants "in the know" are more likely to be united rather than alienated. Each component of the campaign must act consonantly or harmoniously with other components to avoid a split personality projected by the campaign.

The Fayol Theory

Henri Fayol, a French engineer who served as the chief executive of a large coal and steel combine from 1888 to 1918, suggested the existence of a single "administrative science."[8] Its five primary elements or functions of management—plan, organize, coordinate, command, control—were part of fourteen principles Fayol enunciated.

Unity of Authority. *Authority is not to be conceived as apart from responsibility; those with authority to issue orders should accept responsibility.* Today, especially in the political campaign, the other side of the coin is also stressed—those with responsibility to do the job should have sufficient authority. Given the short time span of the campaign, it is imperative that authority and responsibility be closely correlated in staff positions. Gray areas of uncertainty, including any deliberate ambiguity to allow for flexibility and development, may cause intolerable delays in implementing the campaign plan. Although initial ambiguity may encourage competition among staff members to originate ideas in fields outside their responsibility, staff members should not be permitted to second-guess their colleagues at the expense of getting their own jobs done.

In appointing volunteer campaign chairmen, responsibility and authority must be correlated. The chairman for a state, region, county, or other subdivision should not be given responsibility for the area unless he has the authority to make essential decisions. The same applies to chairmen of adjunct groups. If a volunteer chairman is only "window dressing"—someone who lends his good name and prestige to enhance the campaign's image in the area or among the constituency—then another person—a co-chairman, vice chairman or staff member—should have the clear responsibility and authority. In this case the person with the status and recognition does not have the responsibility and authority.

Unity of command. *An employee is to receive orders from one superior only.* The political campaign should have appropriate divisions within it so that staff members do not have to worry about conflicting orders from two different superiors. A staff member who is required to clear his actions with more than one superior is wasting precious time. His immediate superior should generally have the responsibility and authority to "sign-off" on the project; otherwise, he should not be in the superior slot. If a problem arises, the campaign manager or other high level staff member should find out the facts from the ranking staff member, both because he is responsible and to protect his morale (by going through and not bypassing him). Generally, no staff member should be censured or embarrassed in front of other staff members.

Unity of direction. *"One head and one plan" should apply for a group of activities having the same objective.* Within the limited time span of a political campaign, crash projects arise. For example, research may be required immediately on an item dominating the news or before a major television debate; a major speech may need to be drafted within a day or two; a television spot to capitalize on a news development may have to be produced and ready for distribution to television stations within a few days. The person directing the crash program should oversee staff working on it, and they should be told to report to this individual. For example, a single staff member may organize a major rally; everyone in the press office, scheduling, advance, campaign supplies office and mailroom, etc. may be instructed to cooperate with this person on matters petaining to the rally. There may or may not be temporary and obvious changes in the customary superior-subordinate relationships indicated by the formal organizational chart. If possible the changes should be avoided. The project manager (e.g., for the rally) should *approve* all phases of the campaign that affect the rally.

In the general course of the campaign, the structure should encourage unity of direction. Staff members should be reporting through the hierarchical chain, not randomly to staff members throughout the organization.

Chain of command. *Gangplanks should be used to facilitate a scalar chain of command.* Staff members should deal directly with each other provided each has informed his superior. The superiors' time may not even have to be taken if the matter falls within a defined area of expected cooperation.

Division of work. *Specialization is required for optimum output.* Staff members within a given sphere of competence should allocate their time within their specialty. For example, schedulers develop proficiency and confidence in scheduling; they should concentrate there. Above all, staff members should not be preoccupied with whether other staff members are doing their job. The individual who can afford the luxury of worrying about the performance of someone other than a subordinate is either not doing his own job well or does not have enough to do; most likely the former, since there is always more to do in a campaign.

Discipline. *Discipline is essential in the political campaign.* Discipline should not function solely from the choice and degree of sanctions (warnings, criticism, demotion, suspension, dismissal . . .), but from the knowledge that self-discipline is the best discipline. Staff members who need discipline should not be in the political campaign. The more self-discipline, the less discipline is required from campaign management; and extremely valuable management time is not wasted.

Subordination of Self-Interest. *Subordination of the individual interest to the general interest is important in the organization; it is crucial in the political campaign.* For Fayol, this subordination is achieved by firmness and good example on the part of superiors, by their fairness, and by their constant supervision of employees. In the campaign individuals must perceive that it is in their self-interest to subordinate their individual pursuits over the very short term to the overriding goal of electoral victory. If the right people were recruited for the campaign they are mentally prepared to subordinate individual interest. The campaign must "fuse" the individual's goals and aspirations with its goals. This is first done by recruiting sympathetic staff members committed to the candidate; it is reinforced by motivating staff.

Remuneration. *Remuneration should be fair.* The absolute level of remuneration in the campaign is less important than the *relative* level. Modest salaries are accepted as fair if (a) the campaign can in fact afford only modest salaries; (b) the staff members understand and accept this fact; (c) no individuals are compensated by a different standard. For example, if salaries are roughly 80 percent of the salary that each individual could earn in private employment (but the individuals are so highly motivated that they are willing to work for less than they could earn in the alternative nonpolitical pursuit), this standard may be unacceptable if some individuals are paid at 100 percent of what they could earn elsewhere, or even more than they could earn elsewhere. Sometimes, extra compensation may be required to recruit talented and needed staff members, and the only solution is a rigidly confidential payroll.

Fayol placed too much emphasis on monetary compensation, as this must be balanced with other forms of compensation. In the political campaign, these other forms might include status, access to the candidate, access to information, privilege of traveling with the candidate, the opportunity to attend receptions and even the opportunity to acquire experience. The latter can be very appealing compensation to the aspiring young staff member.

In an incumbent's campaign, government salaries may unduly influence the salary structure of the campaign. The high salaries of former government bureaucrats recruited to work in a campaign may offend the other staff members who are paid much less; or, especially, the volunteers who work without monetary compensation. The bureaucratic mentality and the inflated salary structure of the government can have a crushing effect on the morale of a campaign staff.

Centralization. *According to Fayol, centralization is natural.* In the campaign centralization insures that the campaign operates consistently with the campaign's theme. Consistency applies to news releases, speeches, brochures, advertising, interviews; it applies to local campaign headquarters and adjunct committees. The theme or array of issues, or the precise treatment of certain issues, must be uniformly pursued because (a) the theme or choice of issues, or treatment of issues, is strategically optimum; (b) repetition helps to get the message across to the electorate; (c) consistency aids the credibility of the campaign and the candidate; inconsistency impairs credibility; (d) local autonomy may cause embarrassing inconsistencies, even outlandish or intolerant statements or materials to be disseminated from a local headquarters or an adjunct committee; (e) at the very least, additional materials produced will probably be inferior to the primary campaign materials (unless the campaign is ineptly run, or did not seek out local input at the outset), and their creation consumes additional time that could better be devoted to other pursuits.

Centralization should not preclude sufficient local autonomy, or autonomy within adjunct committees, so that practices and materials can be tailored to local and specific constituencies. A control system must be devised to set the limits of autonomy, and define when the authorization of the central headquarters is needed.

Order. *The right person should be in the right spot.* An individual in the spot that optimizes the use of his background, aptitude, skills, and interests can be immensely productive for the campaign; a person mismatched for a job could even be counterproductive. The mismatched person could be frustrated if the job is too easy or too difficult, or outside his interests. His morale could be depressed; the job is done poorly, or at least much below optimum, and he may even damage the campaign effort. The campaign is deprived of the productivity it would have had if the individual had been placed in the right spot.

Within the volunteer sector of the campaign, this principle is vital. No more certain occurrence is found in a campaign than a volunteer with considerable intelligence, a splendid background and high skills engaged in a monotonous, routine chore like stuffing envelopes. Even if the individual is so sincere and interested that he returns to the campaign headquarters for more of the same, little can be said of the campaign that cannot find a better way to utilize this individual. The campaign staff must define several levels of volunteers suitable for different, even specialized assignments. The creative campaign manager and his staff thrive on imaginative approaches to the use of volunteer manpower. The motto is, "There is always a unique position optimally suited to each volunteer." The position is based on many variables (Table 3-7).

The campaign manager or his staff may assert that they are too busy to recruit, or to find tasks for, volunteers, or that matching the right volunteer with the right slot is too time consuming. Another assertion is that volunteers require too much supervision. These complaints have a basis in fact: an individual volunteer may require more supervision or explanation than the task is worth. More

Table 3-7
Evaluation of Volunteers

---

1. Background: intelligence, education, aptitude, skills, ability, experience.
2. Personal qualities: character; motivation, interest, persistence, dedication, dependability, amount of supervision required.
3. Trust: integrity, honesty, loyalty, discretion.
4. Operational: time commitment, regularity, precise factors (days of week, hours).
5. Human relations factors: ability to get along with peers, avoid conflict, sensitivity.

---

likely, the management is incapable of harnessing and motivating volunteers and placing them in appropriate slots. Many routine chores performed by staff could be delegated to volunteers, just as many lower priority tasks left undone by harried staff could be done by volunteers—if they are recruited, motivated, and put in the proper positions.

Equity. *Equity was defined by Fayol as justice tempered with kindness.* The ideal campaign manager is not so goal-oriented that he pursues political victory at the expense of equity; the result may be defeat at the polls. The manager who is viewed as cold and insensitive will find it difficult to motivate and inspire the staff and volunteers.

Stability of tenure of personnel. *This principle of Fayol is the least applicable to the political campaign, which itself is not a permanent organization.* It should be applied in the following way: staff people need time to adapt themselves to the campaign, the candidate, and the leadership style of the manager. Hopefully, most of this adaptation should be done earlier in the less visible phase of the campaign. During this time, as well as later, staff members need to know that their position is secure as long as they perform competently. They need to know that no one is likely to be dismissed, or have his salary cut because of lack of funds. Competent campaign managers never overhire and then cut back; each new increase in the staff or their compensation is predicated on the assumption that the level can be maintained or increased during the duration of the campaign.

Initiative. *The manager should encourage the staff to show initiative, even at the expense of his own vanity.* A vain manager lacking in his own confidence or taking advantage of the candidate's trust and confidence can become too infatuated with his infallibility. He can even be jealous of the talents of subordinates. Instead, the manager should zealously encourage initiative and creativity—even if he is shown to be in error.

Espirit de corps. *The manager must encourage cohesiveness among the staff.* The campaign can only succeed without espirit de corps if it is lucky!—as with an auspicious political environment, a blundering opponent, or incompetent

opposition. Espirit de corps affects motivation, which in turn affects productivity. The candidate and his manager set the tone for espirit de corps.

The Taylor Theory

Frederick W. Taylor,[9] termed the founder of the "second industrial
revolution," began his career in the 1870s as an apprentice in a Philadelphia
machine shop. As a young, ambitious foreman from a middle-class, hard working
family, he noticed that if new laborers worked harder, they gained nothing; the
other men even broke machines to keep production down. Taylor's system of
"task management," commonly called "scientific management"—a term coined
by Louis Brandeis—focused attention on the need systematically to study each
element of production. Time-motion studies analyzed each component and sub-
component of production to determine each step involved and to suggest an
optimum method of production. Taylor's theories failed to consider human relations problems; his "mental revolution" in which management and labor worked
together to increase production never really occurred. Taylor failed to grasp that
greater specialization in routine tasks produced monotony.

In the political campaign no dichotomy exists between management and
labor. To achieve the kind of team spirit Taylor sought in industry the campaign
must motivate staff and volunteers. Staff morale is boosted by minimizing
routine chores—which can be diverted to volunteers. Simple, labor-intensive tasks
(folding and stuffing envelopes, collating, stapling, distributing campaign material
door-to-door, in shopping centers, at rallies, etc.) are volunteer-oriented work.
Volunteers are compensated by the satisfaction derived from their work, the
pride they take in it, and the recognition they receive from their volunteer coordinator, the staff and campaign manager and, most importantly, the candidate.

Sometimes less productive volunteers deserve recognition. An excellent
example is the senior citizen who works less quickly than his younger counterpart but who faithfully donates each afternoon. The volunteer's self-esteem is
immensely important.

The more routine the volunteer task, the more production-oriented the
system can be. Here, Taylor's separation of planning and doing is helpful; he
sought to determine what was a reasonable amount of work for people to do; he
timed motions with a stop watch so that he could understand each step of the
process. Such approaches might be laughable today; in the political campaign,
volunteers who graciously donate their time would, upon being timed by a stop-
watch, disperse immediately and probably never return to such arrogance. People
who donate their time do not want to be treated as if they are liable to be fired
lest they keep a frenetic pace. They should be treated as if their labor is warmly
appreciated. Knowing that others care about their output, their morale will be
higher. Concern about productivity should be stated in terms of concern for the

campaign and for victory: that what they do will make a significant difference in the outcome of the election, i.e., that they are important.

Nothing is more heartening in a campaign than seeing the enthusiasm and excitement engendered by espirit de corps and teamwork. Volunteers compete against one another to see who can be more productive; volunteer headquarters compete in voter registration or literature distribution; groups of volunteers try to get out a mailing before a deadline. Productivity should be used as an incentive: the pride of accomplishment, the feeling of contributing to the campaign effort. Within this behavioral context, Taylor's system can spur productivity; in the campaign, basic motivation is already there, it simply needs to be exploited.

One final point: Taylor's *management-by-exception* is valuable for the campaign manager. Here, the exceptional situation or development is what occupies the manager's attention and time. He permits the smoothly functioning operation to run its course, as he looks for the extraordinary situation, the out-of-place development, something that does not fit in with the strategy. Perhaps a headquarters is not performing up to par, a county organization is not distributing enough campaign literature, or a fund raising component of the campaign is not raising its share of the expected revenue. He pinpoints the problem and resolves it. The management-by-exception approach requires control mechanisms to help discover what situations or developments merit the manager's attention.

The Mayo Theory

Elton Mayo,[10] who served as an associate professor at Harvard University's Graduate School of Business Administration, conducted his famous Hawthorne experiments (1927–1932) to measure the influence of social interaction on productivity. He was criticized for usually assuming that management was logical. Both he and Taylor wanted to show workers that it was in their self-interest to be productive. In a sense, this is what the campaign seeks to do among its volunteers. Their self-interest depends on the election outcome, which they must perceive as important to their welfare, and on their volunteer work, which they must perceive as important to the election outcome.

Mayo found that economic incentives were not the sole determinants of individual motivation. Persons within the work situation carry social meanings; sentiments, desires, and interests are also important. The social organization of the campaign represents values; the social demands of the worker are influenced by social experiences. The campaign is a social system. Observe any group of volunteers working in a headquarters, and the need for group affiliation is apparent. Volunteer work is a social experience. Volunteers are less concerned with the formal structure of the campaign than they are with the informal work group and with the people who deal with them—their fellow volunteers and the staff members with whom they come in contact.

Formal structure and authority relationships in the campaign must consider social factors. The feelings and aspirations of the volunteers and their need to affiliate with like-minded individuals must be considered as part of their group needs. More than mechanical supervision is required; management requires effective social skills to maintain harmony among the volunteers and rapport between the volunteers and the staff. Worker satisfaction leads to high productivity. Volunteers whose social needs are met are more likely to be motivated. They will contribute more time to the campaign, and the time they contribute will be more productively spent.

Taylor's scientific management suggests that working conditions, illumination, rest periods, monetary incentives, and various physical and physiological variables are the primary influencing factors on output. Mayo's social interaction model suggests that group needs must also be considered; his theory helps explain why volunteers or staff working in a sparsely furnished, run-down headquarters can be more highly motivated than their counterparts in a comfortable office suite in the suburbs. Even the most intelligent and capable staff members are motivated by a need for "togetherness"; social interaction is not limited to the volunteers.

The Weber Theory

German sociologist Max Weber,[11] influenced by the Kaiser era, proposed a bureaucratic form of organization to do away with the favoritism and depotism rampant in government agencies. The Weberian model assumes that the environment is known, relatively fixed and predictable. Since any contingency can be anticipated, the bureaucratic model provides for any eventuality. Bureaucratic rules also provide a rigidity incapable of adapting to circumstances or unanticipated situations. Weberian bureaucracy depends on rational-legal authority and rejects charismatic authority. In contrast, the political campaign manager's authority is partly based on his charisma and his ability to serve as a surrogate for the candidate. His authority reflects the staff's belief that he represents the will of the candidate, as well as the staff's perception that he is competent.

Weber believed that the existence of the informal organization, i.e., the spontaneous, unofficial relationships that arise, indicated something was wrong—that the formal or authorized organization was working improperly. In the campaign an informal organization arises to complement the formal organization, which could not have been structured to consider every possible interpersonal relationship. The informal organization is the campaign's method of improvising to consider fully the capabilities and personal qualities of each staff member; there is insufficient time to structure a new formal organization.

The campaign should act as a unit or, as Weber said, it should be *monocratic*. However, its cohesion and consistency cannot be achieved by rules and rigidity and an inflexible structure that presumes omniscient knowledge of the future.

Weber correctly required a clear definition of purpose and boundaries for any organization's participants. Since people act spontaneously, the boundaries must be broad to encourage initiative, quick response, creativity, and innovation. The bureaucratic structure carried to its extreme favors authority based upon hierarchy or position over authority based upon knowledge or competence. Despite bureaucracy's emphasis on specialization, its emphasis on hierarchy suggests an inherent tension between specialists and those in hierarchical positions of authority.[12] In the campaign it is therefore helpful for the generalists in charge to have experience in specialized fields.

Bureaucracy is found in government and in permanent, ongoing party organizations like the Democratic and Republican National Committees. These organizations have quasi-governmental status conferred by their protected and favored legal status and the trend toward taxpayer funding of their operations. Incumbents should avoid transferring their bureaucratic government mentality to the campaign. All candidates should resist the bureaucracy and resulting inflexibility characteristic of many party officials. Finally, no campaign structure can be so wedded to a hierarchy based on position that incompetents once appointed continue in positions of authority.

The Barnard Theory

Chester Barnard,[13] who served as President of New Jersey Bell in the 1930s, defined his "system of cooperation" to redefine authority as the character of a communication order in an organization. It involves two aspects: the subjective or personal acceptance of a communication as authoritative and the objective character in the communication that causes it to be accepted. The *authority of position* is often insufficient; individuals with superior ability, knowledge, or understanding can command respect regardless of their position. This is the *authority of leadership.* When authority of position and authority of leadership are combined, subordinates will accept orders far outside what Barnard called the "zone of indifference."

Barnard's four conditions of the acceptance of an order were probably met in the Committee to Re-Elect the President. It was not only hierarchy that justified the authority; staff members believed the orders to be compatible with the organization and also with their own advancement in the Nixon administration. Barnard wrote that a person can and will accept a communication as authoritative only if:

> (a) he can and does understand the communication; (b) *at the time of his decision* he believes that it is not inconsistent with the purpose of the organization; (c) *at the time of his decision,* he believes it to be compatible with his personal interest as a whole; and (d) he is able mentally and physically to comply with it.[14]

Barnard's conception of authority is an *upward* process, not the traditional *downward* process in which superiors order subordinates.

Barnard recognized that the informal organization must exist to satisfy the interpersonal needs that the formal organization cannot meet. Barnard maintained that the organization depends on an equilibrium between the contributions and satisfactions of its participants, and that persuasion is preferable to coercion as a motivator. Unless the staff and volunteers in a campaign receive what they regard as satisfaction commensurate with their contributions, they will produce at a suboptimal level or even quit.

The Drucker Theory

Peter Drucker has written that managing a business cannot be a bureaucratic, administrative, or even a policy making job; it must be creative, i.e., the manager must innovate.[15] Innovation is the *only* way of effectively managing a political campaign. Only the most secure candidate assured of victory regardless of what his opponent does can retain a manager lacking creativity and innovation.

Drucker insisted the business firm has no single objective. However, the campaign has victory as its paramount objective. To win intermediate goals must be pursued, and Drucker's *management-by-objectives* (MBO) insures that each level of the campaign achieves *its* objectives to make more probable achieving the ultimate objective on election day. Short-term results must be measured by their impact on the long-term objective of winning the election. For example, inroads among voters within a certain ethnic bloc may appear to be desirable. Perhaps a survey showing new support may be cited as an indicator of progress. However, if such inroads are at the expense of the campaign's base of support, which may numerically dwarf the newly-converted, the long-run objective may be sacrificed when the base of support evaporates by election day. The battle for a small number of votes is won; the election is lost. Just as the business firm has diverse criteria, the campaign also has standards by which to measure its progress (Table 3-8).

The Simon Theory

Herbert Simon of Carnegie-Mellon University explained that survival or self-perpetuation is the organization's objective.[16] This is true of political parties and their bureaucratic, administrative organizations like the Republican or Democratic Senatorial Campaign Committees. It is untrue of the dynamic campaign seeking victory at the polls.

Simon recognized that specialization, which is needed in the campaign, conflicted with unity of command, required by the campaign to respond quickly

Table 3-8
Drucker's Objectives and the Political Campaign

For the Business Firm	For the Political Campaign
1. Market standing	1. Identification of candidate; popularity
2. Innovation	2. Popularity of candidate among certain
3. Productivity	geographical, ethnic, etc. sectors
4. Physical and financial resources	3. Fund raising
5. Profitability	4. Penetration of news media
6. Manager performance and development	5. Level of paid media advertising
7. Worker performance and attitude	6. Distribution of campaign materials
8. Public responsibility	7. Staff performance and attitude
	8. Use of volunteers
	9. Efficiency of campaign schedule
	10. Conformity to law, ethical standards

with a single voice to developments in the political environment and to actions of the opposing candidate and campaign. Simon's decision making approach focused attention on where decisions are made, and at which level different kinds of decisions are made. What Simon proposes is relevant to the campaign organization: that one should define the structure by examining the points at which decisions are made and the persons from whom information is required for satisfactory decisions.

For example, should the central campaign headquarters determine the level and nature of advertising in a particular county or area? If so, what influence, if any, should the local chairman have? Should he have veto power, the power to adjust upward or downward within certain limits? Should the local chairman select issues, write his own copy for advertising? What if he can raise earmarked issues for such purposes? What happens to contributions earmarked for local advertising; can they be channeled to the campaign's central war chest? Advertising provides an illustration of decision points within a recent statewide campaign (Table 3-9). The central headquarters controlled all news releases except those concerning headquarters openings, announcements of local chairmen or committee members, local endorsements, an upcoming visit by the candidate, etc. These releases could be mailed locally if certain guidelines were understood and satisfied, and if the local activists used the thorough and personalized media list supplied by the central campaign office and prepared releases according to a prescribed format. Thus, the public information program decision points were roughly consistent with the advertising decision points.

A doctrine of subsidiarity is applied to insure that no decision that can be made at a lower level of the campaign should be required by the structure to be made at a higher level. The structure should connote varying points where different kinds of decisions can be made. Otherwise, valuable time is wasted when superfluous authority is invoked to make a decision that could have been made at a lower level.

Table 3-9
Decision Points in the Political Campaign—Advertising Example

1. All decisions regarding overall theme were made by the candidate, campaign manager, campaign director, news director (press secretary).
2. Advertising and media consultants and volunteers, as well as friends and family of the candidate, occasionally advised on theme.
3. A mathematical formula to determine the level of media buying and choice of media (TV, radio, newspaper, etc.) was formulated by a media committee, which made operational media decisions. This committee's decisions were ratified by the campaign manager, campaign director, and news director.
4. The local chairman could recommend modest advertising to be placed in local media. If he raised the funds himself, he could decide to place such advertising without authorization from the central headquarters. Such advertising was controlled (see below).
5. The central headquarters had sole decision power over television; the media committee made television decisions. The local chairman could recommend supplementary radio, newspaper, outdoor or other advertising; however, the television budget involved such significant spending that it was governed by the mathematical formula, subject to revision.
6. No authorization from the central headquarters was needed for the placement of advertising *if* the material (radio tapes, advertising mats, photo-ready copy, etc.) had been provided by the central headquarters.
7. The local chairman did not need central authorization if he raised the funds locally for advertising and the subject matter did not concern issues; examples would include announcements of headquarters openings, or announcements of the candidate's upcoming visit (which advertisement would have to be okayed by the advance man in charge of the visit).

Simon's concept of "satisficing"—looking for a "satisfactory" or "good enough" course of action—is useful for the political campaign. For example, a campaign speech may be suboptimal but it is the best that could have been done in the limited time given the speechwriter. A news release needs improvement but it was well written considering that it was issued almost immediately following a news development that required the candidate's reaction statement. Goals of quality, quantity, consistency, and deadlines must be satisfied under given circumstances. The objective is to satisfy each criterion; when all criteria are considered *together,* allowing for trade-offs among competing criteria, the product is optimal.

Simon examined the nature of goals, and he suggested that official goals be stated in broad and ambiguous terms. Narrowly stated goals prove to be constraints rather than incentives; they institutionalize the means required to achieve them, and they stifle creativity. Simon explained that it is rarely possible to maximize the goals of any one individual or group. Individuals have a variety of personal goals. Divisions within the political campaign have their own goals— press wants coverage, scheduling wants on-time events, advance wants crowds at events. The goals may be complementary; they may at times conflict. The objective is to "satisfy" all goals, rather than optimize in any one field. For example, press coverage might require altering the schedule to permit an important interview; scheduling people are upset at the alteration of their carefully planned schedule, the change even affects the advance people who were gearing for a crowd at a different time. Everything is not concurrently maximizable, and priorities must be set, choices made. In this particular example, media coverage is still the preeminent intermediate goal.

The individual can develop a personal commitment to meet the organization's goals. To the extent this is done, and in the political campaign it should be done, the individual acquires Simon's "organization personality" and is motivated to work toward the organization's goals. Within the political context, this "internalization of goals" is another way of saying that staff and volunteers must be thoroughly committed to the goal of electing the candidate. Next, they must be committed to the *means* of electing the candidate. These means become intermediate goals that must be attained for the overall goal of electoral victory to be achieved. In order for the "internalization" to occur, organizational participants (staff and volunteer) must understand what the intermediate goals are, perhaps why they were chosen, and definitely how each of them can help achieve the goals.

In Simon's view of authority the subordinate "holds in abeyance" his own critical faculties for choosing between alternatives and uses the receipt of the command as the basis for his choice. Each time a superior in a political campaign requests a lower ranking staff member or volunteer to do something, he is asking that person to trust his superior judgment. If that trust is not present at the outset, the command is either grudgingly obeyed, which is bad for morale and will influence the way in which the command is implemented, or the command is not carried out at all (especially in the case of the volunteer who quits).

The Contingency View

The elements of management are as applicable to the political campaign as to any other organization. Our brief survey of management theorists has shown that each theory offers some guidance for managing the campaign. Their relevance is partially circumscribed by the role of ideology, which plays a minor role in most campaigns, which we shall call *Type I* campaigns. Ideology plays a dominant role in left-wing/liberal campaigns (*Type II*) and right-wing/conservative campaigns (*Type III*). The 1972 McGovern Presidential campaign was primarily Type II; the 1974 Goldwater Presidential campaign was primarily Type III. Many ideologically based candidates alter their campaigns to appeal to a far broader base. These hybrid campaigns, including the Ronald Reagan Gubernatorial (1966) and Buckley Senate race (1970) may rely on an ideological base, but their theme is nonideological (Figure 3-1).

Ideological campaigns are rare because voters tend to reject candidates who

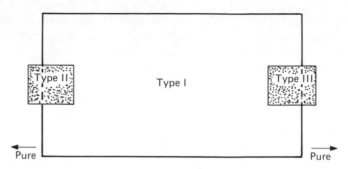

Figure 3-1. Types of Campaigns.
Note: Most campaigns are nonideological (Type I); few campaigns are pure
ideological liberal/left-wing (Type II), or conservative/right-wing (Type III).
Some campaigns are part ideological or hybrid (gray area).

stray from the electorate's perception of the center.[f] Ideological supporters inevitably find dissatisfaction with the positions taken by their candidate, even if
he is an ideological candidate. One can never satisfy ideological supporters; each
is more "purist" than his colleague. Victory inevitably brings disenchantment
with the elected candidate; defeat permits ideologues to say, "I told you so."
Ideologues are so rigid and self-assured that they often have difficulty understanding the perspective of (most) citizens who are less committed or who have a
different viewpoint. Ideologues who "think, sleep, and eat" politics find it difficult relating to citizens with diverse interests—the job, family, sports, church,
education, social, charitable activities. They cannot relate to the independent
voter, nor do they accept the phenomenon of the apathetic voter.

Ideological campaigns compromise the efficient management of the political
campaign. Volunteer chairmen are chosen not so much on the basis of their
leadership ability and community support, but on the basis of their ability to
meet a changing ideological litmus test. The campaign is an in-bred group of like-
thinking individuals who communicate only with themselves and their ideological
bedfellows. The campaign becomes one more battle for the ideologues, many of
whom would otherwise be writing letters to the editor, supporting and reading
publications which extol their viewpoint, visiting their Senator or Congressman,
listening to radio "talk" shows, or demonstrating in support of a cause. Some
ideologues are professional incompetents, masochistically conditioned to losing
causes. Others are highly competent professionals who resent being termed "sell-
outs" by other ideologues who oppose their professionalism.

The hard-core masochistic ideologues depict the fight within a campaign as
between volunteers motivated by noble purpose and the management and staff,

---

[f]As Richard S. Scammon, Democrat and master demographer put it, the candidate who
is able to find the "middle" on as many issues as possible has the best chance of winning.
(*Christian Science Monitor*, Sept. 23, 1975)

motivated by greed and power. No campaign manager can afford to have the debate argued on such an absurd level. Professionalism is not only compatible with volunteer politics; it makes volunteer politics possible.

The ideological campaign offers an independent base of support, as evidenced by both the Goldwater and McGovern campaigns, which raised tremendous sums from small donors. Masses can be highly motivated by a campaign with ideological overtones: people prepared to support the "real thing." Volunteers can work long hours for ideological campaigns, even if victory is unlikely. Even some large contributors, such as the businessmen who gave to Goldwater in 1964 and McGovern in 1972, can be ideologically drawn to the candidate.

The management of the campaign reflects the ideology, if any, of the candidate, and his relationship to ideological movements. Any campaign reflects its "core constituency" or base of support. This core constituency affects the kind of staff and volunteers recruited, the level and type of fund raising, relations with the news media, and ultimately the public's perception of the candidate and the campaign. It is possible, but unlikely, for a candidate, his campaign manager, senior staff, and chief financial supporters to be ideological but to be perceived by most voters as nonideological.

The contingency theory of management not only selects the appropriate portions of various management theories, but it understands the need to treat staff and volunteers differently. It also understands the need for specialization or differentiation, and the concomitant need for integration or unity of purpose. As the organization is fragmented or differentiated into separate parts, each with its own performance goals and standards, there must be some way for them to work in unison and in harmony. The division of labor among departments or volunteer components of the campaign and the need for unified effort lead to a state of differentiation and integration.[17]

The hierarchy within a campaign at both the volunteer and staff level imposes a *vertical* differentiation. The campaign's departmentalization, that is, its different divisions—press, scheduling, finance, etc.—impose a *horizontal* differentiation. There are differences in goals, time, interpersonal, and structural orientation (Table 3-10).[18] Pressures for differentiation in the campaign include: (a) hierarchy within staff, (2) hierarchy within the volunteer organization, (3) geographical division of responsibility, (4) separation of the campaign into spheres of task responsibility, (5) separation of fund raising from budgeting, (6) separation of soliciting large donors from direct mail solicitation, (7) the role of free versus paid media. . . . This list is far from complete.

The process and organizational devices used to achieve collaboration and the level of collaboration that exists among divisions within the campaign is *integration*.[19] Within the campaign as in a business firm, certain individuals must be assigned liaison functions to communicate with other staff members. To the extent the campaign is viewed as a marketing operation, everything is subservient to, and integrated with, the marketing function—maximizing the number

Table 3–10

Differences Within the Campaign in Goals, Time Orientation, Interpersonal Orientation, and Structure

Divisions	Goals	Time Orientation	Interpersonal Orientation	Structure
Press	Coverage by media	Daily, by event, and long-term	Personal contacts with media	Creative part unstructured; typing, duplicating, etc. highly structured
Advertising	Reach certain segments of electorate	Phases throughout campaign; then divided week-by-week	Spirit associated with creativity	Creative unstructured; mechanical, e.g., shipping, very structured
Scheduling	Planned travel and exposure; punctuality; media oriented schedule	Long-term goals set for campaign; short-term involves daily and event puntuality	Firm, but cordial relationship with others	"Tight ship" run by scheduling director
Finance 1. Big donors	Dollar target	Phases and events	One-on-one	Finance committee
2. Direct mail	Dollar target and in statistical terms	Letter projects; daily returns	Mass solicitation	Mechanistic, data-processing; small group which subcontracts out

of votes the candidate receives in his electoral victory. Every component of the campaign directly or indirectly gets votes. For example, finance does not directly secure votes, but it secures dollars that fund programs to get votes. Votes must be the quantitative standard of integration.

The most common and practical method of integration is connecting each *staff and volunteer department and level* within the campaign organization by a *matrix* form (Figure 3–2).

In sum, the political campaign requires more than a structural matrix. It requires a structural-behavioral-quantitative matrix integrating the organization, the people, and the methodology. The structure, the way in which authority is delegated, the interpersonal relationships, motivation, the nature of decision making, and the nature and methodology of the tasks are interrelated and inseparable. The campaign's management system must fully consider all aspects of the modern political campaign.

State Leadership \\ County or Area	Smith for Senate	Organization Divisions (*Example:* Press)	Adjunct Committees (*Two Examples*)	
	State Chairman	Press Secretary	Doctors for Smith	Veterans for Smith
County A	County Chairman (County A)	Publicity Chairman (County A)	Chairman, Doctors for Smith (County A)	Chairman, Veterans for Smith (County A)
County B	County Chairman (County B)	Publicity Chairman (County B)	Chairman, Doctors for Smith (County B)	Chairman, Veterans for Smith (County B)
County C	County Chairman (County C)	Publicity Chairman (County C)	Chairman, Doctors for Smith (County C)	Chairman, Veterans for Smith (County C)
Congressional District #1	District Chairman (District #1)	Publicity Chairman (District #1)	District Coordinator (Doctors)	District Coordinator (Veterans)

Figure 3-2. Matrix Form of Organization.

Note: If Congressional districts were merely subdivisions within counties, then Congressional District #1 shown would be depicted within the appropriate county.

4 The Political Campaign System

The organization can be viewed as an open system in interaction with its environment and composed of five primary components—goals and values, and technical, structural, psychosocial, and managerial subsystems.

—Fremont E. Kast and James E. Rosenzweig
Organization and Management: A Systems Approach

There are two central questions for any organization. How effective is the organization? How efficient is the organization? *Effectiveness* is getting the job done; *efficiency* is getting the job done well. For the political campaign effectiveness is winning the election; efficiency is winning the election with the best use of available resources.

If the election is won, does it matter if victory could have been achieved at less expense or if a more efficient campaign would have produced a higher margin of victory at identical expense? Efficiency is important and efficient management matters. First, the intelligent use of resources affects, and is not independent of, the ultimate outcome of the campaign. One does not know at the beginning that the campaign will be victorious. Resources squandered or imprudently deployed compromise the goal of victory. As the finite supply of campaign funding is apparent in the final days before election and the value of time is inescapable, it becomes painfully obvious that one cannot always compensate for lost time. If the political environment changes, the candidate leading marginally has no cushion upon which to fall; his thin lead can be transformed into defeat. An inefficient campaign can be effective, i.e., win the election, only if one or more of the following obtain: (a) the opposition campaign is more inefficient; (b) the political environment favors the candidate or changes to favor the candidate; (c) the opposition candidate makes a series of blunders. Generally, inefficient campaigns are ineffective, i.e., they lose.

Second, financial contributors and volunteer workers are not satisfied, especially during the course of a campaign, with effectiveness; they often demand efficiency. Rarely does a contributor say, "Spend the money any way you like. Do not give the matter much thought. As long as we win." Or: "Do the best you can, but don't worry. I will give you more money if you spend it inefficiently." Contributors want to be assured that their money is spent efficiently. Volunteers want to be assured that their time is spent in the way most beneficial to the campaign. Both contributors and volunteers may not judge the manager just by the victory; they may feel that another manager could have achieved the same at less cost or with a superior use of the volunteers' time.

Third, the number of votes received is important, because no opinion survey can be a perfect predictor. The manager who can cover the margin of error several times over can feel more secure about the outcome. Moreover, a higher victory margin can have added benefits—producing a "mandate" or coattails effect.

Performance analysis of political campaign managers cannot be in a vacuum but must consider the environment. For example, one campaign manager might boast that he won 15 of 20 campaigns. Another manager has a seemingly less impressive record, 15 of 30. No judgment can be made without additional information, which might reveal that Manager Number 1 turned away campaigns that were long shots; most of his candidates were incumbents favored by a big edge in party registration. Manager Number 2 preferred more challenging campaigns; 20 of his 30 campaigns had been written off as losers, five were toss-ups, and only five were favored to win. Performance analysis must consider additional qualifying data (Table 4-1).

Traditional management theories, similar to performance analysis without considering the environment, were closed-system views. They emphasized the organization's internal operation, as if physical science models could be expropriated to apply to the organization. Only the structure, tasks, and formal relationships of the organization were considered—and these were analyzed independent of the (external) environment. Modern theory, beginning with Chester Barnard, moved to utilize a systems, or unified, approach. Herbert Simon and his associates viewed the organization as a complex system of *decision making* processes. Management scientists emphasized the economic-technical system, and behavioral scientists emphasized the psychosocial system. The management scientists sought to establish normative models of managerial and organizational behavior. Systematic analysis and quantitative techniques were used to focus on the decision maker and optimize his performance. The behavioral scientists,

Table 4-1
Performance Analysis of Campaign Managers

	Total	*Wins*	*Losses*
Manager No. 1	20	15 (75%)	5 (25%)
Manager No. 2	30	15 (50%)	15 (50%)
Adjusted Score:	*% of Certain Wins*	*% of Toss-Ups*	*% of Predicted Losers*
Manager No. 1	15/15 = 100%	0/4 = 0%	0/1 = 0%
Manager No. 2	5/5 = 100%	5/5 = 100%[a]	5/20 = 25%[a]

[a]Manager No. 2 far exceeds the performance of Manager No. 1 in winning elections considered toss-ups or certain defeats. Both managers won elections their candidates were expected to win.

primarily interested in the human components, studied organizations in the real world rather than try to establish normative models.[1] No attempt has been made systematically to examine one of the most ingenious forms of organization—the contemporary political campaign.

Open Systems

The political campaign organization is an open system that interacts with its environmental suprasystem. Because the political environment is changing and uncertain, the campaign organization must be open, rather than closed, in order to survive and to win the election. As the open, adaptable system seeks to deal with the environment, it becomes segmented into specialized units (*differentiation*). This division of labor results in a countervailing need for united effort (*integration*).[2]

Differentiation by function can lead to conflict within the political campaign. For example, maximizing the performance of one functional department, scheduling, may adversely affect another department, press. Schedulers may be more concerned with punctuality than with media coverage; in their zeal to be on time, they may needlessly sacrifice important interviews. In their eagerness to move the candidate around quickly, they may not permit him enough time in one area to generate coverage; in their desire to placate conflicting factions, they may overschedule the candidate in a given area, resulting in more appearances than necessary to stimulate the desired level of media coverage. This kind of conflict can be partially resolved by the formulation of goals that are compatible with both divisions of the campaign. A *media oriented schedule* is most likely to stimulate news coverage, presumably favorable news coverage, and preferably television. If the two divisions of the campaign can agree on the imperative of a media oriented schedule and a common definition of its characteristics, they will resolve part of the conflict. To the extent that the conflict is resolved by appointing one or more staff members to specialize in this kind of scheduling, or serve as liaison between the two divisions, the *structural* subsystem is being employed.

Twelve major concepts of general systems theory can be applied to the political campaign (Table 4-2).[3]

In an integrated systems view the political campaign organization is a system within the environment or suprasystem. The campaign includes five basic subsystems.[4] The *managerial* subsystem is at the core of the campaign. It plays the central role in planning, organizing, and controlling the campaign's activities and in relating the campaign to the political environment. It unites the four other subsystems. The *structural* subsystem regulates the way in which people work together. The *psychosocial* subsystem accounts for the social relationships within the campaign. The *technical* subsystem supplies the knowledge, techniques, equipment and facilities for the campaign staff. The *goals and values* subsystem

Table 4–2

Application of Systems Theory to Political Campaigns

Key Concept	Application
Subsystems or components	The political campaign has managerial, structural, technical, and psychosocial subsystems, and other components, all of which are interrelated in the campaign's performance and are interconnected.
Holism, Synergism, Organicism, and Gestalt	One cannot look at a part of the political campaign and comprehend the breadth of its function. Alone, it does little or nothing; as part of the whole campaign, it helps elect the candidate.
Open Systems View	The political campaign must cope with the political environment and with the total environment. Its manager must understand the environmental suprasystem. The campaign constantly exchanges information and energy with the environment. In contrast, campaigns that lack innovation and are bureaucratic are relatively closed; they operate as if the environment did not matter.
Input-Transformation-Output Model	Based on survey research and information received from the environment, the campaign produces output (what the candidate says, how he says it, scheduling, advertising, etc.).
System Boundaries	In political campaigns in which the environment is assumed to be static, and managers lack innovation, the personnel are not highly motivated, and things are done as they always have been, the boundaries are more rigid, sometimes impenetrable; in the relatively open system, boundaries are permeable to permit the campaign to adapt, change, and perform in an optimal fashion, to make more likely victory on election day.
Negative Entropy	In the relatively closed system, the political campaign approaches irrelevance. For example, if the independent voter becomes dominant, but party type campaigns ignore him, the campaign, adequate for the old party era, is impotent. In the relatively open campaign, entropy—the movement toward disorder and irrelevance—is arrested as the campaign adapts its organization and strategy to survive and thrive.
Steady State, Dynamic Equilibrium, and Homeostasis	The closed system—the political campaign that does not seek to understand and monitor changes in the environment, and that lacks innovation—approaches an equilibrium of disorganization and failure. The relatively open system is in a dynamic equilibrium, where it must "keep going to stay still": the only way for it to remain in equilibrium is to keep adapting and innovating as circumstances dictate.
Feedback	Positive feedback tells the political campaign its strategy is correct; negative feedback indicates the campaign should reconsider its strategy, or its means of achieving the strategy.
Hierarchy	The political campaign, as a system, is part of the environmental suprasystem; the political campaign's components are subsystems.

Table 4–2 (continued)

Key Concept	Application
Internal Elaboration	Relatively closed systems move toward disorganization and disorder: in political campaigns, such an organization will lose the election. Relatively open systems adapt by greater specialization (differentiation), elaboration, and new, more relevant forms of organization, such as different geographical or functional subdivisions, new adjunct committees for support groups for the candidate, etc.
Multiple Goal Setting	The political campaign must recognize the diverse goals of its participants and seek to "fuse" their goals with the overriding goal of electing the candidate.
Equifinality of Open Systems	The election of the candidate is not uniquely attainable by a single strategy or set of means or methods; alternative strategies may be successful; many methods may be employed to achieve identification, issue penetration, etc. The campaign can start at a handicap or at an advantage and still win or lose the election. Different initial conditions can still, in different ways, achieve victory; victory can be achieved in different ways (reacting to the environment).

applies to both the participants and constituents of the campaign. The subsystems of open systems theory[a] are relevant to the campaign (Table 4–3).

Subsystems

Because the subsystems overlap it is difficult to consider any one subsystem without considering at least one more subsystem. This will become apparent as each subsystem is discussed in the remainder of this chapter. In addition, Chapter 5, although it is primarily concerned with the *psychosocial* subsystem, relates to the *structural* and *technical* subsystems. Chapter 6, which covers finance, is primarily concerned with the *managerial* and *technical* subsystems. Chapter 7 on the marketing function discusses strategy, techniques, and methodology in terms of the *technical* subsystem. It is the closest any chapter comes to "how to" campaigning. Chapter 8 on decision making relates the *technical* subsystem to quantitative techniques, but its organizational implications are part of the *structural* subsystem, and its strategic implications are part of the *managerial* subsystem.

---

[a]The subsystems enumerated reflect the definitions of Kast and Rosenzweig. The conceptual model of general systems theory is based on their synthesis.

Table 4-3

Subsystems and the Political Campaign

Structural Subsystem: Includes the organization chart for the political campaign, the slots to be filled, with their job descriptions, the authority attached to each staff position or volunteer chairmanship; the organized methods of communicating from one level of the campaign to another; the patterns in which tasks are assigned, and specializations arise, including the different task divisions within the campaign, such as finance, scheduling, press, advertising, volunteers, adjunct groups, etc., and the geographical divisions within the volunteer sector, such as local chairmen; includes the professional relationships between consultants and the campaign, advertising agency and the campaign, printers, vendors and other contractors and the campaign, etc.; includes the planned means of liaison and coordination between different sectors of the campaign and different geographical levels to assure unity of purpose (integration); includes the way area and committee chairmen are appointed, their responsibilities, privileges, formal relationships to the campaign and each of its divisions; any structural means or devices set up to facilitate coordination and integration, such as a matrix organization.

Psychosocial Subsystem: Includes the make-up, personality, temperament, behavior and motivation of each individual staff member and volunteer who comprise the political campaign; their aspirations, and how they relate to the status and role given to them in the political campaign, especially the hierarchy, or organized way in which positions relate to status or roles; social needs and group influences, both among the staff who need to work harmoniously and among the volunteers who have social needs; the social interaction of the staff and volunteers, within the staff and within the volunteer sector, especially among the volunteer chairmen; the relative influence that different volunteers and staff have within the political campaign; the influence of the environment—in terms of the way things need to be done—on the attitudes of the political campaign's staff and volunteers; the relationship of the environment, and the attitudes and personal make-up of the electorate, ethnic groups, key individuals, journalists on the political campaign, and the behavior of its staff and volunteers.

Goals and Values Subsystem: This can be viewed as part of the psychosocial subsystem; concerns the goals and values of the individual staff members and volunteers, and the need to "fuse" them with the campaign's goals and values; the goals and values of the candidate, his family, his friends and associates, the campaign manager, the staff, etc. and the need to reconcile these goals and values, especially relative to the goals and values of the electorate, which should perceive that the candidate has similar goals and values; the goals and values at different levels within the staff hierarchy or volunteer leadership hierarchy; short-term versus medium-range versus long-term (within the campaign context) goals at different levels of planning within the campaign.

Technical Subsystem: Includes the professional and specialized knowledge required within different levels of the political campaign; among outside consultants in media, direct mail, management, demographics, an advertising agency, and other specialties, as well as further specializations within the aforementioned; includes the techniques and methods used to communicate, secure identification among the electorate, persuade voters, measure public opinion, measure and control progress; the technology required, varying from certain types of aircraft for major campaigns to auto caravans and shopping center tours at the local level; the telephone system, including telephone banks and get-out-the-vote campaigns, drivers; headquarters deployment and modus operandi; kind of duplicating equipment, use of automatic typewriters, telecopiers, telephone call-in messages for the media, etc.; data processing, list maintenance, mailing programs, including fund raising techniques and programs.

Managerial Subsystem: The strategy of the campaign is influenced by, and determines, the other components of the campaign; here, goals are established, priorities set, choices made; the manager gathers the input, plans, organizes the campaign and seeks to devise methods of controlling; here, the campaign seeks to analyze the environment and its changes, and to adjust the other phases of the campaign to keep in tune with the changing environment; all the other subsystems are coordinated at this level and, as a whole, they represent the campaign, of which the candidate is an indispensable part; at this level, the campaign is related to the candidate.

Goals and Values Subsystem

Systems theory suggests that commitment to the campaign's goals on the part of staff and volunteers not only helps achieve goals, but such *internalization* is a major method of integration within the campaign.[5] It has already been emphasized that staff members should be recruited not only on the basis of their professional competence, but on the basis of their philosophical motivation, interest in politics, and favorable view of the candidate. Although individual staff members may vary widely in their personal goals, their common denominator of commitment to the candidate provides a valuable basis for internalization.

Internalization cannot be viewed in a void. Since the political campaign is an open system, the attitudes and behavior of its staff depend not only on the formal organization, tasks and assignments and social interaction, but on the environment. Furthermore, the behavior of any participant in the campaign is determined not only by his own personality needs and motives but also by those of his colleagues.[6] As an individual internalizes the campaign's goals, he influences his peers to "get with it" in working as hard as possible to elect the candidate. Internalization of goals occurs at three different levels.

> The strategic level relates the activities of the organization to its environmental system. The goals at this level are broad and provide substantial flexibility as to the means for their attainment.
>
> The coordinative subsystem translates the broad goals developed at the strategic level into more specific operational goals. The primary purposes of this subsystem are related to the coordination of activities between levels and between functions.
>
> The operating subsystem is involved in actual task performance. The goals at this level are usually very specific, short-term, and measurable. . . .[7]

The political campaign manager sets his goals at the strategic level. He deals with campaign strategy, the selection of theme, the choice of issues, the emphasis on particular issues, and the setting of priorities that govern the entire campaign. Once the strategic goals are set, they can only be attained by setting more specific goals to be implemented by others at a lower level. The middle managers in the campaign coordinate these goals within their respective divisions, e.g., fund-raising or finance, press or media, outside support or adjunct committees, get-out-the-vote drives or voter registration, etc. At the operating level, each staff member sets his own individual, specific goals, or is given goals or objectives to measure his performance. The strategic, coordinative and operating levels of goal setting can be applied to a Congressional campaign (Table 4-4).

Each individual has his own goals apart from the political campaign. These goals relate to ambition, lifestyle and social desires, monetary reward and other personal objectives. To the extent they relate to behavior, they are part of the

Table 4-4
Goal Setting in a Congressional Campaign

Level	Who Is Involved?	Examples of Goals
Strategic	1. Candidate and his family 2. Campaign Manager 3. Campaign Chairman (volunteer) 4. Campaign Finance Chairman and/or key financial backers (Probably no one else will be involved in strategy.)	1. Strategy and approach to issues is . . . . 2. Choice of issues to include . . . . 3. Amount of money needed to be raised is $_____. 4. Time commitment of candidate and family to campaign will be . . . . 5. Reach ____ percent of the electorate in person; reach ____ percent by other methods. 6. Achieve _____ percent identification among electorate. . . .
Coordinative	1. Campaign Manager 2. Key Staff 3. Others listed above, as required	1. Hire _____ people in the following slots in the campaign: . . . . 2. Raise funds with the following projects: . . . . 3. Appoint chairmen in each part of the Congressional district to recruit volunteers. 4. Set up a telephone campaign in the following areas: . . . . 5. Visit every service club (Kiwanis, Lions, Optimists, etc.) in the Cong. Dist. at least once. 6. Visit each of the following shopping centers and campaign at each one for several hours. . . .
Operative	1. Area coordinators 2. Individual staff members 3. Individual volunteers 4. Others listed above, as they perform their own individual chores	1. Approach the following individuals and ask for funds during this week: . . . . 2. In the next four weeks telephone the following service club presidents to arrange appearances by the candidate: . . . . 3. By next week call the telephone company to install the following telephones: . . . . 4. Get a list of all the major shopping centers in the Congressional District. . . .

psychosocial subsystem. As these goals and values relate to the organization, they are part of the *goals and values* subsystem. For example, the candidate's goals and values, including his ideology, have a pervasive influence throughout the entire campaign.

Goals and values at the strategic level are established within the *managerial* subsystem. At the coordinative level they are more likely to be established within the *structural* and *technical* subsystems. Goals and values at the operative level relate closely to the tasks at hand—the *technical* subsystem.

Managerial Subsystem

Since the political campaign is a relatively open system, the manager must understand the environment or suprasystem. Then he can develop goals and strategy and plan, organize, and control the campaign's activities to achieve its goals and implement its strategy. He can organize the structural and technical subsystems, design information gathering and decision systems, shape influence systems and leadership, and design a feedback system to see how the campaign is doing. These managerial tasks explain this book's emphasis on information and survey research, decision making and control.

The open system and a philosophy of innovation do not preclude acceptance of stable conditions within some part of the campaign. A *mechanistic* management system must be rejected, but some elements of mechanistic management usually associated with stable conditions[8] can apply to the political campaign (Table 4–5).

The managerial subsystem includes Peter F. Drucker's management-by-objectives (MBO): "Objectives are needed in every area where performance and results vitally affect"[9] the political campaign. Each division or component of the campaign must have objectives related to the overall objective of electoral victory. Geographical components have objectives stated in terms of vote quotas, as well as in terms of advertising, candidate appearances, etc. Objectives can be set in two ways—top down and bottom up (Figure 4–1).[10]

The strategy chosen by the manager reflects the realities of the political environment. He applies the elements of management to the task of electing the candidate. In sum, the political campaign as an open system is related to the environmental suprasystem (Table 4–6).

Structural Subsystem

A capable businessman would not necessarily make the best political campaign manager. First, learning the intricacies and details of campaigns is time consuming. The most perceptive businessman with a high learning curve still

Table 4-5
Elements of Mechanistic Management Applied to the Political Campaign

Element	Application to Campaign (Examples)
Specialized differentiation	Divide campaign into press, finance, scheduling, adjunct committees, volunteers, etc.; divide also by geographical responsibility.
Technical improvement of means rather than accomplishment of ends	Press division must also concern itself with technical means of information distribution (mail, hand delivery, telephone, telecopier, recording, etc.).
Reconciliation of individual and division tasks with main task	Each volunteer chairman is responsible to a volunteer chairman at a higher level.
Precise definition of responsibilities and methods for each role	The local coordinator of a campaign, or the local publicity chairman, has specific responsibility and is given an approved methodology for his tasks.
Hierarchic structure of control, authority, and communication	Facilitates control of local organization; established communications channels lead to quick implementation of command decisions; too much structure can stifle local adaptibility to developments.
Reinforce hierarchy by locating knowledge exclusively at the top	Satisfies campaign's problem of information security and confidentiality of plans; however, isolation can lead to decisions out of touch with reality and to morale problems within staff and volunteer leadership
Tendency for vertical interaction (between superior and subordinate)	Enables "chain of command" structure to transmit policies and plans through volunteer hierarchy— even in the smallest campaign.
Insistence on loyalty and obedience	Absolutely essential, especially to avoid leaks of information to media and others, and to insure quick response to orders.

would have to master a new specialty. Second, a businessman may lack the judgment and temperament of a political strategist. Third, although a businessman may be a good judge of the demand curve for his product, he may be unable to relate conceptually to ideas, political parties, candidates, and the political marketplace.

Occasionally businessmen are tempted to do more than raise campaign funds.[b] Their political adventures are usually doomed to failure, if only because of a stubborn self-assurance that they have all the answers. Typically, businessmen underestimate the importance of the news media; nor are they able to comprehend the phenomenon of rapid public opinion shifts to or away from a candidate, i.e., momentum. One of the most famous exceptions was entre-

---

[b]Southern California businessman and veteran fund raiser Henry Salvatori became so obsessed with winning Los Angeles Mayor Sam Yorty's 1971 re-election campaign that he switched from finance chairman to campaign manager; consequently, Mr. Yorty's losing campaign was assured of financing.

	TOP DOWN	BOTTOM UP
ADVANTAGES	Provides clarity; has force of authority; can produce quicker response; produces obedience; tells participants what limitations are.	Permits lower levels to participate and helps their morale; may motivate them; gets input and insights from lower levels; gives lower levels greater sense of participation in formulating objectives, hence greater stake in outcome.
DISADVANTAGES	Objectives imposed may not reflect reality perceived at lower levels; may be resented by those who have no voice in formulation; may be unrealistic, impractical, unattainable; may result in feedback only when it is too late, because participants do not feel they have a voice and hence do not venture feedback.	Lower levels may set objectives that are too modest, or not in accord with rest of organization; may break down discipline, command nature of hierarchy; may take more time than available in political campaign; may not fit in with overall strategy, which *is* formulated at top.

Figure 4-1. MBO Program: Advantages and Disadvantages of Top Down and Bottom Up.

preneur Mark Hanna, William McKinley's chief financial angel who also placed himself at the top of the campaign structure.[11] Business and sales people can act as finance chairmen, fund raisers, dinner chairman, campaign and committee chairmen, advance men and a variety of other roles. But the Mark Hanna example should be viewed as an exception to the rule that a businessman should not manage a political campaign.

Any campaign has an umbrella committee, which unites and oversees all campaign activities, including adjunct committees. Recent campaign laws force the candidate to designate one committee as his "principal campaign committee." [c] Whether this committee is Smith for Congress or the Committee to Re-Elect the President, it will have functional divisions and geographical subdivisions. It may spawn numerous adjunct committees, depicted for media purposes as autonomous and authentic, but creatures of, or encouraged by, the principal campaign committee. In sum, a functional division exists within the committee; examples would be media, scheduling, or finance. A geographical subdivision is simply a smaller, local version of the principal campaign committee and usually bears the

---

[c]The designation of a principal campaign committee was explicitly called for in the 1974 federal legislation (Public Law 93-443).

Table 4-6
The Political Campaign and the Environment[a]

The Political Environment = The Environmental Suprasystem
 I. Nature of government and politics
   A. Democratic consensus
   B. Evolution of political campaigns

 II. Ethics
   A. Society
   B. Political
   C. Candidate
   D. Manager
   E. Staff
   F. Volunteers

 III. Legal
   A. Federal campaign laws
   B. State and local campaign laws
   C. Applicable portions of other laws (e.g., IRS)

 IV. Macro-Factors
   A. Domestic (economic and social)
   B. Foreign (and national defense) policy
   C. Relationship between events and trends and government policy

 V. Macro-Political Factors
   A. Political parties
     1. Structure
     2. Status and support
   B. Effects of macro-policies on public opinion and attitudes
   C. Opinion of electorate on issues
   D. Relationship of opinion to voter preference, apathy, voter turnout, candidate preference, party preference
   E. All of above related to demographic factors, and voting behavior, including:
     1. Age
     2. Sex
     3. Income level
     4. Education
     5. Religious affiliation
     6. National origin
     7. Area of residence
     8. Prior voting habits; party registration
     9. Union member or union member in family
     10. Other factors as relevant

 VI. Media (both news media—free time and space—and paid media—advertising)
   A. Electronic media
     1. Television
     2. Radio
     3. Other subdivisions (networks, bureaus, commentators, correspondents)
   B. Print media
     1. Daily newspapers
     2. Weekly newspapers
     3. Magazines
     4. Specialty publications (ethnic, house organs, interest groups, trade publications, business, labor, . . .)
     5. Other subdivisions (columnists, political reporters, editors, key correspondents, favorable media)
   C. Other
     1. Outdoor (billboard)
     2. Bus and subway
     3. Miscellaneous

Table 4-6 (continued)

The Political Campaign = The System
I. The Candidate
    A. Incumbent or challenger
    B. Record and history
    C. Personal assets and liabilities

II. The Campaign
    A. Ad hoc
    B. Short-term
    C. Mixture of staff and volunteers
    D. Ideology—Type I, II, or III

Political Campaign Management = The Managerial Subsystem
I. Integrate and coordinate other subsystems
    A. Goals and values subsystem
    B. Structural subsystem
    C. Psychosocial subsystem
    D. Technical subsystem

II. Elements of management
    A. Planning (forecasting, budgeting)
    B. Organizing
    C. Staffing
    D. Direction
    E. Control (and reporting)
    F. Innovation
    G. Representation

III. Theorists (including)
    A. Fayol (and traditionalists)
    B. Taylor (scientific management)
    C. Mayo (social interaction)
    D. Weber (bureaucracy)
    E. Barnard (behavioral)
    F. Drucker (MBO)
    G. Simon (decision making)

IV. Differentiation and Integration
    A. Geographical (by region, state, county, district, ward, precinct, etc.)
    B. Personnel (staff versus volunteer)
    C. Vertical (by hierarchy, especially among volunteer campaign leadership)
    D. Horizontal (by function, e.g., press, finance, advertising, scheduling, etc.)
    E. Committee (regular committee versus adjunct groups, e.g., Doctors for . . . ,
       Lawyers for . . . , Veterans for . . . , other specialty committees)
    F. In-house versus outside consultants (including pollsters, management consultants,
       media experts, advertising agency, etc.)

 V. The opposition candidate(s)—nature of candidate(s) and campaign(s)

[a]The campaign is an open system that must continually adapt to the environmental supra-system.

same name as the principal campaign committee. An adjunct committee broadens the principal campaign committee's base and secures media publicity; examples would include "Doctors for . . ." or "Veterans for. . . ." Functional committees are for particular projects, such as dinner or rally committees. The interlocking nature of multiple committees is more than organizational: committees provided convenient mechanisms to route large contributions, both to preserve anonymity and to escape the gift tax. One of the earliest examples of multiple committees, organized along geographical and functional lines, was the 1828 Andrew Jackson campaign.[12]

Nearly 150 years later at the headquarters of Presidential candidate George McGovern there was no structure or organizational chart. ("We don't fit people into boxes here.") At Richard Nixon's Committee to Re-Elect the President, "everyone fitted into a box on a table of organization which defined his function—or he left."[13] The Nixon structure reflected (a) the influence of incumbency; (b) the style of administration of White House chief-of-staff Robert Haldeman, who administered a highly structured operation; and (c) Nixon's preference for structure. It also reflected this inescapable fact: *precision requires a formal decision making structure.* Leadership positions must be arranged in a known hierarchy. Responsibility and commensurate authority must be vested in specific slots to insure a quick response to strategic decisions made at the highest points in the hierarchy and to make less likely inconsistencies at the campaign's lower levels.

The structural subsystem should reflect the principles enunciated in the following pages.

1. Traditional management theory is useful. Fayol's fourteen points are, with some reservations, useful in the campaign. The principle that authority and responsibility should flow in a direct line vertically from the highest level of the organization to the lowest level, establishes the hierarchical structure of the organization. The hierarchy can be modified to permit adjunct committees, consulting arrangements, and other variations, but it cannot be discarded. Authority and responsibility are delegated from the candidate to the manager and from the manager successively through the hierarchy.

2. Span of control: no one should have more subordinates than he can effectively supervise. At the staff level, the campaign is divided vertically by the hierarchy, horizontally by deparmentalization or specialization. At the volunteer level chairmen are divided vertically by hierarchy, as well as horizontally by a committee structure based upon appeal to different constituencies. The span of control suggests that vertical or horizontal differentiation should be structured so that a staff member or volunteer leader is able to supervise the number of staff or volunteers for whom he is responsible (Figure 4-2).

3. The insistence on a formal organization structure does not preclude the development of an informal structure. The planned, formal structure is needed to establish patterned relationships to provide the precision needed in the campaign. To insure that such a structure does not stifle creativity or initiative, the manager should emphasize the importance of input from throughout the campaign organization. The structure itself may not be entirely appropriate; no manager can predict the future with absolute certainty. Spontaneous relationships arise in response to the manager's emphasis on *competence, initiative* and *hard work.* Spontaneity also reflects the social interaction of the participants.

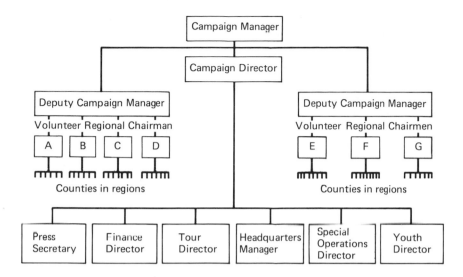

Figure 4-2. Span of Control.

Note: This partial organization chart for a campaign in a large state illustrates the span of control, which would also be reflected in components within divisions, e.g., finance director would include in his span of control direct mail fund raisers, dinner chairmen, etc.

The informal organization is healthy because it helps the campaign cope with the political environment.

4. Authority should be based on position only if position is based on competence. An incompetent in a position of authority endangers the campaign's mission. Real authority in the campaign should be based on competence, respect, and trust, as well as position. Competent staff and volunteer leaders derive *natural* authority from their ability, dedication, and perseverance. In a well-run campaign these individuals rise quickly within the "hierarchy" of an *informal* organization. But the deck should not be stacked against such informal adjustments by placing incompetent political hacks in positions of responsibility and authority.

5. The organizational chart in a campaign should not indicate the degree of authority that a superior has over a subordinate. Jurisdictional disputes are kept to a minimum if the campaign is differentiated by appropriate geographical, functional, or other lines. Within the staff itself the informal organization clarifies authority relationships. The campaign's initial phase tests the authority relationships *implied* in its organizational chart. Since rigid definitions of authority in the beginning may prevent the campaign from growing into a more adaptive structure, the initial phase should permit the development of the informal organization.

6. *The campaign structure must evolve.* Staff members are recruited and hired as needs require *and* as the budget permits. Most campaigns begin with a basic staff and then augment it. The organizational chart should provide for growth without altering the basic skeleton of the chart. A priority group of staff members, designated the *core* group, is initially recruited. By definition, the campaign cannot function without this core group. The core group should not include volunteers, and it should include staff members who will remain throughout the campaign—to assure continuity. Occasionally, a division within the campaign may grow so large that it is divided into two or three sections, e.g., finance into dinner committees and direct mail, as well as an on-going finance committee, or scheduling into a scheduling office and advance staff. Ideally the structure should grow in such a way that core staff members assume additional responsibility or added staff.

7. *The manager must decide which positions should be staff and which volunteer.* People who seem willing to volunteer their time should not be paid unless the monetary reward provides for (a) full-time, steady, and reliable work, rather than occasional contributions of volunteer time; (b) continuity—the same person does the same task each day; (c) greater loyalty and motivation. Problems arise if a staff member is put in charge of volunteers, since volunteers relate best at most levels to volunteer supervision and coordination. The staff must provide direction at some point; preferably, a minimum of staff members should deal with a few senior volunteers who, in turn, communicate directions to greater numbers of volunteers. Once a volunteer is placed on salary, the individual is no longer a volunteer—either in fact or in the eyes of his volunteer peers.

Any position essential to the campaign's basic functioning—such as a key secretarial slot—should not be volunteer. Volunteers should supplement regular staff, not take their place. It may seem costly to hire a staff person rather than use a volunteer. However, even ignoring the fact that the volunteer may be less skilled and reliable, additional staff members, if properly deployed, represent an *investment.* In certain divisions, notably finance, they pay their own way many times over in raising funds. In other divisions, they may contribute indirectly to fund raising (e.g., greater publicity for the candidate may spur contributions) or to securing votes (at a cost, in terms of their salaries, cheaper than the cost of advertising).

8. *Staff salaries should be evaluated on a cost-benefit ratio.* This principle follows closely the point just made: the relative value of substituting paid staff for volunteer workers. It is tempting to use volunteers as receptionists, secretaries, mailroom clerks, and in other positions. Most volunteers lack professionalism and, by definition, they cannot provide the continuity of regular full-time staff. In crucial positions the substitution of staff for volunteers may vitally affect the campaign's effectiveness. For example, a single individual working in

the press section of a Senate campaign could achieve radio news coverage with an advertising value many times the individual's salary. It makes sense to hire an individual for full-time work with radio stations rather than to rely on the sporadic assistance of unprofessional volunteers. (Table 4-7).

9. *The staff should be professional, but professionalism should never obscure the search for and use of volunteers.* Professionals are highly skilled, trained, and experienced in their field and also satisfy other criteria.[14] For example, F. Clifton White and other prominent political campaign consultants and managers have formed professional associations, which meet regularly to exchange knowledge and information.

Staff members and volunteers, no matter how competent, must be matched for the right position. Sometimes an individual does not fit neatly into a pre-constructed box in an organizational chart. If the box is too small the individual is prevented from contributing to his full ability and will lose interest even in his modest contribution. If the box is too large, the individual will devote most of his time "to covering up his inadequacies and neglect the parts of his job he really might handle capably."[15]

In the rush to recruit competent professional staff, the manager should be concerned that the campaign does not acquire an elitist, antivolunteer image.

Table 4-7
Cost Effectiveness of Radio Feeds

Description of What Staff Member Would Do:
A staff member would be hired to call radio stations around the state. Each day the staff member would provide stations with a short and longer taped version of an "actuality"—a news event involving the candidate. The recording would be the candidate's own voice—related to a news conference or excerpted from a speech; it would relate to major stories in the news. A special WATTS (unlimited) telephone line would cost $800 a month for three months; the salary of the staff person would be $1,500 for a total of three months; a consultant would charge $1,000 for ideas for possible statements.
Treating the first month as a breaking-in period and a less active one, the analysis shall ignore the benefits for that period, but consider the cost.

Estimate of Minimum Benefits
60–70 stations called each day; at least 30 stations will use feed daily.

Worth of each feed in advertising time (conservatively-estimated average)	$13.33
Multiplied by allowance for worth of extra credibility	×1.5
	$20 × 30 stations = $600 daily × 40 days in 2 months
Minimum Benefits:	= $24,000
Estimate of Cost	$800 telephone × 3 = $2,400 + $1,500 (staff person) + $1,000 (consultant) = $4,900.

The staff is, in this respect, like the military which is subservient to the civilian authority. The staff is subservient to the candidate and his campaign committee. The campaign manager and his staff may be given a broad charter and considerable discretion, but they only exist to elect the candidate. Volunteers must be actively recruited, and they should not be turned off by professionals with an attitude of superiority.

10. Staff members should be judiciously screened before being put on the payroll; their pay must be perceived as fair by their peers. The recruitment process should be extensive and seek out philosophically motivated, politically aware individuals who are competent and trustworthy. Selection should also be based on past records and experience, appraisal of qualifications and, often especially important in the campaign, a personal interview. The selection procedure in a large campaign could include testing for intelligence, aptitude, personality, attitude, skills. The compensation must be based on several factors including (a) alternatives the individual has in the private sector or in government; (b) the seasonal nature of the campaign work; (c) the level of competence or professionalism required, the applicant's suitability, and the supply of similarly qualified individuals available (or unavailable); (d) the aggregate campaign budget; (e) the salaries of other staff members in roughly comparable positions, and in higher and lower positions within the hierarchy; (f) the nonmonetary benefits the individual desires and will receive from the position, including experience, exciting work, access to the candidate, etc. The individual may be willing to forego present monetary compensation for these nonmonetary benefits, or because the candidate's victory might afford him or her a postelection job.

11. The manager must be able to plan ahead. He must delegate authority down the hierarchy so that he is not preoccupied with details. The cliche, "He can't see the forest from the trees," aptly describes the situation when a manager who tries to resolve every detail himself cannot adapt the structure to resolve major problems. If the staff is too incompetent or insufficiently motivated to handle chores, the fault lies with the manager who hired them or approved their hiring. The structure designed to delegate responsibility progressively down to the lowest levels reflects a consistent management-by-objectives (MBO) approach. This MBO approach facilitates planning by the manager and senior staff, whose judgment is required to anticipate and cope with contingencies arising from alternative states of nature.

An appropriate structure may facilitate planning; it does not guarantee it. Nor does appropriate structure insure thoughtful, prudent planning; it only insures that staff members are in a position to participate in and implement planning. Planning may fail because the planner (a) lacks knowledge of the organization; (b) takes an unrealistic approach (asks for information that is unavailable, time consuming to get, or simply not worth having); (c) follows rather than leads—so that his passive role makes him a captive of events; (d) produces alibis rather than corrects mistakes, which he is therefore doomed to repeat; (e) takes a short-run view, trying to achieve too much too soon, and compromises the ultimate objective.[16]

12. The structure must provide for both differentiation and integration. Competence and professionalism breed the specialization needed within the campaign, but specialists may regard their activities as ends in themselves rather than as means to an end.[17] The structure must provide not only for the different divisions within the campaign—functional sections, committees, headquarters, adjunct committees, etc.—but also the means to direct and unify these components. This includes the control function to measure whether the department or committee is doing its job.[d]

The structure suggests the need for an appropriate communications program to keep staff and volunteer participants informed. Telephone calls, memoranda, correspondence, bulletins, newsletters, personal visits, meetings, conferences, etc. form a common basis for all participants. An interlocking committee or headquarters structure, perhaps like the matrix organization suggested previously, is helpful. The higher level of staff or volunteer, the more information this person requires and is entitled to; the higher level staff person, the ranking volunteer chairman or coordinator, should receive information *as soon as possible.* Established communications links and procedures should provide for priority messages, e.g., that the candidate is coming to a given area. Volunteer leaders especially are very sensitive about not being kept informed, about "doing all their work for nothing . . . without even being given the courtesy of being told that. . . ." Key people do not want to read in the newspapers, hear on television, or hear from someone else what they should have been told. The effect on morale, as well as on direct operations, could be serious.

The hierarchy of structure should be used, not bypassed, so that no one is "stepped on." Channels make sure that ranking volunteer chairmen are not bypassed, that higher level staff members find out about projects and developments that affect their operations.

Psychosocial Subsystem

Leadership style is what the leader does to lead; in the campaign, the manager's style depends on how much power he has, the structure that has been established, the tasks that need to be performed, and the interpersonal relationships among staff and volunteers.

Trait theory ("what a leader is") lists character and personality traits com-

---

[d]In one Senate campaign the manager claimed that each of several auxiliary groups would distribute hundreds of thousands of campaign brochures relating *their* issues. These groups included Catholics (on abortion), Protestants ("A Christian's Role in Politics," brochure), law enforcement groups (anticrime literature), etc. The campaign had a weak structure and was unable to harness these outside groups. A small fraction of the material was actually distributed.

mon to leaders. These traits, which apply to the campaign manager, might include: (a) intelligence (not always on an absolute level, but relative to a group) within an area of competence; (b) social maturity (based on whether the person has an adult perspective); (c) motivation, drive, and initiative; (d) human relations attitudes; and (e) self-confidence or at least the conveyance of that impression.[18]

Charisma—the magic, magnetic attraction of followers for their leader—is intangible. The campaign manager's charisma is based upon the staff and volunteer perception of his competence, judgment, and leadership. Staff and volunteers are drawn to a person they perceive as able to cope with the political environment. The manager's confidence reassures them that the strategy or plan will prevail, and that their role in the campaign will affect the outcome.

Contingency or situational theory of leadership suggests that the style of leadership is contingent upon the task to be done and the process used. Management should identify where it feels most comfortable to operate, i.e., how authoritarian or participative should its style be? The manager should be confident and secure in applying his style, and the group should know what the style is. The creative and innovative campaign manager may be a failure in a bureaucratic environment that discourages spontaneity; in the political environment, his encouragement of subordinate participation in formulating goals and decision making can be very.successful. His initial charter is given to him by the candidate, but he can operate in an even wider area of freedom if the staff and volunteers have confidence in his ability and are prepared to follow his leadership within wide limits.

The campaign manager has many of the same qualities common to the chief executive of a successful corporation. He should be articulate, persuasive; he should set difficult goals, be achievement oriented, more competitive than most people, and prefer win/lose situations. He is likely to have a tremendous amount of energy, want near-term feedback to gauge his performance, be able to make quick decisions under crisis. There is a certain loneliness in his top spot; it is where "the buck stops." The fusion between the political manager and the political campaign is like the fusion between the chief executive and the corporation: the two are almost inseparable.

The successful campaign manager, relying on his own example, knows that the fusion of individual and organizational goals throughout the campaign will help to integrate the organization. He confronts five sets of values:[19]

1. *Individual values:* the individual holds these values, which affect his actions.
2. *Group values:* small, informal, and formal groups hold these values, which affect the behavior of individuals and the actions of the organization.
3. *Organization values:* These values held by the organization represent a composite of individual, group, total organization, and cultural inputs.
4. *Values of constituencies of the task environment:* these values are held by

those in direct contact with the organization—customers, suppliers, competitors for the business firm; in the political context, the voters, opposition candidates and managers, special constituencies (ethnic, labor, business, etc.).

5. *Cultural values:* These are the values of the total society.

All five sets of values interact with each other and determine the way in which individuals act within the political campaign organization. The campaign manager has little influence on the values of constituencies: he needs to determine what they are and make the best of them. Within the staff, the individuals recruited should have certain values. Over the short-term existence of the political campaign, the campaign manager may have some effect on these values; however, the staff should have basic, commonly shared values at the outset.

The focus on leadership styles is a way of emphasizing how the campaign manager can motivate staff and volunteers. What makes a staff person work harder? What makes a volunteer put in more time? Productivity is a function of ability *and* motivation. The staff may have ability, but without motivation inspired by leadership, productivity will suffer.

Authoritarian leadership style is inappropriate for a politically aware and motivated staff. Participative, or relatively participative, leadership style is more appropriate; but it should not be construed to mean imprecise goals, lack of direction, inattentiveness to detail. Nor does it suggest that staff members *choose* whether to participate. Participative leadership style gives staff and volunteers a greater sense of identity by giving them a greater voice in the campaign, especially the tasks most relevant to them. By making them feel more a part of the operation, because they are told more about why things are done, the role they can play, why it is important and how they can modify it, they feel their participation is valued by the campaign.

The general democratic, even egalitarian, trend, coupled with greater education and mobility in society, favors greater influence by participants in the organization. The factors, as well as innovation and the information/technology explosion, also apply to the political campaign. The increasing popularity of behavioral scientists, including some mentioned below, also has spurred the trend toward greater participation. These behavioralists and their leadership styles are relevant to the campaign.

Tannenbaum-Schmidt continuum of leadership behavior.   Different leadership styles are appropriate in different situations (Figure 4-3).[20] In the campaign, time may not always permit subordinates to be included in the decision making process. Volunteers performing simple repetitive tasks may require a rigid, bureaucratic leadership style. Some volunteers have to be told, and want the security of being told, exactly how to perform their tasks. Indeed, since they may be doing the same task repeatedly, it would be a problem if the task were done

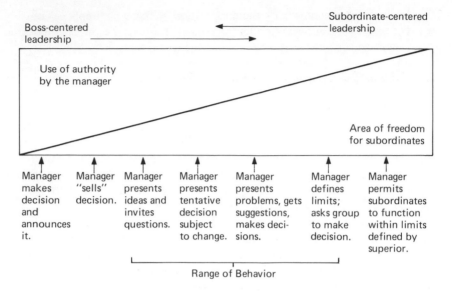

Figure 4-3. Continuum of Leadership Behavior.
Source: Robert Tannenbaum and Warren H. Schmidt, "How to Choose a Leadership Pattern," Harvard Business Review, March–April 1958, p. 96. Reprinted with permission.

wrong each time (e.g., every enclosure in a mailing collated erroneously). The manager must select leadership styles appropriate for the different volunteer organizations—volunteers in one area, division, or adjunct committee may need more direction than other volunteers.

McGregor's Theory X and Theory Y.   Douglas McGregor suggested two alternative views of people.[21] The first and more traditional view holds that the average human being inherently dislikes and will avoid work. Accordingly, most people must be coerced and threatened with punishment to force them to put forth sufficient effort toward achieving the organization's objectives. This view, called "Theory X" by McGregor, holds that rewards alone will not produce the necessary effort; only the threat of punishment will work. Finally, the average human being prefers direction and wishes to avoid responsibility; he has little ambition and values security above all.

The second view, called "Theory Y," places the problem of motivation with management. It suggests that lazy or indifferent employees are partially the result of poor management. The assumptions of Theory Y may not apply to workers as a whole, or to a majority of workers, as McGregor might suggest. But the kind of staff recruited in the political campaign (presumably, motivated at the outset) should be more responsive to a Theory Y leadership style than a Theory X. The assumptions of theory Y are: (a) work is natural; (b) the threat of punishment is not the only motivator; (c) workers can accept responsibility; (d) imagination, ingenuity, and creativity are widely distributed in the population.

Theory X may apply to some volunteers and Theory Y to other volunteers, but Theory Y should apply to virtually all staff members in political campaigns. However, it would be as inappropriate to apply Theory Y across the board as it would be to apply Theory X to everyone. Although McGregor's concern was principally with industrial workers, his theories serve as models of extreme views of treating the campaign's staff and volunteers. Theory X, Theory Y, and mixed approaches can be used—where applicable—in different sectors of the campaign.

McGregor assumed that when man's physiological needs are satisfied and he no longer fears for his physical welfare, which is certainly the case with staff members in a political campaign, *social needs* become important motivators of behavior. These include the need for belonging, for association, for acceptance by one's peers, and for giving and receiving friendship. These needs should be satisfied by a political campaign that recruits and hires motivated staff members and seeks to sustain and increase their motivation, especially by instilling an espirit de corps.

Above the social needs, McGregor also identified the *egoistic* needs. These relate to self-esteem, self-respect, self-confidence, autonomy, achievement, competence, and knowledge. In addition, egoistic needs also relate to needs for status, recognition, appreciation, and the respect of one's peers.

Maslow's Hierarchy. Just as Theory Y applies to people within the political campaign who are imaginative, seek responsibility, and possess intellectual potential and thrive on creativity, there is a corresponding theory that depicts those who seek self-fulfillment.[22] Whether everyone, or most everyone, seeks "self-actualization" or should be treated as if they are seeking self-actualization is not the issue here; the issue is that creative and bright staff members are needed in the political campaign organization, and they are essential in responsible positions and at the highest levels.

Psychologist Abraham Maslow suggests a hierarchy of needs; once a lower need is reasonably well satisfied, the individual can only be motivated by a desire to satisfy the next higher need (Table 4-8). The physiological needs, and

Table 4-8
Maslow's Hierarchy of Human Needs

Self-Actualization (Truth, goodness, beauty, individuality, perfection, completion, order, meaning, etc.)
Self-Esteem (Esteem by others)
Social Needs (Friendship, etc.)
Safety and Security (Basic needs)
Physiological (Air, water, shelter, food, sleep, sex . . .)

Note: Self-actualization is at the top.

the need for safety and security, are usually reasonably well satisfied. The political campaign should endeavor to satisfy the social needs for association with one's peers and for friendship. Although Maslow's framework is too compartmentalized for the campaign, i.e., a participant may proceed to a "higher" level without satisfying totally a lower level, the framework suggests the importance of social needs, which are partially satisfied by the campaign's team spirit. It also suggests a higher level of needs: the need for self-respect, self-esteem, the respect of one's fellows, status. The campaign manager should recruit staff members who will take pride in their position; an individual placed in too demanding a position in which he will fail will not gain self-respect; he may lose it. Similarly, status should be accorded particular positions; as a motivator, status is a cheap method of compensation. This is one reason why the shrewd campaign manager conjures up titles to suit everyone and make them feel important.

Finally, the highest need, according to Maslow, is for self-fulfillment through the development of skills and the opportunity to be creative. Some positions allow for more creativity; speechwriting, advertising, and scheduling strategy are more creative than operations in the mailroom or walking precincts. As a motivator, the need for self-actualization should be applied to every staff member and volunteer. There is some way every person can feel creative. For the individual less endowed with intelligence, less experienced in political campaigning, and less capable of more sophisticated tasks, even "mundane" and "routine" chores can allow for some creativity—if the tasks are so structured to allow for some independence.

Blake-Mouton Management Grid. The political campaign manager needs to conduct sessions, especially in the campaign's formative phase, to explore participants' interdependence in electing the candidate, which leads to mutual trust and respect. This situation is equivalent to Robert R. Blake and Jane S. Mouton's "9,9" position on their management grid—maximum concern for both people and production.[23] The manager should meet with leaders of each division, separately and together, to explore ways of reaching the "9,9" position. In addition, each division head should meet with his staff members to explore how that division can maximize its contribution to the campaign's goal of electing the candidate—without compromising its concern for the participants within that division. Similarly, volunteer chairmen need to secure input from their participants.

Fortunately, the manager who recruits highly motivated and committed staff members and volunteer leaders is already in a much better position to confront the tension and stress of the campaign. These dedicated staff members and volunteer activists *want* to produce for the campaign.

Herzberg's Hygiene Theory. Frederick Herzberg, a psychologist like Maslow, divided the work situation into "hygiene factors" and motivators.[24] The hygiene factors included pay, working conditions, and the superior's attitude. These factors, Herzberg pointed out, could cause dissatisfaction and destroy motivation; but improving the hygiene factors would not increase motivation. Positive motivation could only be produced by self-actualization and achievement—comparable to the higher levels of Maslow's hierarchy. The hygiene factors—including the working conditions—can be dissatisfiers; however, job content, achievement of an assignment, the nature of the assignment, responsibility, opportunity for growth, recognition . . . these are *satisfiers.*

Call it McGregor's Theory Y, or the higher level of Maslow's hierarchy, or emphasis on Herzberg's satisfiers, these leadership styles and methods of motivation inspire and encourage participation and creativity. The campaign may be top down in terms of authority, but it must be bottom up in terms of feedback from the lower levels, and the campaign leadership must be accessible for such feedback. Even if Theory X is suitable for some volunteers who require considerable direction, it is often better that they not perceive all of the subtleties inherent in a Theory X approach. Part of the way this is done is to encourage individuality even in the routine tasks. Individuality may take the form of varying tasks, alternating among volunteers, requesting feedback and suggestions from volunteers; participation may be encouraged by recognition of achievement, especially by the candidate, campaign manager, or higher level staff. One of the mistakes made by most campaigns is that most thank you letters come *after* the election, rather than *during* the course of the campaign, when they could serve as motivators.

Herzberg's formulation helps explain why good working conditions, satisfactory or even outstanding compensation, and other hygiene factors may still be accompanied by uninspired productivity. These factors keep campaign participants from being dissatisfied, but they are not *motivators.* Staff and volunteers need jobs that they perceive as important and meaningful. The manager must structure jobs and assignments and recruit staff and volunteers so that individuals have responsibility or recognition. Positions should provide for growth so that the individual has plenty of satisfiers to keep him or her challenged and motivated.

Likert Scale. Rensis Likert, another behavioralist who has emphasized that employees should understand objectives and have a chance to express their own opinions, has developed a scale that proceeds from (1) exploitative-authoritative to (2) benevolent-authoritative to (3) consultative to (4) participative-group.[25] In the first two, there is virtually no confidence in employees; in the campaign, such a situation would be intolerable. More likely, the manager places "substantial" confidence (i.e., 3) or "complete" confidence (i.e., 4) in staff. The extreme level of participation in which goals of the organization are established by group action (i.e., 4) is possible in certain cohesive volunteer components or adjunct committees operating within the campaign, but such extreme participation is impossible in terms of involving lower level staff in strategy formulation.

Input is helpful and required to assist in formulating strategy, but only the manager and a limited number of staff have the perspective and adequate information to make major strategic decisions and set principal objectives. No group can decide what percentage of the vote the candidate needs in a given area or from a particular demographic constituency.

The motivational goal is for staff and volunteers to feel they are an indispensable part of what is happening, i.e., what they do matters. When they participate, they should experience self-actualization.

Technical Subsystem

More detailed discussion of the technical subsystem—people using knowledge, techniques, equipment, and facilities—is found in a variety of "how to" methodological books and manuals, many published by the Democratic National Committee, Republican National Committee, and local party organizations. Direct mail, marketing, fund raising, press relations, and other topics have been the subject of entire books.

The technical precision required in a political campaign should not obscure the need for social interaction. A spirit of teamwork is compatible with a goal oriented work environment. What matters is not the long hours and demanding labor, but whether the goals are commonly shared, and how well each person relates to others on the staff. The technical subsystem cannot work effectively unless highly motivated people can utilize the knowledge, techniques, equipment, and facilities available. In addition, the finest technical subsystem exists in a void without the *structural* subsystem, which permits particular individuals to use their knowledge in specific positions; the *goals and values* subsystem, which explains why staff members are involved, and how their goals and values affect their performance; the *managerial* subsystem, which provides unity. In short, all the "how to" knowledge in the world, the finest techniques, latest equipment, etc., are irrelevant for the campaign that cannot motivate people to work together in an appropriate structure, individuals with common goals and values who cooperate to implement a strategy.

In George McGovern's 1972 Presidential campaign the preconvention period of delegate hunting and primary elections was notable for its strong technical subsystem and weak structural subsystem, incapable of supporting the subsequent general election campaign. The managerial subsystem was entirely geared to obtaining the Democratic nomination and virtually collapsed at the convention. In contrast, perhaps the strongest component of the Committee to Re-Elect the President was its technical subsystem,[e] which in turn was well integrated with the other subsystems.[26]

---

[e]Survey researcher Arthur J. Finkelstein of DirAction Services, Inc. analyzed survey data from throughout the nation to provide recommendations for the Nixon Re-Election

Victory in the political campaign does not simply happen. Voters do not mysteriously find their way to the polls and, by some unknown process, vote for a particular candidate. There are two important kinds of voters. First, there are those who usually, or in the particular election, plan to vote and go to the polls and *then* vote for a candidate because he is a member of their political party. For these voters, one need only find them and make certain they get to the polls. Surveys can indicate the relative statistical importance of this group—the straight-line party voters whose election preference is a foregone conclusion.

A second group may vote *because* they are motivated. Members of this group become so excited and enthused about a candidate that they are motivated to turn out at the polls. Without the inspiration of the candidate, they might not turn out to vote at all. In a small city council election, or special election, it is important to motivate people who will turn out to vote because they are interested in the candidate; given the small number of voters or the small turnout, these votes may make the difference.

The marketing function in any campaign is primarily a part of the technical subsystem. It is "how to" reach these two different groups of voters and the subgroups within them. It is also the means to turn out those already committed to the candidate; sometimes, these voters must be discovered by door-to-door and telephone campaigns, or by lists based on relative support within certain constituencies, as shown by survey research. Marketing is also the merchandising of the candidate: what issues does he emphasize, especially relative to each other, with what intensity, and in which areas and to which constituencies?

The technical subsystem includes direct mail; get-out-the-vote; voter registration; telephone campaigns and telephone banks; computer letters; special telephone recording machines to deliver messages; data processing and list maintenance; survey research; advance manuals and advance man techniques; methods of advertising; methods of using messengers, the telephone, telecopiers, the mail, the wire services, special services, etc. to get out news releases from the campaign; the way in which the press list is formulated, revised and updated; the way in which letters are addressed—by typewriter, by automatic typewriter, by addressograph plates, by computer, etc. The technical subsystem includes the state of knowledge, the multitude and array of techniques and methods, the mechanics and equipment and facilities available for political campaigning. The technical subsystem is constantly changing; it depends substantially on the state of knowledge, which is changing; on new ideas, which are always being developed; and on new equipment or the adaptation of older equipment and their application to the political campaign.

Committee's $12 million direct mail program—a brilliant marketing/targeting effort aimed at specific constituencies. Recipients of particular "personalized" form letters were screened by computer regarding key attributes, e.g., age, income level, area of county, ethnic origin, etc.

5 The Psychosocial Subsystem

Research shows that both the amount of influence that a leader exerts and the amount he attempts *to exert increase with group acceptance of him as a person.*
—Robert K. Presthus
The Organizational Society

The psychosocial subsystem of the political campaign consists of individual behaviors and motivations, status and role hierarchies, group dynamics, and influence systems. The political environment affects this subsystem, as does the interaction between the technology available to the particular political campaign, the tasks (especially the level of office sought) and the structure of the campaign.[1] This chapter concerns the individual's communication with others in the organization and his own motivation; and the relationship between behavior and the technical subsystem (the way in which things are done in the political campaign); and behavior and the structural subsystem (and the impact of the political campaign's structure on planning, budgeting, and controlling). Because of their importance in the political campaign, stress and conflict are also discussed.

The ideal political campaign motivates *all* of its participants: both staff and volunteers, and at all levels of the organization. Repeatedly the importance of initially recruiting staff committed to the candidate has been emphasized. Some hero worship of the candidate is healthy; his charismatic appeal can stimulate the spirit and camaraderie conducive to high motivation and productivity. The participants in the political campaign come from different backgrounds; within the staff, they may be relatively higher paid and higher skilled or limited to lower paid, lower skilled roles. Volunteers could include prominent and affluent community leaders, consultants such as advertising executives or other skilled individuals willing to donate some counsel to the candidate and campaign, and retired citizens or students willing to do almost any task to help the campaign. (In future large-scale campaigns, mundane volunteer tasks will become less prevalent or be modified; collating, folding, and other equipment will become more prevalent, and the volunteer labor will be diverted to other uses.) The participants in the political campaign are different; hence, the only way to motivate each participant is to treat each staff member or volunteer as an individual.

The challenge is to have the proper mix of motivational factors for each individual staff member or volunteer. As the last chapter indicated, pay (for staff), working conditions, and other "hygiene" factors are limited motivational factors. The excitement of the campaign, the charisma of the candidate, the choice of issues raised by the campaign, access to the candidate, and the opportunity to achieve self-actualization in one's work in the political campaign are more likely to be motivational factors. Although the psychosocial system may be viewed as irrelevant to smaller campaigns by campaign managers who feel they have enough immediate problems without behavioral theory, such disdain is ill-founded. The smaller and more local the campaign, the smaller the staff and the more volunteer-intensive the effort. The more modest campaign relies less on the structural subsystem and the technical subsystem; it needs to utilize to the utmost the human resources available. Behavioral theory supports improved human relations and higher motivation; the result is increased productivity. Moreover, the problems of interpersonal relations, especially the stress and conflict aggravated by the political campaign's work environment, can, in a small campaign, threaten its efficiency. With only a small staff, stress and conflict reverberate throughout the limited staff operation.

High motivation, achieved principally (but not solely) by the fusion process, in which participants fuse their individual goals and aspirations with the political campaign's overriding objective of victory and its associated goals (e.g., raising certain issues), does not guarantee victory. The political environment, including the competition posed by the opposing campaign, can dominate the election. The best functioning psychosocial subsystem cannot surmount overbearing influences of the political environment: the most highly motivated campaign staff may be buried by an avalanche of adverse public sentiment about Watergate, the economy, or some other macro-factor. Nor can the best group working conditions supplant structure (the structural subsystem), technique (the technical subsystem), or strategy (the managerial subsystem). The manager who understands the psychosocial subsystem can select appropriate individuals for positions within the campaign and strive for the kind of interpersonal communications that best motivate participants. Staff members and volunteers will maximize their efforts if they are happy within the work environment and can closely identify their personal goals with both the candidate and the campaign. Indeed, volunteers are drawn to the kind of work environment that explicitly values them not only for their donated labor but for their worth as human beings.

The political campaign manager must be physically able to work long, intense hours. From the broader perspective provided by the psychosocial system, he must also be mentally able to manage the campaign. His leadership ability and style must inspire and motivate staff and volunteers, and he must be able to anticipate and resolve the human relations problems that are inevitable products of the tense campaign environment. He must develop and sharpen keen communications skills, and he must set an example in human relations for others to emulate.

The Individual and the Group

Managers and staff members who function well in the political campaign can cope with its stress and tension, because they do not permit human relations problems to affect their own authentic, thoughtful outlook on life. The manager or staff member should be a source of strength; even temperament and tolerance should cushion the impact of flare-ups. This self-assurance extends, especially at the managerial level, to confidence that the campaign strategy should be implemented as envisioned. The constant temptation to react to every nuance of the opposition and every criticism from a volunteer chairman who second-guesses strategy is rejected. The manager does not ignore valuable counsel, and he is accessible and open to new evidence or data. Nevertheless, he does not react hastily to the actions of the opposition candidate or campaign; such reaction may be precisely what the opposition wants. Just as he is confident and even tempered in his human relationships, the manager is confident that a prudently formulated strategy appropriate to the political environment will work. Tremendous self-discipline is required to adhere even to an ideal strategy; the unremitting second-guessing and emotional pressures to modify strategy are sometimes too much even for seasoned managers. In sum, the ideal manager is confident of both his human relationships and his campaign strategy, because both are based on reality.

In winner/loser psychological semantics, a winner "responds authentically by being credible, trustworthy, responsive and genuine, both as an individual and as a member of society." A loser "fails to respond authentically." Within these two extremes, few if any people are always winners or losers. The campaign needs staff members who come closest to being winners, i.e., it needs someone who "does not dedicate his life to a concept of what he imagines he *should* be, rather he is *himself* and as such does not use his energy putting on a performance, maintaining pretence, and manipulating others into his game."[2]

The implications of being a winner are important for the political campaign. Because he assumes responsibility for his own life, the staff member can choose to postpone enjoyment by exercising discipline in his work situation. His future orientation suggests he can conceptualize in working toward a future goal. He does not waste the campaign's valuable time, a finite resource which is the primary constraint on the campaign, by pretending. He is respectful and considerate of others, honest and authentic; it is not surprising that he is more likely to get along with his peers. The winner is, in short, a very good person to have around the political campaign headquarters; he does not waste time manipulating others and generating or engaging in personal disputes that compromise the campaign's goal of electing the candidate. He is prepared and willing to allocate his time to goal oriented productivity, and a minimum amount of time to conflict. No one is a one hundred percent winner or loser; but it makes sense to recruit and hire staff members who are winners or who seem to be, on net balance, winners.

The group, i.e., the political campaign, is only as strong as its individuals working together. "Winners" can work much better together than "losers." Just as winners reject pretence and performance in their personal lives, they reject the delusion and staging characteristic of managers or staff who will not admit erroneous perceptions or defective analysis. Often the most absurd campaign strategies simply reflect the unreal world in which the self-deluded strategist puts himself.

Interpersonal Communication

People assume "roles" which they act out as they play games."[3] In any organization, including the political campaign, staff or volunteers may assume roles or play games (Table 5-1).

Ego state theory helps us to understand the barriers between communication. Each person has three ego states—parent, adult, and child. The parent ego state incorporates the attitudes and behavior of people who served as the individual's parent figures. The adult ego state is used to reason, evaluate stimuli, gather and store information for future reference, and to enable a person to survive independently and be more selective with his responses. In contrast to the adult, who is objective and clear thinking, the child ego state results in immature, childlike behavior. The adult's clear thinking can be spoiled by *contamination,* i.e., "when the adult accepts as *true* some unfounded parent beliefs or child distortions, and rationalizes and justifies these attitudes."[4]

The constant adult may be so objective that he is unable to empathize with someone who has a problem. The constant adult will experience problems, especially if he is in a supervisory position, e.g., overseeing volunteers. His unfeeling and detached attitude and appearance may antagonize others. The adult ego state, which is the most desirable, "does not mean that the person is always acting from the adult. It means that "the adult allows appropriate expression of all ego states because each has its contribution to make to a total personality."[5]

The individuals acting roles and playing games (Table 5-1) are acting not as adults but on the basis of their parent or child ego states. They seek to be dominant, authoritarian, or manipulative; in other cases, they act immaturely in refusing to recognize reality. They seek protection from others and refuse to live in the real world. These games and roles, which reflect serious contamination by parent and child ego states, not only impair the individual's human qualities, but they can adversely affect the political campaign of which he is a part.

The campaign manager, although no psychologist, should understand ego theory and apply it when making hiring decisions or resolving human relations questions within the staff and volunteer ranks, or when deciding if someone needs to be fired. To understand ego states does not mean that they should be

Table 5-1
Examples of Games and Roles in the Campaign

Game or Role[a] (Description)	Implications for Campaign
Clown	Prevents realistic appraisal, especially in crisis, of situation facing campaign.
Competitor	Antagonizes fellow workers, but win-lose orientation may benefit campaign, since individual could be veritable workhorse.
Cynic	Can turn difficult work situation into pervasive defeatist attitude.
Delicate	Definitely should not be hired or retained because this individual is forever offended by others and unable to cope with stress and tension.
Dogmatic	Will not admit mistake, hence unable to adapt to change; disastrous in manager because he cannot grow into crisis management.
Dominator	Partially acceptable in aggressive volunteer coordinator, but unhealthy in staff; causes resentment among peers.
Dreamer	Impairs operation if dreamer is in "dream" slot for him, but inappropriate slot, from campaign's point of view.
Gossip	Dangerous in campaign's close quarters; reprimand for first offense, then dismissal before disruption to campaign is overpowering.
Indecisive/ Uncertain	Prevents staff from taking responsibility or making essential quick decisions under stress; such a person can only operate at low level.
Intellectual	Acceptable for certain research, writing assignments, but "realist" must supervise, oversee, or edit work before release or production.
Loner	Can be conducive to productive work, especially in volunteers seeking work as an antidote to loneliness.
Procrastinator	Unsuitable for any staff or volunteer slot, since campaign has limited time span and is results/deadline oriented; if prominent individual who has volunteer leadership position is procrastinator, he should be backed up by a real performer/activist.
Sentimental	Inattentive to matters at hand and therefore prevents others from working.
Worrier	Unproductive if worrying does not lead to action; very productive if leads to attention to detail, e.g., in scheduling, advance work, press relations.

[a]For a more complete listing and description of games and roles that inspired these examples, see John Powell, S.J., *Why Am I Afraid To Tell You Who I Am?* (Niles, Ill.: Argus Communications, 1969), pp. 38–39.

unnecessarily challenged. Confronting an ego defense mechanism is not always the best course. Since the person who operates the mechanism, i.e., who plays the game or acts the role, has felt the need to repress something, he would not be comfortable with some realization. "In one way or another, he keeps his psychological pieces intact by some form of self-deception. . . . If the psychological pieces come unglued, who will pick them up. . . ?"[6]

Despite the manager's emphasis on hiring individuals with effective communications skills, barriers to understanding may arise. These barriers, by preventing communication, make it difficult for people to work together, hence to work productively. The lone creative genius is rare in the political campaign. Even the most creative advertising copywriter requires some direction and feedback; the most eccentric speechwriter must work and communicate with others.

The manager, by his attitude, example, and sometimes by explicit discussion, should stress the need for optimum communications in the campaign. He should emphasize the need for open, honest communication. The campaign is too short and its objective too easily compromised by internal misunderstandings and conflicts. The tension and rivalries within and between staff and volunteer ranks produce enough conflicts within the natural course of the campaign; these problems need not be compounded by poor communications.

Individual Motivation

Work is a powerful force in shaping a person's sense of identity. We find that most, if not all, working people tend to describe themselves in terms of the work groups or organizations to which they belong. The question, "Who are you?" often solicits an organizational related response, such as "I work for IBM. . . ."[7]

Work in America, the HEW study quoted from above, contains valuable research material for any political campaign. The findings preview a potentially exciting political issue: the relationship of work to the quality of life. A recession or depression temporarily discourages concern about improving the quality of jobs; people are happy just to be employed. The issue of making work more interesting and meaningful is a long-range political issue. But our focus is not on work as a campaign issue, but on the work within the political campaign. The political campaign is not so different from other organizations that we cannot gain from a general study of work.

A survey undertaken by the Survey Research Center, University of Michigan,[8] sampled over 1500 American workers at all occupation levels. These workers were asked how important they regarded some twenty-five aspects of work. Here are the first eight, in order of importance:

1. Interesting work.
2. Enough help and equipment to get the job done.
3. Enough information to get the job done.
4. Enough authority to get the job done.
5. Good pay.
6. Opportunity to develop special abilities.
7. Job security. (Limited relevance to campaign.)
8. Seeing the results of one's work.

Excepting job security, the items on the list comprise priorities for the manager seeking to motivate staff members and volunteer leaders and workers. Virtually every item is controllable by the manager, who can disseminate information, grant authority, develop special individual talents, and structure and modify job descriptions.

The HEW study also listed factors that have a high degree of probability of determining worker satisfaction and dissatisfaction.[9] These factors also can be applied to a campaign (Table 5-2).

Individuals need not be mentally healthy to be motivated. Well-adjusted staff members may have fewer emotional problems to interfere with their work, but their opposites may use the campaign as therapy for their problems. Assuming it is desirable to have mentally healthy, satisfied participants in the political campaign, it is worth noting that the HEW study reiterated that many mental health problems are related to an *absence* of job satisfaction. A person unsatisfied with his job is unlikely to be motivated; therefore, he is unable to produce as much for the political campaign as someone highly motivated.

The campaign manager must understand socially acquired motives—including the needs for *achievement, affiliation, power,* and *competence.* Two other important needs are the need to reduce anxiety and the need to reduce dissonance (internal conflicts). Since a need amounts to a propensity to act in a cer-

Table 5-2
Factors That Probably Determine Worker Satisfaction and Dissatisfaction

Factor	*Application to Campaign*
Occupational status (prestige, ego gratification from work)	Titles and job descriptions are important (and are usually "cheap" forms of compensation).
Job content (fractionation, repetition, and lack of control versus variety and autonomy)	Repetition OK at certain volunteer levels, but staff should utilize volunteers for the repetitive tasks to free themselves for more challenging tasks.
Supervision (participative management or delegation of authority)	In staff and volunteer operation, authority should be delegated to subordinates, especially to volunteer chairmen for area.
Peer relationships (interaction with congenial peers)	Sensitive, mature staff and volunteers are likely to interact congenially with their peers and make for more productive work relationships.
Wages (to support a certain standard of living; then "equity" is consideration)	Equity is often judged relatively in the political campaign, i.e., by the compensation that others receive.
Mobility (chances for promotion)	Competence should be recognized quickly by increased responsibility or promotion.
Working conditions (hours, temperature, ventilation, noise)	These are important in avoiding physical problems that might lead to complications.
Job security	This is not important, except the assurance that employment will not be terminated arbitrarily.

tain way, the manager should try to understand what kind of behavior will lead to improved performance. He should understand what structure, working conditions, delegation of authority, designation of title, etc. will help to stimulate the desired behavior in specific staff members. Most Americans are "proud of having a need to achieve," but they "dislike being told they have a need for power."[10] The campaign manager should reject the popular perceptions of the need for power—that it is harsh, sadistic, neurotic, Machiavellian. The need for power is a motivational force for many people, very likely for the manager himself.

Individuals who have the needs for achievement or competence are prime recruitment material for the campaign staff. Why some people possess these needs or why others need relatively more or less power than others is beyond this discussion. The manager seeks staff who need achievement, competence or power, and he seeks to satisfy those needs in the political work environment. When these needs are satisfied the participants should feel self-esteem and experience self-actualization as they take pride and feel joy in making a real contribution to electoral victory.

Expectancy theory offers one explanation for motivation. People behave as they do because they expect their behavior will lead to a desired reward.[11] Expectancy theory suggests a number of questions for the manager considering hiring someone. First, what are the person's needs? Second, does the individual perceive that the job will satisfy his needs? Is the job so designed that when he tries to succeed, he can succeed? Does the person have adequate staff support and technical support, e.g., telephones, typewriters, folding machines, etc.? If he gets the job done, can he realistically expect that the reward will satisfy his needs? If he wants monetary compensation, will performance result in a raise? If he wants status, will performance yield a superior title? If he wants proximity to the candidate, will performance permit him to attend a private reception with the candidate, or travel occasionally with the candidate? If he wants a job in Washington (or Sacramento, or city hall) should the candidate win, will performance result in a job offer? Does the person expect such an offer will result?

How should the manager structure the campaign? Titles, offices, compensation, and perquisites can be determined in different ways. Status is partially a function of these factors, and status can be a motivating factor. Dr. Alvin Zander has suggested that individual achievement motivation is not the sole determinant of performance. Group position, team spirit, and team work can alter achievement motivation. His findings implied that transferring an individual from a peripheral position to a more central position can significantly stimulate the individual's motivation for achievement.[12] Individuals working at the "center of action" in the campaign enjoy greater status and may be more highly motivated than those who rarely see the candidate.

Those who hold the Puritan ethic may work hard and do well at any job; it is also possible that a person who does not do well in one job can be transferred

to another, or have his responsibilities modified, or perhaps simply be given a
new title, and, as a result, perform much better. The political campaign manager
should be wary of imposing his own Puritan work ethic on everyone; he should
be flexible enough to see that a different title or work location may significantly
affect the staff member's motivation and productivity.

Compensation should not be automatically tied to position, nor can it always be based on a sliding scale, with the manager at the top of the scale, and
each successively lower position in the hierarchy at a commensurately lower level
of compensation. When the manager spots exceptional talent, especially in a
creative field, he should make every effort to compensate the individual based on
the contribution to the organization, even if the compensation is comparable to
the manager's compensation.[13]

A trade-off exists between various types of needs and individual motivation.
A high degree of structure (rules, regulations, going through channels) will
reduce affiliation and achievement needs but simultaneously make the staff more
power oriented. Risk or challenge will arouse achievement motivation but have
little or no effect on affiliation or power needs.[14] People with relatively low
achievement motivation will work harder for increased financial rewards, but if
there is any way to get the reward without working, they will look for that way.
They must want something that money can buy; obviously money cannot buy
tolerable working conditions or friendship.[15]

The campaign that can only motivate its staff with monetary compensation
lacks, by definition, a candidate, ideas, issues, or party that are motivating forces.
It follows that the staff whose sole motivator is money will have a negligible
need for achievement. In politics such individuals are more likely found in on-
going, permanent political organizations rather than in campaigns.

Call it McGregor's Theory Y or the highest level of Maslow's hierarchy, the
manager should direct staff members toward achieving self-actualization. Even
after lower level needs are satisfied, "we may still often (if not always) expect
that a new discontent and restlessness will soon develop, unless the individual is
doing what he is fitted for. A musician must make music, an artist must paint, a
poet must write if he is to be ultimately happy. What a man *can* be, he *must* be.
This need we may call self-actualization."[16] Since a satisfied need is not a motivator, Maslow's theory presents the hypothesis to explain why individuals can
still be motivated although their needs seem to be satisfied. When lower
level needs are satisfied, higher level needs are activated, and the individual
is motivated to satisfy them.

An individual's level of aspiration is influenced by his position in his life
cycle. *Conservors* merely wish to retain their present position and continue
enjoying their present satisfaction. *Backsliders* lessen their efforts because they
have lowered their level of aspiration. Conservors and backsliders, regardless of
their performance in prior campaigns when they were *climbers* activating higher
level needs, are no longer high achievers. The manager should recruit climbers;

they are usually, but not necessarily, young. Their temperament is reflected in a relentless pursuit of goals compatible with electoral victory. If the goals are achieved before deadline, they look for something else to do. They continue striving because they experience satisfaction at achieving their objectives and immediately set new, higher objectives or meet new, higher objectives defined by the manager. They seek a higher position in the life cycle as their level of aspiration is raised.[17]

The manager seeks to influence staff members and volunteers by appealing to their individual needs.[a] Needs proceed in hierarchical fashion—(a) physiological, (b) safety, security, (c) social, affiliation, (d) esteem, prestige, (e) power, autonomy, (f) competence, achievement and, finally, (g) self-actualization. The manager and his senior aides are concerned only with the higher needs, because the staff and volunteers have most of their lower needs (especially physiological and safety) satisfied. Hence, the leadership style rejects fear, tradition, and, to a great extent, blind faith as the method of influence. Instead, the hierarchy reflects influence processes compatible with greater movement toward self-actualization, i.e., proceeding from rational faith and rational agreement to joint- and self-determination. The manager's style advances from autocratic/authoritarian/manipulative to persuasive/collaborative/democratic. It is difficult to conceive of total self-actualization for staff and volunteers, since the appropriate leadership style would be abdicative.[18]

Although the manager wants staff and volunteers to approach self-actualization, he realizes that total self-determination is impossible: it would lead to a breakdown of the discipline required for the political campaign organization to accomplish its goal in the limited time span. His style is rarely *authoritarian* or *autocratic,* but circumstances may require the kind of firm, decisive leadership that can reasonably be termed authoritarian or autocratic. Often, such a leadership style is evidenced by the manager in the campaign when time pressure is so intense that there is no reasonable alternative to order by fiat.

Manipulative style may be a compromise between the more authoritarian and more democratic styles, but the campaign manager should seek the *persuasive* style as the most comfortable compromise position. He influences staff members and volunteers by the rational faith they place in his ability and competence, and his surrogate role as the candidate's spokesman and representative. Because the campaign manager has (presumably) chosen dedicated, competent staff members who are both creative and highly motivated, a *collaborative* style, which depends on rational agreement, may be useful. This is especially true among the senior staff, e.g., tour or scheduling director, press secretary, deputy campaign manager,

---

[a]The correlation of hierarchy of needs with a manager's process and style has been illustrated by Hampton, Sumner, and Webber, *Organizational Behavior,* p. 143. Their chart of influence processes indicates the continuum of process and style throughout the ascendancy of the hierarchy of needs.

etc. This management team must understand why the manager's actions are necessary and agree that they are proper. When the manager tries to convince or persuade a staff member, he is complimenting him by saying in effect, "I think you have the ability and the knowledge to understand what I am asking, and I respect you enough to take the time to explain."[19]

In coping with the need for power among staff and volunteers, the manager should recognize that he himself has several bases of power. *Reward* power is based on the subordinate's perception that he has the ability to give him rewards. *Coercive* power is based on the subordinate's perception that he (again, the manager) can punish. *Legitimate* power is based upon some legitimate right for the manager to influence and the subordinate to accept that influence. These three types of power should not be utilized very often by a political manager who has recruited the kind of competent and motivated staff members previously described. Instead, he may rely on *referent* power, based on the subordinate's desire to identify with the manager, or *expert* power, based on the subordinate's perception that the manager has (as he should have) special knowledge or expertise.[20]

In the campaign as in any organization, the manager's effectiveness, based upon his choice of influence processes, depends on his leadership style, the reaction of staff and volunteers to it, and the tasks to be done. As the tasks assume a certain urgency in crisis situations, a more authoritarian style is acceptable. The successful manager adjusts his leadership style for different situations. For example, he may come in contact with volunteer chairmen he did not appoint or volunteer workers accustomed to different leadership. Similarly, each individual county chairman in a statewide campaign may have his own peculiar leadership style. Individual motivation is a product of a variety of needs peculiar to each individual. To motivate individual county chairmen who have different needs and desires, they must be treated uniquely. Similarly, they must modify their own style to accomodate unique volunteers in their area.

The manager best motivates volunteer leaders and staff by a participitory leadership style, rather than an authoritarian leadership style. The assumption is that the volunteer leadership of the campaign and the staff members, especially the higher level staff, are ideal or near ideal participants in the campaign organization. They should have a motivation based on their perception of the candidate, their interest in ideas and political philosophy, and perhaps their loyalty to the political party. Second, they should be bright, competent, and capable of relating their needs to what the campaign can provide. Third, they should have the key personal characteristics—persistence, determination, attentiveness to detail, etc. Finally, they should have certain needs, primarily the need for achievement and the need for competence.

Greater freedom for subordinates should result in higher individual motivation, if the subordinates were well chosen in the first place. If these subordinates have relatively high needs for independence, a readiness to assume responsibility, a strong identification with the campaign, and the necessary knowledge and experience to deal with the problem at hand, and if they expect to share in decision making, they should be permitted greater freedom. To the extent that these characteristics do not obtain, they should be permitted relatively less freedom, since freedom is less of a motivating factor.[21]

Behavior and the Technical Subsystem

The *technical* subsystem must emphasize jobs that are more than the mere expenditure of energy or faculties to accomplish a task. Tasks must be structured in such a way that participants have a voice in planning the task. The assumptions of the *job-design-for-motivation* movement[b] are: (a) most jobs can be improved (the inherent potential); (b) job content is related to job satisfaction; (c) motivation is a function of job satisfaction; (d) motivation and productivity are inextricably linked; (e) people seek and need meaningful work. Although job design and redesign, a relatively new field, seems more appropriate to the business sector, especially in manufacturing and assembly line situations, it can be applied to the volunteer sector of a political campaign and, to a lesser extent, to the staff of a political campaign.

The basic methods of job design are job enlargement, job rotation, job enrichment, "plan-do-control" concept of work, and work simplification. *Job enlargement* implies the lengthening of the time cycle required to complete a certain level of work. Within job enlargement, the degree of specialization is reduced in order to reduce repetitiveness and monotony. Each individual is responsible for more tasks. The variety of tasks spurs motivation. In volunteer headquarters work, for example, a trade-off may have to be made between short-term production objectives and job enlargement. The specialization increases production, but it also increases monotony and threatens morale. Eventually, if the jobs are boring enough, the volunteers may stop coming in. Job enlargement, like the other methods listed below, may better serve long-term needs.

Job rotation implies rotating an individual through a series of departments for short periods. Job rotation also means greater variety; this variety can attract volunteers who want to learn about different facets of the campaign and acquire experience in different tasks. Assuming the time required to learn new tasks is minimal, job rotation could be a motivational tool to increase the productivity of those working and to encourage existing volunteers to donate more time and new volunteers to enlist in the effort. In this case, as with the other methods, some form of job design or redesign should be employed if the alternative is to lose *volunteer* help.

At the staff level, some job rotation is essential, especially among key

---

[b]The discussion of job design methodology is synthesized from a variety of conferences and exchanges with other students of management and from *The Conference Board*.

secretaries, for reasons independent of motivation. For example, if a key person is absent for illness or another reason, there is at least one other person who can substitute in the key slot. Job rotation, in this form, assures the campaign manager that each key individual has a trained "second" to substitute in case of absence.

Job enrichment delegates to a staff member or volunteer functions that are expected to be managerial. Since the manager (i.e., the campaign manager or a middle level manager) plans, organizes, leads, and controls the work of others, a program to give participants some planning or control role enriches the job. Herzberg's "motivation-hygiene" theory is the inspiration for many job enrichment projects, which seek to provide "satisfiers" or motivating factors (achievement, recognition, interesting work, responsibility, etc.). Volunteers should be encouraged to help plan and organize their workloads, and volunteers should help to supervise their peers. Competent volunteers can control, i.e., check and verify, the work of their fellow volunteers to maintain quality control. Volunteers acquire a vested interest, not in a narrow monetary sense, but in the personal sense of pride and satisfaction, in seeking to maximize output. For example, the volunteer placed in charge of an afternoon work shift at a campaign headquarters has a personal interest in organizing the volunteers to fold as many news releases as possible, stuff envelopes, prepare special information packets, and reach or exceed the goals assigned. He or she has more of an incentive to see that assignments are done correctly.

Plan-Do-Control, developed by M. Scott Myers of Texas Instruments, is a kind of job enrichment. It assumes that meaningful work is a motivator *and* that lack of meaningful work demotivates. This approach implies that the staff member or volunteer should have as much control as possible over planning, doing, and controlling. The individual who helps plan what he is to do, and whose ideas are actively solicited by his superiors, will be more highly motivated. Ideally, the individual should also influence his working conditions and the way in which work is checked (i.e., quality control).

Work simplification, which has its roots in Taylorism, uses industrial engineering techniques to study jobs and break them down into the smallest possible segments. The difference between this method, as a motivator, and Taylorism as a "scientific management" tool to increase productivity, is that the staff or volunteers *participate* in improving their own jobs. Work simplification, like the other methods of job design or redesign, assumes a relatively free and open relationship between the managerial level in the political campaign and the staff and volunteer levels. Participants in the political campaign should be actively encouraged to originate and suggest ideas for improving their staff or volunteer jobs. Volunteers are often in the best position to suggest a better way of doing their jobs. Sometimes, a volunteer can suggest *new* tasks suitable for volunteer help; the volunteer may even take the lead in recruiting volunteers for the new tasks.

Another term sometimes mentioned is *autonomous* or *semiautonomous* work groups. Assuming that participants can more easily identify with smaller organizational components in which results are more easily observed and measured, this work group encourages a sense of "togetherness." Its participants decide how to establish and meet objectives and which individuals perform which tasks at which particular times. Examples in a campaign might include volunteers who associate in groups to accomplish specific campaign projects; groups that work at the same time in campaign headquarters; groups that undertake a local project, such as distributing campaign material in a neighborhood; groups that form adjunct committees (e.g., Lawyers for . . . , Teachers for . . . , etc.); a group that runs a local campaign headquarters. In each case, the major qualification is that, within broad limits, the members of the work group set their objectives. Their participation in goal setting, the division of labor and assignment of tasks, and the measurement of the quality and quantity of their own work, serve as motivators. Within such a group, job rotation or job enrichment naturally arise, as volunteers rotate jobs or give each other increased responsibility. Often, people who feel they have their *own* project, for which they are responsible and for which they can reap the glory of success, work harder than if they were integrated in an amorphous whole in which they seem to lose their identity.

The Bankers Trust case exemplifies organization change through job enrichment.[22] Bankers Trust, a New York City commercial bank, had made the decision in late 1969 to begin job enrichment in the division handling stock transfer operations. Production was low, quality was poor, and absenteeism and turnover were high. In the political campaign, careful recruiting and screening of staff should prevent deterioration of operations to such a low level. In a campaign, with its brief time span, absenteeism and turnover can be very disruptive. Among volunteers especially, absenteeism and turnover can be minimized if volunteers are motivated by job enrichment. The motivators used in the Bankers Trust case can be applied in different form to secretaries, typists, receptionists, clerical workers, etc. working in the campaign, as well as to volunteers involved in a broad range of tasks.

In the Bankers Trust case, the motivators were: (1) allowing certain typists to change their own computer input tapes; this had always been the responsibility of a group leader, and no one felt responsible for their own work; (2) groups or teams were formed, and errors were picked up by teammates; (3) more typists were allowed to do "special" (i.e., unique) orders, making the work more interesting and satisfying; (4) experienced typists were allowed to train others in more challenging jobs, and their morale improved with the trainer status. What is important is not the precise mechanics of job enrichment, but the *philosophy* behind it. Each campaign has its own tasks and technology, its own equipment and facilities; but each lends itself to a unique program of job enrichment.

In the Bankers Trust case, time was saved by eliminating and combining functions. Quality was more carefully measured, and individuals were prepared to assume responsibility for their own errors. Previously, it was impossible to tell which typist had prepared an erroneous stock certificate. After job enrichment, it was possible. Employee attitudes improved; they found the work more interesting; they felt they had greater freedom in planning the job and had a reasonable say in how the job was being done. The job provided feedback and opportunities for recognition and even advancement. It was no longer so closely supervised, and it was a job worth the effort.

Job enrichment should be applied in finance, direct mail fund raising, advertising (invoices, insertion orders, etc.) and any other field in which individuals can be more highly motivated if their jobs can be enriched in the political campaign.

Behavior and the Structural Subsystem

The campaign structure, like the structure of any organization, should fit the goal being pursued. In the bureaucracy of permanent political party organizations resistance to change may be exaggerated by insecure "bureaupathic" individuals. Because innovation is uncontrolled behavior, it threatens the bureaucracy. Minimal standards become *ceilings* on performance.[23] In contrast, the structure of the political campaign must encourage creativity and innovation, not bureaucracy and stability.

The demarcation between the authority of full-time staff and the functional authority of experts, either on the staff or retained on a consulting basis, should be clearly established early in the campaign. Misunderstanding, stress, and conflict can be minimized if participants in the organization, including "experts," know what is expected of them and to whom to report. It is preferable for expert staff or consultants to report to a single individual within the campaign. This need not mean that everyone reports to the same person, but that no one reports to more than one person.

This is not always possible. For example, the advertising agency may need to deal with the campaign manager, his immediate staff, the press secretary, the campaign's accounting office and treasurer, etc. The goal should be to restrict contact between the agency (or any outside consultant) to the smallest possible number of individuals in the campaign. This avoids contradictory direction, confusion, and the feeling among staff that orders are being given by an outsider. Since staff members usually have qualified or restricted authority, coordination is enhanced when they report such contacts, in an established fashion, to the campaign manager. For example, when the advertising agency seeks payment from the accounting office to purchase time and space, the campaign manager's authorization may be required.

Administrative practices may appear satisfactory from a technical, accounting, or information systems point of view, "but organizations are not only technical, accounting or information entities, they are *social* systems. So the manager needs to know how administrative practices affect motivation and behavior." Referring to a series of laboratory experiments, the authors point to the study's conclusion that ". . . prolonged discussions between superior and subordinates to set goals and explore means of arriving at them may not be more motivating, but they may help the subordinate develop a much clearer idea of what he is supposed to do."[24]

One does not have to be a behavioralist or believe that a structure that encourages superior/subordinate goal setting increases subordinate motivation, to accept the merit of a structure that encourages "give and take." The opportunity for subordinates to understand more fully what their assignment is will help them to complete the assignment more efficiently. The manager may find his time well spent in one-on-one meetings with key staff members to discuss their assignments. The first step is to define their assignments, explain their importance to the overall effort, then discuss the best way of getting the assignments accomplished. Such discussions take time, but they give the subordinate a sense of importance, the explanation helps the individual do a better job, and the rapport helps integrate the campaign effort. (Often the manager can deal with staff members first on a one-to-one basis, later in groups. In this way, the most troublesome questions are resolved on a more intimate basis; the group meeting is shorter and more productive.)

The manager sometimes plans a structure independent of individuals selected for positions; other times, slots are constructed or modified in planning to accomodate individuals the manager wishes to hire or has hired. Often the manager hires someone he can "find a spot for." Care must always be taken not only to ostensibly satisfy the campaign's needs but also to slot individuals in positions that fulfill *their* needs. This is no act of altruism on the manager's part; it is for the campaign's benefit.

Ideally, the staff members in a political campaign should not be compelled to take a given position. An individual staff member should have the right to accept or reject a position; the person may not have such a prerogative if the position offered is itself an accomodation—an attempt to work out a difficult situation such as a personality clash within the organization. A staff member may have personal reasons for not accepting a slot that seems, from the manager's point of view, to be the right one for the individual. The manager should try to determine these reasons. The manager who is extremely confident that the staff member is misjudging the situation, either because he wrongly perceives the job as too much or too little, or is letting personal considerations unduly interfere, can use his persuasive ability to suggest a trial effort. If the manager makes a mistake, the blunder could be costly for the campaign; the short time duration of the political campaign leaves little time for correcting personnel mishaps.

Stress and Conflict

The political campaign organization is characterized by stress and conflict. The campaign's short time duration, the intensity of the work and the need for precision, and the pressure to win aggravate the tension within the campaign. Although no objective measures have been taken of stress associated with different positions within the campaign, the scheduling and press divisions may be the most stress-intensive. Scheduling staffers must resolve an immense quantity of conflicting, all seemingly important, invitations for the candidate. They must deal with precise details and minute-by-minute time blocks. Errors in verifying information or arranging transportation can significantly affect the schedule for several hours or the entire day. Sometimes, there is no way to compensate for missing a flight and foregoing an important campaign appearance. The scheduling staff must confront "acts of nature": changes in the weather, automobile accidents and traffic tie-ups, etc.

Down the corridor in the press office, staff members are given seemingly impossible deadlines to create, research, write, and edit statements; often ordered to produce "reaction statements" responding to a news development on the wires, and to produce such a statement, thoroughly researched, facts and data verified, and accurately reproduced, within a couple of hours or even within ten or twenty minutes. Moreover, the press secretary must accomodate scores of reporters who must file reports within their own deadlines; the nature of competing media suggests that reporters all stop by or call in to make requests or demands in the same "peak" periods. The press secretary and his staff must return dozens of telephone calls, review the upcoming schedule, oversee the mailing of releases and schedules, meet with the candidate, answer requests for the candidate's biography, his photograph, statements on issues, etc., and assorted other tasks—and do everything virtually simultaneously.

Stress can be created by job insecurity, uncertain professional status, exorbitant work demands, and insufficient authority to get a job done. Stress can also be created by over- or under-utilization of an individual's skills. An individual not fully utilized feels tension and stress, as much or even more than the individual who has "too much to do." Mentally healthy individuals may be better able to cope with the stress and tension of the political campaign, and they may be more likely to avoid conflict or escalating minor disputes into serious conflicts. It is also possible that neurotics can perform well in the political campaign, precisely because the long hours and intense work are a form of therapy.

Schaffer and Schoben have listed eight ways to practice good mental health. Because of the importance of stress and tension in the campaign, the manager should be aware of this list: (1) practice good physical health; (2) accept yourself (hence you are better able to accept other people as they are); (3) maintain at least one confidential relationship (i.e., there should be at least one person in whom you can confide); (4) constructive action must be taken to eliminate stress; (5) interact with people other than those with whom you are forced to interact at work; (6) creative experience contributes to mental health; (7) meaningful work contributes to mental health; (8) use the scientific method to solve personal problems.[25]

The political campaign will hopefully provide creative experience for the staff member, but its crash program nature may leave little time for interaction with people outside the work environment. Its work may also be meaningful and, in that respect too, contribute to good mental health. But the inherent demands of the work environment, which may compromise, at least over the short term, an individual's physical health and his equilibrium, suggest that the individual should be in good mental health at the outset to weather the campaign.

Constructive action may be taken to eliminate some sources of stress, but the fast-moving, goal oriented campaign cannot change its innate characteristics or repudiate its overall objective of electing the candidate by election day. People who work in a campaign usually know its characteristics—and knew those characteristics before they joined the organization; they may even enjoy the combination of high goals, long hours, excitement, tension, and stress. Creativity and meaningful work, which should be ingredients of the well-managed political campaign, suggest that the campaign has within it elements that contribute to good mental health.

Stress can lead to conflict which, in turn, feeds upon itself. Within the campaign, different divisions compete for funds. Geographical regions or counties also compete for the budget dollar, just as operating sections in the campaign headquarters compete for the payroll dollar, or the use of the mailing and shipping facilities. Specialized support groups or committees compete for grants from the general campaign budget. Everyone competes for the candidate's time, and everyone and every section of the campaign compete for the campaign manager's ear. Many staff members and volunteer leaders want to play strategist and oversee the campaign; they second-guess the candidate, the campaign manager, and their superiors.

A primary responsibility of the campaign manager is to gather input and evaluate it, so that he has the best information and a sound interpretation of it, in order to work with different leaders and individuals within the campaign, to negotiate, compromise, and arbitrate differences to prevent conflict or escalation of conflict. A conflict between two individuals can usually be resolved more easily than a conflict between two groups or *sets* of individuals, e.g., one group representing one county or component of the campaign, and the other group another county or component. For example, certain individuals within the media or advertising section may lobby intensively for television to be the dominant advertising medium. These television oriented media advisers may have logic on their side, but they should not be permitted, by their *style* of argument, to disrupt the entire media operation. Disruption can occur if the discussion is personalized; if conflict results and is not controlled, and if scars remain after the debate is resolved. Conflict can also occur if the individual cannot satisfy his needs within the political campaign, if he "wishes to satisfy security, affiliative, or esteem needs through the group, but his associates demand excessive conformity or stressful behavior."[26]

Conflict also arises when traditional management principles are applied when they cannot or should not be applied. For example, "unity of command, or one should have only one boss" is a valid principle. But if it is formally asserted when it need not be, a well-intentioned staff member may find himself in the middle of a dispute. Consider a secretary who works in one division (scheduling), but must interact with another (press). The scheduling director should not insist on a confrontation over the unity of command principle if part of the secretary's responsibility is liaison with the press division. Similarly, the old-line political campaign manager, conditioned to worrying about getting-out-the-vote, not television and radio and their array of creative specialists, would make a mistake in trying to treat these part-time consultants and technical aides as full-time employees who can fit neatly into an organizational box. Attempts to do so can create conflict.

Each individual has a different level of stress compatible with his temperament and personality. For an individual who thrives on stress and tension, the campaign can (for a limited time period) be healthy. The knowledge that the campaign will end around election day provides an element of certainty that enables some individuals to keep pushing themselves. They put off rest and relaxation until the end of the campaign. For these individuals, the manager seeks to create a certain amount of stress—as a dynamic, motivating force. Unless the stress is calculated and controlled, organizational life can deteriorate into a series of short-run upsets and long-run conflicts.

Conflict is a powerful process for desirable or undesirable results. The desirable results include creating superior ideas, forcing people to search for new approaches and giving them a chance to test their capabilities. The undesirable results include creating distances between people, developing distrust among people, and making them feel demeaned and defeated. Any conflict involves four elements. *Frustration* is when people feel blocked out. *Conceptualization* involves determining the nature of the problem. *Behavior* flows from the conceptualization of each party to the conflict. *Outcome* includes the feelings of the parties involved following the decisions or actions taken; residual frustration may lead to another conflict.[27]

Any political strategist who has ever negotiated, searched for delegates, or brokered votes in a convention knows the five basic ways of handling conflict. These same ways of resolving conflict can be utilized in any organization, not just the political campaign. *Competing* presupposes a clear definition of the objective and reasons for its importance. A strategy for winning is formulated and it is pursued, even at the expense of the other party. *Accomodating* is pursued when the relationship is more important than the point at issue. The other party is permitted to get his way. *Avoiding* is a method chosen when the conflict cannot be resolved without significant adverse consequences, or if the person does not consider the issue to be critical, or the time to be ripe for another method of handling the conflict. *Compromising* is simply picking some middle course in which neither party wins or loses entirely. *Collaborating* is a form of mutual problem solving in which each party accepts the other's goals. Both parties work together to achieve a solution.[28]

Generally, the manager, as conflict arbitrator, seeks solutions that involve compromising or collaborating. In some cases, such as a squabble between two county organizations supporting the candidate, he may try accomodating or avoiding. Only rarely will he try a competing solution, because he is usually not interested in solutions won by a party to the conflict, because that means some-one else lost. He may opt for a competing strategy to win when the conflict threatens his own leadership in the campaign. Alternative viewpoints and additional inputs should be encouraged, but once a strategic decision is made by the manager and the campaign committee, the decision should be supported. Dissent may engender conflict that can only be resolved by a readical competing solution, in which the dissenters are vigorously contested. In short, the manager's approach to conflict resolution depends a great deal on whether he is a party to the conflict.

Radical solutions are sometimes necessary to discourage others from resorting to conflict. Individuals working under the difficult conditions of a campaign may find they have a lower toleration level and greater propensity to dispute. If staff members A and B conflict, perhaps either A or B can be moved to another part of the campaign headquarters, or their responsibilities can be altered. If A or B conflicts with another individual, C, then the person involved in the two successive conflicts is presumed to be the problem. The clear enunciation of such a firm policy early in the campaign may encourage staff members to work out their own problems without letting them degenerate into a conflict that can only be resolved at a higher level.

The way to avoid conflict is to recruit staff members who are reasonably well adjusted adults who can work as part of the political campaign team. If great care is given to the recruitment process, then the next major step in avoiding conflict is to create a work environment that motivates each person and introduces no more tension and stress than is necessarily required in the political campaign. Such a work environment places a premium on high standards of interpersonal communication, in which games or roles that damage others in the campaign are frowned upon and discouraged. For example, the campaign manager makes it clear in the beginning of the campaign, and as each new staff member is hired, that manipulation of others, gossip, complaining about other members of the staff not doing their work instead of doing your own, etc. will not be tolerated.

There is no magic way to eliminate all conflict, but since it consumes valuable time, a precious asset in the political campaign, it should be minimized.

6 Political Campaign Finance

The Barry Goldwater Presidential campaign was an artistic flop and a political disaster, but it was a fund-raising masterpiece the like of which may not be seen again in politics during the lifetime of his youngest contemporaries.

—Herbert M. Baus and William B. Ross
Politics Battle Plan

Baus and Ross were wrong. The Goldwater fund-raising totals were exceeded by both Richard Nixon and by George McGovern in 1972. In each case, a key component of fund raising was the use of direct mail—the mass solicitation of small givers. The 1964 Goldwater campaign ushered in that era. An ideological candidate with little chance of victory appealed to masses of givers, at least 650,000 individuals, with about 560,000 of them contributing $100 or less.[1] Direct mail, which is becoming more important than ever, partly due to laws favoring its use, illustrates the impact of the political environment on fund raising or revenue raising in the political campaign.[a] The state of the economy determines how much some contributors are prepared or able to give; the perception of the candidate and view of his political party, sometimes related to the perception of his chance of victory, may affect how much they *want* to give; legislation may limit how much they *can* give, although in direct mail, the typical modest contributor is not directly affected. He is, however, indirectly affected in that legislation limiting affluent givers encourages greater solicitation of small givers.

Each subsystem is utilized to measure, estimate, plan, and control fund raising and expenditures. The *goals and values* subsystem is reflected in the priorities of the budget. The *technical* subsystem provides the alternative means and methods to raise funds: the dinners, the finance committee receptions, direct mail solicitation, etc., as well as the quantitative tools and technology required. For example, mail houses, data processing list maintenance, bookkeeping systems, etc. are all highly relevant. The *structural* subsystem provides the kind of organization or committee required. For example, a finance committee structure may be utilized, with local components; a consulting arrangement may be

---

[a]Laws that ban large contributions or provide matching public funds for small contributions derived from many contributors favor direct mail solicitation. For an excellent account of large-scale direct mail, see Christopher Lydon's special report, "Credit System Fuels Wallace Fund Drive" (*New York Times,* May 23, 1975).

set up with a direct mail fund-raising consultant; a treasurer may be appointed
to be accountable for funds; a controller or chief bookkeeper may be responsible
for the technical disbursement of funds and record keeping. The *psychosocial*
subsystem reflects the attitudinal makeup of organization participants. For example, decisions to raise and expend funds will profoundly affect components
of the campaign, beginning with the payroll of staff and extending to the funding of the programs in which they are involved. The *managerial* subsystem involves the strategic decisions regarding which methods of fund raising will be
employed, what programs will be included in the budget, and for how much, etc.

Within this chapter, the three basic elements of political campaign financing
will be considered. These three elements are fund raising or the *revenue* function,
expenditures or the *budget* function, and accounting or the *control* function.

Revenue

Revenue in a political campaign is primarily raised through contributions.
Some campaign materials may be sold, especially from an umbrella committee to
local committees or adjunct committees. There may also be miscellaneous income.
For example, reporters may reimburse (drawing on their media outlet's expense
account) the campaign for seats on the campaign plane. But the overwhelming
proportion of revenue derives from contributions of one kind or another.

Before considering the methods of fund raising, we shall consider the types
of givers to political campaigns. The classifications presented are not discrete,
and a giver may easily fall into one or more classifications. Moreover, he may not
be the ideal case within a classification, but he may be "substantially" that kind
of giver.

Classifications of Givers by Motivation

The Ideological Giver.   This contributor identifies with the candidate's
ideology. He prefers a Type II or Type III candidate (e.g., Barry Goldwater,
George McGovern). Often he accepts a hybrid candidate, Type I, ostensibly
nonideological, but with strong ideological overtones, i.e., a very liberal or very
conservative candidate whose views seem to him to be ideologically based.
Edward Kennedy or John Tunney might fit this classification on the liberal side;
Bill Brock or Carl Curtis might fit this classification on the conservative side. All
four United States Senators' voting records are very liberal or very conservative,
respectively.

At a lower level, for Congress or for local office, the candidate is not as
likely to galvanize ideological financial support. It is more difficult to draw
attention to ideological issues. In addition, the ideological giver is more likely to

think big than to think small: he wants to elect a Governor or Senator, or, more often, the President of the United States—offices offering more dramatic means to "save the country."

The Single-Issue Giver. This contributor is so interested in a single issue that he is prepared to support a candidate whose position on that issue pleases him; or a candidate who is running against someone with the "wrong" position on the issue. It can be seen that the single-issue giver, like the ideological giver, can contribute funds *against* the election of a candidate as well as *for* the election of a candidate. In the ideological case, he is determined to defeat a "left-wing" Assemblyman or an "ultraconservative" State Senator; in the single-issue case, he wants to defeat a United States Congressman who favors abortions, or a United States Senator who voted against a defense program. In past years, abortion, the Vietnam war, the SST, the Lockheed loan, aid to Israel, etc. have all been single-issue orientations for some contributors. In the case of the SST or the Lockheed loan, there may have been some economic involvement, but sometimes the issue exemplified what was perceived as a pro- or anti-environmentalist position, or a pro- or anti-national defense position.

The Party Giver. This contributor is loyal to a given political party, and he supports the candidates who are endorsed by that party, running on that party's line or, in his mind, identified with that political party. This giver is likely to be a regular contributor to the Democratic National Committee or the Republican National Committee, or to local components of each organization, or national fund-raising instruments, such as the Republican Congressional Campaign Committee or the Democratic Senatorial Campaign Committee.

The Candidate Giver. The candidate holds major appeal for this contributor. His personality, his style, his charisma, his disposition or temperament, his issue orientation, his way of speaking, his ideas (this borders on ideology), and his overall image are what may attract this giver. This contributor may be drawn into politics for the first time as a supporter of this candidate. He may have little or no loyalty to a political party; or, he may be loyal to a party but especially attracted to this candidate.

The Favor-Seeker Giver. This contributor seeks access to the candidate. If the candidate is elected this contributor wants access to present his views. Although it is fashionable to dismiss such contributors as "special interests," they often are engaged in hedging operations—giving to both sides to achieve some minimum level of recognition to guarantee basic access to the candidate should he be elected. These contributors should not be confused with the small minority who seek more than access or influence, but who seek to bribe a candidate in exchange for his future decision or vote favorable to their interests.

As long as government grows larger and larger and exerts such pervasive influence over the economy, special interests will, if only as a matter of self-defense and self-preservation, support candidates who are more sympathetic to their viewpoint. The only way to achieve real reform is to curtail drastically the responsibility of all levels of government, thereby removing the incentive for special interests to be active in politics. Regardless of any reforms in campaign contributions laws, there will always be some way that special interests can influence candidates and elected officials.

The Social Giver. This contributor supports a campaign because it is socially acceptable or a way to indicate "good citizenship." The rationale may be that "good citizens take an active part in supporting deserving candidates for public office." In other cases, money may be the least costly means (compared to time) of supporting a candidate and demonstrating "civic mindedness." Then, there are the socially prominent citizens who give to hospitals, universities, charities; within the same circles are peers who encourage them to support candidates. Many of the same people who attend a $100-a-plate political dinner might also attend a dinner in behalf of a local hospital.

Repeatedly, the term "giver" has been used. Actually, the giver need not be an individual; it could be a corporation, labor union, group of citizens banded together in a committee, an organization, or whatever. Particular laws, part of the political environment, dictate the conditions under which givers, including organizational units, may contribute to campaigns. For example, both corporations and labor unions are prohibited from contributing to candidates for federal office. However, corporate executives may contribute their own personal funds, and labor unions may raise political war chests through voluntary contributions. In addition, many states permit corporations and labor unions to contribute to candidates for state and local office.

These classifications have made no reference to the *size* of a giver's contribution. The classifications are more concerned with *motivation* than with the size of the individual contribution, or the aggregate amount of contributions given by those with that motivation. Nor has any reference been made to the *method* of fund raising. It is difficult to segregate and correlate each of these factors. For example, ideological liberals helped provide McGovern's seed money, as did single-issue contributors concerned about the Vietnam war. Within the McGovern direct mail campaign, the motivations of givers were also diverse; someone giving $5 might have the same antiwar motivations as one of McGovern's heaviest financial backers.

The Power-Seeker Giver. There is one additional *kind* of giver who is almost totally correlated with the size of contribution. The power-seeker giver wants the feeling of proximity to the candidate; he wants recognition; he wants the feeling of power that his money offers. This person wants to feel that he has the power to affect destiny; for example, that his contribution may determine whether the local candidate can mail his literature to every household in the district, or whether the candidate for Governor can begin his statewide television advertising campaign. Sometimes, the difference between the status sought by the social giver and the power sought by the power-seeker is difficult to discern. It is important to recognize that we are not talking about a special interest contributor, but someone who wants to play "king maker" or be one of several "king makers."

The power-seeker giver tends to give a contribution large in absolute terms, and always large in *relative* terms. For example, a $5,000 or $10,000 contribution would be insignificant for a candidate running for President. However, for a candidate running for city council in a small city, it might comprise a quarter or third of the campaign budget. Some individuals who cannot acquire the status and power in a large statewide or Presidential campaign may concentrate their resources in a single, smaller campaign. Often, this is the case with a finance chairman of a campaign; he works for one candidate and one campaign, and he does not get involved in any other campaigns or political races.[b]

Individuals who contribute "seed money" to start a campaign can fall into almost any motivational classification. A group of businessmen representing special interests may persuade someone to consider running for office by offering a campaign "kitty." A group of ideologues may recruit an ideological candidate to run for office, and they may contribute, or raise, an initial campaign war chest. What is generally true is that seed money, almost by definition, comes from a small number of (presumably, large) givers.

At the other extreme, the small giver, usually solicited by direct mail, could also be motivated by a variety of considerations, though he is rarely a favor-seeker or power-seeker. Most direct mail givers are ideologically inspired. Their names are often drawn from computer lists of individuals with a record of "cause" giving. On the liberal side, they may include subscribers to *The New Republic* or *The Nation,* or supporters of past liberal causes—civil rights committees, antiwar committees; on the conservative side, they may subscribe to *National Review, Human Events,* or *Conservative Digest* and support favorite conservative causes, or organizations like Young Americans for Freedom.[c]

A common fallacy assumes that any large contributor is necessarily acting

---

[b]When industrialist David Packard became President Ford's interim campaign finance chairman he indicated that all of his political efforts would be directed at the singular goal of funding the Ford re-election effort. However, since the federal law then in effect limited individual contributions to $1,000, Packard himself could not contribute more. His value was not in what *he* could contribute, but in what he could *raise* from individuals giving no more than $1,000 each (*Los Angeles Times,* Sept. 7, 1975). Because Packard could not adapt to the Federal law then in effect (i.e., the $1,000 limitation), he was replaced as Finance Chairman.

[c]List owners and brokers maintain an extensive national market in lists of every kind. However, most publications only rent lists of former, not present subscribers.

unethically or even illegally. Ideological and issue oriented givers are only two examples of potentially substantial supporters who do not seek government contracts, grants, or other favoritism. The social giver who seeks status and the power seeker who seeks control may not be so different if the power seeker settles for proximity to the candidate/elected official and the *perception* of others that with access comes influence. Contributors who hope for social access to the Mayor, a coveted invitation to a White House dinner or reception, or who want an elected official to attend the wedding of one of their children do not compromise the public interest.

A contributor may be motivated by several reasons. He may not only favor the candidate's political party, but he may feel strongly about an issue prominent in the campaign. He may also seek the social prestige associated in some circles with large giving. Whatever the level of campaign, the manager or fund raiser must analyze the role of different motivational forces, both for individual givers and for givers studied as a group, e.g., a mailing list. The next logical step is to target fund-raising appeals so that once issues are selected to appeal to a particular constituency, words, slogans, phrases, examples, and anecdotes are selected for particular effect.

In fund raising the manager works closely with the candidate, finance chairman, and other volunteer fund raisers to evaluate the "market." The finance chairman and members of the finance committee should always be volunteers, although secretaries and clerks are salaried. In larger campaigns a full-time, salaried finance director oversees the day-to-day fund-raising operation. In any campaign the candidate should spend as little time raising funds as possible; generally, surrogates, such as his finance chairman or other substantial supporters should seek funds in his behalf. Everyone involved in this fund-raising process must consider the political environment at the outset and during the campaign. Obvious examples include the state of the economy and its effect on ability to give; domestic and foreign policy developments, and their effect on attitudes of givers; changing ethical perceptions and laws affecting fund raising; the relative importance in the public consciousness of certain issues, and how they affect the giver's propensity to support the candidate; media coverage and its effect and on whether potential givers are aware of the candidate and are favorably disposed toward him.

For medium to large givers, the question of whether a candidate has a real chance to win is important. "Early money" reflects in part the contributor's perception that the campaign is a serious, viable effort. Such perceptions may be stimulated by syndicated columns or news articles by respected political reporters, especially if these stories indicate that funding might make the crucial difference. Even smaller givers prefer not to give to a losing cause. Moreover, the ideological giver is encouraged when the same issues emphasized in his direct mail solicitation are also emphasized by the candidate in his "visuals"—the unstructured news events that are covered by the evening news. Media affects the

Table 6-1

Classification of Givers (By Motivation). Every contributor to a political campaign falls into at least one of these classifications.

1. The ideological giver
2. The single-issue giver
3. The party giver
4. The candidate giver
5. The favor-seeker giver
6. The social giver
7. The power-seeker giver
8. The three-issue giver

timing of contributions, i.e., the relative cash flow over time is related to the quantity and quality of coverage. Lack of, or unfavorable, coverage not only discourages prospective donors from giving, or causes them to give less, it may discourage fund raisers from approaching new prospects.

After considering the total political environment, fund raisers must relate issues to issue oriented givers. Even givers motivated for other reasons may prefer to rationalize their contribution by expressing interest in several campaign issues. The first differentiation of givers is by motivation (Table 6-1).

The Three-Issue Giver.   One additional classification has been added—*the three-issue giver.* This contributor is not quite an ideological giver: he does not have a fixed, rigid philosophical frame of reference, nor is he part of a (liberal or conservative) movement. At the same time, he is attracted to the candidate not because of his position on a single issue of paramount importance to the giver, but because the candidate's position on several issues attracts him. Usually, the number of issues is small—two, three, or four, and more likely three—which can be easily remembered and associated with each other. This giver is more *issue oriented* than the candidate giver, but less issue oriented than the ideological giver. A few key issues may provide the means to reach voters and potential contributors who cannot, over the short term, be reached with an ideological message.[d]

One cautionary note: although it is often desirable to emphasize different issues or the same issues differently in appealing to potential contributors in contrast to appealing to the electorate, major inconsistencies, when reported in the media or when they are so apparent that the contributors see them, can erode the fund-raising base or the electoral base.

---

[d]For example, in the late sixties and early seventies several campaigns emphasized urban crime, drug abuse, and campus unrest. These issues, as well as civil turmoil, pornography, and, in some cases, abortion, were related to Wattenberg's "social issue"—also called the *stability* theme.

Table 6-2

Classification of Givers (By Size of Contribution). The figures are cumulative during the course of a political campaign.[a]

1. *King maker:* This is the highest contributor, or among the top several, usually not to exceed half a dozen.
   a. Presidential campaign: $100,000+ (e.g., for the Nixon 1972 campaign, W. Clement Stone contributed $2,000,000+; Richard Scaife $1,000,000; John Mulcahy $600,000)
   b. U.S. Senate: $100,000+ for large state
                     50,000+ for small state
   c. Governor: same as Senator
   d. U.S. Congress: $25,000

2. *Very large:* For President, $50,000+; for Senator or Governor, $20,000; for Congress, $10,000

3. *Large:* For President, $10,000; for Senator or Governor, $5,000 (or $1,000+ for small state); for Congress, $2,500

4. *Generous:* For President, $5,000; for Senator or Governor, $1,000; for Congress, $1,000

5. *Good size:* For President, $1,000; for Senator or Governor, $500; for Congress, $500 or $250, depending on type of district

6. *Medium giver:* For President, $250; for Senator, Governor, $250; for Congress, $100

7. *Average-to-modest:* For President, Senator or Governor, $100–$250; for Congress, $50–$100

8. *Small:* For President, Senator or Governor, under $100; for Congress, under $50

9. *Very small:* Under $25

10. *Direct mail per capita contribution:* $5–$20

[a]These figures are given without reference to contribution limits set by law; should such limits continue to be imposed and sustained constitutionally by the courts, the historical figures would be revised drastically, and these classifications would be relegated to history.

Classifications of Givers by Size of Contribution and Method of Solicitation

The second differentiation of givers is by size of individual contributions (Table 6-2). In evaluating the market the manager and fund raisers must estimate how many contributors will give different dollar amounts, i.e., how many will give $50, how many will give $100, etc. These figures may be adjusted if givers will be approached to give more than once, so the cumulative figure reflects the campaign's expectation.[e]

Some campaigns have several large contributors without any single individual

[e]When the 1974 federal campaign legislation was first challenged, one of the major issues was the constitutionality of limitations on individual campaign contributions. Interestingly, at an early stage of the case, the Department of Justice modified its prior position in defense of the law and moved toward a neutral posture. (Christopher Lydon, *New York Times,* May 25, 1975; Jules Witcover, *Washington Post,* May 28, 1975; John P. MacKenzie, *Washington Post,* May 29, 1975; Lawrence Meyer, *Washington Post,* May 31, 1975.)

playing a central (king maker) role. The time frame is also important, i.e., the contributor who gives $10,000 to a Senate candidate just after he decides to run may have more influence than the contributor who gives $25,000 in the campaign's final week when it is apparent the candidate will win. It is often easier for a manager to abbreviate classification of givers by size in the following broader categories:

1. *Elite* (highest contributor or top two or few givers)
2. *Large* (very large, large, generous)
3. *Medium* (good size, medium giver)
4. *Small* (average-to-modest, small, very small, direct mail per capita contribution)

The campaign manager can then adjust his "sights" on target dollar amounts to fit each of the above four classifications. He can then decide on an optimum method of solicitation (Table 6–3).

The mechanics of fund raising are beyond the scope of this discussion. Political party organizations provide manuals detailing specific fund-raising methodology. Direct mail specialists are qualified to answer questions about postage, printing, list rental, labels, mail houses, copy-writing, etc. Our concern is analysis of the revenue base (Table 6–4).

Analyzing the Revenue Base

Given an aggregate fund-raising goal based on a budget formulated to achieve electoral victory, this budget is still not a fixed figure, but an aggregate figure *over time* requiring a certain cash flow to maintain desired rates of spending and meet commitments for payroll, headquarters, telephone, advertising, candidate's travel expenses, etc. If funds are not raised on time, the aggregate budget may have to be reformulated; a reduced budget would not necessarily reduce each budgetary item by the same percentage. For example, television time might be so important that TV spending might remain constant, while radio and newspaper advertising expenditures are cut or eliminated; also, some expenses, such as headquarters rent, may be totally fixed costs, and other expenditures, like payroll, may be so difficult to cut or eliminate that they too must be viewed as fixed costs.

What meaning can be attached to the budget if the revenue is not raised? As much thought as goes into a budget, it is only a goal which can be realized *if* the funding is there. Visionary budgets in a political campaign are usually visionary not because of the components of the budget, but because of the assumption that the aggregate figure will be raised *or* the cash flow will be raised within specific time periods to support the budget. In the political campaign, the fund-

Table 6–3
Classification of Givers (by Method of Solicitation)[a]

1. Personal approach (at top level)
   a. By candidate
   b. By campaign manager
   c. By finance chairman or ranking finance committee members

2. Personal approach by peers
   a. Finance committee members and others approach prospective donors in the same income/asset range as themselves
   b. Finance committee members and others approach prospective donors who are similar in other respects (e.g., attorneys approach attorneys)

3. Telephone solicitation (before and after personal visits, attendance at events, etc., including by finance committee)

4. Mail solicitation (small mailings, individually typed letters, follow-up to personal visits, telephone solicitation, attendance at events, etc.)

5. Campaign literature (solicitation within brochures and other campaign material)

6. Door-to-door (only worthwhile in areas with high support)

7. Party organizations (grants, gifts from organizations, campaign committees, local party clubs)

8. Direct mail (mass solicitation to large lists; usually using mail houses and data processing)

9. Advertising (solicitation in newspaper advertising, television, radio, etc.)

10. Projects (dinners, receptions, cocktail parties, auctions, breakfasts, luncheons, use of advance ticket sales, ticket sales at door; ticket sales and contributions; "free" attendance, with solicitation at event, or following event; headquarters donations and the provision of in-kind services, such as free rent of headquarters, donated equipment, etc., if law permits; fashion shows, book sales, car washes, and any other event suitable at the local level)

---

[a]These more common methods are not mutually exclusive, i.e., a giver may be solicited by more than one method. Some methods are more or less appropriate for different kinds of campaigns.

raising goal is determined by the budget; however, alternative budgets based on different environments and fund-raising shortfalls must also be prepared. The implications of fund-raising shortfalls can be ominous. For example, television time is finite and if funds are not raised far enough in advance to purchase the time, it will be sold to commercial advertisers and other candidates. If adequate funds are subsequently raised, it may be too late to purchase the time.

The example of a Congressional candidate with a general election campaign budget of $100,000 illustrates several points. Assume the candidate's best friend, a prominent businessman, becomes finance chairman. He wishes to contribute $5,000, but assume the relevant law (constitutionally upheld) limits him to $1,000, so his wife and three relatives each give $1,000. Assume no cash flow calculations.

Who will contribute to the campaign? Ideological givers? Single-issue givers? Favor-seekers? How should the givers be approached? Should there be a telephone campaign? Should there be groups of meetings at homes of different

Table 6-4
Steps in Analyzing the Revenue Base

1. Analyze each component of the political environment, with special emphasis on the media. Forecast how the environment may change, especially the media coverage of the campaign, and the effect on fund raising among different types of givers (by motivation, size, and method).
2. Analyze the appeal of the candidate to different types of givers by motivation, and estimate the percentage of revenue to be provided by different types.
3. Analyze the appeal of the candidate to different types of givers by the size of their contribution, i.e., based on their past history of giving, their feelings about the political environment and the candidate, their capacity to give, etc., estimate likely target goals for which they should be solicited.
4. Analyze the alternative methods of soliciting contributions, and the relevance of each method to the campaign, and its relative importance to the total revenue base.
5. Divide the aggregate fund-raising goal to reflect, first, the number of contributors who will each give a certain amount, e.g., the number of $10,000 contributors, the number of $5,000 contributors, the number of $2,500 contributors, . . . the number of $5 contributors, etc.; correlate these figures with the method of soliciting those contributions; or, second, divide the aggregate figure by the methods, then correlate those figures with the number of individuals (of firms, associations, unions, etc.) giving certain dollar amounts.
6. Adjust the overall figure into components that are based on time periods: months, weeks, days to reflect actual cash flow, rather than work-in-progress or commitments made but not yet kept.

members of the finance committee? Should they hire a direct mail consultant to mail to smaller givers in the area with a proven record of backing the party's candidates for different offices? How successful will these methods be, i.e., what is their *probability* of success? If they involve costs, are these costs taken into consideration?

No matter which method is chosen, considerable technical expertise is required. For example, a telephone campaign requires the compilation of lists of prospects, the use of cards or some other system to measure the progress of solicitation, the assignment of lists to different fund raisers for telephoning, a program of follow-up, a thank you program, even a program to get a second contribution before the campaign ends. These are all "how to" details of methodology that are indispensable to any precision fund-raising operation.

Forecasting Revenue

Any fund-raising strategy requires forecasting, and forecasting is inexact. It does not rely on 100 percent certain data; instead, all data should be viewed as probabilistic. The first major mistake made in forecasting revenue in the campaign is to view a goal or target as 100 percent probable, or to view a promise, commitment, pledge, or hint of a contribution the same as having the money in the bank. Another mistake is in treating *gross* fund-raising revenue as *net* fund-raising revenue. In the case of this hypothetical fund-raising chairman who wants to raise $95,000, should he hire a professional fund raiser who will be paid no salary, expenses only, plus 20 percent of the funds he raises? For the campaign, only 80 percent of the gross funds would be net—*before* expenses; i.e., if the fund raiser's automobile, travel, entertainment, telephone, etc. expenses equal the net before expenses, the campaign breaks even. The implication is that some subjective probability must be assigned to the fund raiser's success, since his expenses may not be covered unless he raises a certain amount of funds (Table 6-5).

When the finance chairman was first approached by the professional fund raiser, he was offered a plan to net the campaign $12,720; a more realistic assess-

Table 6-5
Should a Professional Fund Raiser's Proposal Be Accepted?

	Projection of Returns If Fund Raiser Is Hired				
Size of contri-bution	*Original Fund Raiser Figures*			*After Using Probability Weights*[a]	
	Number	*Total Dollars*		*Number*	*Total Dollars*
$5,000	2	$10,000		0	$ 0
$2,500	1	0		0	0
$1,000	5	5,000		2	2,000
$ 750	0	0		1	750
$ 500	4	2,000		2	1,000
$ 250	1	250		2	500[b]
$ 100	4	400		1	100[b]
under $100	3	100		8	250[b]
		$17,650			$4,600
	Total expenses for travel and entertainment @$350 per week—for four weeks	1,400		Total expenses for travel and entertainment $250 per week—for four weeks	1,000
	Commission (20% of $17,650)	3,530		Commission (20% of $4,600)	920
	Net to campaign	$12,720		Net to campaign	$2,680

Note: He wants to add the campaign account to his other nonpolitical accounts, as he travels around the state. He plans to allocate part of his expenses to the campaign.

[a]Each figure in the projection using probability weights was arrived at by using a Bayesian formulation (described in chapter 8).

[b]The fund raiser would be using lists of prospects supplied by the campaign. The manager decided that givers of more modest means should not be approached by a professional fund raiser, but should be approached by mail. As for those with a greater ability to give, the list was so small he would turn it over to the finance chairman. When he adjusted the projections for this fact, he discovered gross contributions of $850 (composed of under-$1,000 givers); less $170 for commissions, leaving only $680 to cover at least $1,000 of expenses the fund raiser would run up.

ment was $2,680. Finally, the finance chairman realized that party givers outside the congressional district were not prone to support the candidate; they had their own local races. Hence, he and his colleagues could approach the potentially larger givers themselves; as for the smaller givers outside the district, the cost of reaching them, given the 20 percent commission and the expense contribution, which would be a minimum of $250 a week, was not worth the effort. In other words, only a few people outside the district might give $1,000 or more, and to reach these people, the campaign did not require the services of the professional fund raiser. As it turned out, the "professional fund raiser" was both a traveling salesman and a commission fund raiser for certain charities with high overhead expenses; the campaign would have been a convenient vehicle to permit him to support his other endeavors.

Principles of Fund Raising

Our hypothetical finance chairman might do well to bear in mind the following principles of campaign fund raising:

1. *Any fund-raising project must be weighted by the probability of success.* That is, the probability of each alternative outcome multiplied by that outcome and summed (see chapter 8). At the very least, he should allow for low, medium or expected, and high returns from the program or project.

2. *Any fund-raising project or program should consider both gross and net revenue raised.* If a budget requires $95,000, this is the *net* figure required; depending on the method used, some figure greater than $95,000 will have to be raised. For example, a finance committee may only need to raise $105,000 to net $95,000; the $10,000 would provide for the salaries for a secretary and clerk for two months to help the campaign, plus telephone, rent, postage, and food and cocktails for various receptions and miscellaneous expenses. On the other hand, a direct mail program might only net 25¢ for every $1 raised, so that a net of $95,000 would require $380,000 to be raised.

3. *Fund raising must be related to cash flow over time.* If funds are raised too late to be effectively spent, or too late to meet payroll and other obligations, then the funds are worth less to the campaign than if they had flowed in to be spent on budgeted items or to meet commitments. Any aggregate fund-raising goal must be divisible by timed intervals: months, weeks, days; otherwise, the figure cannot be related to the needs of the campaign. There is some *time value* to funds raised; it is as if there were a discount rate to measure the present value of future dollars.

4. *Any fund-raising committee must be more than names.* Individuals on a committee who do not give funds can hardly solicit from others. No committee can pledge to meet a fund-raising goal if that goal is not capable of *successive subdivision* within the committee. For example, $95,000 might be raised if each

member of the committee agreed to raise a *specific* quota; if he, in turn, were chairman of a finance group in his area, he should be able to *subdivide* his quota into smaller figures for his colleagues to share in the effort. Unless an aggregate fund-raising goal of *any* finance committee can be divided and re-divided successively until its components are manageable figures that can realistically be related to very small groups of individual donors, the aggregate fund-raising goal is visionary and will never be fulfilled.

5. *Staff members can pay their own salaries many times over, if they are effectively used for fund-raising support services.* Telephoning, mailing letters of solicitation, follow-up, securing lists, maintaining prospect cards, etc. cannot be done totally by volunteers. A modest investment in staff to assist the volunteer members of a finance committee may enable those volunteer fund raisers to be substantially more productive in dollars raised.

6. *A commitment is not the same as money.* Hints of contributing, expressions of interest and good will, promises to contribute, oral or written agreements to contribute—all of these implied contributions are not and cannot be treated as contributions until and unless the funds are actually received. By implication budgetary decisions based on promises of financial support are only as prudent as the individual or individuals behind the commitments are dependable. Well-meaning supporters and well-intentioned fund raisers will probably be unsuccessful unless they have a *proven* record of success (though exceptions exist).

7. *No fund-raising project will be successful without attention to details.* Unless the finance chairman or the chairman of an event is personally involved, or can delegate assignments to a staff person or someone else, the project or event will collapse. An elite gathering of affluent givers may net a small amount of money if no one makes the fund-raising "pitch" or if there is no campaign literature or contribution blanks present.

8. *No "free" event will be successful unless there is follow-up.* Merely getting an elite group of possible givers to attend a reception to meet an out-of-state Senator campaigning for the local Senate candidate will not spur them to contribute to the local campaign. If there is no program to solicit funds at the invitation-only event, then a precise and methodical program of personal visits, telephone calls, and correspondence must be pursued following the event to make it a fund-raising success.

9. *The market must be segregated by ability to give.* The political campaign must seek out givers with varying ability to contribute to the campaign, and specific individuals must be assigned and put in charge of givers with different dollar amount potentials, just as different projects, dinners, receptions, etc. must be structured to reach different levels of givers.

10. *The market must be divided by motivation.* The "pitch" must be varied, depending on what part of the market the campaign is trying to reach. Essentially, this involves evaluating prospective givers on the basis of motiva-

tion or interest in different issues, and appealing to them on the basis of what is important to them.

11. *Substantial contributors may require briefings on legal and accounting questions, and a review of the campaign budget.* The larger the contributor, the more information he and his associates may require about relevant legislation and the campaign's budget.

12. *Any adjunct committee should be self-financing.* When an auxiliary committee is formed, such as "Doctors for . . ." or some other support group, it may not be able to raise a great deal of money for the campaign, but it should be (preferably) self-financing, i.e., there should be enough interest among its constituency that it can at least raise enough funds to pay for its own programs, newspaper ads, clerical help, etc.

13. *Fund-raising costs should be correctly matched against fund-raising revenue.* As closely as possible, the costs of fund raising, e.g., salaries, rent, telephone, postage, etc. should be correlated with the revenue for which the costs were expended. Sometimes, this may involve partially allocating expenses to one fund-raising project and the remaining expenses to another fund-raising project. In other cases, it is easier to allocate costs or expenses that are clearly attributable to a single fund-raising project, such as the cost of printing tickets for a $100-a-plate dinner. Only when the costs include considerable fixed costs, i.e., costs that would be present with or without the fund-raising project, is adjustment required in order to assess accurately the benefits of a project and measure the net revenue raised.

14. *The net fund-raising revenue should be applied to the net budget, exclusive of fund-raising expense.* As much as possible, the expense of raising funds should be segregated from regular campaign expenditures; the latter is the campaign budget, the former the cost of raising revenue. This segregation is to discourage fund raising to raise money not merely for the campaign's budget, but to meet *expenses* of other fund-raising programs. The budget should be formulated as a net figure; the cost of raising funds should be listed separately, to be deducted from gross fund raising.

15. *Fund-raising projects should be tailored to local needs and individual tastes.* Programs should be geared to the interests of local givers to spur them to contribute more generously. For example, givers may be reluctant to contribute more funds if virtually all the money is taken out of the area or county and spent in some other part of the state. Individuals with pet interests may contribute to campaigns that incorporate their interests in programs. For example, an individual who wants a local campaign headquarters may help fund expenses for that headquarters.

It needs to be emphasized and reiterated that any fund-raising committee requires a detailed plan; the greater the detail, the more likely the probability of success. The same generally holds true about any fund-raising project. It is rare that a fund-raising program, project, dinner, or reception fails because there was too much detail, or planning started too early. Usually, the detailed planning is lacking, or the timetable for the event begins too late. Any fund-raising program or event, particularly a dinner or reception that involves advance ticket sales, requires a detailed, step-by-step plan, with interim goals and objectives closely correlated to particular dates (and days prior to the event).[f] Details are not left to chance because the "bottom line"—how much money is raised—depends on whether the details are handled properly. A reception with an exciting guest speaker to draw affluent potential campaign donors could be a disaster unless a date is set early enough and invitations mailed, sufficiently in advance and followed up by telephone calls, to assure attendance. The best ideas, with tremendous fund-raising potential, will fall flat without advance planning and attention to details.

Relationship of Spending and Revenue

The success of the campaign's fund-raising program is not independent of the success of the campaign as a whole. This point has already been stressed regarding the media/fund-raising relationship. The kind of precision and detail work that characterizes an efficient campaign will carry over to its fund-raising operation; the reverse is not usually true—many campaigns that excel at fund raising, primarily because they have superb fund-raising chairmen or a secure ideological base for direct mail givers, are poorly run in other spheres. As noted earlier, the overall success of the campaign, including media coverage, affects the morale of volunteer fund raisers. Also, when the campaign is going well, they feel the money is being put to good use. The momentum generated by the campaign provides a climate conducive to giving. Campaign spending can help fund raising, e.g., advertising visibly demonstrates that funding is being used effectively.

One of the most difficult management decisions is how closely spending should be related to revenue, i.e., how much, if any, debt to incur. Debt must be based on a realistic appraisal of fund-raising expectations. It is said that a victorious candidate can always raise funds to repay his debt, but a loser will always have problems. Recent changes in the political environment make it more difficult for campaigns at almost any level to get direct credit, although alternative arrangements are possible.[g] An example of fund raising and expenditures

---

[f] An excellent example of a fund-raising dinner countdown was prepared by the Republican National Committee (*Mission '70s Manual and Workbook*, 1971). Beginning 60 days prior to the dinner, each day shows the progress expected to be made, in terms of speaker and program details, ticket sales chairmen and ticket sales, printing, publicity, etc.

[g] The 1974 federal legislation made corporate loans illegal; also, any loans are illegal if they exceed limits applicable to contributors. Vendors dealing with any campaign, especially

Table 6-6
Fund Raising versus Expenditures

	Funds Raised (Cash)	Funds Disbursed (Cash or Credit)
May	$ 50,000	$ 14,000 (includes survey)
June (No contested	10,000	30,000 (includes direct mail and
July primary)	50,000	60,000 other start-up costs)
August	200,000	175,000
September	300,000	350,000
Oct.–Week 1	100,000	125,000
Oct.–Week 2	100,000	150,000
Oct.–Week 3	200,000	250,000
Oct.–Week 4	350,000	275,000
5 days thru election day	200,000	255,000
after election	150,000 (for debt)	26,000 (transition and misc.)
	$1,710,000	$1,710,000

Note: These figures are based on a real statewide campaign (major state) with activity commencing late Spring following nomination by a party convention (rather than primary election).

from a recent statewide campaign (Table 6-6) indicates that despite the momentum near the end (the candidate barely won), about $150,000 had to be raised after election day.

This example illustrates two important points. First, most spending and fund raising occurs in the latter part of the campaign. Second, fund raising usually lags behind spending. In this example the manager could have been (wrongly) criticized for not accumulating a surplus, since he had no guarantee funding would be raised in the final weeks to support heavy spending. If fund raising had proved disappointing in the end, the campaign's spending curve would have collapsed near the end, when it should have peaked. The example reflects the manager's recognition that funds had to be spent as fast as they were raised during August and September, although the campaign was on the verge of bankruptcy throughout its limited existence. The manager decided that the level of early and September spending was the absolute minimum required to support the *momentum* required for victory. Without that momentum, the campaign

---

federally regulated vendors (airlines, telephone company, etc.) selling to a federal campaign, cannot extend credit or, if the bills are unpaid, they can be charged with making a contribution (in the form of the unpaid debt). Because of the long standing ambiguity of who really is responsible for campaign debts–the candidate, campaign chairman, treasurer, campaign committee, individual staff members–vendors are increasingly reluctant to sell to campaigns, or their prices are adjusted upward to reflect possible nonpayment. Nevertheless, "normal trade credit" during the campaign's short time period permits some "floatation." Major expenditures, such as television and newspaper advertising, must be paid in advance. Payrolls usually cannot be deferred. Printers and other vendors now seek partial payment on order and remaining payment on delivery or possibly within five or ten days. One of the initial problems of the Federal Elections Commission (created by the 1974 law) was to determine what is "normal" trade credit (Christopher Lydon, *New York Times*, May 23, 1975; R.W. Apple, *New York Times*, May 18, May 19, May 20, 1975).

would not be able to raise much in October and near the end. The campaign would not necessarily win with the early spending, but would definitely lose if funds could not be raised to support the final advertising "blitz." The early spending did not guarantee victory, but without it, defeat was assured, because the campaign could never hope for sustained momentum.

The real campaign budget is determined by the revenue and the cash flow over time. If actual revenue equals planned revenue, then the actual budget equals the planned budget. An example (extrapolated from an actual campaign) of forecasting campaign revenue (Table 6–7) demonstrates errors common to many campaigns. The candidate and his inept manager agreed on erroneous forecasts and rejected the counsel of an outside consultant. The item explanations of the discrepancies yield valuable lessons for even the smallest campaign. No campaign can accurately forecast revenue without the discipline provided by realistic projections—not the wishful thinking of candidates or managers trying to prove they are right.

Analysis of Forecasting Errors

(A.) The consultant knew that the Republican Senatorial Campaign Committee, which typically earmarked $5,000, $10,000, or $15,000 to a Senate campaign, would most likely contribute nothing to this campaign. The RSCC would not fund a campaign that lacked professional direction, refused outside counsel, and insisted on a strategy based almost totally on disseminating a wide range of brochures personally written by the candidate. Although there was a slight chance of a $5,000 contribution, the consultant felt safer in simply estimating zero. He knew that the decision makers in Washington believed, as he did, in the necessity for a formal campaign structure and the need for survey research, which were both publicly held in contempt by the candidate and his campaign manager.

(B.) The campaign, with little publicity, especially from out-of-state media, would not attract more than $5,000 in out-of-state contributions, excluding the national direct mail program. The consultant gave the campaign the benefit of the doubt and estimated the full $5,000.

(C.) The error in considering gross revenue rather than net revenue is most significant when considering any direct mail fund-raising program. The consultant's detailed computations are discussed in the direct mail example at the end of this chapter; final receipts reflected strong ideological appeal.

(D.) The consultant knew that most of the larger in-state contributors would not contribute early. Since the campaign did not understand the concept of *momentum,* the consultant knew that time would be the campaign's major enemy. Each survey would look worse, and the probability of contributions from major donors would decline. Only their commission would spur the two

Table 6-7
Forecasting Campaign Revenue[a]

Source of Revenue	Manager and Candidate*	Outside Consultant	Actual
A. Republican Senatorial Campaign Comm. grant	$ 15,000	$ 0	$ 0
B. Misc. out-of-state contributions (large)	15,000	5,000	5,000
C. Direct mail contributions (nat'l consultant)	500,000	104,500	120,000
D. Large contributors in-state (via two prof. fund raisers on commission)	75,000	25,000	30,000
E. Three fund raiser receptions/dinner parties for each of eight out-of-state Senators campaigning for candidate @$5,000 each	120,000	10,000	10,000
F. "Retirement Parties" to defeat incumbent; 200 such events, each organized by an individual chapter of a Republican volunteer organization; average 100 people at $5 per person; club contributions	100,000	10,000	12,500
G. Direct mail (in-state only) thru a local direct mail consultant	50,000	35,000	40,000
H. Unsolicited responses to television, newspaper advertising and coverage of campaign	15,000		
I. Response to pamphlets on issues and those who buy pamphlets in bulk quantity	30,000	10,000	15,000
J. Contributions from special interests	20,000		
K. Rebate from advertising agency	35,000	7,500	6,000
(Manager and candidate computed fund-raising cost of $157,500, leaving a net of $817,500.)	$975,000* $817,500 Net (Rough)	$207,000 Net (Rough)	$238,500 Net (Rough)

Note: *Manager/candidate calculations are *gross* figures before allowing for cost of fund raising.
[a]Two alternative forecasts compared to the actual revenue generated by the political campaign.

part-time fund raisers to seek out new sources, with a net to the campaign of about $25,000. The commissions proved more of an incentive than the consultant had anticipated, and about $30,000 was netted.

(E.) The consultant estimated that only four Senators would come into the state to campaign for a candidate with a near certain chance of defeat *and* whose unorthodox approach indicated he would not affect that chance. In addition, the campaign manager's reluctance to hire two clerk/secretaries for work before and after the receptions or small dinner parties for the Senators suggested that the events would barely raise any funds; perhaps a total net of $10,000. Also, each event was planned at at the last minute, too late to turn out a crowd.

(F.) These "Retirement Parties" were the most unrealistic of all the projections. The following assumptions would have to hold for so many volunteer clubs to take such an active role in the campaign: (1) the campaign should have momentum and generate enthusiasm; (2) the campaign should have field representatives to service the clubs and clerk/secretaries to help plan the events. The consultant knew that the candidate's strong ideology would attract contributions from club treasuries to total about $10,000, but there would be few organized parties to net $100,000—possible conceptually, but not for this campaign.

(G.) This projection, when adjusted for the cost of fund raising, was on target. In fact, greater reliance should have been placed on direct mail within the state, using a local direct mail consultant with more reasonable rates, rather than the national consultant (see end of chapter).

(H., I., J.) These figures were visionary. The campaign did not expect to have much advertising, and it clearly would not raise funds to support more than minimal advertising; hence there would be little response. Moreover, the lack of momentum and interest suggested there would be little *autonomous* giving, i.e., those who were not solicited. In addition, wide circulation of pamphlets written by the candidate would generate few responses in contributions or sales of the pamphlets. As for special constituencies or special interests contributing, the total failure of the campaign would generate almost no such contributions except from a few loyalist constituencies.

(K.) The rebate from the advertising agency was based on a larger media budget than would actually exist. In addition, the agency head was expected to do free work for the campaign in return for this commission. Once the media billings were not generated, he deducted other charges from the rebates owed to the campaign, which received only $6,000 back.

Budgeting

In any campaign, regardless of its size, a budget is required. The budget is a formal statement of priorities and a precise statement of planned spending for payroll, rent, telephone, postage, etc. It includes certain fixed costs, such as headquarters rent, which are constant, regardless of the level of activity of the campaign. It also includes variable costs, such as media advertising, which may vary with the level of activity of the campaign and the amount of contributions raised. Certain committed costs are treated as fixed or sunk costs, although they can be curtailed or eliminated. For example, the budget for payroll may allow for different contingents of staff, depending on the level of activity, but once a staff position is created, and someone is hired for that position, it is likely to exist for the duration of the campaign.

Hiring staff leaves less resources available for printing brochures or buying advertising. Nevertheless, the campaign cannot function without a minimum (core) staff. This staff can always be enlarged, but it cannot be cut without affecting the campaign's momentum. When a campaign retrenchment eliminates any staff, even "surplus" originally hired imprudently, the media will treat the story negatively, reporting that the campaign is in trouble. The rumor can become reality.[2] The manager should never budget for or hire more staff than can be retained for the duration.

A budget in itself is not the answer to financial planning and accountability in the political campaign. If it is formulated on the basis of historical data no longer relevant, its own relevance is questionable. Comparisons to prior campaigns may be artificial; dollar amounts may reflect quantitative changes, but not qualitative changes. Nor can the budget make particular people responsible for costs; only a managerial system can allocate responsibility for costs. The budget has little utility if individuals are given responsibility for costs they cannot control, or if timely feedback is not given to staff members responsible for cost control. Underages and overages are not necessarily objectionable; the campaign manager needs to know the reasons for the deviation from the budget, e.g., an overage may be required to cope with the opposition's strong inroads in an area. The long-term interest of the campaign, precisely, victory on election day, cannot be sacrificed to keep within a short-term weekly or daily budget. The problem is the reason or justification for the deviation from the budget, not the existence of it; otherwise, a budget paralyzes the campaign's ability to cope with the changing political environment.

Budgetary Concepts

The following budgetary concepts are useful for the political campaign.

Zero-Based Budgeting. Historical data is ignored; the budget is treated as a unique formulation. It is imprudent to ignore completely the benefit of past experience, but since each campaign is unique (laws are changing, costs are rising, etc.) one should not be frozen into budgeting for programs that have proven useful or were pursued at a certain cost in past campaigns. Arbitrary budgetary allocations to advertising or specific forms of advertising, e.g., television time, without regard to the specific political campaign, are as unwise as arbitrary allocations to get-out-the-vote drives or any other traditional campaign strategy.

Functional Budgeting. Resources are allocated by determining what will be done, at what cost, and what each expenditure will accomplish. Functional budgeting is useful in the campaign if expenditures relate to its overall purpose—

to get votes. Each budget item must relate directly or indirectly to the vote total on election day. Overhead that is not easily allocated should be minimized, unless it relates clearly to fund-raising programs, or is part of the core budget (see below).

Core Budgeting. The absolute minimum required for the campaign to function is the core budget. This budget varies from campaign to campaign, but normal components would include: the headquarters expenses (rent, telephone, supplies, duplicating, etc.), the candidate's basic expenses (travel, lodging, parking, food), the basic payroll, basic campaign literature. Contributors who give seed money to the campaign are underwriting the core budget for the first part of the campaign and, possibly and hopefully, for the duration. Other sources can be tapped to supplement the core budget and to provide for special projects, such as advertising. In some campaigns, a minimum level of advertising is included in the core budget.

Project Budgeting. Like functional budgeting, project budgeting allocates dollars to particular projects, each with goals and a budget to implement the goals. The projects include not only the apparent, direct costs of the project, but the indirect, attributable costs. For example, secretaries who spend half of their time on one project and half on another project would have their salary evenly allocated to each project. Fund-raising projects would have costs imputed to them from the general headquarters operation in order to determine what their net dollar return really is. Adjunct committees that are loaned personnel or supplies would have costs imputed to them, as would local committees. It should be noted that imputing additional costs to projects may also be a fund-raising device; e.g., if someone or some group agrees to underwrite the costs of a project, the more dollars that can be imputed to the project, the greater the contribution that can be rationalized.

Geographical Budgeting. Dollars are allocated on the basis of states, regions, counties, districts, or some other geographical or political/geographical subdivision. Such budgeting, common practice in past campaigns, is only useful if there is a rationale behind the subdivisions. One rationale may pertain to the sources of funds: contributions raised from an area are earmarked by agreement to an area; this could be an inefficient proposition. Another rationale may be the number of votes that past candidates of the party received in the area. The major problem with political/geographical division is the failure to recognize that *media markets* are not congruent with political districts or city borders. (This deficiency is noted and considered in media market budgeting, explained in chapter 7.)

Time-Flow Budgeting. Dollars are allocated over a period of time—years, months, weeks, days. Few political campaigns are more than two years duration;

generally, only Presidential campaigns can be budgeted to begin that early. Time flow budgeting reflects the following considerations. (a) people are more conscious of campaigns near the end of the campaign period, hence more funds should be budgeted and spent in the closing weeks and days; (b) funds cannot be spent if they are not raised (although borrowing is possible under certain legal and fiscal conditions), and since most funds are raised near the end of the campaign, this is another reason for budgeting greater spending at that time; (c) a desired level of momentum (publicity, name identification and recognition, interest in the campaign, development of issues, enthusiasm, etc.) requires certain levels of expenditure over different phases of the campaign, especially in advertising; (d) expenditures may coincide with strategic planning, proceeding from an introductory phase to more graduated phases, leading to a climax around election day, at which time all facets of the campaign "peak" or reach their crescendo.

Revenue-Based Budgeting.   The campaign budget is closely related to the success of fund raising. Alternative budgets are formulated based on the aggregate number of dollars raised and on cash flow—the rate at which the funding is received. As new contributions are received, they are deployed based on pre-established incremental formulas. Revenue-based budgeting may be adapted to permit new operations, such as adjunct or auxiliary support committees that are self-sufficient. For example, committees formed to consolidate labor or business support or stimulate support among certain ethnic or religious constituencies should raise at least as much as their own budget.

Cash Budgeting.   Promised or hoped for contributions are different from actual cash received; expenditures that require payment in advance or coincident with delivery are different from expenditures with credit arrangements.

Probabilistic Budgeting.   A specific line entry in a budget or a budget as a whole may have a low, medium, or high probability of being correct. These subjective probabilistic assessments lead to formulating alternative line entries or budgets, based on different sets of assumptions, including fund-raising assumptions, and on alternative political environments forecast.

Show Budgeting.   This unreal budget, often used to impress journalists, publicized to affect somehow the opposition or used to inspire fund raisers to higher goals or givers to be more generous, should generally be avoided. It compromises creditibility, confuses the more valid budgeting concepts and may have precisely the opposite effects of those intended. It can cause dissension within a confused staff unable to reconcile real and "show" budgets.

Ratio or Formula Budgeting.   At its primitive level ratio budgeting suggests the proportion of a budget to be allocated to different types of spending. It can be a minimum, maximum, fixed or variable proportion; e.g., at least half of the budget should be devoted to advertising, no more than five percent to survey research. It may allocate resources proportionate to the desired election day results; e.g., a certain percentage of electoral support will come from a given area or ethnic group, hence that same percentage of resources should be so directed to make the goal a reality.

Media market budgeting combines ratio or formula budgeting, which involve much more than geographical budgeting, with geographical budgeting. Dollars are allocated where the votes are, but not necessarily where they have been (past electoral performance). By spending in a certain way the strategist wants his formula to become a self-fulfilling prophecy.

All of these budgeting concepts except show budgeting (Table 6-8) are not mutually exclusive but can be used jointly. For example, cash budgeting and geographical budgeting can be used to *plan* and *control* (the traditional purposes of budgeting) expenditures correlated to geographical breakdown (e.g., media market) that require advance payment (e.g., newspaper advertising). Cash budgeting charts the required cash flow needed to support the advertising, budgeted by media markets, a variant of geographical budgeting.

Budgets must include performance standards or targets that enable management to anticipate and adapt to change. As results are compared with budgetary plans ("controlling to plan") the dialogue permits reassessment as differences are explained.[3] What is true of the business firm is true of the campaign: relevant standards, i.e., neither too high nor too low, are best insured by involving volunteers and staff in the planning stage for their budgetary components. They should also be involved in "controlling to plan."

Budgets have behavioral implications. The budget is a motivator if its high standards challenge staff and volunteers. Its standards may be deliberately set "too high" and are therefore never met. Budgets always met or met easily may indicate not that the campaign is well-run, but that the system is unhealthy be-

Table 6-8
Political Campaign Budgeting[a]

---

1. Zero-based budgeting
2. Functional budgeting
3. Core budgeting
4. Project budgeting
5. Geographical budgeting
6. Time-flow budgeting
7. Revenue-based budgeting
8. Cash budgeting
9. Probabilistic budgeting
10. Ratio or formula budgeting

---

[a]These concepts are useful as appropriate; the methods are not mutually exclusive but complementary and can be used jointly.

cause its goals or standards are set low. Motivating, high standard budgets should be adjusted by a risk factor when actual performance is calculated and evaluated.[4]

Budgetary programs too complete and detailed are unwieldy and require bureaucracy and paperwork to implement. As a tyrannical instrument the budget wastes valuable campaign time by instilling a bureaucratic mentality in a work atmosphere that should be creative, innovative, and adaptive. When individuals are reluctant to do anything, no matter how worthwhile, to upset the budgetary plan, then the budgetary goals supersede the campaign's goal of electing the candidate. Staff members may hide inefficiencies by continuing spending at a budgeted rate, although it should be revised upward or downward. As a coercive instrument the budget can lead to resentment and frustration.

The campaign must constantly reevaluate programs. As political conditions change, funds must be shifted from one area or project to another. Given scarce resources the campaign must spend dollars in their highest valued uses, i.e., where they will directly or indirectly result in the most votes on election day. The use of a budget merely as a pressure device and not also as a measuring device defeats its basic planning purpose.[5]

As participants directly affected by decisions, volunteer leaders and staff should be encouraged to be their own advocates and defend their requests for funds. Regardless of the ultimate budgetary decisions, they will be more easily accepted and implemented by participants if (a) they feel they had an opportunity to make their case; (b) they are given an explanation and understand the reasons for budgeting decisions, e.g., limiting the number of staff in a given campaign division. The manager can justifiably plead confidentiality and security, but this rationale should not be a devious ploy to obscure the fact that there is no strategy or that it cannot be defended.

The probing manager may find that individuals request more than they need "to be on the safe side." Volunteer leaders or staff may overstate needs and work requirements or understate their own ability to cope with the workload. This *organizational slack,* if it does not exist in their original requests, may arise as resources are allocated imperfectly during the campaign.[6] In a competitive race rampant organizational slack could mean electoral defeat.

Regardless of the budgetary method or combination of methods used, the budget must reflect the campaign's strategy. The political environment generally requires greater spending at the end, when public consciousness and interest is heightened and when revenues are the greatest (Figure 6-1). Usually only certain losers (who are so perceived) face a declining revenue curve, which may in turn result in a declining spending curve near the end.

Momentum—the upward movement toward victory—and *peaking*—the high point of campaign activity—are essential ingredients in any campaign budget. Momentum is characterized by substantial news coverage, predictions of victory, more contributors and larger contributions, more volunteers, and general enthusiasm and high spirits. As the candidate exudes confidence, draws crowds, and

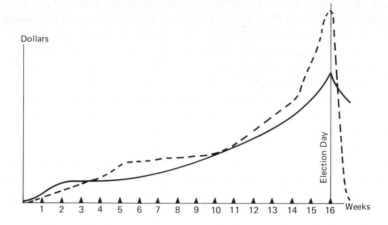

Figure 6-1. Revenue and Budget Curves of a Campaign.
Note: The curves imply that spending (broken line) rises even faster than fund
raising (solid line) near the end, resulting in a deficit to be offset by post-election-
day fund raising.

picks up support, the momentum feeds upon itself and builds to a climax as the
campaign peaks. The closer to election day the peak, the better for the campaign. Ballots cast on election day are equivalent to a public opinion survey for
that day; hopefully, at that instant, the strength of the candidate is at its highest
level.

As a statement of intentions, the budget cannot guarantee momentum,
which is a product of complex forces. These forces include the reaction of voters
to the candidate and what he is saying, the actions and reactions of the opposing
candidate and campaign, the quantity and quality of the news media coverage,
the inroads the candidate is making among uncommitted voters and within particular demographic and ethnic groups, or in particular parts of the congressional
district or state. Another factor is the relative effectiveness of the advertising:
how many people is it reaching, with what message, and how is the message
received?

What the budget can do is provide the foundation for momentum: it can
plan for a graduated increase in expenditures to generate greater public awareness of the candidate, to reach more people when they are most interested, to
get more literature out at the same time that other campaign activity is at its
higher level, etc. A television advertising budget (Figure 6-2) should have the
following important characteristics:

1.   The curve slopes upward: *more* money is always spent in each successive
      week.

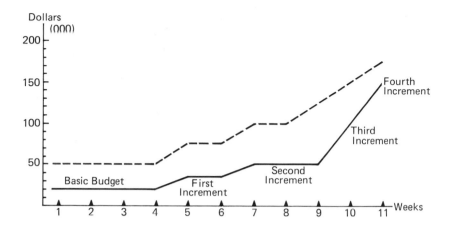

Figure 6-2. Television Advertising Budget.

Note: This graph reflects approximate television spending of an actual Senate campaign which purchased $550,000 of television time over 11 weeks prior to election (heavy line). The strategists knew that TV spending had to be increased, not merely sustained, but they never spent more in any given week than they felt they could sustain. They needed the momentum of early spending but could afford no more than the basic budget for the first four weeks. If the strategists had $1,000,000 for television time *with certainty*, they would have spent more throughout (dotted line). The weekly figures, in thousands of dollars are (dotted line in parentheses): $20 (50), 20 (50), 20 (50), 20 (50), 35 (75), 35 (75), 50 (100), 50 (100), 50 (125), 100 (150), 150 (175).

---

2. The basic budget requires a weekly level of expenditure that has a very high probability of being maintained; thus, at no time will *less* money be spent.
3. Each increment in the budget reflects a new budgeting target, i.e., each time weekly television spending is raised, the assumption is that the *new* level will be equalled or surpassed the following week, never lowered.

When funds are in hand, they can be spent with certainty for future use, i.e., in this case, television time could have been purchased in advance for the campaign's closing weeks. Instead, the campaign in question was unable to buy more than $150,000 the final week, although it actually had the funds, which were then coming in very quickly (approximated by Table 6-6). The campaign would have preferred higher spending even in the earlier weeks, but it was always fearful of not being able to sustain, let alone surpass, a high initial spending level.

In the process of formulating and implementing a budget, *dollars in hand are worth more than future dollars.* There is a present value of dollars in the political campaign which is higher than dollars that are received later. One reason for the discounting of future dollars is that they are *uncertain* dollars. When dollars are certain dollars, planning and budgeting can proceed within those newly established rational bounds, rather than the bounded rationality of the more speculative case. Dollars that the campaign has can, if its strategists so choose, be spent today. Dollars that come in later cannot be spent yesterday, unless the money had been borrowed. Time is precious, and usually momentum cannot be generated late but requires graduated growth over a period of time. In addition, although dollars should be able to be deployed efficiently in the last few weeks and days, additional practical difficulties prevent deployment. For example, finite television time may already have been purchased by others; or the campaign's momentum may have been so lacking that it lost the initiative and the trend toward the opposing candidate is irreversible.

Line items in a campaign budget can best be understood with experience in campaigns. Personal involvement best acquaints the individual with the diversity of budgetary components, technical language, and logical division of budgetary items (Table 6–9).

Control

Every political campaign must have a control system to (a) insure that revenues and expenditures are properly accounted for *and* satisfy legal require-ments; and (b) to measure expenditures against standards of performance. The smaller the campaign, the *more closely* expenditures must be tied to getting votes. Policies and control procedures have major dollar implications for a major campaign. For example, the 1968 Republican Presidential campaign reportedly had $3,000,000 of unexpected debt when credit card invoices continued to pile up after election day; the campaign had lost its ability to control expenditures by distributing the credit cards.[7] Although this example from a major campaign is dramatic, *any* campaign requires a control mechanism, not just for accounting purposes, but to tie expenditures to votes.

Accounting

Since new legislation requires more comprehensive accounting systems, data should be compiled on a regular basis, not only to satisfy legal reporting require-ments, but also to measure performance and facilitate decision making. The importance of budgets as a control device has already been discussed. One CPA firm has even compiled a manual for political campaigns, which urges that an accounting system be created simultaneously with the early formulation of a budget, and that the budgetary system should include weekly projections of con-tributions and expenditures. "Frequent and accurate reporting is essential to good campaign financial management, particularly in large campaigns involving a

Table 6-9
Examples of Campaign Budget Items

1. *Headquarters*—rent, telephone, utilities, insurance, telephones, printing of letterheads, etc., signs, decorations, supplies, equipment rental, security, misc.
2. *Personnel*—management, consultants, secretaries, fieldmen, publicity, scheduling, part-time help, expenses for staff, payroll taxes, travel and lodging, etc.
3. *Candidate*—personal expenses, travel, telephone, meals, lodging, reimbursement for expenses caused by campaigning, entertainment, etc.)
4. *Special Events*—sound trucks, meeting hall rentals, reimbursement to volunteers for receptions, coffee hours, receptions/dinners for supporters, travel reimbursement for volunteers
5. *Research*—subscriptions, purchases of publications, survey research and polls, payroll, clipping service, etc.
6. *Advertising*—purchase of media time and space, commissions, creative costs, production of materials, duplication costs
7. *Print Materials*—typesetting, layout, creative costs, graphics, printing, photography, shipping of brochures, handout cards, bumper strips, signs, etc.
8. *Mail Program*—creative costs, typesetting, printing, etc.; folding, stuffing, mail house, data processing, list rentals, postage
9. *Precinct Work*—production of door-to-door distribution material, telephone campaigns, mailing of kits to workers, election day get-out-the-vote activity, reimbursement of expenses to volunteers
10. *Division Costs*—scheduling and advance work, e.g., expenses for advance men, rental of plane or helicopter for candidate's use, purchase of airline tickets, etc. (see No. 3); press: preparation of press information kits, rental of special telephone WATTs lines, purchase of tape recorders, rental of telecopier, receptions and entertainment for press, etc.
11. *Finance*—cost of raising funds: printed materials, postage, entertainment and receptions, reimbursement of expenses to volunteers; direct mail fund-raising expenses: list rental, postage, consultant fees, mailing costs, etc.
12. *Contingency Fund and Allowance for Specific Programs as Funds Become Available*—adjunct committees, campaign rallies, special mailings, etc.
.
.
.

headquarters staff and many supporting committees," the firm has pointed out. "Since campaigns are typically short in duration, the financial position should be reviewed on a weekly basis."[8]

In fact, the review may be on a daily or even hourly basis, especially when direct mail contributions are received in more than one mail delivery, and envelopes must be opened, sorted, the funds counted, bank deposits prepared, etc. The time lag between securing data on performance, evaluating it, and acting on it may be too long for a week to pass between reviews.

The campaign's financial activities can be divided into three basic functions: treasury, control, and office management (Table 6-10). The thorough, accurate, and timely accounting system is best able to develop reliable forecasts of revenue and spending, within the strategic forecasts of the manager. The accounting and control systems become increasingly important as legislation makes the candidate responsible for his campaign. The candidate's responsibilities include: (a) directing the manager and staff to maintain open, honest records of financial activities; (b) specifying in writing the authority of the campaign committee and key

Table 6–10
Typical Financial Functions in Campaign

Treasury	Control	Office Management

1. Cashier functions
  a. Receipts
  b. Disbursements
2. Cash books
3. Cash management
  a. Transfer of funds
  b. Bank relations
  c. Temporary in-
    vestments
  d. Borrowings and
    lines of credit
4. Legal records
	1. General books of account
	2. Report preparation
	  a. Statutory reports
	  b. Budget reports
	  c. Operations reports
	3. Mailroom operations
	4. Contribution records
	5. Disbursement processing
	  a. General expenditures
	  b. Payroll expenditures
	  c. Media expenditures
		1. Personnel management
		2. Control of property
		3. Office services

Source: These typical financial functions reflect the views of the certified public accountants, Arthur Andersen and Co. in their manual, *Financial Management System for Political Campaigns* (New York: Arthur Andersen & Co., 1972), pp. 18–19.

individuals, reserving certain prerogatives for the candidate; (c) opening and maintaining communication with both legal counsel and outside auditor; (d) establishing and communicating broad financial policy, e.g., regarding deficits, disposition of surplus, etc.; (e) personally reviewing relevant legislation.[9]

When a local volunteer chairman raises and spends campaign funds the campaign is usually responsible. The classic illustration of the need for control is volunteer processing of large-scale direct mail fund raising. The issue is rarely theft, but the need for accountability of contributors by name, address, occupation and other data, and the date received, opened, processed, and deposited. In a well-functioning campaign all four dates are the same, and all contributions are promptly acknowledged, especially when there is time for a second solicitation during the campaign.

Control is more than bookkeeping or accounting; it measures in dollar terms the discrepancy between goals and performance and among individual goals, a division or adjunct committee's goals, and the campaign's goals. Management control includes, but is not limited to, financial control through responsibility centers and full and direct program costing. Full program costs measure the total costs involved in a program in contrast to direct program costs, which measure the variable costs associated solely with the program.[10]

An example of a responsibility center is a headquarters manager responsible for office supplies, petty cash, maintenance, security, office equipment, utilities, telephones, office hours, basic mailroom facilities and postage, etc. An advertising agency could be a responsibility center for typesetting, graphics, layout, camera work, television spot production (music, announcer, recording, editing, photography, etc.).

Apportionment of Costs

Full program costs can be illustrated by an example based on an actual Senate campaign in which four incumbent United States Senators agreed to visit the state (at different times) in behalf of their party's Senate candidate. Since the campaign was poorly organized and insufficiently staffed, its fund-raising events to feature each Senator were always planned too late. Events with ticket sales were disasters, and the receptions with free admission were successful in terms of attendance, but there was no plan to solicit the crowd at the event or subsequently. The events raised $6,500; direct program costs were $5,225, but the net of $1,275 was illusory when full program costs were considered (Table 6-11).

The calculations do not include any dollar allocation for the use of the candidate's time, which might have been better utilized elsewhere, nor an allowance for use of the volunteers' time. The calculations do include the valuation of staff members and consultant's time allocated to the project. *At the minimum, the use of paid staff must be assigned a dollar value, because they can be used for some other purpose. Assigning a zero value indicates the staff members are idle (and the campaign is mismanaged).*

Despite the calculations showing a deficit for the project the Senators' trips might have been worthwhile if they produced significant favorable news coverage for the candidate (the value of which exceeded the project's deficit). Unfortunately, the campaign was unable effectively to exploit these Senators for media coverage. (Evaluation of news coverage in dollar terms is discussed in chapter 7).

Direct or *variable* costs are incurred only if a project or program is implemented. For example, direct costs of a candidate's trip into an area are the expenses directly associated with the trip—transportation, hotel lodging, printing of material and advertising to promote the visit, etc. In contrast, *overhead* costs are not easily allocated to specific ventures but relate to the general level of campaign activity. *Fixed overhead* costs are predetermined and constant, regardless of any change in the level of activity.[11] Headquarters rent and basic monthly telephone service are examples of fixed overhead.

Normally, when making a decision, or evaluating a decision that has been made and seeking to exercise some form of control, the manager looks at the variable costs only. Fixed costs are sunk costs, or past history. It does not matter what has been spent or committed for headquarters rent; the question now is not whether too much was spent, or whether the headquarters should have been placed somewhere else. The question is how to make the most efficient use of

Table 6–11

Analysis of Net Fund-Raising and Full Program Costs–for Visit of Out-of-State Senators

Total revenue raised (ticket sales to events, contributions made at events, contributions made before and following event by individuals invited to event; total of 8 reception events)	$6,500
Direct costs	
Roundtrip airfare for each Senator and aide or spouse (first class)	3,600
Hotel lodging, meals and ground transportation	450
Charter of private plane for two intrastate trips	175
Reimbursement to volunteers for food and liquor	900
Miscellaneous	100
	$5,225
Additional costs	
Printing of invitations (contracted for by campaign headquarters)	250
Postage (taken from stamps at campaign headquarters or use of postage meter) for invitations mailed at last minute to lists	250
Telephone (allowance for numerous calls to offices of Senators, and calls throughout state for arrangements and toll calls to prospective attendees)	175
Allowance for use of scheduling secretary's time, and other (paid) clerical help; and use of press secretary's time[a]	1,250
Allowance for time utilized of outside consultant[a]	1,000
Production and postage for news releases announcing visit of each Senator, additional releases, biographies, telephone calls, rental of facilities for news conferences, etc.	250
Additional travel for candidate and staff from campaign who traveled with Senator during joint swing through state, and lodging, food, etc.	600
	$3,775
Full program costs	$9,000
Net revenue derived (net loss)	($2,500)

[a]Time charged was not idle time and could have been devoted to other campaign activities.

the headquarters. It is important not to be a captive of past spending decisions, which are irrevocable. Decisions to spend or not to spend, to embark on a project or not to embark on a project, cannot be biased by asking, "What if the money had not been spent on that other wasteful project?"

For example, a survey costing $12,000 may produce information so important to the campaign that it saves many times its cost in avoiding wasteful advertising directed at the wrong target groups. Hence the survey should be commissioned, although the campaign may have foolishly spent $100,000 on surveys that asked the wrong questions. The choice is not whether to spend $112,000 on survey research but $12,000. The question concerns the benefit/cost ratio of the *contemplated* decision.

To make a rational decision it is often necessary to assign a value to overhead or fixed costs to the extent that they represent manpower or resources that could be utilized elsewhere. The previous example illustrates the point that the time of the outside consultant, press secretary, and others could have been devoted to alternative vote producing fund-raising projects. Many campaigns mistakenly assign *zero* value to such costs simply because funds have already been budgeted for them. When a value is placed on the time of staff allocated to a project, the decision maker may reach a different conclusion. Given a choice between two alternative campaign swings, Trip A may cost less than Trip B in terms of direct costs, but it may require so much staff time that Trip B represents the preferable allocation of resources.

As in economics, cost is measured by alternatives foregone. The cost in staff manpower is the best alternative foregone in utilizing the manpower. Manpower should not be deployed simply because a project or idea is good—if another project or idea is *superior*. The objective is not for the benefit (votes or funds raised) to outweigh the cost (dollars or manpower), but for the benefit to exceed the cost by the greatest margin.

Methods of Control

In order for the control system to monitor the allocation of all campaign resources, the time lag between receiving information and correctional steps taken, e.g., redeploying staff, should be minimized. The *time span* is the length of time that elapses before a superior can evaluate the discretion being used by a subordinate. For example, suppose a survey or input from local volunteers shows that greater inroads can be made in the Italian community rather than in the Jewish community. The survey or input performs a control function that can lead the campaign to move field men from the Jewish community to the Italian community. They may be effective where they are but they can be more effective elsewhere. For these field men or any staff mambers to be used in their highest valued pursuit, their superior or the manager must regularly receive and evaluate reports of time allocated and results achieved.

Any control system should provide for (1) accurate and *timely* feedback; (2) honest, objective feedback with as little bias as possible; (3) the superior to act quickly based upon the data; (4) subordinates to implement quickly the decision reached. Finally, evaluation requires resources to be measured in dollars and time based on their *marginal* impact on votes (chapter 8).

Another control method, ratio analysis, is of limited use for the campaign. Ratios defy the unique character of each campaign. Moreover, the experienced manager does not need a ratio to know that insufficient funds are being spent on media or too much of the budget is payroll. No leverage ratio can indicate if the campaign has too much debt; no liquidity ratio can indicate if the campaign has enough cash, nor can an activity ratio measure how effectively the campaign is using its resources. The most useful ratios are performance ratios, e.g., the ratio of the cost of fund raising to total funds raised. Other ratios, e.g., that advertising should be half the campaign budget, or survey research should not exceed five percent of the budget, are useful general guides which must be adapted to the specific campaign.

Cash

The importance of cash and cash flow in the political campaign has been repeatedly emphasized. The lack of credit, for legal or practical reasons, and the need to pay for many services in advance, suggest that cash flow must be accurately forecast and measured. In the political campaign, the *transactions* motive for holding cash is to enable the campaign to conduct its ordinary operations—funding its weekly payroll, paying the headquarters rent, paying for the candidate's travel, purchasing advertising time and space, etc. Since the campaign is so fast-moving, cash is usually in and out very quickly. The *precautionary* motive relates to holding cash because of the possible margin of error in predicting cash inflows and outflows. Even in the most fast-moving campaign, some reserves, however small, must be maintained to meet a short-term gap if promised contributions are late in arriving and an advertising budget must be sustained. The *speculative* motive is the accumulation of a cash reserve to exploit opportunities that present themselves. For example, someone suggests an important advertisement to be placed in newspapers, or a new television spot to relate the candidate to an unforseen news development; without any funds, there is no way to exploit these opportunities, outside of raising the funds.

A trust fund for certain "mandatory" expenditures can fulfill all three motives by setting aside cash reserves for television or other anticipated critical expenditures to keep the resources from being eaten up by bureaucracy.[h] Instead of accumulating cash for the speculative motive, the prudent manager *budgets* contingency funds for special purpose projects, especially advertising, or he budgets higher levels of television and newspaper advertising. Thus, more space and time may be provided for in the budget, although the precise advertisement or television spot is yet to be produced. The manager transfers the speculative motive from holding or accumulating cash to budgeting for an advertising program whose content is speculative. Since contributors are more likely to give for specific projects rather than for a general fund, funds may need to be diverted from special projects whose priority has diminished to new projects.

The campaign manager forced to choose between meeting the payment

---

[h]If the law permits the campaign to earn interest on funds, the campaign should explore certificates of deposit and short-term savings accounts; ideally, the law permitting, it would be advantageous to borrow funds to draw interest, then return the borrowed funds and net the interest.

deadline for a week's television spot buys and possibly losing the spots to commercial advertisers or the opposition, may resort to *float*—the difference between the campaign's checkbook balance and its bank balance. Often the campaign takes advantage of the time it takes for checks to clear with the expectation that additional contributions are in route. This procedure is not unusual for a campaign dependent on mass direct mail. Once the mailings are "dropped" and costs expended for postage, printing, etc., a cycle of fund raising begins during which the contributions arrive. Float can be dangerous if a check is returned for insufficient funds and other vendors or the media are apprised.

The campaign should exploit its disadvantage of paying cash in advance or on delivery by negotiating for cash discounts reflecting the payment schedule. Otherwise payments to vendors should be delayed as long as possible (a policy easier to implement if the campaign uses the same vendors throughout its existence). The campaign's collection and clearing process should emphasize prompt conversion of pledges to cash contributions and rapid deposit of all funds, especially direct mail.

The manager's financial planning must allow for postelection cash needs, especially the bills, some unanticipated, sent by local headquarters and adjunct committees, the need to remit income taxes and payroll taxes to federal, state, and local government, and a variety of delayed charges. The major delayed charges are telephone bills, credit card bills, and credit travel. These cash needs may be partially met by the conversion of deposits—typically for rent, telephone, and leased equipment. In addition, purchased or donated equipment and furniture can be sold to provide postelectoral cash.

The inventory problem—brochures, bumperstrips, signs, stationery, etc.—is a cash problem. A *basic* stock can meet expected demand, a *safety* stock can meet unexpected demand, e.g., a volunteer group requests a large shipment of material for distribution at a state fair. The *anticipation* stock is needed for the campaign's anticipated growth, primarily related to its momentum. The manager weighs the need for inventory with the cash investment required, with the qualification that the per-unit cost is much lower with large initial orders.

Direct Mail

A superb example of the problems of financial control is the entire field of direct mail. The problem of forecasting cash flow is always subject to error, regardless of the probability that the flow will be at a given amount. Some direct mail contracts remove the element of control from the candidate, campaign manager, and campaign and transfer it to a direct mail consultant, whose own interests may not be wholly congruent with those of the political campaign. Once the element of control is removed, the campaign is virtually powerless; its lack of control is caused by its own negligence in signing a contract to its dis-

advantage. Then it can only make the best of the situation and attempt to forecast the net funds, and their flow, to the campaign. On the other hand, if the
direct mail operation is internal, or if the contract gives the campaign greater
power of control, control mechanisms must be set up to monitor the aggregate
amount of funds being received, including counting the money and sending
thank you notes, measuring the per capita return, the return over time and per
day, the number of contributors, the return from particular lists, the varied
returns in response to different kinds of mailings, etc. These kinds of controls
require considerable expertise in the field of direct mail fund raising.

Consider a specific example based substantially on an actual political campaign—a race for the U.S. Senate in a major state. The campaign had signed a
direct mail contract with a major consultant. The projection was for a gross of
$500,000. The campaign manager and his associates estimated expenses at 25
percent, or $125,000, leaving a net of $375,000. They thought the contract was
a good one, since it cost only six cents per name rented, and the consultant was
only getting a fee of four cents per name mailed. On closer inspection, the
contract revealed that the direct mail consultant had virtual carte blanche on
mailings; that he controlled all printing and data processing, the relationship
with the mailing house, etc. (and these operations were subsidiaries of his own,
or were involved in rebate arrangements with him). The campaign did not consider the cost of mailing (10¢ first class at that time and the cost of mail processing (printing, typesetting, creative costs, folding, stuffing, business reply
envelopes, covering envelopes, etc.). Nor did it consider that the latter cost, perhaps a six cents per unit cost at large quantities, would be exceeded by the cost
(18¢) for any semipersonalized "computer" letters—prepared by a computer to
look personal, otherwise with the same enclosures.

Every Friday the campaign paid the consultant money due for list rentals,
printing bills, etc. out of a checking account that the direct mail consultant
controlled. The cash flow implications for the campaign were ominous. The
direct mail consultant, however, was in far better shape. Although he seemed to
be doing the campaign a favor by paying for all "up front" costs of the mailings,
all of the vendor services, such as printing and mail house, were on 30- or 60-day
credit. As for the lists, they were rented exclusively from himself (his own firm).
Thus, each Friday he withdrew funds toward invoices that did not yet have to be
paid, or for invoices (principally, list rentals) that represented his own profit.

The contract also provided for a four cent fee to the direct mail consultant
for every thank you letter, plus reimbursement for expenses (travel, telephone,
messenger service, etc.). The campaign was responsible for opening, sorting,
counting, and depositing the mail contributions—monopolizing the time of staff
and volunteers who could have devoted their time to other campaign pursuits.

The outside campaign consultant's projections (Table 6–12) reflected his
assumptions, e.g., 800,000 would receive the standard package, with an average

Table 6–12
Outside Consultant's Projection of Direct Mail Program[a]

Projected Revenue	
Standard lists: 800,000 names × 2½% response factor times $11 per capita contribution	$220,000
Better lists: 200,000 × 5% × $16 (using "personal" letter)	160,000
Second letter: second solicitation to all givers above (20,000 + 10,000 = 30,000) × 15% × $10	45,000
Gross contributions	$425,000
Expenses	
List rental (1,000,000 names at $0.06 each)	$ 60,000
First class postage (10¢) for 1,030,000 letters	103,000
Package costs (printing, envelopes, stuffing, mailing house, etc.) 800,000 × 6¢ (per package) + 200,000 × 18¢ + 30,000 × 18¢	89,400
Fee to consultant for each name mailed to (4¢ × 1,030,000)	41,200
Postage for business reply envelopes received with contributions (10¢ + 2¢ special postage = 12¢ postage) × 34,500	4,140
Thank you letters (34,500 × 18¢) (18¢ = 10¢ postage, 4¢ package cost, 4¢ fee)	6,210
Reimbursement to consultant for travel, telephone, messenger, etc.	1,050
Total expenses	$305,000
Net Contributions (= 28.2% of gross)	$120,000

[a]This data is based on a projection made by an outside campaign consultant to a candidate and campaign manager. He projected the results of a direct mail program contracted for by the campaign with a direct mail consultant. The campaign's outside consultant, advising management, suggested legal grounds be used to break the contract, and the campaign set up its own direct mail operation. (Postage rates were those in effect at time.)

2½ percent response, giving a per capita contribution of $11, etc. Anyone responding to the solicitations would receive a second letter (computer "personalized") asking for a second contribution. The outside consultant suggested legal ways to break the contract, which he recommended be replaced by an internal operation that could rent comparable lists at $45 per thousand (4.5¢ per name) and avoid many fees charged by the direct mail consultant. He calculated the net proceeds would have been at least $43,000 more, especially if test mailings were used to guide the program. Under the present program the direct mail consultant had no incentive to test mail to gauge responsiveness of any given list, since the more he mailed the higher his fee—as long as the mailings produced enough to cover postage, printing, mailing costs, and a portion of his list rental, and explicit fees.

When the outside consultant estimated the direct mail firm's profit on the account (Table 6–13), the candidate and his campaign manager were amazed. They had not understood the subtleties of the contract, especially its provisions giving the direct mail consultant first claim on receipts.

Table 6–13

Gross Profit Earned by Direct Mail Consultant–Projections of Outside Management Consultant to Political Campaign

1,000,000 names × (6¢ per name rented + 5¢ "fee" per name mailed)	$100,000
30,000 names follow-up mailing × 4¢ fee	1,200
34,500 thank you letters × 4¢ fee	1,380
Rebates from printers, mailing house, data processing, etc. = 15% gross bills ($89,400 + $1,380)	13,617
Gross profit to direct mail consultant (27.3% of gross contributions received)	$116,197

Note: Since this consultant only rented lists which he owned, he was not acting as broker and did not have to split a list rental fee with a principal.

Systematic Accounting and Control

To understand the need for a comprehensive and relevant control system for the political campaign, it is instructive to compare past practices with current or recommended accounting and control procedures (Table 6–14).

Table 6–14

Accounting and Control–Traditional versus Modern

Criterion	Traditional or Classical Approach	Modern, Systematic Approach to Accounting and Control
Motive of participants	Salary or profit for staff; power for volunteers; favors for givers	Complex motivation for all participants; varied motivation depending on goals
Objective	Maximize for a particular phase of the campaign; forget about other phases or components or effects of one action on others	Satisfice–or do the best under the circumstances for each phase or part of the campaign; maximize as a whole; check for effects of actions on rest of campaign
Accounting	Bookkeeping; neutral; no significant role	Subjective, advisory, seeks to influence financial decisions and control system and to forecast and monitor progress, e.g., in direct mail fund raising
Behavior	Based on simple conception of motivation	Based on complex and varied motivation; behavior affects actions, accounting, and control systems
Budgets	Imposed; automatic; absolute	Participative; probabilistic; alternative types; motivating

Table 6-14 (continued)

Criterion	Traditional or Classical Approach	Modern, Systematic Approach to Accounting and Control
Authority	Imposed as with budgets	Based upon competence
Rationality	Rationality assumed	Bounded rationality: decisions are rational within the time span, and given imperfect knowledge and information
Environment	Static, stable; political parties certain, predictable	Changing, subject to national and international events; demographic shifts and patterns
Control	Strictly downward; automatic, regimented; or no control because everything is assumed to be satisfactory	Requires human interaction, constant feedback, exchange of views; possible reconsideration of plans; decisions to be made reacting to input
Campaign's goal	To elect candidate	To elect candidate, but the goals of individuals must be fused with the campaign's overriding goal
Effect on participants	None or do not worry about effects of actions on participants	Staff is relevant; actions do affect them; volunteers are important, and effects of decisions on them affect their attitude and motivation also
Staff	They work for the campaign and should take orders	They work for the campaign, but the organization must seek to motivate them to higher levels of aspiration and offer them inducements to spur them on
Performance	Measured against present goals	Measured against changing political environment and goals and objectives tailored for political campaign and time period
Programs and Projects	What worked in the past will work again	Thorough knowledge of what worked in the past and study of alternatives, but exploration of new methods, programs, and projects to get votes, to improve functioning of press department, scheduling, finance, etc.
Forecasting	Things will happen or they will not	Probability must be considered to evaluate what will happen
Revenue	Promises and commitments and goals are important	Unless goals can be successively subdivided so that they are in smaller, manageable units for which small numbers of individual fund raisers are responsible, they are visionary
Expenses	Direct costs considered	Full costs considered to reflect alternatives available

7 The Marketing Function

*Psephology . . . is defined as "the study of elections," and it derives from the
Greek word* psephos *which means "pebble." The derivative comes from the
custom of ancient Greece for citizens to vote by dropping colored pebbles into
the Greek equivalent of our ballot box.*

*Putting things . . . in their Greek context one might say this volume asks
three questions about the American voter:*
—For whom did he cast his pebble?
—Why did he cast his pebble as he did?
—How will he cast his pebble in the years to come?

Richard M. Scammon and Ben J. Wattenberg
*The Real Majority: An Extraordinary
Examination of the American Electorate*

*Marketing—the performance of business activities that direct the flow of goods
and services from producer to consumer or user. . . . Marketing also influences
demand . . . by manipulating consumer taste.*

—Walter B. Wentz and Gerald I. Eyrich
Marketing: Theory and Application

The political campaign's overriding goal is to elect the candidate. The noble
ends of democracy aside, the campaign is a marketing organization. The *product*
is the candidate—his physical appearance, image, rhetoric, positions on issues,
background, experience, education, party affiliation, family. The *consumer* is
the voter—he supports the candidate or one of his opponents or supports no
one. His support can range from a single vote to persuading friends and relatives
to vote for the candidate; he may even volunteer to work in the campaign, contribute funds, or assume a leadership position.

The manager is the campaign's administrator, but he must be something
more. If he is not a psephologist, he must find someone who is. He must study
electoral trends as an economist studies economic trends if he wants to relate
the campaign to the political environment. Since his emphasis is on marketing
the candidate to the voter-consumers, he is, in that sense, a marketing executive.

The candidate compromises his own views and his private life to be a public
figure. He must emphasize not only the issues that concern him but those that
concern the electorate. What finally emerges is someone who in the public's
mind is known or unknown, stands for something or nothing, seems intelligent

or stupid, honest or dishonest, or not very clearly any of these things. When he emphasizes issues and takes particular positions, his posture, including his forthrightness and candor or evasiveness and deceit, are as much characteristics of the candidate as product as size and weight are physical characteristics of a consumer product.

The campaign's staff and volunteers, and its geographical and functional divisions and adjunct committees are the means of *distribution* for the product. *Promotion* is principally achieved through the news and advertising media, although personal selling—door-to-door crusading of precinct workers, pamphleteering of youth volunteers at a shopping center or telephone canvassing—can never be replaced.

Like marketing research for the demand curve for any product, research is needed in the campaign. Campaign research includes the political environment—ethics, relevant legislation, macro- and macro-political factors, specific issues—and survey research relevant to the election at hand. Psephology defines the broad outlines of the marketing campaign, but only specialists can devise the means to reach specific voter-consumers (Table 7–1). As the campaign progresses it reaches more voter-consumers who "adopt" its candidate. If the campaign continued past election day, the losing candidate might in turn become a winner. Such common speculation assumes the opposition candidate and campaign do nothing during this extension of the campaign period. The ceteris parabus assumption does not apply.

The marketing plan must overcome three barriers that may prevent communication through mass media. *Selective exposure* is an individual's tendency to see and hear only material conforming to their beliefs. *Selective perception* is the tendency to interpret new information in favor of present attitudes. *Selective retention* is the tendency to retain only information that reinforces present beliefs.[1] Although political party organizations, cause organizations, and a variety of service, community, civic, and religious groups form an interconnecting communications network to disseminate information, personal contact and influence can best overcome these barriers.

In deciding the most appropriate combination of methods to reach the electorate, the manager should realize that the smaller the constituency, the more important the *communications network* of activists, group/club joiners, and opinion molders. These people are more likely to socialize, talk about issues, and influence others. In smaller campaigns the diminished importance of media is correlated with the greater importance of personal contact. Similarly, the impact of volunteer workers in a small campaign can be overriding. In a city council race, one hundred volunteers donating an average of 10 hours a week each can probably reach at least 20,000 households, each with about two votes. If there are several candidates in the race this concentrated volunteer effort could make the difference.

Marketing in the political campaign includes:

Table 7–1
Different Kinds of Adopters and Their Counterparts among Voters

Different Kinds of Adopters	Implications for Political Campaign
Innovators: venturesome people who try things first; possibly young; high social status; successful members of multiple reference groups, willing to take risks.	Political activists who are among the candidate's initial supporters; they are also active in community, civic, and religious groups, or antiwar groups, or educational organizations, etc.; they may be on the candidate's initial steering committee or those first urging him to run.
Early adopters: similar to innovators, but more cautious; usually have high social status; respected as opinion leaders within a social group; well-educated, more creative than people in categories below.	Like the innovators, these people may be money people, willing to support the candidate financially; in fact, they have one of three things: money (to contribute), time (to volunteer in a leadership position) or influence (with which to spread the word and persuade others that the candidacy is viable and worth supporting); in a less active sense, they may simply be among the first "to see the light" before it is fashionable or there is a great deal of publicity.
Early majority: observes experience of early adopters, waiting until a substantial number have accepted the innovation before they acquire it themselves.	These people need a great deal of reinforcement before making a commitment; however, the reinforcement may come from a source other than the candidate, such as party label; the innovators and early adopters form the leadership and financial support of the base; the early majority forms the voting support of the base for the candidate.
Late majority: below average in nearly all characteristics such as social status and income; display little leadership; require pressure.	These people are needed to win any election; an intense campaign, with a great deal of advertising and travel by the candidate, will eventually reach these people; their social status and income may not be uniform, but they tend more and more toward apathy.
Laggards: tradition-bound and socially isolated.	In a close election, these people may make the difference between victory and defeat, unless they are so apathetic that they sit out the whole election; they are, relatively, lower priority than others; often, they support the candidate favored to win at the end, or, more likely, they may still hold out, or not bother to vote at all.

Note: Differentiation and description of adopters is based on marketing theory, e.g., Walter B. Wentz and Gerald I. Eyrich, *Marketing: Theory and Application* (Harcourt, Brace & World, 1970), pp. 215.

1. Utilizing research to understand the political environment, the consumer (the voter), and the opposing candidate.
2. Presenting the product (the candidate) in an effective way to the consumers (the electorate).
3. Using traditional methodology—volunteers, precinct work, billboards, brochures, get-out-the-vote—to make the final sale on election day.
4. Emphasizing scheduling the candidate and presenting him through the media—news and advertising—to penetrate the market.

Political campaigns become more independent as the environment becomes more unpredictable, voters become more independent, and the influence of political parties, or at least the two major parties, declines. If the number of people who are committed, by reason of political party, to the candidate is unknown or small, simply registering new voters or getting-out-the-vote will not win the election. In addition, it is possible for media, through news and advertising, not only to affect voter preference but to motivate citizens to vote for the candidate.

The Consumer

Public opinion proceeds down a hierarchy. Overall public feelings and attitudes are a function of the political environment. At lower levels in the hierarchy attitudes and issue concerns coalesce and relate to the specific election, campaign, and candidate. Survey research enables the campaign manager to understand each level within the hierarchy, and to delineate "target groups"—a winning coalition with certain identifiable characteristics: X percent Republicans, Y percent Catholics, Z percent $15,000+ income level, etc. In other words, the goal is the support of a certain percentage of the voters who are registered Republicans; a certain percentage of those who are Catholics, a certain percentage whose family incomes are $15,000 or more a year, etc. The more overlapping goals, the more precise and methodical the goal setting can be.

For example, in a Congressional district, the strategy may call for a certain percentage of the vote in each of five different areas within the district. The percentages might be, let us say, 36 percent, 57 percent, 52 percent, 49 percent, and 40 percent. Because each area does not have precisely the same number of registered voters, it is not the average of the percentages (46.8 percent) but a weighted average that is important, that is, the percentage of support in an area times the number of registered voters in that area (assuming the voter turnout ratio is constant in all areas). However, there must be something behind the aggregate percentage figures in each area; otherwise, how were they computed? What are the characteristics, e.g., age, income level, housing status, educational level, party registration, etc. of the voters in each areas? How are these characteristics correlated, even *roughly,* with candidate preference (or hoped for candidate preference)?

Marketing methods must be employed, regardless of how appealing the candidate and his positions on issues are (potentially) to the target groups. This appeal may be based on survey research or on the judgment and experience of someone who lives in the area; but the appeal is only potential, as yet unrealized, until the target groups find out who the candidate is (identity and recognition . . . that he exists) and what he stands for (positions on issues). For some voters, mere identity and recognition may be sufficient, if they are only looking for an alternative to a candidate who turns them off; but the alternative must *exist* not just on the ballot, but credibly in their consciousness.

Often a candidate must make news to be taken seriously by the voter. A voter may not like Candidate A but vote for him simply because Candidate B is an unfamiliar commodity; this is often true in local elections. If he knew Candidate B was a real i.e., visible, alternative, he might vote for him at the polls or even be motivated to turn out and vote; certain statewide elections support the theory that television visibility correlates with identity.[a]

Survey research helps define the campaign's market and its target or subgroups (Figure 7-1). Even without survey research, discerning strategists in a local race can identify a base of support for the candidate and both the issues and means of communication to expand that base to reach important target groups. Sometimes, a single demographic variable supersedes other variables, e.g., area of residency might be a more important variable than sex, age, income level, or religion in determining voting behavior for a certain race.

Media markets are not congruent with political boundaries, and the "reach" of individual stations or newspapers must be considered in any marketing plan. For example, a newspaper published outside a congressional district may reach registered voters within the district; a newspaper published in the district may be circulated mainly outside it. A television station may broadcast mainly to out-of-state residents, or a station outside the state may broadcast mainly or partially to residents within the state. An extreme example is the populous state of New Jersey, which has no commercial television stations and relies on stations in New York City and Philadelphia.

The question is not whether someone should be reached by television,

---

[a]For example, in the 1974 Gubernatorial race between Edmund G. Brown, Jr. and Houston Flournoy in California, Flournoy began the race behind but moved quickly near the end to almost win. Surveys indicated Brown's base of support was soft, but people did not sufficiently identify Flournoy. Neither newspaper nor radio advertising in Flournoy's campaign was targeted; its theme was general or ill-defined, its audience or readership general. Surveys (Field Poll, Decision Marketing Information) indicated that Flournoy's rise in the polls, largely a function of his identification, closely paralleled his rise in television spending. If little or no funds had been spent on newspapers and radio and the funds added to the television budget, Flournoy probably would have won.

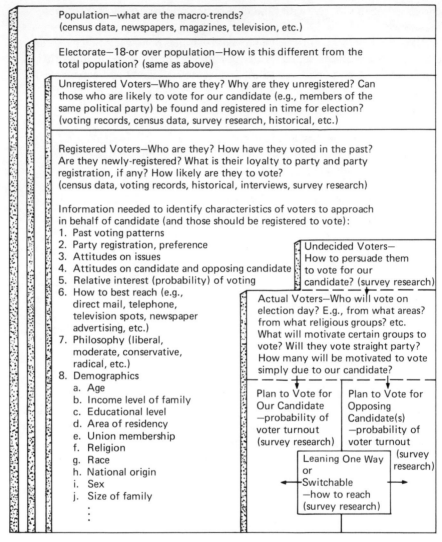

Population—what are the macro-trends?
(census data, newspapers, magazines, television, etc.)

Electorate—18-or over population—How is this different from the
total population? (same as above)

Unregistered Voters—Who are they? Why are they unregistered? Can
those who are likely to vote for our candidate (e.g., members of the
same political party) be found and registered in time for election?
(voting records, census data, survey research, historical, etc.)

Registered Voters—Who are they? How have they voted in the past?
Are they newly-registered? What is their loyalty to party and party
registration, if any? How likely are they to vote?
(census data, voting records, historical, interviews, survey research)

Information needed to identify characteristics of voters to approach
in behalf of candidate (and those should be registered to vote):
1. Past voting patterns
2. Party registration, preference
3. Attitudes on issues
4. Attitudes on candidate and opposing candidate
5. Relative interest (probability) of voting
6. How to best reach (e.g.,
   direct mail, telephone,
   television spots, newspaper
   advertising, etc.)
7. Philosophy (liberal,
   moderate, conservative,
   radical, etc.)
8. Demographics
   a. Age
   b. Income level of family
   c. Educational level
   d. Area of residency
   e. Union membership
   f. Religion
   g. Race
   h. National origin
   i. Sex
   j. Size of family

Undecided Voters—
How to persuade them
to vote for our
candidate? (survey research)

Actual Voters—Who will vote on
election day? E.g., from what areas?
from what religious groups? etc.
What will motivate certain groups to
vote? Will they vote straight party?
How many will be motivated to vote
simply due to our candidate?

Plan to Vote for
Our Candidate
—probability of
voter turnout
(survey research)

Plan to Vote for
Opposing
Candidate(s)
—probability of
voter turnout
(survey
research)

Leaning One Way
or
Switchable
—how to reach
(survey research)

Figure 7-1. Marketing Subgroups.
Note: Parentheses indicate sources of information.

newspapers or both, but more specifically, which stations, newspapers, programs, or sections of the newspaper.

Targeting Subgroups

Which subgroups can be reached with specific issues in the most efficient,
i.e., cost-effective, way? It is important not to confuse the percentage of support

within a demographic group with that group's contribution to the winning vote. For example, assume the following: Smith is running for Congress in a district with 250,000 *registered* voters. Their religious breakdown is shown in Table 7–2. (The actual population of the district is higher than 250,000, just as the religious distribution is different.) In this simplified example, which uses a voter breakout by religion, Column (C) is the percentage of support candidate Smith has in each religious group. However, each group's actual contribution to Smith's 96,000 victory reflects:

1. How important is the group to the total of registered voters (Column A)?
2. What percentage of the group is supporting Smith (Column C)?

Table 7–2
Percentage of Support within a Group versus Percent of Winning Vote

Religion	(A) % of Total	(B) Number of Voters	(C) % of Group for Smith	(D) % of Group Who Go to Polls to Vote	(E) Number Who Go to Polls
Protestant	70%	175,000	60%	75%	131,250
Catholic	15	37,500	40	60	22,500
Jew	5	12,500	30	70	8,750
Other	10	25,000	45	50	12,500
	100%	250,000		$D' = 70\%$[a]	175,000

Election Results: $(F) = (C) \times (E)$ (G)

Religion	Number of Votes for Smith	% of Winning Votes (96,000)
Protestant	78,750	82.0%
Catholic	9,000	9.4
Jew	2,625	2.7
Other	5,625	5.9
	96,000 = 54.9% of the vote[b]	100% Total

Note: The attribute or characteristic of religious preference is used for illustration only.
[a]D', a weighted average = 175,000/250,000 or [(A) × (D) for each group] summed.
[b]54.9% = 96,000/175,000, or to arrive at a percentage regardless of the absolute numbers,

$$\% \text{ of Votes for Smith} = \frac{\text{the sum of each of the four components: (A)} \times \text{(C)} \times \text{(D)}}{D'}.$$

$$= \frac{(0.7 \times 0.6 \times 0.75) + (0.15 \times 0.4 \times 0.6) + (0.05 \times 0.3 \times 0.7) + (0.1 \times 0.45 \times 0.5)}{D'}$$

$$= \frac{0.384}{0.7} = 54.9\%$$

3.   What percentage of the group will go to the polls and vote, i.e., voter turn-
      out (Column D)?

Note that the total voter turnout figure of 70 percent is obtained by
setting the number of people who voted over the number of registered voters.
It is a weighted average, also computed by multiplying (A) × (D) for each
group, and adding the four figures. In like fashion, the victory margin of 54.9
percent is obtained by setting the number of people who voted for Smith over
the number who vote. It too is a weighted average, computed by adding (A)
× (C) × (D) for each group and dividing the sum (0.384) by the voter turnout
(0.700).

In this example Smith obviously did poorly among Catholics, Jews, and
Other (which includes declined to state); he still won. All factors considered,
Protestant voters provided more than four-fifths of his winning margin (Col-
umn G).

This example indicates the strategist must "go where the ducks are" and
concentrate on areas and constituencies with the greatest number of voters likely
to turn out and support the candidate. This does not mean ignoring other areas or
constituencies but giving priority and greater resources to cultivating constituencies most likely to support the candidate. Although this simple example
depicts religious "breakouts," it is difficult to target an appeal to discrete religious groups, even assuming their preferences for a candidate are clear. Generally the campaign must relate to a series of demographic characteristics that
describe voters more or less likely to support the candidate.

The psephologist, demographer, survey researcher, and pollster all try to
identify different voter groups. Their data and counsel should be used to assign
different probabilities to different kinds of voters, in terms of their likelihood of
supporting the candidate. The campaign will more efficiently use its limited resources by concentrating, as much as possible, on voter groups with higher
probability of supporting the candidate.

The political environment affects marketing subgroups (Figure 7-1) in
various ways. For example, the changed age requirement for voting from 21 to
18, revision of residency requirements, and proposals to register by mail affect
subgroups.[b]

Incumbents.   Incumbents can use their power to change laws or exploit
existing laws. Reapportionment or redistricting political boundaries is the most

---

[b]In recent years proposals for postcard registration were advanced in both Congress
and state legislatures. Proposals to register by mail change the relative strengths of political
parties to the extent that registration by mail encourages more registration by members of
one party than another; or to the extent mail registration favors politicians with access to
strong party organizations and labor unions to help circulate the cards.

blatant example of affecting the electorate and its subgroups. Incumbents thus act to change the rules of the game, i.e., the way in which subgroups are determined, or they make it easier for them to reach subgroups. In the former case, they decide who the consumer will be; in the latter case, they use traditional perquisites or "reform" legislation to make it easier to market themselves.

Once incumbents define the electorate and subgroups, they use all their resources and privileges to disguise a marketing program as public service. For example, when Sen. Jacob Javits (R., N.Y.) was a candidate for re-election in 1974, he hired direct mail expert Lee MacGregor to prepare a "master plan" using franked mail to achieve "the kind of identification that can be translated into a vote at the polls on Election Day." Sen. Javits approved mailing 700,000 reelection messages disguised as official business and targeted to places "where the Senator isn't strong politically."[2] In another case, a defeated Congressman planning to run again in the same district invoked a legal technicality permitting him unrestricted franking for 90 days after leaving office to mail newsletters to the electorate.[3]

In contrast to the short-term marketing effort of the political campaign, the incumbent is always involved in marketing. Recent trends have been to avoid salary increases for legislative officials in favor of higher fringe benefits, part of which are used to market the incumbent. After one major increase in allowance passed in May 1975, one Congressman observed, "The majority party is slipping its hands into taxpayer's pockets and will use public funds in an attempt to re-elect the freshmen."[4]

Mistaken Perceptions. Both incumbent and challenger must reach beyond their base of support to less committed voters. The candidate should never sacrifice that base to get new support. Four main reasons account for candidates and campaign managers believing they are making inroads where they are not:

First, candidates and campaign managers are more often blessed with optimism than pessimism (or realism).

Second, candidates and campaign managers want their strategy to work, so they convince themselves it is working, regardless of how unrealistic it is.

Third, candidates, campaign managers and their closest supporters are so close to the situation that they cannot relate to the average voter. The voter is mildly apathetic or very apathetic; in any case, he is not a stalwart supporter of the candidate or the opposition. He is preoccupied with himself, his family, his friends, his job, his church and group memberships, etc. His interest in government is not enthusiastic, and he is not excited by political campaigns. Nevertheless, the candidate and others in the campaign are so thoroughly engrossed in the effort, giving considerable time in the most intense fashion, that they believe there is a growing bandwagon of support. Too often, they spend most of their time associated with others intimately involved in the effort or with partisans of the candidate.

Fourth, candidates and campaign managers usually start out thinking more people know who the candidate is than in fact know who he is; they continue overstating identification and recognition among the electorate, and even on election day they exaggerate the number of voters who can identify the candidate. Pride, ego, and arrogance are reasons for this miscalculation. People will not admit that after so much time and work, only a limited percentage of the electorate can identify the candidate.

A candidate's ego is hurt when he learns that a small percentage of the electorate can identify him. For statewide or national office significant identification cannot be achieved without television. For lesser offices significant identification is difficult to achieve unless television can be involved. Otherwise, the principal means are other media and direct mail. In any case, identification only measures the 18-or-over population at that point in time; since people have short memories and the 18-or-over population itself is changing from year to year, it is possible for the identification of incumbents to decline considerably following their hyperactive election campaign. One final caution: identification questions in surveys that do not have follow-up questioning may overstate identification, i.e., voters say they know who the candidate is when they are told his name, but when pressed they cannot identify him as a candidate, but as someone else (actor, baseball player, etc.)

Mistaken perceptions affect the campaign's choice of issues and the candidate's rhetoric, especially in terms of reaching the uncommitted voter. Mistakes in perception lead to mistakes in tactics.

Issues. Candidates and campaign manager's may talk about issues that do not concern voters; i.e., their marketing strategy disregards the consumer. They may talk about issues of concern to themselves or their partisans—the most adamant, diehard supporters—but not issues of concern to the electorate. Another problem is talking to themselves as they speak again and again to groups composed mainly of their partisans. Even candidate debates are usually before audiences composed of partisans on both sides—committed (usually irrevocably) to one or the other candidate. Any marketing strategy to reach the consumer must do more than reinforce the committed or encourage volunteer workers to work harder or financial contributors to give more. The strategy (specifically choice and use of issues) must reach those who are neither volunteers nor contributors; their votes numerically dwarf the partisan activists.

Rhetoric. The consumer must be reached (a) by issues that concern him, (b) with simple arguments and in simple language, and (c) with points repeated for emphasis during the campaign (although the context, such as a variety of "visual" events, may be different). Emotive language, compelling facts, and lucid examples must be used in an effort to sway the uncommitted and convince the skeptical, not merely reinforce the committed.

Uncommitted voter.   Because the "switchable" voter may not take the
initiative to learn about the candidate, he must be aggressively sought out and
reached by advertising. Traditional means of distribution—precinct work,
pamphleteering, to some extent newspaper advertising—may not reach these
people. The candidate's message may not penetrate the voter's consciousness—
even assuming the people receive the material.

Myth of conversion.   This is the evangelical belief that everyone, or nearly
everyone, would vote for the candidate if only they saw the light, if only they
were reached. Perhaps they need to read a newspaper advertisement, or see a
television spot, or read a long position paper. This mythology ignores the central fact that most people do not want to see a television spot, they do not want
to read a newspaper advertisement for the candidate, and they certainly do not
want to read a position paper or any other campaign literature. In fact, most
people will not read the lengthy position papers or newspaper advertisements,
even if the position papers are given to them, or the newspaper advertisements
run repeatedly. The partisans on both sides read such materials, the press com-
ments upon them (they may serve other uses, such as giving the candidate
stature, credibility, substance, . . .), but such tracts do not reach the uncommitted or the switchables.

The *uncommitted* voter has not made up his mind.

The *switchable* voter has made up his mind, but he can be reached within
the short time span of the campaign, if he is reached with the right message and
using media *relevant* to him.

The *committed* voter will not change his mind. Some candidates do not
recognize this fact. They always maintain that other candidates, inept and
ineffectual, and other campaigns, poorly run, could not reach him. Somehow,
this messianic candidate will win in a Congressional district with registration
overwhelmingly in the other party's favor. *The burden of proof must be on the
person making such a claim.*

The consumers who are most likely to decide elections are those who require the greatest effort and expenditure of funds to reach. Although they
may, in a particular election, lend themselves to description and identification
by certain demographic characteristics, newspapers and television stations can
achieve only *some* targeting, as can other methods of marketing, but there is a
limit, and there is a wastage factor. One simply cannot reach individuals with
precise demographic characteristics and reach all or nearly all of those individuals,
and no others. Targeting is almost always probabilistic: one advertises on a
television show that is likely to have certain types of viewers or has a higher
percentage of viewers with certain characteristics than an alternative program.
Other forms of targeting can be more certain (i.e., with a higher probability
factor) such as going door-to-door in a neighborhood with an 80 percent Jewish
residency in order to reach Jewish voters; or reaching veterans by mailing to a
mailing list of veterans who live in the area.

Survey Research

Survey research has many uses for the political campaign. It can help a prospective candidate decide whether to make the race. It can suggest the magnitude of the election task, funds required to change the candidate's identification or support. It can, if shown to prospective donors, raise funds, especially if it is interpreted to show how a certain number of dollars can change the figures (e.g., by lifting the candidate's identification, by providing the advertising fund to dramatize issues of concern to certain groups, etc.). The survey can also accurately describe the demographic component of the political environment, especially the attitudes of subgroups on different issues. It can explain what issues are important to different groups, relative to other issues, and which issues are important, or potentially important, in deciding how someone will vote.

The survey can tell a candidate how much time, attention, advertising expenditures, etc. should be devoted to particular areas or to specific subgroups. It can suggest where his strength should be exploited, and in which areas his weakness is so great that resources should only be deployed if other areas have been adequately covered. It can suggest how to reach certain kinds of voters, i.e., what issues will *move* them to the candidate if he is perceived as empathetic. The strategist does not invent positions for the candidate but seeks to select, emphasize, and dramatize precisely those of the candidate's positions and feelings closest to the sentiments of the voters targeted by the survey.

The well-formulated survey can indicate words and phrases the candidate should use or avoid in rhetoric, literature, and advertising. Properly interpreted, surveys indicate what he should *not* do, as much as what he should do. The survey that asks the right questions of the right people can suggest which media are most useful in reaching the target groups—television, newspapers, magazines, direct mail—particular television networks, stations, programs, advertising at certain times of day, specific newspapers, sections of newspapers, days of the week. All of this data, and more, can be inferred from a well-constructed survey that tells something about the viewing and reading habits of different subgroups, as well as from the knowledge and data the campaign strategist already has, e.g., if the survey indicates it is important to reach young males, advertising on televised football games would be appropriate.

The survey is a current status report on the candidate's identification, popularity, preference in the election ("If the election were held today . . . "), and it provides projections or "breakouts" of the undecided vote. It can suggest trends, based upon comparisons with prior surveys. It also provides analogous data on the opponent, and an indication of his strengths and weaknesses.

In sum, it is clear that the candidate and campaign manager who merely use a summary to look at the bottom line (Candidate A, 52%; Candidate B, 43%; 5% undecided) are not making very productive use of survey research. The real message of the survey, if you are candidate B, is how to reach the 5 percent undecided, and how to move some voters out of Candidate A's column into your own, without losing any of your 43 percent support.

It is helpful to use survey research *with* the data and information available from other sources. Historical research and voting records and statistics can be used in conjunction with the latest survey results, both as a means of interpreting and understanding them, and as a way of supplementing the information. The survey itself can include some questions that focus on *motivation:* why individuals are supporting one candidate or another, one party or another, and what will get them to vote on election day. All data should be compared with, and used with, information and input from volunteer leaders and staff members, particularly those "in the field" or outside the main campaign headquarters.

Despite the proven value of surveys in political campaigns, the skeptics remain. In almost every case, the critics of survey research do not understand statistics and polling; they do not appreciate demographics, and they cannot utilize such data. As George Gallup, Jr., once observed, reflecting on the deep suspicion of political pollsters:

> In every presidential election year "open season" on polltakers is declared, with the shooting usually coming from those who don't like the findings. People across the nation write or telephone us to remind us of 1948, to ask why they haven't been interviewed, or just to give us a piece of their minds.
> One person during the campaign wrote my father, "Discontinue this very crooked manner of earning your livelihood, even if it means selling pencils or peanuts, as it will be something earned in an honest manner."[5]

The 1948 election results confirmed what any student of survey research knows: a poll is only a snapshot taken at an instant. If accurate, it is for that point in time, not for a future point in time. The closer a survey is taken to the date of election, the closer its figures will be to the actual results. As Gallup has pointed out, the value of surveys for the candidate and his campaign is *not* to get the latest reading of where he stands relative to the opposing candidate but to find out "where the large and decisive mass of swing voters is located."[6]

The survey itself does not gain any votes for the candidate. It only costs money. The information it supplies, and the inferences drawn from the information, suggest the *marketing strategy* that will gain votes. As new survey methods of questioning are tried, more information can be discovered that is relevant to the demands of the current political environment. For example, voter turnout is, as previously indicated, an important consideration in forecasting election results, especially in a "tight" race. Voter turnout is a function of, among other things:

1. Political party attachment: strong, intense partisans are more likely to vote.
2. Citizenship responsibility: patriotic citizens who feel voting is a solemn obligation are more likely to vote.
3. Concern over the election outcome: the individual that believes, first, that this election is very important to his welfare and, second, that the outcome may be close, is more likely to vote.
4. Interest in the campaign: someone whose interest in the campaign has been aroused by television and newspaper coverage of the campaign, heavy advertising, the dramatization of issues important to him, etc. will be more likely to vote.

All four of these areas are susceptible to questioning in survey research. The questions may not always be direct, but they can measure political party attachment, citizenship responsibility, concern over the election outcome, and interest in the campaign. From the responses to several questions, a probability can be assigned to an individual indicating his likelihood of voting on election day. Thus, survey research can even adjust, within ranges of error, for the turnout factor, both by combining and weighting the responses to various questions as well as asking individuals how likely it is that they will vote on election day (Table 7-3).

Components of Survey Research

The questionnaire. There are two basic types of questions: identification and attitudinal. The former relate to establishing who the respondent is; the latter to what he thinks. A third type of question is more speculative, relating to what he will do; often, it is more prudent to infer or interpret what he will do from his responses, and from cross-tabulation of those responses (i.e., drawing correlations between responses to one question and responses to another question).

Identification questions. These questions (Table 7-4) might include party registration, age, sex, income level, education, area of residency (county, state, district; urban, suburban, rural; upstate, downstate), union membership in family, religion, race, national origin, sex, self-perception (liberal, moderate, conservative).

Attitudinal questions. Tables 7-5 through 7-7 present several sample attitudinal questions. Note that questions are usually tailored for classified responses suitable for data processing; in contrast, open-ended questions, which

Table 7–3
Measuring Voter Turnout Probability

Voter Probability (Very High, High, Moderate, Low . . .) derived from integrating responses
   to the following three questions:
  1. Some people don't pay much attention to political campaigns. How about you? Would
     you say that you usually follow political campaigns with very much interest, some
     interest, or not much interest?
     Very much interest _____
     Some interest _____
     Not much interest _____
  2. We would like to know how strongly you feel about the importance of voting in the
     election this November. Would you say you care a great deal whether or not you vote,
     care somewhat, or don't care too much at this time whether or not you vote?
     Care a great deal _____
     Care somewhat _____
     Don't care too much _____
  3. Generally speaking, do you consider yourself to be conservative, middle-of-the-road or
     liberal?
     Conservative _____
     Middle-of-the-road _____
     Liberal _____

Note: These voter probability questions are extrapolated from 1974 surveys conducted by
Decision Making Information (DMI), Santa Ana, Calif. and are reprinted with permission of
DMI. Evaluating voter probability can be crucial, especially given widespread cynicism.
which has been described as "the bitter edge of the apathetic element which seems so pervasive today" (*Christian Science Monitor,* Oct. 6, 1975).

Table 7–4
Sample Identification Questions[a]

  1. Are you a registered voter in (area or state in which survey being taken)?
     1. Yes
     2. No (If "No," terminate interview).

  2. With which party are you registered?
     1. Democratic
     2. Republican
     3. Other listings might be required, depending on state
     4. Independent

  3. Regardless of your party affiliation, do you consider yourself to be a liberal, a moderate
     or a conservative in your political views?
     1. Liberal
     2. Moderate
     3. Conservative
     4. Not sure/don't know/decline to state

(The following questions might be near the end of the interview; some do not need to be
  asked, or cannot be asked, depending on attitude of interviewee.)

  4. Do you, or does any member of your immediate family who lives in this household,
     belong to a labor union?
     1. Yes
     2. No

  5. What is your religion—Catholic, Protestant or Jewish?
     1. Catholic
     2. Protestant
     3. Jewish
     4. Other (Specify) _____

Table 7–4 (continued)

6. What is your national ancestry? (Limit to one choice)
    1. Irish
    2. Italian
    3. German
    4. English/Scot
    5. French/French Canadian
    6. Polish
    7. Russian
    8. Other (Specify) _____

7. What is your annual family income . . . under $6,000, between $6,000 and $12,000; between $12,000 and $20,000; or over $20,000?
    1. Under $6,000
    2. $6,000–$12,000
    3. $12,000–$20,000
    4. Over $20,000

8. Race
    1. White
    2. Black
    3. Puerto Rican
    4. Other (Specify) _____

9. Age
    1. 18–21
    2. 22–30
    3. 31–40
    4. 41–60
    5. over 60

10. Sex
    1. Male
    2. Female

11. What is the highest grade of formal education you have completed?
    Less than high school graduate _____
    High school graduate _____
    Some college/vocational school _____
    College graduate _____
    Post-graduate _____

Note: This list is not complete. The importance of different questions can vary, depending on the purpose of the survey and the need for certain types of data. No questions are shown which seek to establish prior voting habits ("For whom did you vote for President in the last election? . . ."). Also, the classifications within questions can be broken down differently. Finally, these questions are taken from an *in-person* interview schedule.

[a]These questions are either asked or the answers may be obvious, e.g., area in which interview takes place. Sometimes responses must be inferred (age or income level). Many identification questions, particularly those which do not require follow-up questions, are asked at the end of an interview. (Questions are not in any specific order.)

Table 7-5

Sample Attitudinal Questions—Drawn from In-Person Interview
Schedule (1970) (Instructions to interviewer are in parentheses.)

1. In this year's elections for high office in New York, are you more likely to vote for candidates who generally support President Nixon and his policies or for those who generally oppose President Nixon and his policies?
   1. Support
   2. Oppose
   3. Depends on the individuals
   4. Not sure

2. The following is a list of proposals set forth on Vietnam. With which proposal are you in more agreement? (Read list)
   1. Immediate withdrawal
   2. Gradual withdrawal
   3. Increased escalation
   4. Not sure/depends

3. Now, I am going to read you a list of five subjects of interest. Please tell me which two you consider to be of most concern to you personally: (Read list)
   1. Drugs
   2. Declining morality in America
   3. High cost of living
   4. War in Indochina
   5. Environmental control

4. Here is another list—Please tell me which two of these you consider most important: (Read list)
   1. Crime in the streets
   2. Race relations
   3. Student and education disorders
   4. Crisis in the Middle East
   5. Unemployment

5. From the following list . . . please tell me which one issue concerns you the most: (Read list)
   1. War in Indochina
   2. Declining morality in America
   3. High cost of living
   4. Drugs

6. From the following list . . . please tell me which one issue concerns you the most: (Read list)
   1. Sex morals in America
   2. Environmental control
   3. Crime in the streets
   4. Student and educational disorders

7. In the election for Senator, the candidates are . . . . Which of the three candidates do you feel can best deal with the following list of issues? If you do not know the candidate's positions or have no preference, just say so.

Issue	*Goodell*	*Ottinger*	*Buckley*	*No pref./don't know*

   Eight issues were listed.

8. Are there any other issues of particular importance to you that we haven't mentioned?
   1. No.
   2. Yes (Specify)

9. Now, I am going to read you a list of personality traits. Which, if any, of these traits do you feel applies to the Senatorial candidates: Richard Ottinger, the Democrat, Charles Goodell, the Republican, or James Buckley, the Conservative? (Circle as many as respondent says.)

187

Table 7-5 (continued)

	Goodell	*Ottinger*	*Buckley*
1. Intelligent			
2. Arrogant			
3. Stands up for what's right			
4. Believes in what he's saying			
5. Good appearance			
6. Opportunistic			
7. Immature			
8. Real American			
9. Independent			

10. In the election for Seantor, do you intend to vote for . . . (candidates mentioned)?

11. What are the main reasons why you are supporting (name of candidate)?

Source: These questions, excerpted from in-person interview schedules (1970) prepared by Arthur J. Finkelstein, are reprinted with the permission of Arthur J. Finkelstein and DirAction Services, Inc.

Table 7-6

Sample Attitudinal and Forecasting Questions—from Telephone Surveys (1974)

1. As you know, we will be voting to fill many state offices here in California come November 5th. I am going to read you the names of the candidates in each of several races. For each race, please tell me how you would vote if the election were held today?
   Races and candidates listed.

   Example: If respondent answers undecided in U.S. Senate race:
2. Do you lean more toward H.L. Richardson, Republican, or Alan Cranston, Democrat, in this race?

1. How would you rate the job Gerald Ford is doing as President: excellent, good, fair or poor?
   Excellent _____
   Good _____
   Fair _____
   Poor _____

2. As you know, President Nixon has just received a full presidential pardon from Gerald Ford. Do you agree or disagree with President Ford's decision to pardon Richard Nixon "in full"?
   Agree _____
   Disagree _____
   Don't know/undecided _____

If agree or disagree, then:

3. Would you say that you feel very strongly or not so strongly about the Presidential pardon?
   Very strongly _____
   Not so strongly _____
   Don't know/no opinion _____

Source: These questions, excerpted from telephone surveys conducted by Decision-Making Information in California during September–October, 1974, are reprinted with the permission of DMI.

188

Table 7-7

Sample Attitudinal Questions—from In-Person Interview Schedules (1973 and 1974)

Open-ended questions:
1. What do you consider to be the most important issue facing the United States today?
2. What do you consider to be the most important issue facing New York State today?
3. What do you consider to be the next most important issue facing New York State today?
4. What do you think have been the major accomplishments of James Buckley?
5. What would you like James Buckley as Senator to do for you personally?
6. Who would you like to see the Democrats (the Republicans) nominate for President in 1976?

(Note: No names are given to interviewee.)

Additional sample questions (from different surveys)
1. Would you vote to re-elect Jacob Javits regardless of who ran against him?
   1. Yes
   2. No
   3. Don't know/not sure

2. Would you vote to re-elect James Buckley regardless of who ran against him?
   1. Yes . . .
   2. No . . .
   3. Don't know/not sure

3. If the election for Governor were held today and the candidates were Malcolm Wilson, the Republican and Hugh Carey, the Democrat, for whom would you vote?
   1. Wilson . . .
   2. Carey . . .
   3. Don't know/not sure/undecided

4. Would you say James Buckley is doing an excellent job, a good job, a fair job, or a poor job as United States Senator?
   1. Excellent . . .
   2. Good . . .
   3. Fair . . .
   4. Poor . . .
   5. Don't know

5. Here is a list of items recently prominent in the news. Could you please tell me whether you approve or disapprove of each?

	Approve	*Disapprove*	*Don't know*
Legalization of marijuana			
School busing to integrate public schools			
Stricter gun control laws			
Legalized abortion			
Life imprisonment for drug pushers			
. . .			

6. Now I am going to read you some statements. Could you please tell me whether you agree strongly, agree, disagree, or disagree strongly with each?

	Agree Strongly	*Agree*	*Disagree*	*Disagree Strongly*	*Don't know*
The Republican Party is corrupt					
Jacob Javits represents my views					
James Buckley represents my views					
The Democratic Party is corrupt					
I feel safe while walking in my own neighborhood at night					
Drug use is declining in my neighborhood					

189

Table 7–7 (continued)

---

1. Now I am going to read you a list of names. Will you please tell me if you have a favorable or unfavorable opinion of each. If you have no opinion or have never heard of the person, just say so.

	Favorable	*Unfavorable*	*No opinion*	*Don't know*
Richard Nixon				
Spiro Agnew				
Nelson Rockefeller				
Jacob Javits				
James Buckley				
John Lindsay				
. . . other names of concern to pollster				

2. Now from a similar list of names, could you please tell me which you consider liberal, which moderate and which conservative?

	Liberal	*Moderate*	*Conservative*	*Don't know*
List of names . . .				

Source: These questions, excerpted from in-person interview schedules prepared for New York State surveys in 1973 and 1974 by Arthur J. Finkelstein, are reprinted with the permission of Arthur J. Finkelstein and DirAction Services, Inc.

---

may sometimes be asked, do not present a choice for the respondent ("What do you consider the single most important issue facing the United States?") There are scale questions, in which the respondent must rate something on a numerical scale, 1 to 5, 1 to 10, etc.; probability questions ("Are you more likely or less likely to . . . ?"); conditional ("If President Ford does . . . , would you be more inclined or less inclined to . . . ?"), and numerous other types of questions. *Note:* Sample questions may be out of order and/or taken from *different* surveys.

Media questions. Other questions seek to measure how effectively the campaign has penetrated the news and advertising media. For example: "Have you seen any television commercials this year for any candidates for Governor or Senator?"; if yes, "Which candidates' commercials do you remember seeing?" —(read list of candidates; circle as many as respondent says). Related to this type of question are those which try to find out the sources of news for the respondent, the relative importance of newspapers and television, and the importance of particular newspapers or television programs, the nature of reading or viewing habits, etc.

The formulation of questions is accomplished by the joint efforts of the survey researcher, the candidate, campaign manager, and others. The number and types of questions are affected by the decision to do an in-person interview versus a telephone interview. The questionnaire reflects the cross-tabulations that will be desired, i.e., one reason for asking Question A and Question B is to run both questions through the computer, to measure: of those answering "yes" or "very likely" to Question A, how many answered "poor" or how many answered "excellent" to Question B. Thus, each question is really an almost infinite number of questions, when related to how many times it can be run through the computer, with its responses matched up to the responses to other questions.

As *probability* becomes more important in political analysis, techniques used in consumer research to test intentions to purchase may be adapted to political survey research. For example, descriptive words can be assigned probability values to quantify the likelihood that a voter will support a candidate or switch his vote. In one such probability scale, eleven values, ranging from 0.10 for "no chance, almost no chance" to 0.99 for "certain, practically certain" measured increments in articulated probability (e.g., "fairly good possibility" is equivalent to 0.50, "good possibility" to 0.60).[7] Attempts to quantify subjective opinions represent an evolution toward more precise predictions relating to voter choice, conversion probability, interest in certain issues, and voter turnout probability.

The most competent pollster cannot alone formulate the questionnaire. He must know what information the campaign requires to develop, test, and validate its strategy, and to forecast future trends.

The sample. The sample size is the major determinant of the cost of a survey. The sample error is based upon the sample size, and it is indicated by the term "confidence interval"—a mathematical calculation used to estimate the size of the sample error. Thus, with a sample size of 600, the confidence interval might be ±4%, meaning that if 40 percent of the respondents indicated they would support Candidate A over Candidate B, the figure should be 36 to 44 percent, i.e., the overwhelming number of times a survey is taken, the results will be *within* that error range, but quite possibly less than the error range, and very close to reality. By "overwhelming number of times," we refer to the level of confidence which, for most political surveys, is 0.05, i.e., 95 percent of the time, or 19 out of 20 times, a survey with the particular sample size will be accurate within the confidence interval associated with that sample size, e.g., ±4% for a sample size of 600.

Composition of sample. The validity of the sample is verified by comparing major demographic characteristics of the sample to the relevant universe, e.g., a survey of a Congressional district would compare the sample to the 18-or-over registered voters in the Congressional district. A scientifically selected random sampling technique usually constitutes a fair reflection of the registered voter universe, or the universe of those who voted in the last election; i.e., the same proportion of Republicans to Democrats to Independents; the same proportion of male to female, white to nonwhite, etc., in each case, the same proportion as in the universe as a whole.

Naturally, it is virtually impossible for a sample to be a perfect mirror of the universe in *every* respect, to have the same proportion of Polish nationality respondents as in the universe as a whole, the same proportion of $15,000+ income level as in the universe as a whole, etc. Either due to chance or error, the survey may not represent precisely the proportion of a characteristic in the universe; however, the results of the survey can be adjusted (weighted or post-stratified) to correct the variation.

Quality control. Census Bureau statistics and random sampling techniques are used to determine the size of the total sample, and the proportions desired within it. The determination of the relevant universe is made, and quality control is checked by comparing the *sample frame desired* with the *sample obtained,* which should be very similar.

Technical competence.   This pertains to the sampling error, which has been discussed. It also pertains to *questionnaire* error (poorly worded questions, especially if worded by nonprofessionals); to *interview* error (poorly trained or briefed interviewers, either paid or volunteer); and to *clerical* error (poorly coded responses, errors in entering the data into the computer, etc.).

Interviewers.   Most survey research firms and pollsters have few, if any, interviewers; they contract out this work to services scattered throughout the United States. These interviewers are trained, and their employers are usually able to "guarantee" that the sample will be taken as specified, the questions asked as specified, and the sample taken within a very brief time interval, such as within two or three days. Otherwise, the survey is not an accurate reflection of opinion at a point (i.e., within two or three days) in time.

Interpretation.   This is very important, and many of the most well-known pollsters cannot interpret data as well as their lesser-known counterparts. Interpretation also relates to the utilization of data: how many cross-tabulations are sought, for what purpose; why was the sample structured to include so many Italians and why was nationality asked; why does the computer program automatically provide for so many cross-tabulations.

Conclusion.   It should be emphasized that surveys are used to suggest the ways in which issues are used to stress a theme within the political campaign, as well as to test the identification, popularity, and possible showing in an election (*if it were held today*) of the candidate. Surveys that are conducted in-person rather than by telephone tend to be more accurate (they especially cut down on the number of "undecided" voters), and they can be longer.

It may be advisable for a political campaign with limited resources to limit the number of surveys, or limit the participation of a professional to structuring a sample or providing a computer program, or counseling on the wording of the questions. The actual interviewers can be taken from the ranks of campaign volunteers, especially for telephone surveys. Also, once a major, in-person survey is taken, subsequent surveys to track, monitor, or check the progress of the campaign can be taken on the telephone by *volunteers* who are properly briefed. (Telephone surveys have a natural bias favoring those who have telephones, but this is usually not significant). A major problem is the random selection of the telephone numbers to be called.

The Product

The political organization is the marketing organization delivering the candidate to the consumer-voter. Actually, the product is much more than the candidate (Table 7-8), just as the marketing organization is much more than the formal political campaign. It is all of the volunteers and noncampaign community and support groups mobilized in the distribution process, especially the news and advertising media; the consumer is much more than the voter, for the consumer is also the nonvoter who has not yet registered, but still can, or the registered voter who can be persuaded or motivated to vote. (Once voter registration closes, the unregistered voter is no longer important.)

The inescapable influence of the candidate throughout the political campaign has been stressed. It is all-pervasive because he is the center of activity, the reason for the campaign's existence. There may be "the cause," the national interest," or specific issues, but the campaign is built around an individual. How

Table 7-8
The Product

The candidate is the product:
  A. His physical appearance
    1. In person
    2. On television, in photographs, etc.

  B. His rhetoric and utterances
    1. Positions on issues
    2. Utilization of research materials
    3. Speaking ability and fluency

  C. His background
    1. Experience
    2. Education

  D. Innate ability (intelligence, aptitude, etc.)

  E. Party affiliation

  F. Political philosophy

  G. His family
    .
    .
    .

---

capable, alert, and bright he is; how good a speaker he is, how well he comes across on television; whether he can assimilate material quickly, write prodigiously to turn out statements in quick order, make quick decisions or procrastinate . . . these are all part of the candidate's make-up influencing the entire campaign. Since perception, not reality, is operative, the candidate as a public person and the impression he conveys are more important then the private person.

The Candidate as Product

Campaign strategy should aim to "peak" the campaign as close as possible to election day (Figure 7-2). The momentum should be so strong near the end that the candidate's strength seems to be rising almost uncontrollably. Although "peaking" cannot occur without the campaign first passing through introductory and initial growth phases, campaign activity cannot be characterized by the maturity and decline phases of a commercial product's life cycle. Any campaign that enters a maturity or decline phase prior to election day is losing its momentum.

In other respects, the candidate is similar to a product, as evidenced by the following five primary variables.[8]

Physical properties.   In the television age, no one can dismiss the importance of physical attractiveness and photogenic qualities.

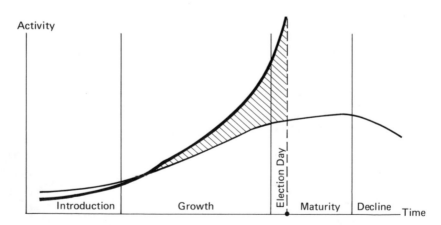

Figure 7-2. Development of Political Campaign
Note: Unlike a commercial product's life cycle with its four phases (introduction, growth, maturity, and decline) the campaign "takes off" (heavy line) as it evidences momentum (gray area) and "peaks" on or just before election day.

Brand and label. Most Americans identify candidates, especially at the local level, by their brand or label, i.e., the identification provided by their political party. Parallels exist: just as a brand not only identifies a product but transfers whatever image the firm or its product family has to the branded good, so the party label both identifies someone who is running for office and transfers to him whatever good and bad qualities are associated with the brand (party label). Just as a firm that has established a brand image of prestige or high quality may damage its premium line by using the same brand on a less expensive product, so too is a party label diluted by making it available even to mediocre candidates.

Packaging. This supplies additional identification for the product; for the candidate, packaging is the kind of campaign organization in which the candidate plays the central role. A highly professional organization is one kind of package; an amateurish organization is another kind of package.

Quality. The reliability and durability of a product are paralleled by the reliability of a candidate and the durability of the positions that he takes on issues. Is the product exactly what it is represented to be, and will it perform as it is intended to perform? Is the candidate what he says he is, and will he, once elected, do what he promises?

Image. Just as image refers to the characteristics of the product as they are perceived by the consumer, so the image of the candidate is how he is perceived by voters. In either case, image may be more a product of advertising and promotion than substance. Sometimes, commercial marketing executives do not have a very good product, so they must manipulate the product's image. Some campaign managers also have only one option available to them; given the nature of their candidate, they must manipulate his image.

The campaign strategist must differentiate among types of voters as any marketing executive segments the market for his product by differentiating price, promotion strategies, packaging, etc. Both strategies analyze consumers by demographic variables to define the market more precisely. Marketing similarities are illustrated by the strategy of a candidate running on a "ticket" headed by a popular candidate. This "coattails" effect follows an established marketing strategy in which a group of products "closely related either because they satisfy a class of need, are used together, [or] are sold to the same consumer groups . . . are marketed through the same type of outlets. . . ."[9] In the political application, candidates might sponsor common headquarters or joint advertising.

Although the incumbent supposedly has the advantage, incumbency has drawbacks as well as benefits. The incumbency matrix (Figure 7-3) includes one incumbent disadvantage peculiar to the television age. The more conscientious the incumbent, the less time he can devote to visual theatrics to draw television

	Advantages	Disadvantages
Incumbent	1. Access to media 2. Stature, position of responsibility 3. Ability to generate news 4. Staff, perquisites, possibly travel allowance, franking privilege, research personnel, etc. 5. Record of accomplishment 6. Can point to experience 7. Probably has name identification	1. Image of invisibility occasioned by lack of sustained, regular television coverage in state or district, especially when compared to campaign periods 2. Staff or privileges can be attacked 3. Associated with present problems 4. Record is there and apparent to media, opposition; can be attacked 5. "Politician" and "establishment" image 6. Official business obligations
Challenger	1. Can be active in district or state while incumbent is away 2. Can go on offensive, challenging incumbent's record 3. Has no record of his own to defend 4. May be able to stress citizen, nonpolitical stance vs. professional politician 5. May be able to go on offensive without any necessity to offer solutions to problems	1. Has no record of experience 2. Has difficulty getting media coverage 3. Lacks government-provided staff and privileges 4. Probably lacks name identification

Figure 7-3. Incumbency Matrix.
Note: The pros and cons of being an incumbent and being a challenger.

coverage. For example, the United States Senator who is preoccupied with the mundane, routine chores of committee work, does not have time constantly to fly into his home state and stage a contrived event, visually appealing to news directors at television stations and suitable for camera coverage. Nevertheless, since more and more voters get most of their news from television, they judge the worth of their elected official by his activism, or *perceived* activism. They decide whether or not an elected official is doing things by whether or not he is visible, i.e., whether he is or is not on the evening television news.

In this sense, then, the incumbent is judged by an unreal standard; the harder he works, the less likely he is to get television coverage, which requires (usually) his presence in the state or district. The real workload of the elected official is dull and routine or, at the very least, it is not visually exciting for television. Thus, the incumbent in the television age is always up against a "do-nothing" image caused by his inability to appear regularly on television news, especially compared to the hyperactive period of his campaign, in which case he was on the television news every evening.

Research

An area too often given low priority is the research behind the candidate. This information is the basis for his speeches, issues papers, brochures, newspaper advertising, etc. Although research is often given scant attention due to the importance of media as the principal means of communication, this oversimplified view ignores several reasons why research is important.

First, a candidate should project confidence and assurance. The candidate lacking confidence in his material will not project confidence in his speeches or in debates. Staff members who deride the candidate's research requests forget that they work for the candidate. If some facts or data will make him feel at ease, the research should be done.

Second, issues can only be dramatized with clever anecdotes, interesting examples or illustrations, and compelling facts. Even inspiration for media "visuals" is often based on research. Research suggests both ideas and proposals the candidate can articulate, as well as practical ways to dramatize issues.

Third, research on the opposition candidate, i.e., not clandestine, Watergate-type snooping but basic knowledge of the individual, his background, positions and public record, is indispensable.

Types of Research. In addition to *survey research* and *opposition research,* there are eight other basic types of research.

General issue research. This pertains to issues of widespread public concern and focuses especially on issues relevant to the office sought.

Political research. An adjunct of survey research, this includes past voting records, voter registration data, and similar historical and present data. It also includes a variety of lists of party leaders, financial contributors, delegates to past conventions, volunteer club leadership and membership lists, etc.

Briefing materials on specific areas. These include maps and the history of states, counties, or other areas relevant to the campaign. It includes census data, business, agricultural, and labor information and trends, major developments and news stories pertaining to the area, etc. This information, constantly updated, provides the basis both for briefing the candidate before he visits the area (so he appears better informed in his conversations and better versed in his public speeches) and for modifying campaign advertising and other marketing to better suit the local constituency.

Anecdotes, examples, facts, statistics. These comprise the priority file of the most compelling such items to substantiate and dramatize the candidate's

points. This file includes jokes, humor, and funny stories, little known facts and
poignant accounts of individuals or organizations dealing with the government.
Such research includes not only compelling aggregate statistics but often trans-
lates the big numbers into manageable, easily understood numbers relevant to the
individual citizen, taxpayer, or voter. Common methods include adjusting
statistics to per capita terms or converting the data (e.g., "If every Form 8052
in the Department of Agriculture were stacked end to end. . . . ").

Groups and lists.   These include the many directories of civic groups,
charitable organizations, social groups, veterans and patriotic organizations,
rabbis, priests, and religious leaders, Chamber of Commerce and similar business
groups, unions and union leaders. Leaders of statewide and local affiliates can
provide valuable support for the candidate, background material and briefings
related to issues concerning their members, and membership lists for special
mailings.

Information on the candidate.   The campaign's most important asset, this
category includes the candidate's biography, writings, public record, family,
past memberships and affiliations, prior correspondence, military record, education, hobbies, photographs, etc.

Media research.   This should include thorough, updated lists of all relevant
media outlets, including verification of personnel, addresses, telephone numbers,
and supporting data (circulation figures, wire services used, columnists used,
frequency of publication, network affiliation, station call letters). Mailings are
personalized to include key media managers, publishers, editors, news directors,
political reporters, columnists, on-the-air reporters, assignment editors. This data
can also be cross-referenced with data to be used in the campaign advertising.

Publications.   A monthly, weekly, and daily watch over relevant publications to look for specific items and clip and file or condense them into manageable form should be closely administered by the press or research division,
especially relating to monitoring newspapers within a state or district.

Priorities.   Issues that emerge during the campaign as overriding and those
which personally interest the candidate determine the campaign's research
priorities. Current events and developments also determine priorities by their
effect on campaign discussion and debate. The research division can utilize
standard sources of information (Table 7–9) to furnish material at the request
of the candidate and on its own initiative. Competent research directors try to
anticipate research requests. They also maximize the use of volunteers, both
high level, well-educated experts who supply invaluable information and less
skilled volunteers who clip, file, type, etc.

Table 7-9
Examples of Sources of Research Information

1. U.S. Census Bureau records and publications (The list is widely extensive.)

2. U.S. Library of Congress (Their summary reports on particular issues are very useful and can be obtained through the offices of a Senator or Congressman who makes the request in his name.)

3. U.S. Government agencies, state, and local government (numerous bureaucrats)

4. U.S. *Congressional Record, Congressional Record* Index; also *Congressional Quarterly* and *National Journal* (private, weekly coverage of Congress and Washington)

5. Private organizations (U.S. Chamber of Commerce, National Association of Manufacturers, AFL-CIO, Common Cause, etc.)
   a. Special interest groups (Protagonists on both sides of a question can be approached for the most cogent material.)
   b. Religious groups, veterans groups, membership organizations, etc. (for position papers, information, lists of leaders and members, or rental of such lists, advertising in house organs, etc.)

6. Volunteers
   a. Experts who are sympathetic to the candidate may donate time, head up a task force, write or edit a speech draft on a specialized topic, etc. (may include professors and foundation allies).
   b. Other volunteers may send in reports "from the field," especially local volunteer leadership seeking to update the file before the candidate's visit.
   c. Volunteers in headquarters may assist in clipping and filing, etc.

7. Political party organizations (regular organizations, volunteer organizations, party campaign committees, e.g., Senatorial Campaign Committee, party caucus organizations in Washington or state capitols, etc.)

8. Campaign reports on file in Washington and at state capitols on prior campaigns; voting registration records in various jurisdictions

9. (Mandatory) publications for candidates running for federal office: *Congressional Record, National Journal, Congressional Quarterly, New York Times, Washington Post, Los Angeles Times, Wall Street Journal, Christian Science Monitor, Time, Newsweek, U.S. News* (and political/educational publications, e.g., *National Review, Human Events, Public Interest, New Republic, Nation*, etc.)

10. Clipping service (a paid, contract service to clip for mentions of the candidate's name, the opponent's name, or any other items, on a local, regional or national basis, with special, expedited service for an extra fee; can be extremely thorough . . . and expensive, depending on the number of clips)

11. General reference volumes (dictionary, Who's Who, collections of quotations, historical outline and summary volumes, statistical abstracts, almanacs, various directories of publications, television stations, journalists, statistical volumes; especially, the volumes put out by government agencies on crime, agriculture, education, etc.—lists and suggestions provided by Senator, Congressman, library or Government Printing Office; not overlooking the *Guide to Periodic Literature*)

12. Opposition (speech texts, news releases, public schedules, clippings, voting record—if incumbent, publicly-filed campaign reports, also voting record analyses—Americans for Constitutional Action-ACA, Americans for Democratic Action-ADA, the AFL-CIO Committee on Political Education (COPE), the American Conservative Union (ACU), the American Security Council (ASC), Congressional Quarterly index, etc., plus counterparts for voting records at state level). Quote books of the opponent's statements, taken from clippings, position papers, past campaigns, speeches, news releases, etc. are valuable, as are annotated records of his voting, if he is an incumbent in Congress or in a statehouse or other legislative body.

(continued)

Table 7-9 (continued)

13. Local publications (if candidate in state or area, special emphasis placed on local publications too important to be delayed by seeing clips thru the clipping service)

14. AP or UPI ticker machine (installed in campaign headquarters)

Note: The actual information retrieval system should be designed for the particular campaign. For a small campaign, a highly organized system can be developed without microfilm or data processing. For the large campaign, microfilm or data processing, especially when used in conjunction with the perquisites of incumbency, can be very practical.

The mechanics of research—filing systems, indexing, and cross-references, information retrieval systems, condensing and editing material into manageable, cogent form for the candidate—reflect the issue priorities, in terms of range and complexity of issues. Although party organizations provide guidance and manuals to structure research operations, the candidate and staff must accept the importance of research. Although survey and related research suggest how to reach the electorate (marketing), additional research (e.g., media directories, like *Editor and Publisher, Broadcasting Yearbook, Ayer's,* and *Working Press of the Nation,* or organization membership and mailing lists) enable the campaign to perform its *distribution* function.

Conclusion.   It should be reiterated that the candidate and the political campaign are inseparable. The candidate cannot isolate himself and disclaim responsibility for an inept campaign. He cannot apologize for not being prepared in a campaign debate and excuse himself because the campaign's research division was not functioning. Nor can he insulate himself from the everyday activities of the campaign's participants—the staff and the volunteers. Each time these individuals come in contact with the electorate, they represent the candidate. Hence informative issues papers should provide background for them; particularly, any speakers for the candidate, including those enlisted in a speaker's bureau, should have a loose-leaf briefing book, regularly updated. The means of *distribution* become part of the product: The candidate and the campaign must both project leadership, confidence, and assurance. When voters see an incompetent campaign, they believe this is the way the candidate will run his office if elected. Similarly, if he recruits and selects incompetent staff, they believe he will choose poorly in government. They see the campaign as a measure of how he will govern.

Distribution

The distribution problem, which is tantamount to the communications problem, confronts every campaign in its marketing process (Figure 7-4). The candidate must somehow reach the electorate and priority subgroups with his message. Distribution brings the product to the consumer, i.e., to registered

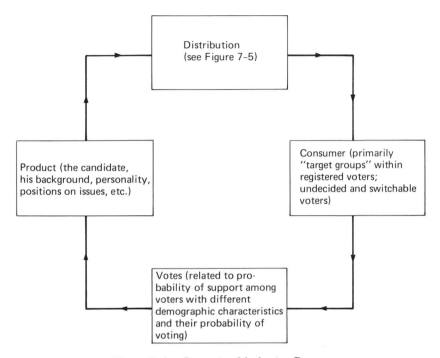

Figure 7-4. Campaign Marketing Process.

voters and those who can be registered, especially undecided voters and "soft" opposition support that can be induced to switch. The marketing process is complete when consumers go to the polls to vote for the candidate.

The distribution process begins at the campaign committee level. This is the candidate's official committee and its geographical subdivisions and local headquarters. The adjunct committees are formed to appeal to special groups broken down by occupation or profession, by special interest or issue interest, etc. Both the campaign committees and adjunct committees place special emphasis on forming a communications network, with active community leaders and the more interested citizens at the top of the network. This network, which utilizes civic and community organizations, although informally and unofficially, is composed of the "joiners" who are members of these organizations or, more likely, leaders. This *network* of religious, patriotic, educational, business, labor, and other groups and associations is an informal method of reaching the electorate, unlike the adjunct committees.

Unlike a consumer product, the *distribution* and *promotion* functions are not entirely discrete, although promotion is staff oriented and distribution, except for direct media activities, is volunteer-oriented (Figure 7-5).

The importance of recruiting volunteers, placing them in the right spot, and motivating them has been noted throughout this volume. A volunteer operation

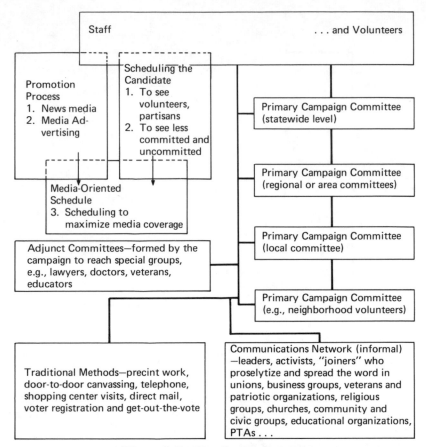

Figure 7-5. Distribution Process.

Note: Just as the primary committee is divided successively into smaller geographical units to reach successively smaller geographical constituencies, adjunct committees can be similarly divided. In any size campaign the adjunct committees must reach the individual . . . veteran, lawyer, educator, etc. (unless the committee is merely a publicity device). The communications network is an informal organization lacking structure and especially potent in the small campaign. It relies on "word of mouth" and other communications among activists, joiners, leaders, and opinion molders who reach and influence others.

requires detailed plans to search out and recruit volunteers, and to match the individual's skills and time availability with the campaign's needs (Table 7-10). Using a comprehensive cross-filing system and data processing, the political campaign assigns volunteers to the slots most appropriate for them, given their background, skills, time availability, location, etc.

Traditional uses of volunteers relate primarily to precinct work—canvassing areas and neighborhoods for unregistered voters. Canvassers do not report those who wish to register for the opposition party but refer cooperating deputy registrars only to those who wish to register in the canvasser's party. In more advanced operations large-scale telephone "boiler rooms" are used to canvass, measure voter preference, and assist favorably inclined voters to get to the polls. Although the volunteers for these operations are usually recruited directly through political party organizations, the imaginative campaign can tap its own sources of volunteer manpower. The charismatic candidate can generate his own following; also, the campaign can mount its own recruiting drive. For example, in direct mail fund raising, respondents can use one side of a card to record their name, address, etc. for giving a contribution, and the reverse side for providing volunteer information, which is subsequently given to a coordinator in their area.

In sum, precinct work usually includes the following steps. (1) Canvass to find favorably inclined unregistered voters and register them. (2) Canvass and telephone voters to determine favorably and unfavorably inclined and undecided. (3) Distribute literature to sway the undecided. (4) Re-canvass the undecided to monitor conversions. (5) Assist favorably inclined with rides, babysitters, etc. to get them to the polls. (6) Deploy volunteers to assist in ballot security to protect against miscount, fraud. Both political parties provide exhaustive manuals on recruiting and utilizing volunteers, the mechanics of voter registration, canvassing, literature distribution, telephone campaigns, and election day activity.[c] The productivity of precinct workers is enhanced with proper guidance, instruction, and briefing materials, updated voter lists, and supporting materials (tally sheets, pens, pencils, precinct "walking sheets," lists of telephone numbers, etc.).

Any special election, i.e., called to fill a vacancy caused by an incumbent's death, resignation, appointment to office, etc., best illustrates the critical role of volunteers. Since such elections are usually characterized by lower voter turnout, the effect is to increase vastly the impact of volunteer manpower. The strategy must deploy volunteers in their highest valued uses. A special election for Congress in 1969, in which seven Republicans competed in a primary to determine who would face the Democrat, exemplified superb strategy.[d] Since

---

[c]These manuals present detailed programs; however, many political campaigns use these manuals as the basis for their own manuals, tailored to the needs of their campaign. An example of a superior manual is Mary Ellen Miller, *Manual for Boiler Room Operation (Telephone Center)* (Washington, D.C.: Republican Congressional Committee, 1974), a 59-page description of a complete telephone operation, with charts, room layouts, sample schedules, suggested telephone conversations, tabulation programs, etc.

[d]The October, 1969 election was to fill the vacancy created in the Thirteenth Congressional District in suburban Chicago when Rep. Donald Rumsfeld was appointed by President Nixon to be Director of the Office of Economic Opportunity (OEO). The district's current Congressman, Rep. Philip M. Crane, won the critical primary election, which virtually assured him of victory in the general.

Table 7-10
Typical Volunteer Information Required

1. Name
2. Work address and telephone number
3. Home address and telephone number
4. Congressional District or area of residence
5. Days and hours available
6. Prior political experience
7. Skills (e.g., typing)
8. Work at headquarters or some other location (home, work, residence of another person)
9. Other members of family interested in helping
10. Groups or committees in which individual is active or a leader (church, education, community, nationality groups, etc.)
11. Special abilities which can be applied to campaign (advertising, graphics, statistics, educational background, foreign language skills)
12. Interest of volunteer in helping in particular areas:
    a. Main campaign headquarters
    b. Typing
    c. Filing
    d. Reception work
    e. Telephoning
    f. Clipping
    g. Research
    h. Surveys—polling in-person or on telephone
    i. Working in adjunct committees
    k. Working with special outside constituencies—such as Spanish-speaking citizens
    l. Precinct work (door-to-door literature distribution, voter registration, etc.)
    m. Putting on rallies, social events, ticket selling, decorations,
    n. Fund raising (solicitation, receptions, dinners, auctions, etc.)
    o. Youth activities
    p. Setting up local headquarters
    q. As aide to full-time staff member in particular section of campaign, e.g., press, scheduling
    r. Major time-commitment—e.g., advance man
    s. Bookkeeping
    .
    .
    .

the district was strongly Republican the primary winner was likely to win the general election. Strategists for the most conservative Republican contender knew the following to be important: (a) The dominant characteristic of their product was conservatism. Above all, their candidate was a conservative Republican. *The product was conservative.* (b) A major portion of the Republican electorate in the district was conservative. If the conservative candidate could win the support of most of this constituency, he could let the other six candidates divide the "moderates" and "liberals." *The consumer was conservative.* (c) The marketing mechanism could not operate unless the campaign could *identify* individual conservative voters. The campaign utilized its volunteers to canvass the district to find Republicans who considered themselves conservatives. Subsequently, the campaign, through mailings, telephone calls, door-to-door work, etc. appealed repeatedly to this conservative Republican subgroup, which had been isolated by the volunteer canvassing. Needless to say, the *packaging* and *image* of the candidate was decidedly conservative.

In the campaign just mentioned, the use of mail was very important. As a means of *distribution* and *promotion,* mail has been a classic tool of political campaigns. The technical aspects of mail could easily be the subject of several books: different postage rates, first class versus bulk rate, sources of labels, drop dates, computer-personalized mailings, household mailings, self-mailers (requiring no envelopes), etc. Some mailings ask for money and volunteer help, others are sent only to specific lists. The mailings may be in the form of newspapers, or three-panel brochures, or six-panel brochures, or fold-out literature. There may be much copy, few photographs; or just the reverse. The mailing may be black-and-white or color. It may emphasize endorsements or simply consist of a letter of endorsement from someone prominent. It may use a commemorative stamp as an attention getter, or it may use a postage meter or simply a printed bulk mail designation. It may be in a large envelope, or it may consist only of a postcard, perhaps to be taken to the polls.

The campaign manager must keep in mind the following regarding direct mail as a means of distribution and promotion:

1. Unless direct mail is highly targeted to certain kinds of constituencies or lists, with an appeal relevant to those constituencies or lists, it is of limited appeal.
2. The smaller the campaign, i.e., the lower level the office sought, the greater the role mail can have, relative to television, radio, or newspapers.
3. The effectiveness of direct mail is limited, first, by recipients who do not open obviously "junk" mail; second, by those who throw it away once opened; third, by those who skim it once opened; fourth, by most of the remaining voters who read it and disregard it.

If the mailing achieves name recognition for the candidate, this may be sufficient in certain races, e.g., a local contest or a primary with no real issues. Mailings can also be counterproductive.[e]

The candidate's scheduling and media utilization are so important that they will be discussed separately. As party structures become less relevant with the ascendancy of the independent voter, media oriented scheduling and creative

---

[e]The hotly contested election for the Fifth Council District in Los Angeles, held May 27, 1975, is instructive. The candidates were Frances Savitch and Zev Yaroslavsky. Mrs. Savitch's campaign flooded the district with computer-"personalized" mailings. Since these mailings were endorsements over the signature of assorted elected officials, they supported Yaroslavsky's theme that Mrs. Savitch was the establishment/machine candidate. Also, since so many types of "personal" letters were sent, each with similar type face and format, the "personal" effect of the letters was severely compromised.

advertising become more important. However, for the small, local race, traditional means and direct mail remain important.

Scheduling

Scheduling, like other topics briefly covered in this book, can be the subject of a volume. Even one component of scheduling can be treated as a separate book—the legendary "advance manual" detailing a campaign's scheduling policy and its inventory of instructions for the advance man whose job it is to make every campaign foray a success.[f]

The value of scheduling is enhanced by research. Survey and political research indicate where a candidate's likely strength is. Data, briefings, and input provided by local leaders suggest possible appearances correlated to issues. Finally, research can discover fairs, conventions, community and service group conferences, and a multitude of other opportunities.

As an art scheduling requires creativity to reconcile conflicting criteria and demands and to invent or exploit opportunities. The schedule must simultaneously provide sufficient candidate exposure to his supporters to maintain morale and motivate volunteer and financial assistance and maximize the time available to reach and convert uncommitted and switchable voters—either by direct appearances or through media related events. These include news conferences, one-on-one interviews with reporters or correspondents, editorial board meetings, television and radio tapings and live shows, preparing television and radio spot commercials, etc. Even the media oriented schedule must still satisfy other demands—meal and nonmeal functions, public and private meetings, ethnic and nonethnic groups, etc. As events are modified or altered to suit strategic guidelines or generate media coverage, the creative genius of the imaginative schedule is evident. In accomodating a last minute opportunity or in revising travel plans, in turning a reception into a dinner event, or a dinner speech into a brief "dropby" at a reception, the scheduler's judgment and persistence are required to search out every alternative use for the candidate's time.

Scheduling is a science because precision is required to satisfy adequately seemingly conflicting demands. The candidate must have time to research and read, confer with his manager, strategy committee, researchers, key financial supporters, scheduling aide, attend to limited correspondence and other nonpublic candidate functions. The competent scheduler understands that privacy, rest, relaxation, and family time are as important components of the candidate's schedule as public events.

[f]These manuals are often condensed versions of comprehensive Presidential advance manuals, which are usually too detailed, especially regarding security references, for most campaigns. Using these manuals experienced advance men can within a few days train aggressive volunteers. Former Nixon campaign advance man George H.C. Lawrence specialized in quickly training such volunteers to become advance men for campaigns.

Scheduling cannot be a creative art unless its mechanical role is fulfilled. The most original visual idea cannot be consummated unless the details are handled. The media oriented scheduler can work with the aggressive press secretary to time a newsworthy appearance to exploit a major news event, but unless all the laborious, methodical, and seemingly mundane chores are done, a triumphant event can become a fiasco. Any scheduling secretary must answer the basic questions (Table 7-11) about the candidate's schedule. The campaign using an advance team to personally "check out" appearances must be even more precise.

Modest campaigns may have limited personnel to follow up on all details, but ignoring obvious questions is inexcusable—despite low scheduling standards in small campaigns. If the obvious questions (Table 7-12) cannot be answered, the candidate should not be there.

Receptions and meal functions present special problems for the campaign—which seeks to maximize the candidate's exposure to individuals. This standard means meeting many people and shaking many hands at receptions and speaking to a meal function without sitting through a leisurely served meal and lengthy program. As implied from the questions on receptions (Table 7-13) and reception-banquet events (Table 7-14), most candidates spend far too much time at such events, and the time spent is usually poorly utilized.

Similar and even more extensive checklists could apply to a variety of campaign events. Here is a summary of other possible items on a candidate's schedule.

Campaign rally. Preparation for such an undertaking is so extensive that an advance man's manual has an appendix—a "rally manual." Outdoor events are more challenging than indoor events, but both require major planning, especially to turn out adequate crowds.

Shopping center visits. These may be combined with a campaign rally. In any case, the projects are complex, often involving girls in decorated uniforms passing out literature, possibly a band, as with a rally, and a great deal of volunteer backup. Like many campaign events, legal questions involving the selection of a location, possible trespass, etc. must be resolved.

Walking tours. These can be highly successful in populous areas, especially at certain times of day. For example, a noon rally at the Federal Building at Wall Street in New York City has an automatic draw of 5,000 people because of the location and time: serious technical questions must be resolved, such as sound. The walking tour, as implied with the Wall Street example, may culminate (or begin) with a rally.

An example of a typical problem encountered in a walking tour is poor advance work in briefing staff. Because they surround the candidate, they prevent him from being seen and discourage average citizens from approaching him to shake hands.

Table 7-11

Sample Questions from a Scheduler's Checklist[a]

1. Has each item on the proposed or final schedule been reviewed by appropriate people in the campaign and approved by the tour or schedule director? Has any controversial item been reviewed by both the manager and candidate?
2. Is the schedule complete, specific, and detailed, and is it rigorously accurate?
3. Does the schedule include each item? Is each item carefully described?
4. Does the schedule include the exact sequence of events (e.g., the Invocation, Pledge of Allegiance, National Anthem, etc.)?
5. Does the schedule include the individual responsible for each item (e.g., the person giving the Invocation, the person leading the Pledge of Allegiance, etc.)?
6. Does the schedule show the exact location of each event? For example, does it show the name of the place, the precise location, the floor of the building, the name of the room, etc?
7. Does schedule show appropriate telephone numbers so candidate and entourage can be reached, and will telephone numbers apply at time of day or evening in which event is being held? Have telephone numbers been tested for accuracy?
8. Who will oversee schedule to keep it moving, i.e., to keep it on time? For example, who will make sure that each speaker or person on the program does not consume more than the allotted time?
9. Has each person on the program, or each person responsible for a part of the program, been thoroughly briefed on his or her responsibility? Does each person know how much time is alloted for his segment?
10. Does the schedule show *arrival* and *departure* time for each segment of the candidate's movement (airport arrival, airport departure, hotel arrival, room arrival, room departure, banquet room arrival for reception, banquet room departure for ballroom (dinner), etc.)? Does the schedule show destination after each departure?
11. If the candidate is accompanied by his staff or others, are these names shown at such points in the schedule?
12. Does each entry on the schedule, if for a new location, specify the change in location; if a new telephone number is relevant, is it shown?
13. After the schedule has been made final, do all parties know what the *final* schedule is, have they been briefed on all changes, and is everyone proceeding on the basis of the same schedule?
14. Is the final schedule final: does it show all changes that have been made?
15. For each time listed on the schedule, and for each amount of time estimated to be consumed by each phase of the schedule, are the time listed and the time to be consumed realistic and precisely accurate?
16. Does the schedule have built-in flexibility to allow for "normal" delays, i.e., does the internal schedule provide time for handshakes and goodbyes, autographs, photo taking, etc?
17. Does the candidate understand each item on the schedule and its importance, does he feel comfortable or at least accept the necessity of each item? Have any commitments been made, or is there any danger of commitments being made, in his name for his time, that do not represent his intentions or desires?

[a]The larger campaign using advance men would delegate many of these questions to them.

Table 7-12
Obvious Questions from a Scheduler's Checklist

1. Who invited the candidate? When? Who responded from the campaign? When?
2. Who confirmed the invitation and the details? When?
3. What is the *purpose* of the event? Who is the host? Who is the sponsor?
4. What type of event is it? Breakfast/lunch/dinner? Reception? Picnic? Parade? Conference or meeting? Rally?
5. Who else is involved?
6. What local person or which two persons will accompany the candidate, take the responsibility for introducing him, etc. during each phase of the schedule? Do these people know and understand their responsibilities? Will they be distracted?
7. In a small meeting, has an attendance list been supplied? Is the list annotated (e.g., corporate, union, or group identification)?
8. In a small meeting, such as a small meal function, cocktail party, fund-raising conference, is there a stated purpose? Do those invited know the purpose? Even if the program is informal, is there a program? Does the host know his responsibilities? Does the host know the duration of the event, the scenario or program, will he begin and end it on time?
9. What is the exact and verified location, day, date, and time of the event?
10. What are exact and verified traveling instructions, plans, and directions?

Table 7-13
Sample Questions from a Reception Checklist

1. Is the reception before the event and not after?
2. Is the reception by invitation only? Is there a price of admission for the reception? Will there be solicitation for funds at the reception? How? What about plans for follow-up solicitation? (If before a dinner, see below, is reception open to everyone who attends dinner?)
3. Is there more than one reception, e.g., a VIP reception and a general reception? What are detailed attendance figures, capacity of rooms, etc.?
4. Who (which person or two persons) will circulate with the candidate, making sure he meets as many people as possible and his time is not monopolized by any one person? (It should be host, co-host or someone prominent who knows most of those attending; they should not be distracted from this responsibility.)
5. Will there be any speechmaking at the reception? If so, what provisions have been made for microphones, introducing the candidate, the order of the program, briefing each speaker, getting the crowd's attention, timing the candidate's remarks at the peak of attendance, etc.?
6. Will the candidate arrive during the latter half or latter third of the reception and use his limited time efficiently, meeting as many people as possible, or will he be forced to be present for a longer period of time or for the entire reception, spending more time than necessary to circulate (if he were properly circulated by a two-person team)?
7. How will attendance at the reception be controlled to limit it to those invited?
8. Is reception open to press? If now, why not? Has news policy been authorized and cleared by campaign news division? What about press photographers?
9. Will there be a professional photographer? Will there be many requests for photographs? From candidates desiring a joint picture or endorsement? Do requests for photos need to be screened? Does number of photo requests suggest need for setting aside a separate room for photo taking, allotting a short time on schedule for photo-taking session? If so, will everyone be ready, in the order scheduled, to have their photos taken?

Table 7–14

Sample Questions from a Reception/Banquet Checklist

1. Have arrangements been made to end any planned reception in time to transfer guests to meal function? Is candidate staying for banquet or leaving for another commitment? When will he leave? How will this be done gracefully? Do hosts know candidate's plans, does group understand or will hosts explain candidate's early departure?
2. Will reception be ended by public address system, hostesses circulating and moving people into the ballroom or banquet room, chimes sounding, lights going on and off, or . . . ?
3. At what point prior to the end of the reception will the bar close, e.g., fifteen minutes before, to assist in ending the affair?
4. How long will it take to move people from the reception to the dinner and for them to be seated? What percentage of the crowd will have moved in that time, and will this interfere with the planned starting time for the banquet?
5. What is the arrangement for taking tickets at the dinner? Do people have to wait in line? How long will that take? Who and how many people will be taking tickets? What about last minute ticket sales?
6. What will be the attendance at the reception, at the dinner? What price? How many tickets were sold? By whom? Is this a reliable figure? What about last minute arrivals at the door?
7. Will rooms be chosen and settings planned so that the event appears to be a capacity one?
8. What about arrangements for the press and a press table? Have all press problems and arrangements, e.g., for television cameras, microphones, etc., been cleared with the press division?
9. Have arrangements been made for prompt serving of the entire meal? Will there be successive serving of each course, without interruption? If an invocation is given before serving, will the clergyman be prepared? Does the program require the dais to march in before dinner can start; if so, will they be prepared, is there an assembly point, someone in charge, etc.?
10. Has time been accurately estimated for the serving of the dinner? If a buffet function, have all problems, e.g., queues, number of servers, etc., been checked out?
11. If the program is long, has it been cut down? If it is still long and cannot be changed, has consideration been given to starting the dull and routine portions, e.g., multiple introductions of party workers, party club chairmen, et. al., during the serving of the meal?
12. What is being served? Will candidate have time to eat? What would the impact be if he ate and worked in the suite and arrived just for the speech?
13. Will liquor be sold during the meal? Wine? Will this delay the schedule and the clearing of tables?
14. Who is master of ceremonies? Does he have program under control? Will it start on time?
15. Will tables be cleared before candidate speaks? Or at end of evening? If former, how long will it take? Or, will tables be partially cleared, and dessert and coffee placed down before he speaks? Are there contingency plans to put candidate on, even if serving is late? Under unusual circumstances, has consideration been given to putting the candidate on first, so he can get to another event the same evening? Has the maitre d' been briefed? The banquet manager?
16. Is a podium needed? What kind is being used? Is lighting required for the podium?
17. What about sound system? What kind? Is it adequate? Has it been checked? What about directional microphones, etc.?
18. Is banquet formal, black tie . . . ? What about dais: black tie, white tie?
19. Who will sit at head table? Has candidate been briefed on list of dais or head table? Has he been briefed about attendance at reception?
20. What time will the candidate leave the event? Is this time absolutely reliable and valid? Do hosts know this?
21. If the candidate has to leave banquet early to go to another event, to catch a plane, to go to hotel to sleep, etc., do hosts know this? How will this be explained to crowd?

Banquet events. These could be for the political party, the campaign, a private organization.

Receptions. These can be held in conjunction with a banquet, or they can be separate. They can be part of the campaign, or the candidate can be a guest. They can be VIP or less exclusive, fund-raising or get-acquainted. If fund-raising, they can require a price of admission, or be free, with funds raised during or after the reception.

Merchant campaigning. This store-to-store campaigning is useful only in smaller campaigns, unless it is used to get media coverage for a larger campaign.

Local forums. Exposure may be the reason for appearing at a forum of the Kiwanis or Lions or some other community organization; press coverage may be another. These groups often include many opinion molders, community activists, and, sometimes, uncommitted or switchable voters.

Commuter stops. Like other types of campaigning, this method is irrelevant in some parts of the country, essential in other parts.

Door-to-door. This could be the most important method of campaigning for the candiate in a minor race; it is irrelevant for any candidate for statewide or national office, often irrelevant for candidates for Congress. In any of the latter cases, it may be used for *media* coverage.

Factory visits. Like any other type of campaigning, this method is useful for meeting a particular constituency. Walking tours and early morning and shift change visits enable the candidate to shake many hands and also utilize the symbolic importance of the visit. Clearly, factory visits, like other scheduling alternatives, are useful both in themselves and as media events.

Coffee hours. These intensive, small groups are only relevant in Congressional or smaller campaigns.

Other events. Examples include appearances at sporting events, exhibitions, rallies of other organizations, meetings of local, regional, state, or national conventions or conferences, ethnic and religious groups, visits to colleges, high schools, senior citizen homes, hospitals, parades, etc. These events should always be judged by the dual standard of their intrinsic worth and their media orientation. Specific media events, e.g., editorial board meetings, news conferences, tapings, news availabilities (news conference without prepared statement) occupy a prominent place in any well-constructed campaign schedule. Also, the many nonpublic components of the schedule, especially interaction with the manager and staff, and the candidate's private time, cannot be compromised. The candidate's time to be alone, to read, prepare for debates, and relax with his family is carefully planned and precisely scheduled to be minimized, yet adequate, so remaining time can be maximized.

Since every minute is important, many candidates are scheduled in five- or ten-minute blocs. Presidential candidates are scheduled even more closely. Because the efficient schedule minimizes travel time to maximize exposure time, the candidate is moved around rather quickly. For the candidate to be as rested, relaxed, and alert as possible, given the intensive schedule, the scheduler or advance man maintains a checklist of travel questions (Table 7–15) and lodging questions (Table 7–16).

Scheduling is a detailed, time consuming, and demanding task in the political campaign, not merely because of the standards required for *excellence,* but

Table 7–15
Sample Questions from a Travel Checklist[a]

Travel—example: automobile (minimum information)
1. Have arrangements been made for automobile(s) and driver(s)? Checked?
2. Is automobile acceptable, e.g., four-door standard size, noncompact, American-made, etc.?
3. Is driver competent (preferably, off-duty policeman or capable volunteer)?
4. Is there a driver and roster of passengers for each car, especially for a motorcade? Is candidate's car limited to driver and three passengers? If not, why the exception?
5. If there is a need for police escort, is it marked or unmarked? Blinking light? Blinking light with siren? Is this essential to schedule and worth the trouble?
6. Have arrangements been made for rapid, unblocked automobile passage into and out of events, and for necessary easy-access, special parking during events?
7. Will drivers be ready for immediate departure, i.e., have automobiles in place and ready to move *before* scheduled departure?
8. Have all automobile routes in the schedule been charted and mapped out, optimum route selected, alternate routes considered and ready for contingency? Has actual route been driven and timed under comparable traffic situation?
9. Does luggage need to be transferred from one car to another? Will it be done during events, so as not to consume time?

Travel—example: airplane (minimum information)
1. Are reservations made, tickets purchased? Alternate reservations made? Has special VIP treatment been secured to expedite entry, exit from airplane, luggage handling (avoid checking), parking, etc.? Who will meet airplane? What is method of communication if there is a delay?
2. Example—if a private plane is used: Do you have following information: type of plane, description—coloring, identification number or marking, name of pilot, co-pilot, number of passenger seats, list of passengers, luggage capacity, cruising speed of plane, air miles for each leg of route, departure and arrival times, expected time of trip, name of airports or airfields to be utilized, precise location of relevant terminal, section of airfield, gate, possible traffic conditions at airport, etc.? Is private plane being used the most efficient considering distance and airfields available for landing relative to ground location of event?

---

[a]These questions are examples of those on a checklist to assure that the candidate and staff move as expeditiously as possible.

Table 7-16
Sample Questions from a Lodging Checklist

1. Even if the candidate is not staying overnight, is there a private room for him to relax, refresh, work, write, telephone, confer privately?
2. If a hotel or motel room is unavailable, does every event have a "holding room" for such contingencies?
3. If the candidate is a male, has the advance man determined the location of the closest men's room during each phase of the schedule? If the candidate is a female, or the spouse of the candidate will be present . . . etc.?
4. Is there a holding room, despite the fact that the schedule does not allow time, just to be on the safe side, in case time opens up and the candidate needs a room?
5. What kind of suite is reserved? Are staff rooms adjacent to the suite? Do they conform to the advance manual specifications?
6. Will the hotel not give out the candidate's room number or connect calls? Which staff room will get queries to the hotel desk?
7. Will the candidate and staff be preregistered? Will the staff be given their keys and the candidate's aide the candidate's keys before they arrive at the hotel? Are the rooms billed in advance? Checked out in advance?
8. Does the schedule list the correct name, address, and telephone number of the hotel? Does the headquarters know the exact room numbers? Does each staff member know the room numbers of other staff members?
9. Do accommodations for the press follow instructions in the advance manual? Are press accommodations, billing to their media outlets, etc., checked and verified?
10. Will luggage be packed for candidate and staff if they lack time to do so? Will it be loaded into automobile in advance of departure?
11. Have special arrangements been made for late room service, early room service? What about double-checked wake-up calls, in case hotel forgets?
12. Will candidate's suite have his favorite beverages, daily newspapers of host city?

because the schedule is constantly changing and being updated. Because the scheduling division must spend so much of its time, in any campaign, at any level, in (a) processing invitation requests; (b) researching invitations and preparing recommendations; (c) accepting invitations and following through on details and correspondence; (d) telephone arrangements and details on tickets, billing, reservations, etc.; and (e) liaison with media, political committees, and other facets of the campaign, it delegates the actual leg work of planning and confirming the plans of events to the advance team.

The advance team does not accept or reject invitations, although advance men may suggest modifications of the contemplated schedule (adding events, dropping events) or ways to get publicity in an area. It is the scheduling division which, based on criteria set forth by the campaign, makes those decisions. This is usually done by a committee composed of the ranking person in scheduling, the tour director or schedule director, the campaign manager, and some others. In certain cases, the candidate may be asked for counsel or decisions. Initially, he authorized the committee to accept certain kinds of invitations in his behalf.

This section, in its general discussion, has omitted two important areas. First, what kind of formula can be used to determine roughly allocations of time? Second, how does scheduling relate to media, generally, and in terms of

details? The model that will be presented to answer the first question also relates to the media—news and advertising; hence, the model will be presented in
the media section. The second question will be also briefly covered in the media
section.

Advance Work

Advance work, like scheduling, will be treated here briefly. The advance
man or woman's responsibility is to make the planned schedule the real schedule.
Although advance work is often associated with maximizing crowd turnout, the
advance man is concerned with all details. He never feels his job is completed
because, as a seasoned professional, he is always on alert, relentlessly pursuing
each component of the schedule. Although he is apprehensive and nervous that
something might deviate from plan, he projects calm assurance and confidence
around the candidate and press. He always seems in control of the situation,
and he usually is.

The most seasoned, competent advance man can only make the best of a
given schedule. He can suggest modifications and even improvise at the last
minute, but his constraints are defined by the campaign's scheduling philosophy
and its choice of events. For example, if the scheduler ignores the principle of
concurrent scheduling, i.e., scheduling overlapping events so that the candidate
has no "dead" time between activities, the advance man can only make the best
of a poor schedule. The difference between a consecutive schedule and a concurrent schedule (Table 7–17) is emphasis on the candidate, not on the event.
In concurrent scheduling, the candidate maximizes briefing time, rest and
relaxation time, and public time. The schedule is intensive without being needlessly prolonged, and the candidate enters each event when activity or turnout
is at its peak. Multiply the block of time in the example throughout the day,
and the impact of just this single principle is obvious: given properly constructed
schedule blocks, the advance man can *enforce* those blocks; conversely, if the
local hosts propose a consecutive schedule, he can modify it to a concurrent
schedule. A summary of the advance man's responsibilities follows.

Detail.   The advance man has checked out every single detail.

Physical Advance.   The advance man has physically "advanced" the candidate's routes and actions; he has driven the route, visited the hotel suite, the
banquet room, the news conference room, etc. Everything is checked according
to exhaustive criteria and specifications. The advance man has seen to it that
local volunteers have specific responsibilities for each phase of the schedule,
e.g., one person is in charge of photo taking, another person is in charge of
assembling the head table, etc.

Table 7–17
Concurrent Scheduling[a]

Poor schedule	Concurrent schedule (briefing provides additional details for candidate)
4:45 Candidate arrives at hotel and in suite	4:45 Candidate arrives at hotel
5:00 News conference begins	4:50 Candidate arrives at suite (time to shower, shave; skim evening newspaper; re-read briefing material on visit, city, evening, local reporters; rest time)
5:30 News conference ends; return to suite	
6:00 Attend reception	6:00 Oral briefing by press secretary and advance man on schedule, local reporters, questions likely to be asked, etc.
6:30 Go to ABC room for 10 minutes of photo taking with local candidates	
6:45 Return to reception	6:05 Advance man departs suite to review room for news conference; verifies everything still proceeding smoothly and in readiness for 6:15 news conference
7:00 Reception ends; head table forms	
7:15 Enter dinner in procession	6:15 Candidate and press secretary enter for news conference (no statement; just brief questions; text of evening speech already distributed) or press secretary enters five minutes prior
Rest of evening schedule omitted.	
	6:35 Estimated time news conference concludes
	6:40 Candidate joins reception (in-progress from 6:00, official time of public invitation); candidate escorted by . . .
	7:00 Candidate departs reception for photo-taking session in . . .
	7:10 Candidate departs photo-taking session for head table formation (50 feet away, in . . . corridor)
	7:15 Head table enters dinner in procession

Notes on the Concurrent Schedule
1. The candidate is given a large bloc of time, uninterrupted for what he must do. (4:50 to 6:10 vs. about 4:50–4:55 and 5:35–5:55; or 80 versus 25 minutes.
2. The news conference is already so late in the day that the 6:15 time will not jeopardize any deadlines; the speech text having been given out earlier.
3. While the news conference is on, the reception has already started.
4. The candidate enters the reception when the crowd is at its peak, and he is efficiently escorted to meet as many people as possible.
5. The candidate leaves the reception for the photo-taking session; those to be in the photos having been assembled during the last few minutes of the reception. While the photo-taking occurs, the head table is assembled.
6. The candidate arrives, joins those assembled for the head table procession, and enters.
7. Candidate is better prepared, better briefed, less fatigued.

[a]This single important scheduling principle has great impact in maximizing the advance man's labor.

Maximum Turnout. The advance man has arranged for the maximum crowd turnout by utilizing the strategy and tactics suggested in the advance manual, with its array of crowd-building techniques for any event.

Media. The advance man has placed special priority on any facets of the schedule that affect the media: advance texts, their hotel rooms, the news conference, telephones, typewriters, press table at dinner, local background, etc.

Schedule Maximization. The advance man has a "bag full of tricks" to maximize the schedule. For example, all events have "standing-room only" crowds because the advance man always arranges for a room too small for the anticipated crowd, especially in terms of the number of seats set up. Thus, news coverage inevitably refers to "packed house" or "overflow crowd." These events are characterized by contrived spontaneity.

A campaign can be rated from one to ten to measure the degree of thorough scheduling and advance work:

1. *Amateurish scheduling.* There is no formula for allocating the candidate's time; let alone handling details.
2. *Poor scheduling.* There is some kind of formula but inattentiveness to detail.
3. *Basic scheduling.* There is a basic recognition that the candidate's time is divided into three major blocks: breakfast and morning, lunch and afternoon, dinner and evening; a set number of days and hours over the course of the campaign, and that these must be allocated. But the criteria for accepting invitations are insufficiently established; the details are poorly handled.
4. *Good scheduling, poor details.* Good scheduling formula, efficient operation with well-established scheduling criteria, lack of attention to details.
5. *Good scheduling, good detail work.* The criteria are established and implemented well, with attention to details.
6. *Good scheduling, good detail, heavy media orientation.* The schedule is oriented for maximum favorable news coverage with emphasis on visuals to draw television cameras. "Advancing" is done on the telephone, because the campaign lacks advance men.
7. *Good scheduling and detail work, heavy media orientation, light advance.* An advance man provides a basic check of all details by visiting the area once.
8. *Medium advance.* The advance man makes two trips into the area, one days or weeks before the candidate's visit and the other just prior to the candidate's visit. As in light advance he stays on the scene until the candidate departs.

9. *Heavy advance.* At least two advance men are used; two, possibly three trips into the area; no detail is left to chance.
10. *Presidential.* This is the highest standard of advance work and includes Secret Service security precautions.

Regardless of the level of the campaign, and whether or not an advance team is used (and whether it is professional staff or volunteer staff), the key to the scheduling operation is the following set of criteria.

1. There must be a formula or a set of rules for accepting and rejecting events, and the schedule must be media oriented.
2. There must be a scheduling secretary, a scheduling director, or a tour director to administer the operation.
3. Ideally, there should be an advance team to furnish backup for details, assure crowd turnout, and supply additional input on structuring *creative* events (which often deliberately appear "unstructured," e.g., a visit to a drug rehabilitation center to "rap" with rehabilitated addicts).
4. The scheduling, advance, and press divisions must combine efforts to supply typewritten and oral briefings for the candidate so that (a) he knows about the area, the schedule, the rationale for it, the people he will meet; (b) he has material to include in his speech, with references to the area, the VIPs, local humor, etc., and the relevance of campaign issues to the area; (c) he knows about the local media, individual journalists, etc.

This review of scheduling and advance has been necessarily brief. For a small campaign, the personnel resources may permit limited detail work and no advance work. Nonetheless, the formula for scheduling must be based on certain explicit critera (Table 7-18). As these criteria are reconciled, schedulers must use tact and diplomacy as they firmly and graciously turn down invitations that do not satisfy the campaign's high standards.

Media

The news media set the campaign's tone not only by reporting what happens but, by the effect of reporting on the campaign's momentum. Not only do the media affect momentum by implying that the campaign is going uphill or downhill; their superiority as a communications vehicle for marketing the candidate suggests that he should be speaking to the media audience, not to the auditorium audience. When George McGovern triumphed at the 1972 Democratic National Convention, the television image was not well-received in middle America. The candidate himself had an opportunity to try to overcome the

Table 7-18

Criteria for Accepting Invitations—a Typical Listing

1. Balance between geographical divisions of the constituency
2. Balance between media markets
3. Balance between committed-partisans and uncommitted-switchables
4. Balance between different ethnic, nationality, racial constituencies; different age constituencies, blue collar vs. white collar, business vs. labor, etc.
5. Aggregate attendance at event: how many are expected at event, how reliable is estimate, how many have heard candidate before?
6. Is invitation important to volunteer leaders, financial contributors, VIP endorsers, party leaders? How important?
7. Is it recommended, endorsed and approved by local volunteer leader?
8. How is candidate doing in area, and what effect will this event have?
9. When was the last time the candidate was in the area? When will he be there next? Does the invitation compromise the intended *frequency* of visits, i.e., too many in too brief a time, followed by too long an interval for next visit?
10. What time of day is event, and how does this fit in with rest of day's schedule? What will he be doing before and after, and will this event have insufficient benefits to warrant the expenditure of energy and compromise the success of more important events?
11. What day/date is the event, and does this day/date compromise events before and after? Does it interfere with private time, family time, research time, preparation for a debate, rest time before a taping of television spots, etc.?
12. Previous history: has campaign disappointed people in this area before by turning down invitations due to conflicting dates, or changing dates? Have people who are extending the invitation proved reliable in the past?
13. Does the invitation blend in well with the travel schedule? How much travel time is required? At what cost? At what times of day or night?
14. What kind of event is it? Dinner? Lunch? Reception? Parade? Rally? How much work will it require on the part of local campaign people? Could their time be better spent?
15. *Important:* What is the media orientation of the event? Will it get good coverage? Why? How? Can it be modified for media coverage? Can it be tied in to release of a statement or position paper or tied-in with an endorsement, a news conference, an issue?
16. What will the event do, if anything, for media coverage, fund raising, boosting the morale of volunteer workers, rewarding local initiative, satisfying the candidate, influencing the undecided, converting the switchable voter, reaching particular groups, etc.? What, specifically, will event do in each of these areas, e.g., how much money will it really raise?

caricature of the convention, but poor planning and convention infighting postponed his acceptance speech until 2:48 A.M.—losing most of the television audience.[10]

The number of television sets jumped from 53 million in 1960 to 88 million in 1970; today, the figure is higher, equivalent to 97 percent of American households having at least one television set. Forty-one percent have two or more sets, and 68 percent have a color television set. Television has become the main source of news for most Americans. Nielsen estimates illustrate television's pervasiveness as an advertising medium: weekly viewing activity is 24 hours and 54 minutes for men and 31 hours and 52 minutes for women.[11] Thus, advertising has impact because so many people watch television so much. Its unique sight/sound/motion combination penetrates even the most apathetic households.

The circulation figures for print media, though dwarfed by television, are very important. Print media is essential in reaching many voters, independent of television *and* reinforcing television. In certain races, print media is critical. Clearly, its audience, i.e., readership, may figure prominently in a race in a small district. Its readers include opinion molders, leaders, and activists. Print media, even more than television, can at the early stages of a campaign set the tone for the coverage during the duration.

News and advertising are separate, but inseparable. They must emphasize the same theme—the same issues—for the campaign to market the candidate successfully. Any advertising that treats the same issues raised by the candidate in the print media (news) and on television news will have its credibility enhanced; similarly, issues featured in news coverage will benefit from the consistent repetition factor provided by advertising.

News. Three essential, related elements must be present in any campaign press operation: personal relationships, professional competence, and a media oriented schedule. The press secretary and his staff must be personable, patient, and persistent. The press secretary walks a tightrope between candidate, campaign manager, and campaign, on the one hand, and the news media on the other. He is protector/advocate for the candidate and campaign and servant/advocate for the press corps. He is tactful and accommodating, even when he skillfully withholds information not directly sought.

The press operation must be service oriented. Journalistic skills required include writing, editing, and proofreading; basic familiarity with reporters' customs and habits; an understanding of determining news, leads, features; comprehension of release times, on-the-record, off-the-record, background, attribution-only, and other critical definitions. Finally, the press secretary must be an *administrator* who can manage the press operation at the same time he generates and provides news, features, news releases, schedules, background material, photographs, etc.

Media oriented schedule. For a national or statewide campaign, a media oriented schedule aims to penetrate two or three media markets per day by in-person appearances in those media markets. Consider the candidate running for office in California: perhaps the campaign's objective for a given day is to penetrate both the Los Angeles and San Francisco media markets. The wire services might cover *statewide* his appearance in either city, if he says or does something newsworthy; but he wants television news coverage, typically correlated with presence in a media market. In other words, to get film coverage of the candidate on the evening news in a given city, the candidate will probably need to be in that city. Therefore, the staff programs a morning visit to a place in Los Angeles that will "draw press," e.g., the site of a recent police shootout with militants, an excellent setting for the candidate's new antiriot proposals.

Then, he scurries to the airport, flies to San Francisco to deliver a luncheon talk with a strong lead to draw the camera crews (e.g., TV assignment editors were stimulated to attend by a briefing indicating newsworthy items in the talk).

One way to understand the high standards of a media oriented schedule is to study a model schedule (Table 7-19).

The example illustrates the need to service the traveling and local press. A news distribution system includes simultaneous release of information from the main and regional campaign headquarters and also from the candidate "on the road." Distribution mechanisms include hand delivery, mail, telecopier, telephone, audio fees. The most emphasized and costly distribution mechanism— the mail— is as necessary as it is outdated. Releases are printed and they do inspire some news and editorial coverage. They also provide background material and affect media attitudes. Releases of the candidate's schedule are critically important to the media. However, the mail is a slow means of distribution. For a statewide campaign data processing can provide the greatest number of media listings and the widest mail distribution (Table 7-20).

As the mailing system implies, media servicing is so important that the most charismatic, charming press secretary is no substitute for creating news and helping the media cover it. The determination of what is news, how to define a lead, how to frame rapid response statements for the candidate to react to news developments, etc. are all within the province of political journalism. The press secretary is a combined journalist/administrator/political technician who operates within a servicing context (Table 7-21).

Press secretary.   The importance of distribution and servicing in the press operation suggests that being a press secretary is much more than "drinking with the boys." The imaginative news or press secretary capable of designing "unstructured" visuals to exploit current, newsworthy events is still the exception, not the rule.[12] The successful press secretary must be both a competent journalist and an amiable socializer, but unless he is also a service oriented administrator, he will be a failure.

A major campaign problem is limiting the number of spokesmen to one— the press secretary. Even the campaign manager should defer to him or notify him before accepting an interview. The candidate, although he speaks for himself, should always be accompanied by the press secretary or his surrogate. Local volunteer leaders should be discouraged from issue oriented releases that might compromise the campaign theme or its consistency. One method to keep local volunteers active in securing publicity without compromising consistency is the *form news release.* Although the volunteers are prohibited from issue oriented releases or must secure authorization prior to their release, they are given form releases (Table 7-22) as guidelines to inspire their own releases. In many cases they need only substitute the name of their county or committee and local chairmen in the form draft, then retype the draft for duplication to the comprehensive local media list supplied by the headquarters.

Table 7–19

Media Oriented Schedule—Sample Day Based Upon an Actual Campaign Schedule from a Major Senate Campaign (*Note:* This schedule is abbreviated just to show key items; *also,* it includes what transpired, in addition to the planned schedule.)

Schedule	*Interpretation*
7:00 Candidate greets workers arriving for 7:15 shift at manufacturing plant.	Television station WXXX has crew for filming to use on afternoon and evening and late evening news, and for shipment to downstate station for evening use.
7:50 Live appearance on "Morning Show" WXXY-TV	Interview format on a television show aired each day; this gets coverage on a second station in the city.
8:30 Breakfast meeting with union leaders in hotel suite	Photographers for various union publications are on hand to take photos; campaign photographer takes photos for use in special statewide mailing to union leaders.
9:35 Candidate tape records a 20- and a 35-second excerpt from statement at his news conference on foreign policy.	This "feed" is given to the campaign headquarters; then it is sent, by telephone, to radio stations throughout the state; it is an "actuality"—as if they had a reporter covering the news conference at 10 A.M.
10:00 Candidate visits office of nationality/ethnic group protesting their status in Communist country; he talks with them, issues statement on foreign policy related to the problems they have mentioned; then answers questions from newsmen at news conference.	Photogenic story—backdrop is at nationality headquarters; scenes of candidate talking to protestors and pickets; then he makes statement, without notes (statement that he stands by is distributed as background for questions) WXXY-TV covers this; also two other television stations; WXXX is undermanned and relies on the early morning story to cover itself; the traveling media send out dispatches, and the wire services and others use the statement, which has been mailed and hand-delivered throughout the state during the morning (mailed day before to arrive today).
11:00–12:00 Candidate rests in suite.	
12:15 Reception for business leaders at Chamber of Commerce luncheon 12:30 Luncheon—buffet 1:00 Speech	This is not much of a television story; there is no new speech; the candidate relies on notes used for prior business-economics oriented groups; however, several proposals he has made in other cities are repeated, and a news release with these proposals is given out and extensively covered by the business editors of both papers, especially his proposals for dealing with unemployment, which are modified to include reference to local problems and statistics.
2:00 Editorial board meeting with publisher and editors of one of the city's two major newspapers	This on-the-record session will result in a large photo spread in the Sunday newspaper, together with a major story based on the lengthy interview; at the same time, the interview provides background for the editors, puts them on a personal footing with the candidate, and may result in an endorsement.

Table 7–19 (continued)

3:15 Rest in suite. Campaign headquarters calls to report a news development has crossed the UPI ticker which requires candidate's comment.	Statement quickly drafted and approved; it is distributed to traveling press, and by telecopier around the state and hand-delivered; candidate records voice feed, and campaign advises AP and UPI to put on statewide ticker that an audio feed is available for radio stations of the candidate's reaction, by calling . . . ; statement in textual form is put on wire service.

During the day, the candidate's visit is saturating radio station news; radio newsmen had been present at various events during the day.

5:00 Private interview with correspondent from *Wall Street Journal*	An important private interview, which will result in a major story for the candidate, the subject of a 2-day field tour by their roving political reporter.
5:40 Tape interview show for television station	Show will be aired Sunday afternoon. (Also, a segment of the show will be "lifted" for use in tomorrow's evening news.)
6:20 Live appearance at same station	Live appearance on the evening news This station had been unable to cover day's events.
7:00 Private meeting with key organizers in area	
7:30 VIP Contributors reception— private	The last media event of the day is the radio talk show; the traveling press has filed its dis-
8:00 Banquet, speech, etc. 9:45–	patches; the candidate has saturated the local press with materials. As for the talk show, it
10:15 Appearance on high rated radio talk show	is one of many talk and interview shows scheduled for the candidate's appearance at convenient times during the campaign.

Servicing and Bias.   Competence and technical proficiency directly confront media bias. For example, media information kits tailored to each type of media (e.g., color slides for television, variable size photos for newspapers, glossy photos for offset newspapers, mats for letterpress, etc.) facilitate media coverage. These and other methods provide the media with supporting materials, just as proper servicing, especially giving journalists timely and accurate campaign schedules, increases the probability that the campaign will be covered thoroughly, accurately, and fairly. Fairness is often related to thoroughness and accuracy, which reflect the quality of servicing. Bias also reflects the journalist's attitude, which will be more favorable if he is properly serviced. The campaign can only determine the existence of bias by isolating every technical/servicing variable to answer the key questions. For example, did the journalist have information? Did he have it on time? Did he have schedule in advance? Was material genuinely newsworthy, i.e., was it current, topical, and new? Rarely can an evaluation of media bias be made on the basis of coverage of a single story; there

Table 7–20

Data Processing Coding for Media Reference and Mailing Lists—Recommended Program Suitable for a Major Statewide Campaign

Objectives
1. To list every relevant media outlet and provide for constant updating of information. Each time a journalist writes about the campaign, telephones the headquarters, attends a news conference, etc., his name, address, telephone number, media outlet, and related information are added to the media list.
2. To distinguish between media personnel rosters stored for reference and computer printout and individuals on the mailing list.
3. To provide for computer printouts on printout sheets and on color coded 4 × 6 cards; thus duplicate reference systems can be provided for county chairman and advance men, with listings for particular counties or zip codes.
4. To provide for printing names and addresses directly onto envelopes or on labels used for large envelopes.
5. To provide that all mailings are to specific individuals, identified by title or position, where appropriate, and media outlet.
6. To provide for targeting special mailings to specific media, e.g., a special weekly mailing to weekly newspapers, which are exempted from the many mailings sent to daily newspapers.
7. To provide substantial background information on each media outlet, e.g., call letters of station, network affiliation, wire services and columnists used by each newspaper, "talk" or interview shows on each station, circulation figures for each newspaper, etc.

Basic Codes (for listings or mailings of particular kinds of media)
1. Television—in-state (commercial and educational)
2. Radio—in-state (mainly AM stations with newscasts)
3. Daily newspapers—in-state (inclusive, modified for joint names, i.e., someone with two titles)
4. Weekly newspapers—in-state (inclusive, modified for chain operations)
5. Bureaus and correspondents—in-state location (AP, UPI, wire and news services, newspapers, networks, etc.)
6. Ethnic media—in-state
7. Out-of-state (political columnists and writers, VIP friendly media and contacts, correspondents from in-state publications and stations who are covering Washington, etc.)

Geographical Codes (for listings or mailings by area)
1. Zip code
2. County (e.g., to mail an announcement of candidate's upcoming visit to county to all relevant media; or produce working list, including background information)
3. Additional, as relevant (e.g., by media market)

Attitudinal Codes (for internal use only, not on computer printouts)
1. Favorable-partisan, partial to party or to candidate
2. Competent, fair, professional
3. Neutral/average/unknown
4. Incompetent, unpredictable, possibly unfair
5. Unfavorable partisan, antiparty or anticandidate

are so many possible explanations that the press secretary can only form a judgment on the basis of a trend.

Proper servicing would probably limit the number of assertions of media bias. Inept campaigns with poor servicing are precisely characterized by charges of bias against the media. When not justified, these charges may become a self-

Table 7-21
Typical Checklist to Service Journalists. The press secretary must be assisted
by scheduling and advance divisions.

---

1. Do all media have biographies, photographs, information kits on the candidate? Both
   local media and travel media? Is information updated? Is schedule updated?
2. Does everyone have the schedule, did they receive it in time to use the information, have
   they been queried for special requests, have their requests, initiated or solicited, been
   fulfilled?
3. For the traveling press, has everything been taken care of—hotel reservations, billing
   instructions, airplane reservations, seats at banquets, press tables, telephones, typewriters,
   survey of local bars, automobile transportation to campaign events, etc.?
4. Have advance texts been given out? Excerpts of texts? News releases? Is the dateline of
   the story correctly stated on the news release? Are releases being distributed by hand
   simultaneously around the state? Did they arrive in the mail the day of, or in some cases,
   day before, the event, with the proper hold-for-release date or, if appropriate, immediate
   release instructions?
5. What about physical facilities? Does set-up of news conference room conform to advance
   manual specifications, e.g., size, number of chairs, aisles, electrical outlets, room tempera-
   ture, etc.?
6. Have arrangements been made to provide access to news conference room to press, and
   not to supporters and others who might take up seats, interfere with questions, applaud,
   or otherwise interfere with the smooth functioning of the event?
7. Has special consideration been given to television? Lighting? Platforms? Backdrops for
   color and photographic quality? Backdrop of candidate's name and photograph?

---

fulfilling prophecy. Fair coverage is best achieved by giving media a media
oriented schedule, offering technical assistance, servicing, and complete background information, and showing a positive, cooperative, and cordial attitude.

Momentum. The discussion of media would be incomplete without reference to momentum—that seemingly intangible movement, normally upward but
possibly downward. When one campaign has upward momentum and the other
has downward momentum, the two movements reinforce each other. The first
campaign is not only converting the undecided, but the second campaign is
losing support to the undecided or to the first campaign. Some strategists can

Table 7-22
Form News Releases[a]

---

1. *Form A:* Local organizing committee forms for campaign
2. *Form B:* Committee formed and local chairman named
3. *Form C:* Prominent citizen endorses candidate
4. *Form D:* Headquarters opens
5. *Form E:* Candidate is coming to area
6. *Form F:* County chairman urges something (related to campaign issue)
7. *Form G:* County chairman urges . . . (related to another issue) etc.
8. *Form H:* Volunteers flocking to campaign

---

[a]These news releases indicate the format and exact wording, including quotations; they only
require local names and references.

"feel" or "sense" momentum, but there are some tangible indications (Table 7-23).

The strategist seeking to orchestrate the political campaign needs the assistance of a press secretary with a keen sense of timing. His promotional effort is a carefully developed, graduated publicity drive, paced and timed to draw increasing attention, yet not peak too soon. Because each campaign and candidate is unique and poses different public relations challenges, the publicist must evaluate their strengths and weaknesses and tailor his strategy to maximize the strengths and obscure the weaknesses. The skillful publicist produces momentum so powerful (Table 7-24) that the weaknesses are forgotten.

Although the momentum example refers to both the news media and advertising, the former offers two distinct advantages. First, it is free. Second, it has greater credibility than commercials. The campaign that refuses to allocate resources to hire talented staff to create visuals and then pleads it needs funds for television advertising is incompetent. Because visuals generate news coverage worth at least as much and probably more than commercials of equivalent time duration, the salaries of the staff and related expenses to generate visuals must be measured by attaching a monetary worth to visual events (Table 7-25).

Advertising.   Political campaign advertising, no matter how creative, does not exist in a void but must implement a strategy. Any advertising must be unified, first in its theme, selection, and treatment of issues, second in its technical aspects, logos, colors, typography, photos, etc. The advertising must be designed to reach both aggregate numbers of people and particular subgroups targeted for special attention. Issues must be utilized selectively, and the ad-

Table 7-23
Indications of Momentum

---

1. The morale of the campaign staff is good and getting better.
2. The candidate is in a good mood, taking his work in stride and looking forward to the results on election day.
3. Crowds are getting bigger at campaign events.
4. Contributions are increasing—the number of them and the average amount; fund raisers find it easier to raise money; some people are giving a second time.
5. Invitations are coming in faster, and they are better quality.
6. The mood in the opposition camp is restless and nervous, and the opposition candidate is apprehensive.
7. Mail volume increases, telephone calls to the headquarters increase, the number of citizens volunteering to work in the campaign increases.
8. Any formal polls taken show an upward trend (the candidate's showing is better than in the last poll taken).
9. The candidate is receiving more coverage from the media, and the coverage, whether favorable or unfavorable, has one thing in common: it takes the candidate seriously, perceives him as viable and sees victory as a distinct possibility or, as things get better, predicts victory.
10. There is a pervasive feeling of teamwork, and individual goals really seem to be fused with the campaign's goal of electing the candidate.

Table 7–24
Momentum and the Public Relations Build-up[a]

Timing	Purpose
1. Settle on campaign theme, slogan, colors, choice of issues; review findings of survey; set out basic course; hire staff, get initial funding; put together massive, up-to-date media list; get background information on key media people, make initial contacts.	To get everything in readiness without alerting the opposition; without generating premature news coverage that *could not be sustained* and would run the risk of collapse. Like a roller coaster the build-up would go up quickly, only to fall down thunderously—unless there were substance to keep it alive.
2. Have the candidate visit groups of editors and editorial boards, accompanied by campaign manager and press secretary; visit is low key; get some TV and other coverage in each city; make it clear campaign begins Labor Day; also cement local organizational and finance contacts. Because candidate is impressive, put him in with as many top editors, columnists, etc. as possible	To orchestrate build-up; to convince the senior editors and top columnists that campaign is viable, candidate is confident of victory, there will be adequate funding, and an organization is being put together; also to get many favorable syndicated columns and photo-interview spreads for future reproduction and to increase name identification. *To take candidate from 'viable' and 'taken seriously' to 'could actually win'; a view first popularized among the elite media, later by the follower media.*
3. Arrange exposure in *Time, Newsweek, U.S. News, Wall St. Journal, Washington Post,* etc. Begin television advertising early—3 weeks before campaign officially begins.	To get a head start; to start the ball rolling; a calculated risk at this point, since financing is still uncertain; this is the *Take-off Stage* of the campaign; the goal is, by Labor Day, to have the candidate considered totally viable and taken seriously.
4. Get everything in readiness for Labor Day; all staff hired, advance/scheduling operations in readiness; schedule one visual after another for opening two weeks, even one visual each day, as long as in different media markets. Campaign has started (Labor Day).	To have a credible campaign opening, characteristic of a serious, well-funded, well-organized campaign; the coverage during the first week will make or break this campaign; it must appear to be professional, the crowds must be big, the schedule must be on time, the traveling press must be impressed and write good accounts . . . .
5. Increase television spending; intensify issue discussion, emphasize repetition of 3 main issues; pressure advance men to increase crowds even more; when attacked by opponents, *Do not go on defensive;* continue circulating massive media coverage reprints throughout state to reinforce journalists who believe the campaign is going places. Polls show candidate climbing.	To keep and build upon momentum; to exceed the performance during the first two weeks; to use the advertising curve (upward, graduated to higher spending levels each week on television) to support the momentum and increase the rate of climb in identification; increase visual awareness of voters and thereby affect crowd attendance; begin to corner voters who are "up for grabs" and get them committed to affect early polls. Pundits say candidate really could win.
6. Begin using the most effective ideas for visuals, schedule visuals more frequently, in more cities; enlarge candidate's schedule; increase advertising budget to whatever funds will allow in hopes that more will come in the final weeks. The	To make the momentum so powerful as to begin to cut away at opposition strength, as well as getting the undecided; also, to go from *viable* and *possibly might win* image, after having been *taken seriously,* to *can win, may win, will win;* thereby, to

Table 7-24 (continued)

public opinion polls finally show candidate is in the lead.	stimulate more and more support of the bandwagon variety, and really start money coming in.
7. *Climax*—The advertising budget slopes upward as much as it will go, money keeps coming in; the opposition camp is depressed and apprehensive.	To peak the campaign at its height.

Note: The publicity/promotion campaign first cultivates editors and editorial boards, publishers, key columnists, respected political writers; then, these senior journalists and "pundits" are used to propagandize the masses of journalists who are followers, and not leaders, in reporting trends; eventually, as the bandwagon sweeps the journalistic community, it becomes more and more fashionable to say that this campaign is heading upward and could win; the mood of the journalistic community and print and electronic media reporting really begins to make its impact on the people. *Thus,* (1) elite media and editors; (2) regular journalists; (3) voters . . . *in that order.*

[a]The public relations/publicity/promotion aspect of momentum is depicted by these abbreviated examples extrapolated from an actual statewide political campaign.

vertising should emphasize the same issues that are given attention in the candidate's speeches, his campaign brochures, his "visuals," and news conferences. The dual uses of media, "free" news and "paid" advertising, should not be at odds with each other or neutral but complementary and reinforcing.

Technical competence in advertising does not substitute for strategy. Although Barry Goldwater would not have won the Presidency in 1964 even with a superb strategy, his advertising was characterized by tactical maneuvering disguised as strategy. The strategy board met for hours each week but discussed mechanics. The finance chairman did not understand the nature of revenue, spending, and advertising curves and insisted that the important television spots booked for the last ten days be cancelled due to lack of funds. When money came in "like confetti" in late October, it was impossible to reinstate the spots that had been pre-empted. The campaign's record surplus in money has been compared with its record deficit in votes and offices lost.[13]

Strategic advertising establishes the campaign's general theme; *tactical* advertising is precise targeting of newspaper advertising, television spots, radio commercials, etc. Tactical questions are best resolved once the strategy is established. Although advertising is only one element in the campaign's marketing plan, which can include precinct work, adjunct committees, informal communications network, news coverage, direct mail, etc., advertising is most closely associated with understanding the consumer-voter's motivation (needs, drives, wants, urges, motives) and perception (his interpretation of stimuli) to induce him to behave in a certain way, i.e., vote for the candidate.[14] The importance of altering "learned tendencies" is applying communications psychology to the voter-consumers with full recognition of their apathy and prior viewpoint, rather than permitting the strategist's preconceptions, and biases to interfere with either what to say in advertising (strategic) or how to say it (tactical).

Table 7–25
Monetary Worth of Visual Events

For simplicity, consider a large city media market.

	Cost for 30-second spot	Cost for 60-second spot (Average cost for spot adjacent or in evening/late evening news)
Station A (CBS)	$2,500	$4,000
Station B (NBC)	2,000	3,500
Station C (ABC)	1,800	3,000
Station D (Ind.)	800	1,500
Station E (Ind.)	600	1,000
Station F (Ind.)	300	500

The minimum value of the television time generated by a news event equals:

Step One
Number of seconds of coverage on a station ✕ Rate per second, figured as average of per-second rate for 60 and 30 second spot at that time of day or evening
. . . for the total number of stations.
(A + B + C . . . for each station that covered candidate.)

Step Two
If all of the coverage was neutral, i.e., straight reporting of the candidate's appeal on a particular issue (presumably, a priority issue in his campaign), multiply the dollar figure by 1.5 to allow for the added credibility given to television newscast. If the coverage was somewhat negative, allow for some subjective value for those stations. If the visual was particularly effective in dramatizing one of the primary campaign issues, multiply by 2.0; if the coverage varied from station to station, use a different factor, ranging from 1.0 to 2.0 for each station.
Unless the visual was poorly designed by the campaign, or the station is biased, the factor should be at least 1.5, and not below 1.0. Only extreme bias and a visual that proved totally counterproductive, e.g., a confrontation resulted in which a pedestrian out-debated the candidate, would result in a *negative* or *minus* factor (which would mean the campaign, in effect, lost money as a result of the visual, or the coverage on a particular station; even so, some monetary allowance would have to be made for name recognition).

Step Three
When many creative visuals are used over a period of weeks to dramatize one issue, or two or three or four issues, the cumulative effect, over time, tends to make each individual visual worth more than originally estimated. The whole is, in effect, greater than the sum of its parts. The reinforcement and repetition value of news coverage, with its credibility factor, of associating the candidate with an issue, is also worth something in dollars. Each such repetition should increase by *10 percent* the value of all prior visuals on the same issue. For example, consider the following (for simplicity, rate per second will be derived from 60-second rate = $3,000 for station C).

A. One visual on candidate touring drug rehabilitation center and attacking drug abuse:
Use one station in example
(Station C, 40 seconds; factor of 1.5) $3,000 valuation placed on coverage of first visual ($2,000 ✕ 1.5)

B. Second visual shows candidate conferring with narcotics agents after a raid, then issuing a statement blasting judges for leniency for heroin pushers selling "hard stuff" to teenagers:
Use same station as example (40 seconds; factor of 1.75) $3,500 valuation placed on coverage of second visual ($2,000 ✕ 1.75)

Add: 10% of ($3,000 + $3,500) = $650 additional
or $3,000 + $3,500 + $650 = $7,150

228

Table 7-25 (continued)

C. Assume a third visual shows candidate listening to drug education class at junior high school and, afterwards, calling for expanded drug education programs:

Use same station as example $4,000 valuation placed on coverage of third visual
(50 seconds; factor of 1.6)   ($2,500 × 1.6)

New total = $7,150 + $4,000 + 10% of ($7,150 + $4,000)
= $11,150 + $1,115 = $12,265

Note: Although the commercial offers a package, with more emphasis on name and extremely favorable content, the *news* spot is more authentic, more credible, more accepted. It should be worth as much, or more, than the commercial rate.

> Opinions, attitudes, beliefs, and prejudices are terms which in general refer to learned tendencies to respond favorably or unfavorably to certain situations, persons, or objects. All involve the positive or negative classification of stimulus objects in relation to the individual's goals, or the making of value judgments that accept or reject stimuli.[15]

In contrast to survey and marketing research used to determine, measure, and describe the voter-consumer market, advertising research evaluates the impact of advertising messages on the market. At the minimum, it identifies the number of times individuals are exposed to the advertising message. Advertising research utilizes psychology and survey research to quantify *qualitative* reactions: how deeply voter-consumers are moved, persuaded, or motivated by being exposed a certain number of times to advertising messages. In the end, the only test is quantitative—how many will vote for the candidate.

The political campaign's advertising program includes the seven components common to any commercial advertising campaign. These include: (1) an analysis of the market situation, (2) determination of advertising objectives, (3) advertising budgeting and control, (4) selection of advertising media, (5) creation of the message or copy, (6) coordination of advertising with other promotional and selling methods, (7) evaluation of the results. In particular, the advertising budget is influenced or formulated by similar methods. The *competitors-expenditure* method suggests the impact of the opposing candidate's advertising expenditures. The *what-can-be-afforded* method is the single most important determinant of advertising in a campaign. The *unit-of-sale* method relates advertising to where the votes are. The *percent of sales* method relates advertising to a percentage of the overall campaign budget. Sound political advertising is based on the principles and methodology of effective commercial advertising.[16]

Structure. A final problem to be considered in this brief overview of advertising is the structure of the advertising agency. The basic argument for creating an in-house agency is the considerable savings in advertising commissions and mark-up fees on contract work. For example, for a statewide campaign in New York or California, total media billings for a candidate could easily exceed one million dollars. The commissions alone on these billings would be $150,000 (15 percent of billings). The most notable and successful use of an in-house agency was the "November Group" created for the Committee to Re-Elect the President.

There are disadvantages to forming an in-house advertising agency. First, money saved in commissions is not all savings. The in-house agency must use part of the gross savings to hire media buyers, traffic managers, and other skilled personnel. It also has telephone, postage, shipping, travel, and other expenses, including some expenses the agency would not bill to the campaign, such as subscriptions to Nielsen reports or other information services. Second, the in-house agency lacks the creative expertise of a professional agency, unless it recruits advertising professionals (as was done in the November Group). Third and most importantly, the in-house agency composed wholly or substantially of campaign personnel may lack the outside perspective required to provide the candidate, manager, and strategy committee with proper counsel. If the in-house agency is owned by individuals who are also part of the campaign, they may be in conflict of interest—urging more advertising to net more commissions for the agency. Because the campaign is so brief, commissions generated by substantial media billings are very remunerative for the time devoted to the account. Hence if an in-house agency is not formed, the campaign should seek some negotiation to limit the 15 percent commission of the advertising agency chosen.

Targeting. Any political campaign advertising must resolve three central questions—how much to spend, which kinds of media to employ, and precisely how the advertising message should be targeted. The level of campaign (national, state, local, district) and the strategy often dictate choice of media.[g] For example in a Congressional race in a rural area, highway billboards may achieve excellent name identification. In contrast, billboards are a cost ineffective media expenditure for a statewide race more suitable for television.

Unless newspaper and radio advertising is highly targeted (e.g., ethnic newspapers and radio, special sections of newspapers, "traffic time" radio in the days before the election to get out the vote) it fails to satisfy certain criteria adequately. These include numbers and kinds of voter-consumers reached, pos-

---

[g]For example, in 1972 the Republican Senatorial candidate in North Carolina faced an uphill battle and was expected to lose. However, the candidate, Jesse Helms, took the offensive. Weekly newspaper ads linked Helm's Democratic opponent with his party's 1972 presidential nominee, George McGovern, who was certain to lose North Carolina. The advertisements directly confronted the Democratic Senatorial candidate's bland image and put him on the defensive. Helms was not tarnished with the problems associated with negative campaigning, because his television spots were entirely positive, and the campaign ended on a positive note following the newspaper advertising.

sible effect on uncommitted or switchable voters, change in candidate's name and issue identification and retention factor. This does not preclude issue oriented advertising specifically targeted to a readership or listenership clearly identifiable by desired demographics. Nor does it include newspapers or radio technically superior to television in reaching voters. For example, newspapers or radio may be the most cost effective means of reaching voters in part of the state reached principally by out-of-state television, which would include a high wastage factor in any television advertising purchased. Similarly, weekly newspapers might best reach a consumer-shopper readership including many housewives interested in inflation, the quality of public education, or some other issue suitable for the particular campaign.

Precise targeting is best achieved by reliance on traditional advertising and political data. The former is needed to secure the best buys in time and space. The latter guarantees that the best buys quantitatively (i.e., cost per thousand readers or viewers) are the best *qualitative* (i.e., cost per thousand readers or viewers with certain demographic characteristics).

Media market budgeting.   Political boundaries do not coincide with media market boundaries. Media markets rather than political boundaries should be used for both scheduling and advertising in statewide and national campaigns. For example, in a statewide race in New York, the candidate's scheduling and advertising in New York City should reflect the expected contribution in votes to the candidate's anticipated statewide total from the New York City *media market,* not merely New York City. Similarly, it is the Los Angeles media market, not Los Angeles, that is the unit of analysis. In each case the candidate's appearances in the city and advertising budgeted for the media based in the city but reaching outside the city limits reflect the relative importance of the areas included in the given media market.

The ideal overall scheduling formula for a statewide or a national campaign is designed to achieve certain levels of exposure in different media markets. Such exposure may require one appearance in a media market, two appearances, or many appearances. The appearances may utilize different events and emphasize different issues. But the objective is programmed exposure, and the principal measuring device is television news exposure. In the case of multiple appearances, i.e., visits to a media market, the *frequency* of such visits must be carefully considered, as it relates to visibility, repetition, and momentum, and as it relates to the probability of news coverage; e.g., all things being equal, coverage is more likely if a candidate's three visits to a city are spaced apart by two-week intervals, then if all three visits are within a short period of time, say ten days.

Importance of Television.   The relevance of television for political campaigns has been cogently explained in a classic memorandum (Table 7–26) written by advertising executive Daniel J. McGrath. Although McGrath ad-

Table 7–26
Importance of Television

Excerpts from Memorandum	Comments on Memo
1. As the business and political communities have demonstrated on innumerable occasions (from Procter & Gamble thru Nixon, the Kennedys and Richard Ottinger) *television is, by many orders of magnitude, the most powerful, effective medium ever known.* Procter & Gamble, acknowledged as the preeminent marketing firm in America, invests *over 99%* of its advertising funds in television. Newspapers, radio, magazines and outdoor *combined* obtain less than 1% of Procter & Gamble's media budget. There is scarcely any mass marketer engaged in selling directly to the consumer who does not direct upwards of 80% of his advertising budget to television.	This basic fact of advertising/marketing is lost on many political campaign strategists who insist on allocating advertising dollars to radio, newspapers, billboards in pre-established ratios.
A professional prepared message which can be placed *quickly* and frequently in virtually every home in America and which embodies sight, sound and motion in engaging formats (every theatrical device is employed) is, quite simply, light years ahead of whatever medium is in second place.	Unless other media are specifically targeted, they are, all things equal, inferior to TV.
2. . . . All of Jim Buckley's high intelligence, warmth, candor and integrity register extremely effectively in television interviews. In filmed commercials which have been carefully produced, Jim Buckley can be presented in a galvanizingly effective manner.	The method of presentation can be adjusted to bring out the best in a given candidate.
3. Television offers to Jim Buckley's candidacy advantages which are absolutely not available to Messrs. Ottinger and Goodell. Consider the following facts:	These specifics are for the Buckley constituency; another candidate might have different specifics peculiar to his constituency; targeting could be achieved by advertising on different television programs.
A. The median age of the voting population is about 44 years, i.e., 50% of the voting population is over 44 and 50% is under 44 years of age.	
B. 95.3% of all households own at least one television set.	
C. The putative Buckley constituency (or, at any rate, a great portion of it) is (1) 35 to 40 years of age and over, (2) with middle annual income . . . and (3) with a modest formal level of education	These statistics only clarified the base, which suggested that persons with similar attributes were more probable to support Buckley, hence should be contacted. Actually, *many others* would also have to be contacted.

D. As a person tends to be . . . older, in the middle-income bracket . . . , equipped with a high school education (or slightly less) . . .
    [*Note:* This is the demographic definition of the apparent "core" Buckley constituency.]
    . . . He (or she) tends significantly to watch television more. This person is thus, significantly, more easily and less expensively reached than the younger, the better-educated and the more, and less, affluent members of the community.
    [The memorandum then reported on weekly viewing habits by age/sex/household income/education of head of household (source: A. C. Nielsen). Statistical tables followed.]	

232

Table 7-26 (continued)

E. It is axiomatic in television that most advertisers seek to concentrate their television messages against the 18–34 and 18–49 age groups because these groups with growing families are the most prolific consumers. These are the groups to whom Messrs. Ottinger and Goodell must appeal. Conversely, the networks and stations have difficulty selling advertisers time in and around programs which attract older audiences (e.g., . . .)	In order to win, the Buckley campaign had to reach a certain number of these people also.
. . . Ottinger and Goodell must compete for essentially the same kind of program and spot availabilities. Moreover, the type of availabilities which Goodell and Ottinger must seek will be precisely those which most of America's mass marketers will desire. Therefore, Ottinger and Goodell will have to pay rate card	
The Buckley campaign, on the other hand, will have many spots available to it which will reach the potential Buckley voter . . . . Expenditures in television *per dollar* will almost inevitably generate significantly more "potential voter impressions" than will either Ottinger's or Goodell's	The key concept is "potential voter impressions" rather than "potential impressions." More precisely, "potential prime voter impressions" might be used.

Source: These excerpts are from memoranda written by Daniel J. McGrath, a New York advertising executive who has been associated with the author in formulating media strategy for political campaigns. The excerpts are reprinted with the permission of Daniel J. McGrath. The memoranda comprised part of the strategy synthesized and implemented by an inhouse advertising agency, the Agora Group, Philip Nicolaides and Patrick Nagle.

dressed himself to a specific campaign, his principles and arguments in the excerpted passages apply to any statewide or national campaign, and possibly to lower level races as well.

McGrath's emphasis on using media markets to allocate television dollars (Table 7-27) was coupled with his own bias favoring television. Diverting media funds to nontelevision media would, he felt, diffuse the campaign advertising effort. It should be reiterated that with some modifications the ratio of the number of votes contributed from a media market over the projected statewide total should also determine the percentage of the candidate's total time scheduled in that media market. Additional key points following from the example include:

Spots. The length should be 60, 30, 20, or 10 seconds. Ideally, shorter commercials can be "lifts," i.e., derived from the longer commercial, to (a) reduce production costs and (b) maintain unity of theme and reinforce prior spots.

Spending curve. In the Buckley case, McGrath recommended that 80% plus of all media spending be concentrated in the last 30 days prior to the

Table 7–27

Media Market Allocation—Additional Excerpts from McGrath Memoranda

Excerpts from Memorandum	*Comments on Memo*
. . . Television, as an instantaneous and ubiquitous medium, is quickly capable of reaching most of the population with frequency. ("Reach and frequency" are, of course, the indispensable goals of any media plan.) As an example of television's reach/frequency effectiveness, $100,000 will put a Buckley commercial message in 85%–90% of all New York State TV households an average of 5.0 times.	The key words for virtually any statewide or national political campaign: 1. instantaneous 2. ubiquitous 3. frequency 4. reach
. . . *A committee of New York State political experts within the Buckley campaign, e.g., . . . , should make estimates of the geographic source of the Buckley vote potential on a county-by-county basis.* These voting estimates would then be laid against a television coverage map of New York State to determine what per cent of available media funds would be spent in each of New York State's eight [sic] discrete television markets . . . . Thus, the committee might determine that while [a] . . . television market has only 8% of New York State's TV households, it can be counted on to deliver 15% of the projected state total vote for Buckley. Therefore, 15% of all media funds would be directed to [the] television market, and so forth	This is the heart of television media market allocation: extrapolate political data to fit the advertising, i.e., television media market data.

election, and that spending within the final thirty days be skewed in favor of drastically higher spending during the final 10 days.

All broadcast dayparts should be employed. Daytime, fringe (early and late evening), weekend, and prime all have different values in reaching particular target groups.

Time buying should be done by professionals. Unlike much of commercial advertising, buying should be done by time buyers who travel to the television stations and negotiate face-to-face with station personnel.

Time buying is highly competitive in September–October. Campaigns geared to the general election compete with the start of the new television season, which puts tremendous emphasis on technical proficiency in estimating how new shows will fare with ratings, and in competing with commercial buyers.

The extrapolation of political data to be used in conjunction with advertising data has been assumed. In the Buckley campaign example, psephologist Arthur J. Finkelstein projected or forecast "reasonable vote totals" for Buckley, broken down by county. As the political data was converted to media markets,

Table 7-28
Information Sources for Voter Projections

---

1. Intuition

2. Recent surveys

3. Statistical bases
   a. 1968 Presidential results, by county and percentage
   b. 1968 Senatorial results, by county and percentage
   c. Correlation between Nixon and Javits votes, by county
   d. Relationship between Buckley percentage per county vote versus Buckley percentage statewide 1968 (Buckley had run as a symbolic, i.e., nonserious, Senate candidate in 1968)

4. Nonstatistical measures
   a. Candidate's home districts
   b. Geographical proximity to weak or strong areas
   c. Publicly expressed or widely conceded local (Republican) support for Buckley

---

Note: Any such forecasts are *not* present alignments of voting patterns, but forecasts or predictions. Such forecasts assume an aggregate number of registered voters, a percentage voter turnout, and either constant voter turnout in each county, or some qualification that may affect the results. This summary from the Buckley Senate race (1970) is based on the work of Arthur J. Finkelstein. However, analogous and more timely information can be utilized for any given election.

some counties were included entirely in one media market, other counties were apportioned to two media markets. Generally, each media market included several or even many counties. Without a detailed methodological discussion, the summary of information sources for Finkelstein's voter projections (Table 7-28) suggests the kinds of information needed in other campaigns.

The objective is weekly allocation of television spending dollars. The allocation remains the same each week unless new data suggests a revision. The actual total dollar level may change but would still reflect the formula distribution in terms of percentage of the total for each media market. Unanticipated weaknesses in certain sections of the state may suggest redeployment of television dollars (Table 7-29). It is important to remember that the estimated (potential) vote for the candidate within each television market, divided by the statewide projected (potential) vote determines the percentage of media (television) dollars allocated to each media market.

Targeting is accomplished by the following steps:

1. Combine the survey research and political data with extensive media data, e.g., Nielsen publications.
2. Examine television programs that other data indicate are likely to be watched by certain constituencies (classic examples included Polish voters watching Lawrence Welk, Italian voters watching Dean Martin).
3. Check television programs for issue identification (classic examples include inflation/food costs on daytime television, ecology spots for nature/con-

Table 7-29
Revision of Media Market Formula

Six weeks before the election, new surveys and data pinpointed weaknesses in certain sections which strategists wanted to correct. Thus, the weekly television spending, at that time $50,000, had to be reallocated.

Television Media Market	Original (%)	Change (%)	$50,000 Weekly Budget (dollars)
Albany/Schenectady/Troy	7%	7%	$ 3,500
Binghamton/Elmira/Ithaca	2	3	1,500
Buffalo	7	10	5,000
Burlington	1	1	500
New York City	66	62	31,000
Rochester	6	6	3,000
Syracuse	8	8	4,000
Utica	2	2	1,000
Watertown	1	1	500

servation television shows, law and order/drug abuse spots during the crime shows).

4. Once profiles and characteristics of voters *already* supporting the candidate are clearly identified, seek to reach viewers, listeners, or readers with the same or similar characteristics. These are most likely to support the candidate.

   a. Define "prime voters" as the most likely to vote for or convert to the candidate; measure the cost of advertising (e.g., a television spot) by the cost per thousand in reaching "prime voters."

   b. Define progressively less probable voters required to expand the sup-

Table 7-30
Allocation of Television Dollar—Diverse Criteria

1. Allocate statewide dollar by media market formula.

2. Consider other criteria:
   a. Television stations (determine programming, ratings, audience profile)
   b. Daytime, fringe, weekend, prime time
   c. Television programs (suitability of particular programs for different issue television spots)

3. Duration of spot (60-, 30-, 20-, 10-second or variations)

4. Cost:
   a. Per thousand viewers
   b. Per thousand viewers qualified by demographic characteristics
   c. Per thousand viewers adjusted to reflect estimate of "prime voter" viewers
   d. Analysis to consider numbers and types of progressively less probable voters watching show

5. Differentiation by issue (percentage of spots devoted to different issues)

port base; determine which media and specific vehicles (e.g., specific television shows) best reach these voters.

c. Stress reaching voters who are more highly probable of voting for the candidate before reaching those less probable.

In sum, the allocation of the media or television dollar must satisfy many criteria (Table 7-30).

Various types of buying methods and negotiating are especially useful in the political campaign. For example, "buying backwards" means buying up time in the last few weeks or few days of the campaign, before the opponent can buy the time, or before a commercial advertiser can buy it. This requires money up front, but it guarantees access near the end. At the very least, time may be held, but as the competition for the time becomes more intense, cash may have to be put up. Other methods are part of the methodology and technology of advertising applied to political campaigns and would require a great deal more space.

8 Decision Making

McGovern's briefing session was held at the Hyatt House with eighteen people present to offer advice. . . .

—Theodore H. White
The Making of the President 1972

Political campaigns characterized by inefficient decision making processes can win only if they are favored by the opposition's incompetence, an auspicious political environment, or other good fortune. In the competitive political environment, skill rather than luck usually is controlling, since the opposition cannot be counted upon to be incompetent. Hence it is valuable to understand the decision making process.

Such an analysis is often prevented by the misconception of judging the campaign's decisions retrospectively by higher standards. It is tempting to second-guess after the campaign is over, when there is time to reflect and ponder over the alternatives, when more information is known, including the results of the decision actually made and the opposition's reaction to it. After the election one can review how the media reacted to a decision. The decision's likely impact on the election can be better evaluated. The real test, however, can never be applied retrospectively but must always reflect the data and information known to the decision maker at the time of the decision.

When a candidate wins, the victors are too preoccupied with celebration to examine past decisions. When a candidate loses, the search begins for scapegoats. Sometimes analysts suggest that a single event marked a turning point (for one or both candidates) in a campaign. The fallacy is that once an event occurs, the subsequent actions and reactions can be held constant. For example McGovern's choice of Eagleton as his Vice Presidential nominee clearly hurt the campaign by adversely affecting the candidate's press coverage, fund raising, staff morale, and his public image. Assume instead that he had chosen a stronger nominee and the "Eagleton affair" had not occurred. The campaign would have been somewhat more competitive *at first*; however, the Nixon organization would have been spurred to a different kind of offensive. Relatively less secure and confident, the Nixon strategists would have modified their strategy, perhaps relying more on television than direct mail, more on confrontation than avoidance. The specula-

239

tion is unimportant; the Nixon strategists would have approached their goal of a record electoral victory by alternative means. Because ceteris paribus (all factors held constant) does not apply, it is unfair to assume the absence of an event and re-evaluate the entire campaign without permitting the opposition the same re-evaluation. If one event were different, an infinite number of actions and re-actions would have been different.

When decisions are analyzed in terms of the information available to the decision maker at the time of the decision, the analysis asks: What criteria did he use? Were the criteria appropriate, well-defined and well-chosen? What was the nature of the environment at the time? Given the environment, information known, and criteria used at the time of the decision, did the decision maker make the right decision?

Principles of Decision Making

Planning and forecasting in a changing political environment are not simple tasks. Political forecasting is inexact and subject to a margin of error. When a turning point has occurred, it takes time to make this realization, time to act on it and, if necessary, to take corrective action. Whatever action is taken, additional time is required for the action to reverberate throughout the campaign. Within the campaign's short time duration, days and weeks, even hours, are precious, and the time required to make decisions, as well as the lag in implementing them, must be minimized. This accounts for our prior emphasis on structuring the campaign in terms of locating where decisions will be made.

The manager and other strategists never have perfect information. The most they can hope to do is to acquire additional information to enable them to make more prudent decisions. Whenever the decision maker searches for additional information, the search costs should not exceed the benefits. A survey costing the campaign $15,000 must provide it with information worth more than $15,000. Also, any search involves a cost in *time,* which partly accounts for the importance of decisiveness in evaluating a manager's ability.

Voter preference in a national or major statewide campaign is a function of many variables, including many uncontrollable environmental factors that indirectly affect voter preference. In simple terms,

$$V = f(E, P, ID, i)$$

where voting preference V is a function of the largely uncontrollable environment E, the support base provided by the candidate's party and organizational base P, the candidate's identification and recognition among voters ID, and his issue orientation i, i.e., voter perception of the candidate associating him with particular positions on a limited number of issues.

In trying to change V, we should look at the variables that can be directly affected. Hence, although we eliminate the environment from the equation, the constraints and opportunities it presents must be studied and understood so we can best affect the remaining variables:

$$V = f(P, ID, i)$$

Past party support is not an infallible guide to the current support base. Voter disenchantment, apathy, and party loyalty are not constants. In addition, the loyalty factor, i.e., the percentage of party registrants who will support the party's candidate in the specific race, reflects party registrants' identification and recognition of the candidate, including their identification/recognition of him as their party's candidate and of the issue orientation: does his choice of issues and does his position on issues enhance or lower his standing with them?

Party registration, to the extent that it implies loyalty, is a stabilizing element. Since certain issue positions taken by the candidate or overall perception of him as a liberal, moderate, or conservative (included within ID in this case) will affect loyalty, adjustments must be made, especially to consider those factions of the party antagonized by the candidate.

If P' is *real* political party support, adjusted for the present (or probable impact of ID, i, and environmental factors like the economy or Watergate), then

$$V = f(P', ID, i)$$

If P' is influenced by largely uncontrollable environmental factors as well as ID and i, which can be influenced, then we can concentrate on ID and i, provided that P' is not radically eroded by the way in which our candidate is perceived. Thus,

$$V = f(P') + f(ID, i)$$

Concentrating on the second half of the equation,

$$V = f(ID, i)$$

This equation merely summarizes the marketing and distribution problem of a national or major statewide campaign. Both identification and issue orientation are a function of distributing the candidate-product to the voter consumer. For the smaller candidates, ID and i are largely a function of in-person campaigning, informal communications networks, direct mail, limited and local media advertising, etc. In cases where party loyalty is high, voter awareness is low, media is insignificant, local races may be decided entirely on the basis of P', which in turn affects what little identification and issue orientation the candidate has. In this case, voters do not really know the candidate, let alone his priority issues and positions on issues. By definition, they are not motivated by the candidate to go to the polls; rather, they are motivated by party and once they get to the polling booth vote for the party's candidate. Merely getting these individuals to vote is the marketing task; in their case, voter turnout is the crucial factor.

In larger campaigns, voters must be able to identify an alternative. Since television is the source of most news for voters and has the most powerful advertising reach, identification is closely associated with the television component of media. Indeed, for the large segment of our population addicted to television, "their political world is in large measure an electronic creation."[1]

For issue orientation, the subgroups that will not vote for the candidate regardless of his position on issues (because they do not like his party, do not trust him, are solidly behind an opponent, etc.) should be written off. These groups are by definition affected by the identification factor. Marginal dollars should be spent on approaching priority subgroups to achieve identification and, if needed, issue orientation.

In sum, marketing discerns (a) those who merely need to be turned out to vote; (b) those who merely need to know who the candidate is; (c) those who also need issue orientation. In the latter cases, the powerful marketing effort actually motivates some individuals to vote because they are so "turned on" by the candidate.

If we accept that

$$ID = f(M)$$

$$i \;\; = f(M)$$

i.e., both identification and issue orientation are (not entirely) functions of media, then by substitution

$$V = f(P') + f(M)$$

We have simply returned to the simplified proposition that voter preference in a large campaign is primarily a function of the political party, adjusted for other influences, and the media. Hence, the lesser role of the party confers a greater role on the media, and the reverse is also true. As P' becomes less important due to voter disenchantment with politics, distrust for established institutions and parties, skepticism of politicians, and the rise in independent voter sentiment, M becomes more important.

If the campaign is considered a marketing organization, every decision directly or indirectly relates to the marketing function. Decisions in scheduling, advertising, and press are more directly related; decisions in bookkeeping or shipping, which are support functions, are indirectly related. Finance decisions reflect the need to raise funds for marketing, which is why net funds, i.e., the revenue after paying the cost of fund raising, are important. Since classical theory suggests that decisions should be assigned to the lowest competent level in the organization, the campaign manager should apply this counsel to his marketing effort. The closer the decision maker is to the marketing activity, the quicker and more responsive the decision can be. The problem is in determining the lowest competent level. The danger exists that the manager, in his quest for close control to assure uniformity and consistency in the market effort, may leave little leeway for decision making at lower levels.[2]

The manager encourages differentiation between creative, judgmental, and unique tasks versus the routine, nonjudgmental, and repetitive tasks. The latter should be delegated as much as possible so that the manager and senior staff can concentrate on management by exception, i.e., pinpointing unique and urgent situations requiring attention. As decision makers seek to influence their subordinates, in delegating and assigning tasks, it becomes apparent that unless human factors are considered, individuals will be unwilling to accept such influence and policy will not be accepted by staff and volunteers.[3]

The decision making model for the campaign, like any decision making model, must distinguish between controllable and uncontrollable factors. The latter includes "the frequent intransigence of society and nature" as well as the *competitive strategies,* i.e., "the competition of rational opponents."[4]

The *risk seeker* prefers risk. The *risk averter* selects the less risky alternative. The person indifferent to risk does not care which of two alternatives he selects.[5] The campaign requires a risk seeker when the campaign is destined for defeat and a risky strategy needs to be pursued for any hope of victory. The risk averter is the more appropriate decision maker for the candidate enjoying a comfortable lead that could be jeopardized by a risky strategy. The manager indifferent to risk cannot equate possible benefits of an action with the risk factor. The decision maker must always consider not only the benefit/cost ratio for any decision, but evaluate the risk factor, i.e., what is the risk to the overall campaign strategy and victory if the action is counterproductive. This requires some probabilistic estimate that the action will succeed.

The principle of *bounded rationality* explains the fallacy of retrospectively judging decisions. Since there is insufficient time for the decision maker to obtain information about all possible alternatives and many factors are outside the decision maker's control, human beings do not try to find the optimum action in a decision problem but define outcomes that would be "good enough." The decision maker cannot indefinitely postpone the need for a decision to search for more information that might change his decision. Otherwise, by the time he gets the additional information, the time for decision is past.[6]

The suboptimization of bounded rationality, i.e., making the best decision with limited information, should not be confused with the suboptimization

when objectives within the campaign conflict. As long as objectives do not conflict, actions to achieve either objective are independent and can be separated.
With dependent objectives, suboptimization means that "the optimization of one
can result in a lower degree of attainment for at least some of the others."[7]

The maximization principles of decision making (Table 8-1) apply to the
campaign's marketing problem—distributing resources (money and time) among
alternative means. The *rule of proportionality* states that distribution of resources between alternative instruments of production is optimum when the
ratio of the incremental change in revenue to the incremental change in cost is
equal for each alternative.[8] In the campaign, resources are allocated optimally
when, all other considerations aside, the ratio of the incremental change in votes
to the incremental change in spending is equal for each alternative or, expressed
mathematically:

$$\frac{\Delta V_1}{\Delta S_1} = \frac{\Delta V_2}{\Delta S_2} = \frac{\Delta V_3}{\Delta S_3} = \ldots = \frac{\Delta V_n}{\Delta S_n}$$

where

ΔV = incremental change in votes, i.e., the number of votes likely to result from
the change in spending, ΔS

ΔS = change in spending and $1, 2, 3, \ldots, n$ represent each of the alternative
spending projects, e.g., television time, radio time, newspaper space, etc.

Since ΔV is primarily a product of the change in identification and issue association, i.e., I and i, then

$$\Delta V_1 = f(\Delta I_1, \Delta i_1), \quad \Delta V_2 = f(\Delta I_2, \Delta i_2), \quad \text{etc.}$$

or the change in the number of votes likely to be received on election day
caused by the spending program is primarily a function of the change in identification and the change in issue association resulting from the particular spending
program.

Thus, if $1,000 in television time is estimated to produce a change in
probable voting strength of 5,000 votes, and an expenditure of $1,000 in news-
paper advertising (all factors held constant, and without specific reference to
advertising content, targeting, or special factors) will produce a change in
probable voting strength of 1,000 votes, the ratio is 5.00 for television versus
1.00 for newspapers. Of course, the ratios are not constant but change at different levels of media expenditure.

Another way of looking at allocation of funds is considering the many
possible combinations of two inputs. For example, what combination of tele-

Table 8-1
Maximization Principles of Decision Making

Maximization Principles	Example of Political Application
1. Choose the objective; specify its dimension and value	1. Victory on election day; 55 percent of the vote.
2. Isolate all of the variables that are pertinent to the attainment of the objective value, i.e., the relevant independent variables.	2. Party registration, voter turnout, candidate's identification among electorate, issue association, media spending, and . . . uncontrollable.
3. Develop the relationships that exist between the independent variables.	3. Examples previously given of conceptual relationship between probable voting strength and actual party loyalty, identification, issue association, media spending.
4. Distinguish controllable variables (which can be part of the strategy) from noncontrollable variables (classifying the latter as either states of nature or competitive strategies).	4. Uncontrollable includes the state of the economy, foreign policy developments, Watergate indictments, budget of opposition candidates.
5. Develop forecasts and predictions for the noncontrollable variables, which should be treated as states of nature. Those variables that have (rational) intelligence behind them must be treated separately by game theoretic methods.	5. The economic situation and the state of the world will be . . . . Hence, the issues of concern to voters will be . . . . The opposition candidate may emphasize the following issues. . . . Financial campaign support will be. . . .
6. Determine whether or not the forecasts and predictions are based on stable processes. This determination can be intuitive, but powerful methods of statistical quality control are available to assist.	6. What is the evidence to support forecasts?
7. Develop the function that relates the independent variables to the dependent objective variable.	7. 55 percent victory assumes 65 percent voter turnout; candidate's *ID* factor of 92 percent, etc.
8. State the restrictions that limit the possible values of controllable variables.	8. *ID* is very difficult to achieve in the 90+ percentile, because of voter apathy and preoccupation with other things, and limits to advertising over time.
9. Choose those values of the controllable variables (i.e., that strategy) that promise to maximize the degree of attainment of the objective, within the limits set by the restrictions.	9. For example, rely heavily on television because print media and radio will not have comparable impact on *ID*.

Source: The nine maximization principles are from David W. Miller, Martin K. Starr, *The Structure of Human Decisions,* © 1967, pp. 34–35. Reprinted by permission of Prentice-Hall, Inc., Englewood Cliffs, New Jersey.

vision and radio advertising should be used to achieve a desired level of identification, issue association and change in voter preference? (Figure 8-1).

In order to make the decision, the decision maker should determine the value of the non-TV components, individually. Also, he must determine if the impact on identification is the same throughout the curve of spending, i.e., does each increment of television time purchased yield the same increase in identifi-

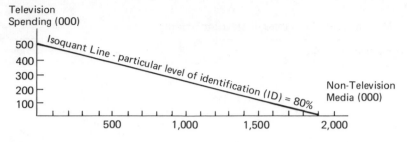

Figure 8-1. Varying Media Inputs.

Note: In this hypothetical diagram, $500,000 of television spending achieves the same level of identification as $1,900,000 of non-TV spending. At any point on the isoquant line, the combination of TV and non-TV achieves the same level of identification, let us say, 80 percent, in this particular large state. (This simplified relationship assumes a constant trade-off between TV and non-TV media throughout the entire range of the curve, an unlikely assumption.)

cation, or does the last $50,000 increment, for example, yield less in identification than the first $50,000 of non-TV spending in radio, newspapers, billboards, etc., or a particular combination?

The overall decision rule that determines the most reasonable way of making a decision is the Bayes decision rule.

1.   List the set of possible outcomes that the state of nature may take on for a period (or periods) in question.
2.   Assign a probability weight to each of the possible states of nature. The probabilities may be subjective weights, though objective information should be incorporated if it is available.
3.   Compute for each state of nature the consequences of the given act. The consequences in certain cases may be in terms of dollars but are more generally in terms of a measure which is called utility, and which incorporates psychological reactions to the monetary gains or losses.
4.   Multiply for a specific act the probability of each state of nature by the consequences of that act and state, and sum these products for all the possible states. The sum is the expected value of the act.[9]

The Bayes decision rule, then, requires multiplying the consequences of each act by the probability of each act, and then adding the products. The act with the largest expected value is the most desirable decision. Other criteria include:[a]

───────────────
[a]These decision making criteria, as well as the conditional value tables and the theoretical approach to conditional and expected opportunity loss and related concepts reflect quantitative methods used in business decision making models. See Harold Bierman,

1. *Maximax.* This criterion chooses the act that maximizes the maximum possible profit, utility (or votes). This criterion ignores possible losses. It would appeal to a campaign going downhill, facing almost certain defeat, and willing to adopt a strategy that, if successful, could win; but if a failure, it could result in a total fiasco.

2. *Equally likely.* This criterion assumes each state of nature has an equal probability of occurrence. However, the decision maker should have *some* idea about the probability of possible events. There is no reason to assume that the most desirable act simply is the one with the most favorable consequences, disregarding probability.

3. *Minimax.* This suggests that the decision maker choose the act with the minimum maximum loss or, alternatively, with the maximum minimum profit. This is a very conservative decision criterion, perhaps embraced by a campaign that is substantially ahead in the polls over the opposition. This strategy is designed to limit the possibility of loss and to not follow any course that could, regardless of the low level of the outcome, result in a loss. It often leads to doing nothing, because doing anything entails *some* possibility of loss. Doing nothing may be a poor decision, because the opposition is doing *something* which could affect the election outcome.

4. *Maximum likelihood.* This criterion only considers the state of nature most likely to occur and chooses the best act for that state of nature. This criterion ignores the *consequences* of all states of nature except the one with the highest probability of occurring. In effect, it ignores the trade-off between reward and risk. If the probability of one state of nature occurring is 0.6, and the probability of another state of nature occurring is 0.4, this criterion would favor the act with the highest profit, utility, or vote outcome for the first state of nature, although other acts might provide a more reasonable trade-off between reward and risk; since, after all, it is possible that the second state of nature may occur.

For example, assume a simplified illustration in which a campaign manager must decide whether to invite the President, the Vice President, or neither to campaign for his candidate two months hence—just before election day (Table 8-2). The event or state of nature that most concerns him is whether the Administration scandals will be or will not be an issue during the latter part of the campaign. Based on the sources of information the campaign manager has in Washington, he has sought counsel on whether there will be new dramatic disclosures, whether there will be any indictments, or whether the scandal has been exaggerated, or indictments will be delayed until after the election. He has concluded that the probability is 0.6 that Administration scandals will be an issue and 0.4 that Administration scandals will not be an issue.

Jr., Charles P. Bonini, and Warren H. Hausman, *Quantitative Analysis for Business Decisions,* 4th ed. (Homewood, Ill.: Richard D. Irwin, 1973), pp. 45–56, 71–74.

Table 8–2

Conditional Values Table and Decision Making

	Conditional Values (in terms of votes)		
Event or State of Nature	Act A: Invite President to campaign (invitation accepted)	Act B: Invite Vice President to campaign (invitation accepted)	Act C: Do not invite President or Vice President to campaign
Administration scandals will be an issue—$P = 0.6$	–50,000	–25,000	0
Administration scandals will not be an issue—$P = 0.4$	100,000	75,000	–25,000

1. *Maximax: Act A,* because campaign could gain 100,000 votes; might appeal to campaign that feels it will lose for certain or near certain without the visit, but that it could win with the visit (if scandals not issue).
2. *Equally likely:* Either *Act A* or *Act B,* because this criterion calls for adding the possible consequences of each act and dividing by the number of possible events. Thus,

$$Act\ A = (-50,000 + 100,000)\ divided\ by\ 2 = \ 25,000$$

$$Act\ B = (-25,000 + 75,000)\ \ divided\ by\ 2 = \ 25,000$$

$$Act\ C = (0 - 25,000)\ \ \ \ \ \ \ \ \ divided\ by\ 2 = -12,500$$

3. *Minimax: Act B.* Since *Act A* could result in a loss of 50,000 votes, that act is ruled out. Yet, under *B* and *C,* –25,000 could result, so either could be pursued, except that *B*'s other outcome is 75,000 versus 0 for *C,* so *B* gets the edge.
4. *Maximum likelihood.* That Administration scandals will be an issue has a probability of 0.6, or the maximum likelihood; given this state of nature, the best alternative is *Act C,* with 0, compared to –50,000 for *Act A* and –25,000 for *Act B.*
5. *Bayesian rule:*
   Expected value of each act is:

$$Act\ A = 0.6\ (-50,000) + 0.4\ (100,000) = \ 10,000$$

$$Act\ B = 0.6\ (-25,000) + 0.4\ (\ 75,000) = \ 15,000$$

$$Act\ C = 0.6\ (0)\ \ \ \ \ \ \ + 0.4\ (-25,000) = -10,000$$

Therefore *Act B* should be pursued.

Note: This is a hypothetical, highly simplified table used for illustration only. The numbers might not be realistic for any given state. Also, it is assumed that a decision on the invitation must be made two months before the appearance. The Expected Value of each act (Bayesian rule), or *EV,* is an important figure which will be mentioned again.

There are three alternative courses of action. (*Act A*) Invite the President (who will accept the invitation). Under any conditions, this will please party stalwarts. But this decision could cost 50,000 votes if the scandals are an issue. (*Act B*) The popular Vice President is also willing to campaign, and his presence would also satisfy the party stalwarts. He is untouched by the Administration scandals, but there would still be some fallout, an estimated loss of 25,000 votes, if he comes into the state and the Administration scandals are an issue. On the other hand, if the scandals are not an issue, he will not help as much as the President. (*Act C*) If neither man is invited in, and scandals do become an issue, the candidate will gain some votes if he exploits his refusal to invite either man in, but he will balance the gains with losses among party stalwarts. On the other hand, if the scandals are not an issue and neither is invited, the candidate will lose the support of 25,000 party stalwarts, who will sit at home, antagonized, because neither the President nor the Vice President were invited into the state to campaign.

The conditional opportunity loss in this case is the amount of votes foregone by not choosing the best act for each event. The conditional loss table for Table 8-2 is as follows:

	Conditional Opportunity Losses		
	A	B	C
Scandals are issue	50,000	25,000	0
Scandals are not	0	25,000	125,000

(These values are obtained by subtracting the conditional value of each act from the conditional value of the best act, given that state of nature.)

The expected opportunity loss (EOL) is the conditional opportunity loss weighted by the probability of the events occurring, and summed for each act. Thus, the expected opportunity loss for *Act A* is

$$0.6(50,000) + 0.4(0) \qquad = 30,000 \ EOL_{Act\ A}$$

for *Act B* is

$$0.6(25,000) + 0.4(25,000) \ = 25,000 \ EOL_{Act\ B}$$

for *Act C* is

$$0.6(0) + 0.4(125,000) \qquad = 50,000 \ EOL_{Act\ C}$$

As noted, the conditional opportunity losses in this simple illustration were derived by subtracting the conditional value of each act from the conditional value of the best or optimum act, given that state of nature. The optimum act if the scandals are an issue is *Act C*, since 0 is better than either −50,000 or −25,000. The optimum act if the scandals are not an issue is *Act A*, since 100,000 is superior to 75,000 or to −25,000. This is consistent with the finding that at these points, *Act C* if scandals are an issue, or *Act A* if scandals are not an issue, the conditional opportunity loss is 0, i.e., there is no loss at the optimum point.

The expected profit under certainty, i.e., the expected votes under certainty, EVUC, weights each profit, i.e., vote item, that is optimal by its probability of occurring.

In this simple illustration, we are dealing with only two alternative *states of nature,* rather than three or four or more, and only three possible courses of action, or *acts.* Thus, in this case, the expected votes under certainty are the product of results for the optimal act for each state of natue times probability of that state of nature occurring.

$(0) \times (0.6) = 0$ Optimal act for state of nature: scandals will be issue

$(100,000) \times (0.4) = 40,000$ Optimal act for state of nature: scandals will not be issue

$0 + 40,000 = 40,000 =$ Expected votes under certainty ($EVUC$)

The *expected value of perfect information (EVPI) is the expected votes under certainty minus the expected votes under the optimum act,* i.e., under *Act B* = 15,000 votes,

$$EVPI = EVUC - EV = EVPI$$
$$40,000 - 15,000 = 25,000$$

Note: EVPI also equals the expected opportunity loss for *Act B.* In other words, the expected votes under certainty must equal the expected votes (by Bayesian rule) for any act plus the expected opportunity loss for that act. As per the Bayesian rule (Table 8-2, Item 5), *Act A* = 10,000, *Act B* = 15,000, *Act C* = -10,000. The expected opportunity loss is : *Act A* = 30,000, *Act B* = 25,000, *Act C* = 50,000, as previously derived. The *EVPI* for *Act B* has already been shown to be 25,000.

$EVUC$ = expected votes (Bayes) + expected opportunity loss
    = $EV + EOL$ for each act

$EVUC_{Act\ A}$ = 10,000 + 30,000 = 40,000 (expected votes under certainty)

$EVUC_{Act\ B}$ = 15,000 + 25,000 = 40,000 (expected votes under certainty)

$EVUC_{Act\ C}$ = -10,000 + 50,000 = 40,000 (expected votes under certainty)

In conclusion, the expected value of perfect information (*EPVI*) is:

1. The expected votes under certainty minus the expected votes under the optimum act; *or*

2.   The expected opportunity loss (*EOL*) of the optimum act.

In both cases, the figure must be the same. In this example, the expected value of perfect information is 25,000 votes.

This formulation is important, because if the campaign had established a ratio of dollars spent per votes, i.e., the *rule of proportionality,* then it would know the trade-off between dollars and votes, at a given aggregate level of expenditure. For example, if survey research could provide perfect information (which, of course, it cannot), the information would be worth no more than 25,000 votes.[b] Should the campaign spend $10,000 for the survey? I.e., should the campaign spend forty cents (40¢) per vote? Not if $10,000 spent on television will yield 50,000 votes (i.e., 20¢ per vote); yes, if the $10,000 will only get 10,000 votes if utilized in newspaper advertising (i.e., $1.00 per vote).[c]

Additional Topics

Survey research is the campaign's marketing research. Modified to include volunteer interviewers, especially telephone "tracking" surveys," its high costs can be reduced. In any case, the cost in time and money is significant. Its gross value is the difference between the expected value of the decision, given research, and the value of the decision without research. The net value is the gross value less the cost of the survey. The major difficulty is in estimating probabilities, including those to be used in the Bayesian formulation.[10] The ultimate question is: can the survey provide information to produce a dollar gain in effectiveness of campaign spending to exceed the dollar cost of the survey? If survey research locates subgroups within the electorate, it can aid the decision maker to target expenditures. Thus, a dollar spent based on the survey research may have a higher value, e.g., $1.25 or $1.50 in purchasing power in terms of effectiveness, than the dollar spent without survey research.

In the simplified decision tree (Figure 8-2), the decision maker must either allocate $250,000 to a television spot campaign on social issues (e.g., crime, drugs, campus unrest, morality, etc.) or opt for present advertising plans. The campaign manager and strategists are certain that the present plans (for spots on other issues) will increase identification and issue orientation so that there is a net change of 500,000 votes (ΔV = 500,000) or a ratio of 2-to-1 in terms of

---

[b]Survey research cannot provide infallible information nor can it predict events, e.g., whether a state or nature or competitive strategy will occur; it can suggest, given proper interpretation, the effects or consequences on public opinion and voter preference of a state of nature or competitive strategy.

[c]The ratio of votes to expenditure for a given project or type of expenditure is not constant throughout the range of expenditure. The final $100,000 increment in television spending, for example, is unlikely to be as effective as the first $100,000, all factors held constant.

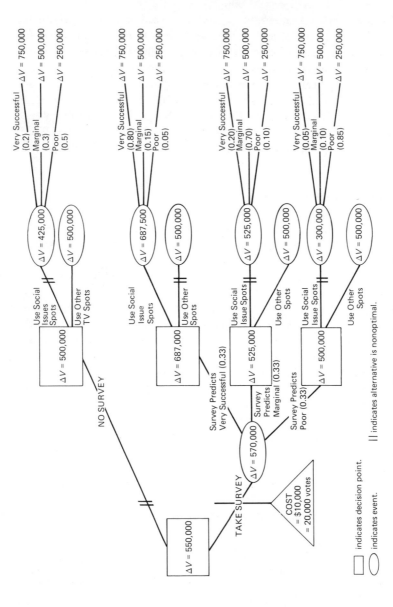

Figure 8-2. Decision Tree.

Note: Simplified example to decide whether to take a survey. If the survey predicts either very successful or marginal returns, he will go with the social issues spots (new advertising campaign); if it predicts poor results, he will use the other spots (present advertising campaign).

votes per dollar spent. (This ratio is used to measure the cost of the survey). Without the survey, the expected value of the $250,000 social issues spot advertising is a net change of 425,000 votes; hence without the survey the manager would stay with the original plans. Using Bayesian formulations, the decision tree suggests that the survey should be taken because its expected value of ΔV = 550,000 votes exceeds ΔV = 500,000 votes.

The survey predictions have a very high degree of accuracy; 0.70 is the lowest figure, for "marginal"—but there is a 0.20 chance that the results could be even better ("very successful"). With perfect information, the survey would not be needed. Moreover, if the survey predicts "poor" reactions to the social issue TV spot campaign, the decision maker realizes there is an 0.85 chance that the results will be "poor," so he will use the other TV spots. Nevertheless, he would still have to pay for the survey, so that the gain in votes would be 480,000, i.e., 500,000 votes less the 20,000 votes equated to the $10,000 cost of the survey.

In equating the $10,000 cost of the survey with 20,000 votes, it should be emphasized that this 2–1 ratio is only applicable at the margin. For example, "core" budgetary expenses, i.e., the basic budget below which the campaign cannot function, cannot be evaluated at that ratio. By definition, those expenses are essential and, presumably, without them there could be no management structure, viable capacity for fund raising, etc. and hence no TV spot campaign.

Obviously, this simple example does not reflect the fact that the TV spot campaign on social issues should not be pursued in a void. It must represent *part* of a campaign strategy in which the candidate would be pursuing the same issues in his speeches, news conferences, visuals, etc. Thus, the survey would provide information useful for those ventures, as well as other information useful to the campaign. Rarely is a survey commissioned to discern the answer to only one question or to provide counsel for only a single activity.

Bayesian statistics and decision trees need not be used formally. For example, when a press secretary considers holding a "visual," he must evaluate the issue and its timeliness, the logistics and mechanics of holding the event, time of day, location, etc. He implicitly estimates the probability that the news conference will be covered. Will the media turnout be poor, low, medium, good, or excellent? Standards must be defined, i.e., how many publications, television stations, radio stations, wire services, etc. must attend for the turnout to be a success? Which media outlets are more important than others? Given the turnout, what is the probability that coverage will be light, medium, or extensive? Given the coverage, what is the chance it will be unfavorable, neutral, favorable, or very favorable?

The press secretary who does a good job considers dozens or hundreds of ideas for news and feature stories, especially visuals. He accepts only a small number which, he feels, can generate substantial coverage, without undue risk of negative effects on the campaign. An "unstructured" situation can compromise the dignity of the candidate, it can cause media criticism of its transparent nature, and unanticipated events, such as picketing, confrontation, or logistic complications can occur. The press secretary considers the probability that unpleasant events might occur, and he weights the estimated cost (in votes) to the campaign by the probability of occurrence.

In forecasting for important decisions, the data used must be accurate, timely, applicable to the specific problems, and inexpensive to collect and to analyze, in terms of the problem. One possible forecasting method, the *Delphi* method, systematically pools expert opinions anonymously and then presents a composite of the predictions to everyone. In subsequent rounds each expert can modify his prediction.[11] Although the Delphi method was originally designed to forecast dates, it can be modified for volunteer chairmen to forecast voter turnout figures, support within particular ethnic groups, or the quantitative impact of certain projects.

Structure

How does the decision making relate to the structure? A simplified organizational chart for a statewide campaign (Figure 8–3) is designed for a staff of forty to seventy-five. Its core group of twenty-four would include: campaign manager/director and one secretary; tour director (or scheduling secretary) and two staff secretaries; press secretary (or news director) and an aide and two secretaries; research director and aide; finance director and two secretaries; special operations director and a secretary; an assistant campaign manager, secretary, and two field men; an office manager/headquarters volunteer coordinator and three staff (secretary/receptionist/telephone operator combination). At least twenty-four staff members would be required to mount a serious campaign in one of the top five states.

Full-time staff positions do not include volunteer advisory committees, outside consultants and fund raisers, volunteer leaders, or county chairmen. The critical elements are management; press; scheduling; finance. If funds can be raised by dependable volunteer chairmen, staff support can be minimized. Management is, of course, necessary to oversee the operation, and press and scheduling are the two primary means of giving the candidate access to the electorate. Paid advertising must be arranged; hopefully the level of advertising would be such that an outside agency would be used.

In this chart, the candidate is placed at the top, and the campaign manager and campaign director are placed below the campaign committee. In fact, the manager and his assistant managers oversee the activities of regional, county, and local chairmen. This hypothetical chart could be modified for a political campaign to centralize authority and decision making. For example, the news director or press secretary could have the research and speechwriting responsibilities within his division. The chart could also be modified for centralization

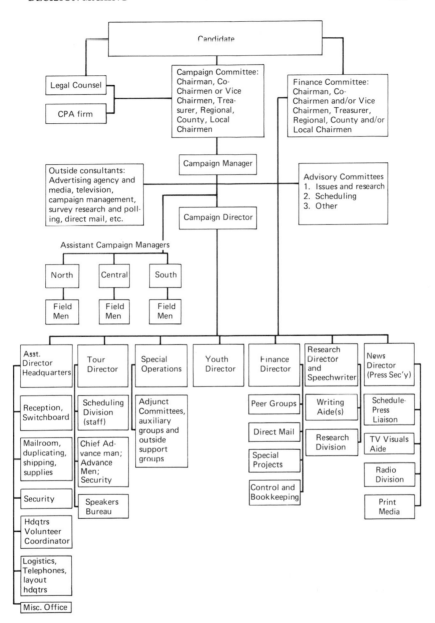

Figure 8–3. Statewide Campaign Organization Chart.

at a higher legel; e.g., the chief advance man could head the advance team, which
is separate from scheduling and which reports to an assistant campaign director,
in charge of scheduling, advance, and press.

This skeleton chart, if supplemented by a complete list, would include a
larger contingent of staff (secretaries, receptionists, aides, clerks) assigned to
each office or division of the campaign. The total number of personnel is the
number in parentheses: campaign manager (2); campaign director (3); tour
director (6)—not counting volunteer advance men; news director (7); research
director (3); youth director (2); finance director (5); special operations (3);
assistant director in charge of headquarters (11); assistant campaign managers
and field men (8). The total minimum staff required for a serious campaign for
Governor or Senator in either New York or California would be about 50, with
nearly all concentrated in a single headquarters.

What each of these individuals do is a function of the degree of differentiation in the campaign. Actual job descriptions can be found in the official manuals
published by political party organizations. The larger the campaign, the more
staff for two reasons: each job is broken down into components, and each component requires an individual, and the larger the campaign, the more components
into which an individual slot is broken down; second, more secretaries, mail
room personnel, receptionists/switchboard operators and other (support) personnel are required.

Fundamental strategic questions must be decided at the highest levels of the
campaign. These questions, and the decisions they produce, result in the daily
activities of the campaign staff. Sometimes, it is difficult to separate *strategic*
questions from *tactical* questions. In Tables 8-3 through 8-8, lists of considerations that are strategic or strategic/tactical indicate some of the strategic and
operating parameters that should govern decision making in the political campaign.

Strategy and Tactics

A brief summary of decision making guides to formulate strategy and to
implement strategy (tactics) follows Tables 8-3 through 8-8. The tables comprise a survey of tips, with minimal reference to "how to" questions of methodology. They are intended as a brief review for the candidate, campaign manager,
and campaign staff.

Models

Progressive spending, i.e., additional increments, in non-TV media permit
the campaign to reach a progressively higher percentage of the readership,
listenership, or billboard scanners. However, the aggregate figure is limited. Even

Table 8–3   Overview of Strategy and Tactics

1. Centralize decision making in matters affecting strategy.
2. Decentralize decision making as much as possible in matters affecting tactics.
3. Encourage the candidate to limit his contacts with the campaign staff regarding substantive matters, and encourage lower ranking staff members to go through the campaign manager or their superior when they wish to see the candidate.
4. There is no substitute for sound strategy, i.e., for a well-conceived, formal plan for winning the election; the plan should be in writing.
5. No amount of technical proficiency will supplant bad strategy.
6. There is no magic gimmick that will win the campaign, i.e., no slogan that will carry the election, no single brochure that will, in itself, convert the skeptical . . . .
7. Strategy, no matter how well conceived, requires an administrator to implement the plan; an administrator, no matter how competent, requires a strategy or plan to implement. Sometimes, a single person can be both strategist and administrator; other times, the campaign splits the functions (as discretely as possible).
8. Separate decision making into areas of judgment and areas of technical fulfillment; the former should require clearance, the latter should involve wide latitude and discretion.
9. The candidate and campaign should act, not react, if possible.
10. When reactions are required, the decision maker should react prudently and cautiously, yet quickly.
11. Decisiveness is required at the highest levels; losses must be cut.
12. Prudence is required at the highest levels; decisiveness means quick decisions, not hasty decisions.
13. If the plan was well-conceived, it should not be altered unless there is new evidence, new data, or unanticipated events that alter the situation.
14. The burden of proof is on advocates of altering the strategy or plan.
15. The plan should not be altered under pressure of supporters, financial contributors, volunteers or others, unless they have evidence and reason, not emotion, on their side. It should not be altered simply to accommodate their inevitable second-guessing.
16. The campaign manager and ranking subordinates should try to be calm and project calm; they should try to be dispassionate, yet decisive.
17. Avoid, if possible, negative statements; if the opponent must be criticized, endeavor to have the campaign manager or volunteer chairman generate the criticism.
18. Get on the offensive, stay on the offensive; if put on the defensive, get off the defensive; generally, don't reply to attacks and give them more coverage and credibility, unless reply is deemed essential; generally, don't mention other candidate's name.
19. Address the opponent's weaknesses, not his strengths.
20. Incumbent should use all the benefits of incumbency *and* as much as possible before election time; his credibility is diminished the closer he gets to election year.

---

100 percent penetration of this group, represented by the tiny circle (Figure 8-4), is only a small fraction of the television universe.

Yet, there is a great risk of understating the importance of alternative media. Non-TV media *are* essential, if one or more conditions obtain:

1. The finite limit of television time prevents any more buying, so funds have to be diverted.
2. Geography favors other media. For example, television produces too much wastage in reaching an area of the state (or, more obviously, in the case of a Congressional District in a big city).
3. The habits of voters do not favor television. For example, farmers may rely

Table 8–4
Strategy and Tactics: Issues

1. Concentrate on a very small number of issues; no more than five, and preferably three.
2. Discuss and be fluent on other issues that are important to people or may come up, but emphasize only a few.
3. Seek a unified theme, within which the issues are discussed.
4. Say the same things over and over again for the value of repetition; but say them in different contexts, settings, visual events, etc.
5. Seek to associate the candidate's name, face, and rhetoric with certain positions on several key issues.
6. Tie issues to current events in order to make them relevant to the electorate and to make them interesting to the news media.
7. Advertising should emphasize the same theme and issues as the candidate emphasizes in speeches, news events, visuals, and as the campaign is covered in the news media.
8. The issues chosen must be "voting issues," "cutting issues," or whatever one calls issues that *move* voters from the undecided to your column or from the opposition column to the undecided, or from the opposition column to your column.
9. It does not matter if an issue is important to a contributor, or to a county chairman or group of volunteers; these are important considerations, but the ultimate consideration is whether the issue is a voting or cutting issue.
10. Using issues is preferable to engaging in a personal campaign; a campaign perceived as personal in nature will be counterproductive.
11. Be credible, especially with the traveling press, and say the same or similar things in different areas; i.e., emphasize the same issues.
12. This does not mean that local issues cannot be added to a basic speech, or substituted for less important parts of a text; or visuals oriented toward local events; however, the basic issues should be of statewide (or national) importance, and hence universally applicable. The goal is to find local implications or examples for the primary issues.
13. Relate issues, therefore, to the schedule, in terms of which of the primary issues should receive more attention in given areas.
14. Do not underestimate the importance of research, in providing issues, providing ways of dramatizing issues, and providing the anecdotes, examples, statistics, etc. to drive points home to an audience or in a commercial.
15. There is an almost infinite permutation of issues, but only a few are capable of affecting the election; in addition, the candidate must not only emphasize these issues, he must have a position compatible with the position of those voters in the relevant subgroups; finally, it is vital that the candidate and the campaign communicate, through the most effective means and media, with the subgroups.
16. Changing the candidate's position on an issue indicates that insufficient planning and research influenced the early course of the campaign; this may be an unfortunate but wise course; however, repeated changes in position have the *cumulative* effect of severely affecting the candidate's credibility.
17. The candidate must project competence in being able to deal with the issues and problems he discusses.

on the radio for weather bulletins and information, and the radio may be the best way to reach them.

4. The message favors other media. For example, the print media is more conducive to detailed discussion of issues.

5. The project favors other media. For example, get-out-the-vote drives, or the distribution of sample ballots, may favor radio and newspapers, respectively.

6. It is important to reach individuals who either do not own a television set or are not regular viewers.

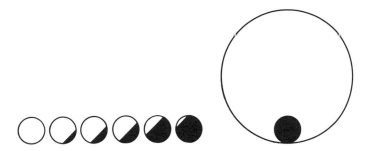

Figure 8-4. TV versus Non-TV Universe.
Note: Progressively more advertising in non-television media results in greater
and greater penetration of a small universe (shown by the progressive darkening
of the small circle). Relative to the large television universe (large circle), even
100 percent penetration of the non-TV universe (total darkening of the small
circle) is insignificant.

7. The strategy or momentum requires voters to be reached by a variety of
    media, for the benefit of repetition and reinforcement.
8. Other media are qualitatively superior. For example, print advertising may
    enable the campaign to reach a more limited, but select, group of voters,
    including those with a higher probability of turnout at the polls.
9. Other media are more issue oriented. For example, advertising on the issue
    of high food prices might be very helpful to the campaign if placed in the
    weekly food advertising section of the newspaper.
10. Response is desired. Print media, in particular, can provide application
    blanks, contribution forms, or other response material within the advertise-
    ment.

    As increased funds become available for the television budget, their deploy-
ment should follow a plan favoring substantially higher levels of spending near
the end. It is important to note that an advertising spending curve is one way to
generate momentum near the end. As funds become available they can never be
spent backward, i.e., time has passed; hence, the curve tilts upward from that
point on (Figure 8-5).
    Previously, we noted that when a state is broken down into media markets
by formula to determine advertising allocation, the breakdown should also apply
to scheduling (Table 8-9). This means a goal of a particular number of visits per
media market and a subgoal of a particular number of visuals per issue per media
market.
    Within campaign advertising there has been no scientific study to quantify
the value of different media; the relative importance of media varies from year
to year, state to state, candidate to candidate. Yet some attempt must be made
to measure, forecast, or at least roughly estimate the marginal impact of expenditures, especially in different media. The model (Table 8-10) is a hypothesis

Table 8–5
Strategy and Tactics: Media

1. Be positive in relating to the media, both in terms of attitude, and in terms of proposals.
2. Personal attacks on the opposition, helpful in generating media coverage, may be counterproductive with the electorate.
3. News media personnel prefer conflict situations and personal contests, but the campaign should not necessarily satisfy these wants.
4. Project confidence and assurance to the media; project competence to the media. What is projected to the media will greatly influence what the media projects about the candidate and campaign to its listeners, viewers, and readers.
5. The candidate and staff, campaign manager and staff, campaign staff members and volunteers, etc. should never argue in front of the media.
6. If possible, segregate the media into priorities; approach the highest priority media first, before the actual campaign or in its early stages.
7. The candidate should establish rapport with editors, editorial boards, publishers, syndicated columnists, veteran political reporters, etc.: these media personnel influence or control those who will cover day-to-day the candidate and campaign.
8. Use the time before the campaign formally begins to establish rapport with editorial boards and to meet privately with key media executives; time becomes more tightly scheduled during the campaign, and prevents too many meetings of this type.
9. Visuals should be the number one priority to generate news—i.e., news on television; a formula should be used to decide how many visuals are needed in which areas, and on which issues.
10. Visuals should be original, creative, daring, current, newsworthy, photogenic, exciting, but not demeaning to the candidate, or undignified.
11. The candidate should relate personally to the media, because their personal impressions of him will color their reporting.
12. Generally, newspaper endorsements are not very helpful; they can help in small communities, in which the newspaper is read more closely or is more influential; also, the endorsements, if exploited, may spur financial support, may spur news coverage as candidate is taken more seriously, may help momentum.
13. It should be a primary goal of the campaign to maximize the amount of free time and space by getting appearances on as many live shows, taped TV and radio programs; by getting newspaper interviews, etc.; no stone should be left unturned in the search for free media exposure.
14. Discriminate between media with large ratings and large circulation and media with relatively lower ratings and lower circulation; allocate time to media on the basis of how many people are reached *and* what kind of people.
15. The objective should be for the candidate and campaign to be so exciting that it is in the media's self-interest to cover the campaign; journalists should be fearful of missing a news conference or an event, because of competitive reasons, i.e., they are afraid of missing a good story.
16. The candidate should be fashionable, in vogue, i.e., the story to cover.
17. Frequency is important: this relates to scheduling; it is imperative that the candidate appear in certain media markets, i.e., be visible on television, at certain minimum intervals; maximum coverage is derived by not appearing someplace too many times in too short a time, and maximum visibility is achieved by scheduling the frequency of the appearance to consider the need for repetition and retention among viewers.
18. In short, it is the appearances *over time,* not just the absolute number, that influence the voter's perception of the candidate, his identification among the electorate, and their retention factor.
19. If advertising is negative, it should still be issue related; preferably, it should be in the print media, and not electronic (this rule, like others listed, is flexible).
20. Generally, the press should not be criticized or attacked; nor should a journalist's boss be told that his staff member is doing something wrong, unless the situation is intolerable.
21. Don't complain about lack of coverage unless it is indeed poor, the candidate and campaign are not the source of the quantitatively poor or qualitatively poor coverage, and a complaint will really do some good (and not harm).

Table 8-5 (continued)

22. It is very important, in terms of the perception of the media, to produce schedules of the candidate, regularly and on time, complete, accurate, detailed; this conveys an image of professionalism and competence, and of activity.
23. Each day, the campaign should have a report of the total media coverage generated that day—local, statewide, electronic and print media, tapings, columns, editorial board meetings, news conferences, etc.
24. The campaign should be able to define its own news stories each day by generating its own news "leads"—e.g., by varying speeches each day by adding dramatic disclosures, important announcements, etc.; by holding visuals, etc.

Table 8-6
Strategy and Tactics: Schedule

1. The schedule should be based on media-market scheduling.
2. The schedule should be based on satisfaction of multiple criteria.
3. The schedule must be media oriented.
4. Scheduling exists regardless of the level of advertising or the level of organization; what the candidate does is basic to the campaign.
5. Schedule to be in the areas of strength (and to address sympathetic groups) in order to boost morale, stimulate contributions, volunteer support, voter turnout, etc.; seek to make the demographic/election day forecasts self-fulfilling prophecies.
6. Schedule to reach the subgroups, which are also part of the demographic/election day forecasts.
7. Schedule a minimum of events to reach extremely low priority groups; e.g., some appearances may be necessary for image, although a certain group has only a 10 percent probability of voting for the candidate.
8. Minimize travel time in the schedule; schedule events so that the time in the air or in automobiles, etc. is absolutely minimized; utilize travel time in some way—for interviews, briefing and writing, staff meetings, etc., or, in some cases, for planned rest breaks.
9. Do not overschedule the candidate so early in the campaign as to jeopardize his physical or mental health; without him, the campaign cannot go on, or cannot be conducted very efficiently.
10. Don't overload the schedule with low priority or lower priority events that jeopardize the success of high priority or higher priority events, such as a television debate or the taping of television spot commercials; both of which require rest and preparation time.
11. Scheduling must reconcile many demands and meet many exhausting criteria, but press coverage, especially on television, is the single most important criterion in judging the effectiveness of the schedule.
12. Seek flexibility and open commitments and open invitations, rather than fixed commitments and closed invitations, i.e., seek events that let the campaign select the date and place, rather than a fixed date and fixed location that must be accepted or rejected.
13. If a suitable event in a suitable location does not exist for the campaign's needs, invent one.
14. Make the scheduling operation as automated as possible, with forms, files, form letters, automatic typewriters, etc., so that staff time can be devoted to overseeing the automated operation, making it as "personalized" as possible, and making critical decisions on whether events should or should not be accepted.
15. The schedule division should work for precise data, as far in advance of events as possible, to help the press division in releasing accurate, complete, and timely schedules for the media.
16. Public schedules should show time fully allocated.
17. Scheduling should go through one person at the top, who has the authority to add, modify or delete items from the schedule; he (the tour director) has a counterpart in the traveling campaign entourage.

Table 8-7
Strategy and Tactics: Momentum

1. Momentum is intangible, but its manifestations are clear (see listing and discussion in prior chapters).
2. Momentum can be affected by the campaign by providing for a graduated advertising budget, which provides a cushion for the campaign.
3. Events should be paced out, so that the campaign does not peak too soon.
4. Advertising should be paced out so that the campaign does not peak too soon.
5. Momentum can be affected by scheduling certain major events at particular times, especially weeks in advance, to give the campaign a rhythm and flow; or by influencing certain key events, e.g., when the television debate(s) will occur.
6. Momentum relates to orchestrating the campaign, timing, use of issues, utilization of visual events, generating news, level of advertising, etc. and the integration of all of these, as they relate to the overall level of campaign activity, especially as perceived by the electorate.
7. Momentum is also important because people want to back a winner.
8. Momentum is more likely to be achieved if the campaign's theme is unified and consistent, rather than confused and erratic.
9. Television advertising affects momentum by giving the candidate star-like quality and prominence, and by directly affecting crowd turnouts (especially by providing visual recognition and identification).
10. Television debates are watched by very few people; mainly, they are committed partisans; however, they can affect momentum, because the "lifts" are seen on the highly rated television news, and journalists report on the debates in the print media; moreover, the psychological effect of losing the debate can be felt in the opposition camp and will affect their campaign. A good showing in the debate will affect positively the campaign of the winner.

based on major campaigns in two similar states, California and New York. Its weights or factors represent the different properties of television, radio, and newspaper spending curves: generally the initial spending is the most effective. Under a variety of simplifying assumptions, e.g., newspapers or radio are not used for special purpose or targeted advertising, no funds should be spent on either newspaper or radio advertising until the campaign spends $350,000 for television or, more realistically, the former expenditures should assume planned television spending of $350,000. At this point, radio has the same *factor of effectiveness*.[d] The figures in Table 8-11 indicate the composition of aggregate media budgets of $350,000 or more. In this simplified example, the candidate will receive 49.55 percent of the vote with a media budget of $1,000,000 (Table 8-12).

An example of one of the simplifying assumptions, efficient media buying (Table 8-13), indicates that the television spot with the lowest cost per thousand viewers is not necessarily the cheapest.

---

[d]When the marginal returns from alternative media are equal, judgment must be made about the media mix. In this model, an increment may have to be divided, e.g., $50,000 TV increment divided into two $25,000 increments in order to compare to a $25,000 non-TV increment. The figures must be extrapolated, e.g., at $375,000 aggregate spending, the last $25,000 TV increment has a factor between 0.035 and 0.030.

Table 8-8
Strategy and Tactics: Marketing

1. It is the perspective of the electorate, especially target groups, that is important, not the perspective of the candidate or the die-hard supporter.
2. On making inroads into electorate support, the survey is much more likely to be right than wrong; if you disagree with the survey, you are probably wrong.
3. The first step in marketing is to find out the characteristics of the individuals who already support the candidate; then identify others who have the same (demographic) characteristics and go after them, or those who have similar characteristics, and go after them.
4. The undecided vote will always be higher in a telephone poll than in an in-person poll; the undecided vote will *usually* split along the same lines as the decided vote; e.g., 40-35-25 would, all things equal, translate into the following on election day, with the 25 allocated: 53.3-46.7.
5. The undecided will not split in the same proportion as the decided if more intensive surveying discerns how the undecided is leaning (and the leaning preference is different than indicated by the split among the decided); or, if massive new developments are expected, or if one candidate has the clear momentum and trend; the burden of proof is on those who suggest the undecided will split in a different proportion than the decided; e.g., will the voter turnout factor of the undecided be different than the decided, in terms of the way in which the undecided splits among the two candidates?
6. The candidate should have a sense of humor and display it, especially in speeches.
7. Speeches should be limited in length.
8. All speeches should be almost the same, adjusted for local color and humor, special emphasis of certain issues.
9. The exceptions are a few major speeches on special topics, e.g., foreign policy, the economy, etc.
10. Speeches should consume the absolute minimum of the candidate's time in preparation.
11. The candidate should rely on sparse notes or no notes in speechmaking; rarely, should he use a text (perhaps a few times during the campaign when delivering major speeches before special groups).
12. Show people that the candidate empathizes with their problems, understands their concerns, and is concerned about the same things.
13. Solutions to problems are not always necessary in campaign rhetoric; if mentioned, they should be simple, easy to understand; the position papers, task force studies, etc. are mainly for credibility and stature for the media.
14. The campaign should feature youth and young people, students—in responsible slots, but they should be the type of youths and students who would elicit favorable responses from adults.
15. The campaign should emphasize women, in management positions and key volunteer slots.
16. The campaign should be broad based, not just to appeal to minorities, but to appeal to the majority.
17. Don't take the base of support for granted; secure it, cultivate it, make sure its voters turn out at the polls.
18. Don't sacrifice the base by going after voters with questionable probability of supporting the candidate, or who do not number very many.
19. The candidate should project an image of decisiveness, but not rashness; firmness, but not inflexibility; honesty, but not gullibility; authority, but not authoritarianism; ability, but not superiority; bright, but not superior.
20. Multiple surveys with similar findings greatly increase the probability that the findings are correct.
21. Accept the results of the survey; don't fight it. Learn from the survey, profit from its information (including the public surveys).
22. Ideally, voters who are liberal should perceive the candidate as a liberal, voters who are moderate should perceive the candidate as a moderate, voters who are conservative should perceive the candidate as a conservative. In other words, under ideal marketing, each voter would see the candidate in his own image.

Table 8–8 (continued)

23. Establish an image of the opponent before he has a chance to establish his own image; then put him on the defensive throughout the campaign. This strategy is sometimes used in a very competitive situation, in which the opponent will win, unless he is shaken out of his noncombatant status.

24. Negative advertising is more likely to work if it reinforces an impression the voters *already* have of the opposition candidate; it may backfire if the voters do not have that impression.

25. Dramatic shifts in opinion *will* show up in surveys.

26. It takes years, often decades, for large demographic groups to shift party loyalty or opinion preference on major issues; sudden changes are possible, though improbable, but they are unlikely to be permanent.

27. In television advertising, prime time must be utilized; fringe, weekend, daytime may be used and may be appropriate for reaching certain types of viewers, but without prime time, there cannot be effective penetration; also, network affiliate stations must be utilized, the smaller stations cannot accomplish effective (i.e., mass) penetration of the market.

28. Advertising in non-TV media should have specific purposes, be designed to reach particular groups, etc.

29. Repetition applies to advertising, e.g., in television, repeat a small number of commercials over and over. ("Repetition is the mother of learning.")

30. In any advertising, seek to use issues relevant to a group, and relate the group's viewing, listening, or reading habits to the method and precise way chosen to reach them; e.g., in television advertising, run spots in or around shows that reach people interested in the issues featured in the spots.

31. A shabbily produced television spot with the right message is more important than a well-produced spot with the wrong or a less effective message; in other words, technical quality is very important, but not as important as the content (although there sometimes is a trade-off).

32. All print and electronic media should be monitored for coverage and advertising to produce data for marketing and re-targeting, in light of penetration of candidate in media, and effectiveness of opposition candidate.

33. Political programs, rather than spots, are wasteful; they drive away viewers to other programs, alienate viewers who are missing their favorite program, which has been pre-empted; most of the total small number watching the program are already committed.

34. Voter turnout is unlikely to have a major effect unless the election is close.

35. Don't push party unless it is an asset.

Present Value. The concept of present value of money presents an apparent paradox. If most of the campaign's budget is devoted to the latter part of the political campaign, why is "early" money worth more than "later" money? Here are the reasons:

1. Early money is needed to fund the campaign in its early stages and to build momentum. When a campaign has momentum, its expenditures seem to exert even more of an effect than if it does not have momentum. The *momentum effect* is so powerful that, in its absence, expenditures may have little effect. This is apparent when a campaign, despite its considerable expenditures near the end, makes no headway. It is too late; the valuable time that was lost cannot be made up.

Table 8–9
Media Market Scheduling

Media Market	Number of Visits Needed	Ideal Interval of Time between Successive Visits	Issue to Be Emphasized in Visual	Number of Times Visual Required for Issue
Syracuse-	5–Syracuse	10 days		
Utica	3–Utica	15 days		
Syracuse:			Crime	2
			Drugs	2
			Campus unrest	1
Utica:			Economy	1
			Crime	1
			Drugs	1
.				
.				
.				

Each media market is listed, broken down into locations, etc.

Note: The political data are utilized to formulate vote projections for election day, assuming victory. The political data is combined with the advertising data (media markets). Just as the media advertising budget is broken down by media markets, allocating funds in the same proportion in which the media market contributes votes to the candidate's statewide vote total, so scheduling is broken down the same way.

2. Sufficient funds are needed to pay cash-in-advance bills at the beginning and to purchase television time near the end. Even if funds do not have to be put up immediately for buying time at the end, such time will be lost if (a) the campaign reneges on any purchases at the beginning, because (b) the stations will demand that money be put up to hold the time near the end.

3. Because public consciousness is highest near the end of the campaign, many strategists tend to hold back some funds at the beginning, unless they have sufficient funding to cover all desired expenditures at the beginning and enough left over to put in a "trust fund" for subsequent deployment.

4. Television time is finite, and purchases missed because of lack of funds may be forever lost. (See number 2.)

5. Time is expendable, and the time lost in the beginning because of lack of funds may not be recoverable. (See number 1.) Time cannot be stored for future use.

6. Certain commitments are unlikely to be made without early money. For example, if efficiency dictates a payroll of sixty staff members, perhaps only twenty will be hired if the campaign manager is worried about subsequent layoffs.

7. Early money is needed for deposits, especially rent and the telephone company.

Table 8–10

Marginal Media Dollars—Model Based on U.S. Senate Campaigns in New York (1970) and California (1974)

Assumptions
1. The issues utilized in all advertising media are also utilized by the campaign in putting together news events and visuals.
2. The media buying in all media is done skillfully. If media buying were not skillful, the television results should be multiplied by 0.8 (i.e., a 0.2 diminution in buyer power); the newspapers by 0.95, and the radio by 0.9; skillful buying is important for all media, but most important for television.
3. Specially-targeted advertising, such as advertisements in ethnic newspapers or spot announcements on ethnic radio stations, are not considered.
4. Special circumstances are not considered, e.g., linking news coverage in a weekly newspaper or on a radio station with the purchase of space or time.
5. The base figure, i.e., the showing that the candidate will have on election day without any communication to the electorate, any campaign, or any advertising, is 25 percent in this example.
6. Since the advertising projections assume commensurate activity in generating news, e.g., using visual events, the level of advertising reflects an analogous level of news penetration.
7. When the *factor of effectiveness* is multiplied against the increment in media spending, the resulting figure is equivalent to a one percent (1%) change in voter preference for each $1,000.
8. No assumptions are made about content of advertisements or issues utilized. (Except that issues utilized in any media will be dictated by survey research and need to reach certain subgroups interested in particular issues.)

Television		Factor of Effectiveness	Radio	Factor of Effectiveness	Newspapers	Factor of Effectiveness
Increments			Increments		Increments	
$50,000		0.040	$25,000	0.030	$25,000	0.020
50,000	1	0.050	25,000	0.020	25,000	0.020
50,000		0.055	25,000	0.010	25,000	0.015
50,000	2	0.050	25,000	0.0025	25,000	0.010
50,000		0.045	25,000	0.0005	25,000	0.005
50,000	3	0.040				
50,000		0.035				
50,000	4	0.030				
50,000		0.020				
50,000	5	0.020				
50,000		0.010				
50,000	6	0.010				
50,000		0.0075				
50,000	7	0.0075				
50,000		0.0030				
50,000	8	0.0030				

Additional assumptions (about this state and campaign)
1. Increments of television reflect divergent influences: repetition helps get the message across, but repetition among some viewers is wasteful, and some viewers are being unnecessarily reached too many times; the factors of effectiveness reflect these divergent influences.
2. About $75,000 in radio provides heavy coverage; beyond $100,000, the audience is reached over and over again, with few new impressions.
3. About $50,000 provides for a good statewide advertising campaign in the major daily newspapers.

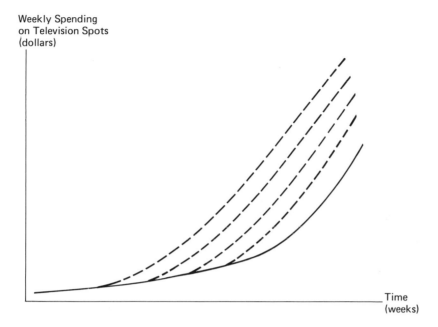

Figure 8–5. Incremental Additions to Weekly Television Budget.
Note: The graph shows progressive increments (dotted lines) to the basic
television budget. It illustrates the obvious fact that as additional funds become
available, they cannot be deployed retroactively. Thus, the dotted line farthest
to the right shows the change in the spending curve when funds become available very late in the campaign.

Table 8–11
Composition of Aggregate Media Budgets

Total	Television	Radio	Newspapers
350,000	350,000	0	0
375,000	375,000	0	0
400,000	375,000	25,000	0
450,000	400,000	25,000	25,000
500,000	425,000	50,000	25,000
600,000	500,000	50,000	50,000
750,000	600,000	75,000	75,000
1,000,000	800,000	75,000	125,000

Table 8–12
Effect of Media Spending on Voter Preference

For television, multiply each increment by the factor of effectiveness; for radio, multiply each increment by its factor of effectiveness; for newspapers, follow the same procedure.

TV	Radio	Newspapers
$ 2,000	$ 750	$ 500
2,500	500	500
2,750	250	375
2,500		250
2,250	$1,500	125
2,000		
1,750		$1,750
1,500		
1,000		
1,000		
500		
500		
375		
375	Radio Total $ 1,500	
150	Newspapers Total 1,750	
150	TV Total 21,300	
$21,300		

$24,550 = 24.55% (Assumption No. 7, Table 8–10)

24.55% gain in voter preference

25.00% base vote (due to party registration, preference, etc.; this is the figure regardless of *any* campaign activity)

Outcome 49.55%

Note: This effort to quantity the curve represented by $V = f(M)$, is based on the simplifying equations, $ID = f(M)$ and $i = f(M)$. The assumption is *competence,* i.e., higher levels of media advertising are accompanied by commensurate news/visual activity; space and time buying are efficient and skillful; issues utilized are priority concerns for the relevant subgroups; these same issues are utilized in both news/visuals and advertising. *Qualification:* If the campaign does not generate news activity to match its heavy advertising and on the same issues, its advertising has diminished credibility.

Table 8–13
Efficient Media Buying

The most competent media buyer can purchase time at the best available rates, in terms of per thousand readers or viewers reached. In the example below, which is the better buy?

	Viewers	Cost: 30-second spot	Cost per M
Television Show A	2,500,000	$2,500	$1.00
Television Show B	1,800,000	$2,000	$1.11

From the information shown, one cannot say which is the better buy, because it is not known what the *composition* is for the audience of each program. What are the demographic characteristics of each audience, relative to those desired for the marketing subgroups sought by the political campaign in question;

8.   Early money may be required to retain a campaign management firm, to pay
      for initial survey work, as an advance against future commissions for an
      advertising agency, etc. In short, early money is required to make commit-
      ments for the duration of the campaign.

      Even if the campaign manager knew for certain that funds would come in
the latter part of the campaign, he might be unable to borrow funds. In fact,
borrowing funds in a federal campaign is virtually illegal. For this reason, and for
some of the reasons mentioned above, *early* money is worth more than late
money. The simple fact of political life is that events must be set in motion, e.g.,
producing television spots, designing campaign materials, surveying the voters,
early enough in the effort so that there will be enough time to exploit the
opportunities. At the same time, "it takes money to make money," especially in
direct mail fund raising, with its heavy start-up costs.
      In sum, the upsurge in contributions near the end of the political campaign
is partially a function of momentum (exceptions include ideological campaigns,
like the Goldwater for President 1964 race). But the momentum cannot be
achieved without expenditures at the beginning. Hence, a dollar at the beginning
is worth $1.10 or $1.25 or $1.50 or more in later dollars, because each dollar
raised and spent at the beginning may result in an additional ten, twenty-five, or
fifty cents raised. These figures may be conservative: $100,000 at the beginning
may permit the campaign to fund a survey, fund all of its start-up expenses, pay
the payroll costs for several weeks, produce its creative material and television
spots, etc. Without all of these efforts, the campaign might not get underway,
and would be able to raise perhaps $500,000. With the $100,000, the campaign
might be able to generate enough momentum to raise an additional $750,000 or
more.
      The closer one gets to election day, the less time there is to plan rationally
the expenditure of incremental dollars. For example, $1,000,000 in contribu-
tions to a statewide campaign the day before election could not be effectively
spent. Two days before election, a small portion could be effectively spent. A
week before election, perhaps $200,000 could be effectively spent, and so forth.
      The short duration of the political campaign suggests that in many cam-
paigns each weekly period, during the September–October general election time
frame, should be regarded as a year, for the purposes of figuring a *discount rate*.
It is even possible to suggest a model in which the discount rate increases to a
higher rate near the end. For example, beginning at week 0, with eight weeks to
go, the value of one dollar ($1) might be one dollar ($1), i.e., the discount rate
is zero. However, look at the dramatic effect of changing both the time period
and the discount rate (Table 8–14).

      PERT.   Another reason for a higher present value of contributions is the
need for early planning, facilitated by cash on hand to finance present projects

Table 8–14

The Time Period and the Discount Rate. What is the present value of each one dollar ($1) in contributions given now, one week hence, two weeks hence, etc.?

	A Hypothetical Model		
	Discount Rate (%)	*"Years"*	*Present Value of $1*
Now (week 0)	0%	0	$1.000
One week hence	2	1	0.980
End of week 2	2	2	0.961
End of week 3	3	3	0.915
End of week 4	3	4	0.889
End of week 5	3	5	0.863
End of week 6	3	6	0.838
End of week 7	4	7	0.760
End of week 8	5	8	0.677

Table 8–15

PERT

Activity	*Immediate Predecessors*	*Estimated Time (days)*
A All materials for mailing written	. . .	2
B Typesetting is done	A	3
C Photographs taken, developed, laid out	A	4
D All materials printed, folded, inserted, ready	B, C	6
E Large envelopes and labels obtained	. . .	2
F Volunteers put labels on envelopes	E	8

In this project, a campaign mailing needs to be done. The campaign manager is willing to pay to have the envelopes stuffed by machine, but the labels for the mailing cannot be put on by machine, but by hand. Therefore, he decides to use the time available while the mailing materials are being prepared to have volunteers put the labels on the envelopes. The project of putting the labels on will consume eight days, because only twelve volunteers can be allocated to the project, each working a full day.

The critical path determines the minimum time needed for the completion of the project, i.e., having everything ready for the mailing to be stuffed by machine. Thus, there can be no delays in A, C or D; however, a one-day delay in B, typesetting, would *not* cause a delay in the 12 days (critical path).

Similarly, if it takes a little longer to obtain the large envelopes and the labels, or if it takes the volunteers a little longer than expected to put the labels on the envelopes, the project will not be delayed, unless the total delay for E and F is more than 2 days.

To reiterate, a delay in any activity on the critical path delays the entire project.

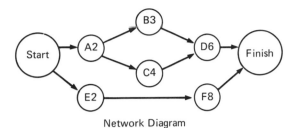

Network Diagram

Figure 8–6. PERT.

Note: A simple example illustrates the application of PERT to a campaign mailing. In a broad sense, the entire campaign is a massive application of PERT, with finish equivalent to election day.

and allow for future cash flow. Planning for projects is aided by PERT (Program Evaluation and Review Technique) to calculate the total amount of time required for a project, detail the sequencing requirements, and pinpoint the bottleneck activities.[12] The *critical* path is the path with the largest amount of time associated with it, e.g., the critical path ACD (12), in contrast to ABD (11) and EF (10) (Figure 8-6 and Table 8-15).

Further research will present additional opportunities for applying management and quantitative techniques to political campaign decision making. Queues, e.g., waiting for campaign materials, may be serviced by Poisson mathematical solutions. Problems relating to inventories of campaign materials may lead to a search for economic order quantities. Regression analysis used to construct models to predict the future value of a variable may help define the relationships between different types of expenditures and candidate identification or voter preference. Linear programming may prove an appropriate mathematical technique to allocate campaign resources, especially given aggregate or cash flow constraints. Simulation or game theory could gauge the relationship between two opposing campaigns.[13]

Data processing can help control the momentum effect by assisting the manager to orchestrate graduated advertising, more intensive scheduling, more visuals. In addition, a wide variety of other methods, including volunteer canvassing, telephone campaigns, mailings to voters, etc. can be choreographed to occur at the proper time. The objective is to assure a course of upward momentum as steep as possible without "running out of steam," i.e., without peaking too soon.

Progress has been made in evaluating voter response to advertisements to correlate response with survey research. If these figures provide enough data they can be sorted by county or media market to determine areas of weakness and strength.[e] These correlations can be quickly drawn using data processing, which is already being used for campaign accounting systems, mailing lists, labels and coding and for finance, including contributor research (e.g., last date of solicitation, response) as well as for up-to-the-minute cash balances.

The most prominent uses of data processing in campaigns are demographics/ survey research and direct mail solicitation. Computers make sophisticated research possible by permitting high speed cross-tabulations, as well as comparing past voting history with current trends. The direct mail field is dominated by computers, which oversee list maintenance, printouts, labels, special mailings, "carbon" mailings, targeted mailings to different groups, contributors of varying amounts, etc. Computers can also be used to analyze response by list, per capita contribution, number of contributors, response correlated to days following the mailing, etc. Ideally, computers could track the progress of individual voters to produce mailings or printouts for telephone banks or get-out-the-vote drives.

The emphasis on quantitative techniques in the final chapter should not obscure the other two essential areas: organization/structure and behavioral/ psychosocial. Only by understanding and applying management principles qualified by the all-important human element, can the aspiring political campaign manager truly hope to cope with the political environment.

---

[e]Arthur J. Finkelstein of DirAction Services, Inc. has evaluated responses to campaign newspaper advertising in terms of relating the cost of the advertisement in the daily newspaper to 3-day/6-day projections of response, number of responses, total amount and per capita responses, number of responses per 1,000 population, etc., then comparing various measurements to forecasted candidate strength in the given area in order to test the hypothesis of strength.

Notes

Chapter 1
Government, Politics and Political Campaigns

1. *The Random House Dictionary of the English Language,* unabridged ed. (New York: Random House, 1966).
2. David R. Hampton, Charles E. Summer, and Ross A. Webber, *Organizational Behavior and the Practice of Management,* rev. ed. (Glenview, Ill.: Scott, Foresman and Co., 1973), pp. 11–12.
3. For theoretical background, Ayn Rand, *For the New Intellectual* (New York: Signet Books, 1961); Ayn Rand, ed., *Capitalism: The Unknown Ideal* (New York: New American Library, 1967); Frank S. Meyer, ed., *What Is Conservatism?* (New York: Holt, Rinehart and Winston, 1964); Frank S. Meyer, *The Conservative Mainstream* (New Rochelle, N.Y.: Arlington House, 1969); Milton Friedman, *Capitalism and Freedom* (Chicago: University of Chicago Press, 1962).
4. For theoretical background, Robert LeFevre, *The Nature of Man And His Government* (Caldwell, Idaho: Caxton Printers, 1963); *This Bread Is Mine* (Milwaukee: American Liberty Press, 1960).
5. For theoretical background, David Friedman, *The Machinery of Freedom: Guide to Radical Capitalism* (New York: Harper & Row Publishers, 1974); Robert Nozick, *Anarchy, State, and Utopia* (New York: Basic Books, 1975); also see reviews of the Nozick book, especially Sheldon S. Wolin (*The New York Times Book Review,* May 11, 1975) and Christopher Lehmann-Haupt (*New York Times,* August 5, 1975).
6. Thomas Hobbes, *Leviathan or the Matter, Forme and Power of a Commonwealth, Ecclesiasticall and Civil,* edited by Michael Oakeshott, with an introduction by Richard S. Peters (New York: Collier Books, 1962).
7. J. Bronowski and Bruce Mazlish, *The Western Intellectual Tradition: From Leonardo to Hegel* (New York: Harper & Row Publishers, 1962), pp. 195–199, 203–215, 280–304.
8. For theoretical background: Frank S. Meyer, op. cit.; F.A. Hayek, *The Constitution of Liberty* (Chicago: University of Chicago Press, 1960); Ludwig von Mises, *Human Action: A Treatise on Economics,* rev. ed. (New Haven: Yale University Press, 1963).
9. Jacques Ellul, *Propaganda: The Formation of Men's Attitudes,* trans. Konrad Kellen and Jean Lerner, with an introduction by Konrad Kellen (New York: Alfred A. Knopf, 1971), p. 233.
10. Ibid., p. 234.

11. Robert A. Dahl, *Modern Political Analysis,* Foundations of Modern Political Science Series (Englewood Cliffs, N.J.: Prentice-Hall, 1963), pp. 1–2.

12. James MacGregor Burns, *The Deadlock of Democracy: Four-Party Politics in America,* with revisions (Englewood Cliffs, N.J.: Prentice-Hall, 1963), p. 27.

13. Ibid., pp. 32–33;

14. Ibid., pp. 33–35.

15. Theodore H. White, *The Making of the President 1964* (New York: Atheneum House, 1965; Pocket Books, 1965); *The Making of the President 1972* (New York: Atheneum Publishers, 1973).

16. Robert V. Remini, *The Election of Andrew Jackson,* Critical Periods of History Series (Philadelphia and New York: J.B. Lippincott Co., 1963), pp. 68, 84–85.

17. Horace Samuel Merrill, *Bourbon Leader: Grover Cleveland and the Democratic Party,* edited by Oscar Handlin (Boston: Little, Brown & Co., 1957), p. 17.

18. Paul W. Glad, *McKinley, Bryan and the People,* Critical Periods of History Series (Philadelphia and New York: J.B. Lippincott Co., 1964), pp. 15–16.

19. Ibid., pp. 20–29, 96–97.

20. Walt Anderson, *Campaigns: Cases in Political Conflict* (Pacific Palisades, Calif.: Goodyear Publishing Co., 1970), p. 95.

21. Ibid., pp. ix–x.

22. Theodore H. White, *The Making of the President 1960* (New York: Atheneum House, 1961; Pocket Books, 1961), pp. 335–336, 340.

23. Ibid., p. 346.

24. Anderson, *Campaigns,* p. 209.

25. Herbert M. Baus and William B. Ross, *Politics Battle Plan* (New York: The Macmillan Co., 1968), pp. 263–264.

26. See Jeb Stuart Magruder, *An American's Life: One Man's Road to Watergate* (New York: Atheneum Publishers; 1974).

27. White, *1960,* p. 107.

Chapter 2
The Political Environment

1. Warren G. Bennis, *Changing Organizations: Essays on the Development and Evolution of Human Organization* (New York: McGraw-Hill Book Company, 1966) argues the need for innovative organizations to cope with the changing environment.

2. Theodore H. White, *The Making of the President 1964* (New York: Atheneum House, 1965; Pocket Books, 1965), p. 96.

3. A controversial and humorous account of journalists covering the Presidential candidates is Timothy Crouse, *The Boys on the Bus: Riding With the Campaign Press Corps* (New York: Random House, 1972). The book illustrates the first lesson of political journalism: unfavorable coverage is more

often the result of a poor candidate or sloppy servicing of the press corps than of bias.

4. J. Bronowski and Bruce Mazlish, *The Western Intellectual Tradition: From Leonardo to Hegel* (New York: Harper & Row Publishers, 1962), p. 38.

5. H.S. Merrill, *Bourbon Leader: Cleveland and the Democratic Party,* edited by Oscar Handlin (Boston: Little Brown & Co., 1957), p. 60.

6. Ibid., pp. 103–104.

7. Muriel James and Dorothy Jongward, *Born to Win: Transactional Analysis With Gestalt Experiments* (Reading, Mass.: Addison-Wesley Publishing Co., 1971), p. 273.

8. George Orwell, "Politics and the English Language," from *Shooting an Elephant and Other Essays* by George Orwell; reproduced in Mark Schorer, Philip Durham, Everett L. Jones, *Harbrace College Reader,* 2nd ed. (New York/Burlingame: Harcourt, Brace & World, 1964), pp. 358–371.

9. Terry Catchpole, *How to Cope with COPE: The Political Operations of Organized Labor* (New Rochelle, N.Y.: Arlington House, 1968), p. 371.

10. Douglas Caddy, *The Hundred Million Dollar Payoff* (New Rochelle, N.Y.: Arlington House, 1974).

11. *Los Angeles Times,* April 24, 1975.

12. U.S. District Court, District of Columbia, Civil Action No. 75-0001: Complaint for Declaratory and Injunctive Relief.

13. *New York Times,* April 20, 1975.

14. Committee on Rules and Administration, U.S. Senate, *Federal Election Campaign Laws* (Washington, D.C.: U.S. Government Printing Office, Jan. 1975).

15. William E. Leuchtenburg, *Franklin D. Roosevelt and the New Deal 1932–1940,* Harper Torchbooks, The University Library (New York: Harper & Row, 1963), p. 1.

16. Ibid., p. 12.

17. James MacGregor Burns, *The Deadlock of Democracy: Four-Party Politics in America,* with revisions (Englewood Cliffs, N.J.: Prentice-Hall, 1963), pp. 11, 47–48.

18. Vincent P. de Santis, "The Republican Party Revisited, 1877–1897," in H. Wayne Morgan, ed., *The Gilded Age: A Reappraisal* (Syracuse, N.Y.: Syracuse University Press, 1963), p. 139.

19. Ibid., p. 101.

20. Robert K. Carr, Merver H. Bernstein, Walter F. Murphy, *American Democracy in Theory and Practice: National, State and Local Government,* 4th ed. (New York: Holt, Rinehart and Winston, 1963), pp. 155–156.

21. David S. Broder, *The Party's Over: The Failure of Politics in America* (New York: Harper & Row Publishers, 1972); David Broder, *Washington Post,* Feb. 12, 1975, July 27, 1975, August 24, 1975.

22. Figures are extrapolated from studies by Arthur J. Finkelstein, a consultant to Buckley in 1970 and Nixon in 1972. Reprinted with permission of Arthur J. Finkelstein and DirAction Services, Inc.

23. *Congressional Quarterly,* Oct. 26, 1974, p. 2965.

24. *New York Times,* Sept. 25, 1975.

25. William A. Rusher, *The Making of the New Majority Party* (New York: Sheed Ward, 1975).

26. *Los Angeles Times,* Nov. 10, 1974.

27. Ben J. Wattenberg, *The Real America: A Surprising Examination of the State of the Union,* with an introduction by Richard M. Scammon (Garden City, N.Y.: Doubleday & Co., 1974, pp. 288–290.

28. William Watts and Lloyd A. Free, *State of the Nation 1974* (Washington, D.C.: Potomac Associates, 1974), pp. 10–11, 14–15.

29. See, for example, Frank E. Armbruster, with contributions by Doris Yokelson, *The Forgotten Americans: A Survey of the Values, Beliefs and Concerns of the Majority* (New Rochelle, N.Y.: Arlington House, 1972).

30. John S. Saloma III and Frederick H. Sontag, *Parties: The Real Opportunity for Effective Citizen Politics,* with an introduction by James MacGregor Burns (New York: Alfred A. Knopf, 1972), pp. 248–249.

31. White, *The Making of the President 1972,* (New York: Atheneum Publishers, 1973), pp. 250–251.

32. Elmer E. Cornwell, Jr., "Role of the Press in Presidential Politics," in Richard W. Lee, ed., *Politics and the Press,* Contemporary Issues in Journalism Series (Washington, D.C.: Acropolis Books, 1970), p. 80.

Chapter 3
The Political Campaign Organization

1. Ernest Dale, *Management: Theory and Practice,* 3rd ed., McGraw-Hill Series in Management (New York: McGraw-Hill Book Company, 1973), pp. 4–6. Also see "Notes on the Theory of Organization," in Luther Gulick and Lyndall Urwick, eds., *Papers on the Science of Administration* (New York: Institute of Public Administration, 1937), p. 13.

2. See F. Clifton White, *Suite 3505: The Story of the Draft Goldwater Movement,* with William J. Gill (New Rochelle: Arlington House, 1967).

3. Dale, *Management,* p. 80.

4. White, *The Making of the President 1972,* (New York: Atheneum Publishers, 1973), pp. 72, 314–315.

5. See Mike Royko, *Boss: Richard J. Daley of Chicago* (New York: E.P. Dutton & Co., 1971).

6. Warren G. Bennis, *Changing Organizations: Essays on the Development and Evolution of Human Organization* (New York: McGraw-Hill Book Company, 1966), p. 53.

7. Ibid., pp. 52–54.

8. Dale, *Management,* pp. 147–154; Fremont E. Kast and James E. Rosenzweig, *Organization and Management: A Systems Approach,* 2nd ed. (New York: McGraw-Hill Book Company, 1974), pp. 58–59. Also see Henri Fayol, *General and Industrial Management,* trans. Constance Storrs (London: Sir Isaac Pitman & Sons, 1949).

9. Dale, *Management,* pp. 113–133, 144–145, 148–149, 173–174, 212–213;

Kast and Rosenzweig, *Systems,* pp. 54–57. Also see Frederick W. Taylor, *Scientific Man* (New York: Harper & Row Publishers, 1947).

10. Dale, *Management,* pp. 111–112, 135–145. Also see Elton Mayo, *The Social Problems of an Industrial Civilization* (Boston: Graduate School of Business Administration, Harvard University, 1945).

11. Dale, *Management,* pp. 153–160, 198–199, 511–512; Kast and Rosenzweig, *Systems,* pp. 30–31, 62–65. Also see Max Weber, *The Protestant Ethic and the Spirit of Capitalism,* trans. Talcott Parsons (New York: Charles Scribner's Sons, 1958); also, A.M. Henderson and Talcott Henderson, trans., *The Theory of Social and Economic Organization* (New York: The Free Press of Glencoe, N.Y., 1964).

12. Robert K. Presthus, *The Organizational Society: An Analysis and a Theory,* A Caravelle, ed. (New York: Random House, Vintage Books, 1962), pp. 29–30.

13. Dale, *Management,* pp. 176–179; Kast and Rosenzweig, *Systems,* pp. 83–84. Also see Chester Barnard, *The Functions of the Executive* (Cambridge, Mass.: Harvard University Press, 1938).

14. Barnard, *Executive,* pp. 163–164.

15. Dale, *Management,* p. 6; Kast and Rosenzweig, *Systems,* pp. 6–7. Also see Peter F. Drucker, *The Practice of Management* (New York: Harper & Row Publishers, 1954).

16. Dale, *Management,* pp. 174–176, 185–186; Kast and Rosenzweig, *Systems,* pp. 88–89, 162–164. Also see Herbert A. Simon, *Administrative Behavior,* 2nd ed. (New York: The Macmillan Company, 1959).

17. Paul R. Lawrence and Jay W. Lorsch, *Organization and Environment: Managing Differentiation and Integration,* with research assistance of James S. Garrison (Homewood, Ill.: Richard D. Irwin, 1969), p. 8.

18. Ibid., p. 9.

19. Ibid., p. 11.

Chapter 4
The Political Campaign System

1. Fremont E. Kast and James E. Rosenzwieg, *Organization and Management; A Systems Approach,* 2nd ed. (New York: McGraw-Hill Book Company, 1974), pp. 77, 106–109.

2. Paul R. Lawrence and Jay W. Lorsch, *Organization and Environment: Managing Differentiation and Integration,* with research assistance of James S. Garrison (Homewood, Ill.: Richard D. Irwin, 1969), p. 8.

3. Fremont E. Kast and James E. Rosenzweig, *Contingency Views of Organization and Management* (Chicago: Science Research Associates, 1973), pp. 40–41.

4. Kast and Rosenzweig, *Systems,* p. 20; *Contingency Views,* p. 13.

5. Kast and Rosenzweig, *Systems,* p. 169.

6. Lawrence and Lorsch, *Organization and Environment,* p. 6.

7. Kast and Rosenzweig, *Systems,* p. 164.

8. Tom Burns and G.M. Stalker, *The Management of Innovation* (Tavistock Publications, 1961) reproduced as "Mechanistic and Organic Systems," in Kast and Rosenzweig, *Contingency Views,* pp. 74–75.

9. Peter F. Drucker, *The Practice of Management* (New York: Harper & Row Publishers, 1954), p. 63.

10. Kast and Rosenzweig, *Systems,* p. 173.

11. Paul W. Glad, *McKinley, Bryan and the People,* Critical Periods of History Series (Philadelphia and New York: J.B. Lippincott Co., 1964), pp. 97–98.

12. Robert V. Remini, *The Election of Jackson,* Critical Periods of History Series (Philadelphia and New York: J.B. Lippincott Co., 1963), pp. 87–89.

13. Theodore H. White, *The Making of the President 1972,* (New York: Atheneum Publishers, 1973), p. 320.

14. Howard M. Vollmer and Donald L. Mills, ed., *Professionalization* (Englewood Cliffs, N.J.: Prentice-Hall, 1966), p. 2.

15. Ernest Dale, *Management: Theory and Practice,* 3rd ed., McGraw-Hill Series in Management (New York: McGraw-Hill Book Company, 1973), p. 274.

16. Ibid., pp. 348–349.

17. Ibid., p. 245.

18. Dale, *Management,* pp. 413–420; Kast and Rosenzweig, *Systems,* pp. 341–349.

19. Kast and Rosenzweig, *Systems,* pp. 155–156.

20. Kast and Rosenzweig, *Systems,* pp. 346–347. Also see Robert Tannenbaum and Warren H. Schmidt, "How to Choose a Leadership Pattern," *Harvard Business Review,* March–April 1958, p. 96.

21. Dale, *Management,* pp. 427–428, 435–436; Kast and Rosenzweig, *Systems,* pp. 258, 260–261; David R. Hampton, Charles E. Summer, and Ross A. Webber, *Organizational Behavior and the Practice of Management,* rev. ed. (Glenview, Ill.: Scott, Foresman and Co., 1973), pp. 173–178, from Douglas McGregor, *The Human Side of Enterprise* (New York: McGraw-Hill Book Company, 1960), pp. 33–48; or see condensation, "The Human Side of Enterprise," *Management Review,* Nov., 1957, pp. 26–27.

22. Dale, *Management,* pp. 430–431; Kast and Rosenzweig, *Systems,* pp. 257–258. Also see A.H. Maslow, *Motivation and Personality* (New York: Harper & Row Publishers, 1964); A.H. Maslow, *Toward a Psychology of Being* (New York: D. Van Nostrand Co., 1962). Also see: Frank G. Goble, *The Third Force: The Psychology of Abraham Maslow—The Science of Self-Actualization* (New York: Pocket Books, 1971).

23. Dale, *Management,* pp. 428–429; Kast and Rosenzweig, *Systems,* pp. 323–324. Also see Robert R. Blake, Jane S. Mouton, Louis B. Barnes, and Larry E. Greiner, "Breakthrough in Organization Development," *Harvard Business Review,* Nov.–Dec., 1964, pp. 133–155.

24. Dale, *Management,* p. 431; Kast and Rosenzweig, *Systems,* pp. 262–264. Also see Frederick Herzberg, B. Mausner, and B. Snyderman, *The Motivation to Work* (New York: John Wiley and Sons, 1959); Frederick Herzberg, *Work and the Nature of Man* (Cleveland: The World Publishing Company, 1966).

25. Dale, *Management,* pp. 183–184, 429–430; Kast and Rosenzweig, *Systems,* pp. 261–262. Also see Rensis Likert, *The Human Organization* (New York: McGraw-Hill Book Company, 1967) and *New Patterns of Management* (New York: McGraw-Hill Book Company, 1961).
26. White, *1972,* pp. 97, 122.

Chapter 5
The Psychosocial Subsystem

1. Fremont E. Kast and James E. Rosenzweig, *Contingency Views of Organization and Management* (Chicago: Science Research Associates, 1973), pp. 14–15.
2. Muriel James and Dorothy Jongward, *Born to Win: Transactional Analysis with Gestalt Experiments* (Reading, Mass.: Addison-Wesley Publishing Co., 1971), pp. 1–3.
3. See, for example, Eric Berne, *Games People Play* (New York: Grove Press, 1974).
4. James and Jongward, *Born to Win,* pp. 101–102, 224–226.
5. Ibid.
6. John Powell, S.J., *Why Am I Afraid To Tell You Who I Am?* (Niles, Ill.: Argus Communications, 1969), pp. 116–117.
7. Report of a Special Task Force to the Secretary of the Department of Health, Education and Welfare, *Work in America,* with a foreword by Elliot L. Richardson (Cambridge: The MIT Press, 1973), p. 6.
8. Ibid., pp. 12–13.
9. Ibid., pp. 94–96.
10. David C. McClelland, "The Two Faces of Power," *Journal of International Affairs,* Vol. 24, No. 1 (1970), reproduced in Hampton, Summer, and Webber, *Organizational Behavior* (pp. 25–38), p. 26.
11. David R. Hampton, Charles E. Summer, and Ross A. Webber, *Organizational Behavior and the Practice of Management,* rev. ed. (Glenview, Ill.: Scott, Foresman and Co., 1973), p. 19. For a detailed, mathematical exposition of expectancy theory, see Mahmoud A. Wabba, Robert J. House, "Expectancy Theory in Work and Motivation: Some Logical and Methodological Issues," *Human Relations,* Vol. 27, No. 2, pp. 121–147.
12. Alvin F. Zander, "Team Spirit Vs. The Individual Achiever," *Psychology Today,* Nov., 1974.
13. Frederick Teague, "Managers Want An Early Payoff," *Business Week,* May 4, 1974.
14. G.H. Litwin and R.A. Stringer, *Motivation and Organization Climate* (Cambridge: Harvard University Press, 1967), quoted in David C. McClelland, "Money as a Motivator: Some Research Insights," *The McKinsey Quarterly,* Fall, 1967, reproduced in Hampton, Summer, and Webber, *Organizational Behavior,* p. 645.
15. David C. McClelland, "Money as a Motivator: Some Research Insights," *The*

McKinsey Quarterly, Fall, 1967, reproduced in Hampton, Summer, and Webber, *Organizational Behavior,* pp. 642–643.

16. A.H. Maslow, "A Theory of Human Motivation," *Psychological Review,* July, 1943 (Vol. 50, No. 4), pp. 370–396.

17. Robert A. Sutermeister, "Employee Performance and Employee Need Satisfaction: Which Comes First?" *California Management Review,* Vol. 13, No. 4 (1971), reproduced in Hampton, Summer, and Webber, *Organizational Behavior* (pp. 197–205), pp. 202–204.

18. Hampton, Summer and Webber, *Organizational Behavior,* p. 143.

19. Ibid., p. 153.

20. J.R.P. French and B.H. Raven, "The Bases of Social Power," *Studies in Social Power,* D. Cartwright, ed. (Ann Arbor: University of Michigan Press, 1959), quoted in Hampton, Summer and Webber, *Organizational Behavior,* p. 154.

21. Robert Tannenbaum and Warren H. Schmidt, "How to Choose a Leadership Pattern," *Harvard Business Review,* March–April, 1958, reproduced in Hampton, Summer, and Webber, *Organizational Behavior,* pp. 625–626.

22. William W. Detillback and Philip Kraft, "Organization Change Through Job Enrichment," *Training and Development Journal,* August, 1971, pp. 2–6.

23. Victor A. Thompson, *Modern Organization* (New York: Alfred A. Knopf, 1961); reproduced as "Bureaucracy and Bureaupathology (pp. 404–415) in Hampton, Summer, and Webber, *Organizational Behavior,* pp. 407, 409.

24. Hampton, Summer, and Webber, *Organizational Behavior,* pp. 520, 523. The study was done by J.P. Campbell, M.D. Dunnette, E.E. Lawler III, and K.E. Weick, Jr., *Managerial Behavior, Performance, and Effectiveness* (New York: McGraw-Hill Book Company, 1970).

25. Lawrence Schaffer and Edward Schoben, Jr., *Psychology of Adjustment* (Boston: Houghton Mifflin Co., 1956), pp. 585–590.

26. Hampton, Summer, and Webber, *Organizational Behavior,* p. 672.

27. Warren H. Schmidt, "Conflict: A Powerful Process for (Good or Bad) Change," *Management Review,* Dec., 1974.

28. Ibid.

Chapter 6
Political Campaign Finance

1. Herbert M. Baus and William B. Ross, *Politics Battle Plan* (New York: The Macmillan Co., 1968), p. 73.

2. Ibid., p. 273.

3. J. Fred Weston and Eugene F. Brigham, *Managerial Finance,* 4th ed. (Hinsdale, Ill.: The Dryden Press, 1972), p. 86.

4. G.H. Hofstede, "The Game of Budget Control: Practical Recommendations," in David R. Hampton, Charles E. Summer, and Ross A. Webber, *Organizational Behavior and the Practice of Management,* rev. ed., (Glenview, Ill.: Scott, Foresman and Co., 1973), pp. 558–564.

5. Weston and Brigham, *Managerial Finance,* p. 92.

6. R.M. Cyert and J.G. March, *The Behavioral Theory of the Firm* (Englewood Cliffs, N.J.: Prentice-Hall, 1963), pp. 126–127, quoted in Michael Schiff and Arie Y. Lewin, "The Impact of People on Budgets" (*Accounting Review,* Vol. 45, No. 2, April, 1970); reproduced in William Thomas, ed., *Readings in Cost Accounting, Budgeting and Control,* 4th ed. (Cincinnati: South-western Publishing Co., 1973), pp. 116–129.

7. Theodore H. White, *The Making of the President 1972,* (New York: Atheneum Publishers, 1973), p. 296.

8. Arthur Andersen and Co., *Financial Management Systems for Political Campaigns* (New York: Arthur Andersen & Co., 1972), p. 19.

9. Arthur Andersen and Co., *Audit Criteria for Federal Political Campaigns* (Chicago: Arthur Andersen & Co., 1974), p. 1.

10. Robert N. Anthony, "Characteristics of Management Control Systems," in William Thomas, ed., *Readings in Cost Accounting,* pp. 28–30. From Robert N. Anthony, *Management Control Systems* (Homewood, Ill.: Richard D. Irwin, 1965).

11. Howard Clark Greer, "Cost Factors in Price Making," (pp. 201–223 in Thomas, ed., *Readings in Cost Accounting,* p. 211. From Howard Clark Greer, "Cost Factors in Price Making," (*Harvard Business Review,* July–August, 1952).

Chapter 7
The Marketing Function

1. Walter D. Wentz and Gerald I. Eyrich, *Marketing: Theory and Application* (Harcourt, Brace & World, 1970), pp. 217–219.

2. *Wall Street Journal,* June 2, 1975.

3. *Los Angeles Times,* May 30, 1975.

4. *New York Times,* May 25, 1975.

5. George Gallup, Jr., "The Influence of Polling on Politics and the Press," essay in Richard W. Lee, ed., *Politics and the Press,* Contemporary Issues in Journalism Series (Washington, D.C.: Acropolis Books, 1970), p. 133.

6. Ibid., p. 140.

7. F. Thomas Juster, *Consumer Buying Intentions and Purchase Probability,* Occasional Paper No. 99, National Bureau of Economic Research (New York: Columbia University Press, 1966) quoted in Roger K. Chisholm and Gilbert R. Whitaker, Jr., *Forecasting Methods* (Homewood, Ill.: Richard D. Irwin, 1971), p. 36.

8. Wentz and Eyrich, *Marketing,* pp. 297–320 explains the five primary vari-ables.

9. Ibid., p. 320; from Ralph S. Alexander and the Committee on Definitions of the American Marketing Association, *Marketing Definitions* (Chicago: American Marketing Association, 1960), p. 18.

10. Theodore H. White, *The Making of the President 1972* (New York: Ahteneum Publishers, 1973), pp. 184–186.

11. Robert T. Bower, *Television and the Public* (New York: Holt, Rinehart and

Winston, 1973), p. 4; "A Look At Television" (*Nielsen Newscast,* Number
3, 1974), Media Research Division, A.C. Nielsen Co., Northbrook, Ill.

12. Rick Neustadt and Richard Paisner, "How To Run on TV," *New York
Times Magazine,* Dec. 15, 1974. Portions of the article are outdated by
changes in television news.

13. Theodore H. White, *The Making of the President 1964* (New York:
Atheneum Publishers, 1965; Pocket Books, 1965), pp. 383–384, 397.

14. Jacques Ellul, *Propaganda: The Formation of Men's Attitudes,* trans. Kon-
rad Kellen and Jean Lerner, with an introduction by Konrad Kellen (New
York: Alfred A. Knopf, 1971), pp. 60–61; John S. Wright and Daniel S.
Warner, *Advertising,* 2nd ed., with a foreword by Norman H. Strouse and
chapter headpieces by Irwin Caplan (New York: McGraw-Hill Book
Company, 1966), pp. 60–61.

15. Wright and Warner, *Advertising,* p. 67.

16. Ibid., pp. 411–412, 434. See also, *How To Create Advertising That Sells,* a
booklet prepared by Ogilvy and Mather, a major advertising agency.

Chapter 8
Decision Making

1. Kurt and Gladys Lang, "Television Distortion in Political Reporting," in
Richard W. Lee, ed., *Politics and the Press,* Contemporary Issues in Journalism Series (Washington, D.C.: Acropolis Books, 1970), pp. 159–160.

2. Ernest Dale, *Management: Theory and Practice,* 3rd ed., McGraw-Hill Series
in Management (New York: McGraw-Hill Book Company, 1973), pp. 552–
553.

3. Edwin H. Caplan, "Behavioral Assumptions of Management Accounting"
(*The Accounting Review,* Vol. 41, No. 3, July 1966) reprinted (pp. 76–96)
in William E. Thomas, ed., *Readings in Cost Accounting, Budgeting, and
Control,* 4th ed. (Cincinnati: South-Western Publishing Co., 1973), p. 76.

4. David W. Miller and Martin K. Starr, *The Structure of Human Decisions*
(Englewood Cliffs, N.J.: Prentice-Hall, 1967), pp. 26–27.

5. J. Fred Weston and Eugene F. Brigham, *Managerial Finance,* 4th ed. (Hinsdale, Ill.: The Dryden Press, 1972), p. 189.

6. Miller and Starr, *Human Decisions,* pp. 49–50.

7. Ibid., pp. 48–49.

8. Wentz and Eyrich, *Marketing,* p. 119.

9. Harold Bierman, Jr., Charles P. Bonini, and Warren H. Hausman, *Quantitative Analysis for Business Decisions,* 4th ed. (Homewood, Ill: Richard D.
Irwin, 1973), p. 7.

10. Wentz and Eyrich, *Marketing,* p. 480.

11. Dale, *Management,* pp. 312–314.

12. Bierman, Bonini, Hausman, *Quantitative Analysis,* pp. 398–399.

13. For a summary of these mathematical techniques and explanatory models, see Bierman, Bonini, and Hausman, *Quantitative Analysis,* pp. 199–200, 337, 359–363, 380–381; also J. Fred Weston and Eugene F. Brigham, *Managerial Finance,* 4th ed. (Hinsdale, Ill.: The Dryden Press, 1972), p. 548; Roger K. Chisholm and Gilbert R. Whitaker, Jr., *Forecasting Methods* (Homewood, Ill.: Richard D. Irwin, 1971), pp. 97–98.

Index

Achievement, need for, 117–118
Activist (joiner), 43, 172, 201–202, 211
Advance men or team, 12–13, 213–214, 216–217
Advertising, 13–14, 21–22, 80t; budgeting, 231; for candidate as product, 194–196; decision points in, 75–76; versus free media, 60–61, 219; print versus electronic, 44, 266–267; rule of proportionality in, 244–246; strategic, 227, 229; targeting, 230–231; television, 11, 157–158, 231–237, 266–267; volunteers in, 58n. *See also* Budgeting of campaign; Media; Media market budgeting; Strategy
Advertising agency, 125, 229–230
Affiliation, need for, 117. *See also* Needs, individual
Authority, 72–74; Barnard's view of, 73–74; charismatic, 72, 102; competence, based on, 97; Fayol's view of, 65; of leadership, 73; Mayo's view of, 72; of organization chart, 97–98; of position, 73; rational-legal, 72; and responsibility, 65; Simon's view of, 77; and social interaction, 72; versus specialists, 73; unity of, 65; upward versus downward, 73–74, 93f Weber's view of, 72. *See also* Structure, campaign

Bankers Trust case, 124, 125
Banquets, 207, 210t, 211
Barnard, Chester, 73–74, 85
Baus, Herbert M., 131
Bayes decision rule, 142t, 246–251, 253
Behavior, individual, and structural subsystem, 125–126. *See also* Motivation; Psychosocial subsystem
Behavior, individual, and technical subsystem, 122–125; autonomous work groups, 123–125; Bankers Trust case, 124–125; job enrichment, 123; job rotation, 122–123; plan-do-control, 123; work simplification, 123. *See also* Motivation; Psychosocial subsystem
Blake, Robert R., 106
Brock, Bill, 132
Broder, David, 36

Brown, Edmund G., 11
Brown, Edmund G., Jr. (Jerry), 175n
Brown, Wilfred, 63–64
Buckley, James L. (campaign), 27, 36, 39, 50, 232–236
Budgeting of campaign, 150–157; behavioral implications of, 155; cash, 153; core, 152; defined, 150–151; examples of, 159t; as forecasting, 51; functional, 151–152; geographical, 152; media, 153–154, 244–246, 266–268; momentum, effect on, 155–157; probabilistic, 153, project, 152; ratio or formula, 153–154, 266–267; revenue-based, 139–140, 153; rule of proportionality, using, 244–246, 251; show, 153; standards of, 154–155; time-flow, 153–154; zero-based, 151. *See also* Control of campaign; Finance, campaign; Fund raising
Burns, James MacGregor, 35
Business and businessmen, compared to campaign, 17, 64, 91–93

Caddell, Pat, 38n
Caddy, Douglas, 19n, 26
Campaign. *See* Political campaign (organization)
Campaign director, 62–63
Campaign manager, 2, 9–10, 62–63; businessman as, 91–93; versus campaign director, 62–63; candidate, limited by, 59; versus consultants, 61; controlling, 54–55; in direct mail, 205–206; directing, 53–54; environment, understanding, 21–22; ethics of, 24–25; factors, legal, understanding of, 31–32; factors, macro-, understanding of, 32–34; factors, macro-political, understanding of, 32–34; forecasting, 40–41, 51, 141–143, 148–150, 254; games and roles, coping with, 114–116; innovating, 55–56; interpersonal communication of, 113–116; limitations of, 56–57; in marketing, 171–172, 179–181; motivating, 52, 53; need for power, 117–118; objectives, outlining, 49–50; organizing, 51–52; performance analysis of, 84; representing, 56–58; requirements,

285

About the Author

Arnold Steinberg has been active in politics, public affairs and journalism since 1963 when he first became interested in volunteer politics. He has been active as a volunteer, staff member and consultant in organizational politics and political campaigns throughout the nation. Once described by the *Los Angeles Times* as a political press relations "wunderkind," Mr. Steinberg has conducted seminars in media, press relations, advertising, scheduling, advance work, demographics and survey research, and overall campaign management. He has served on the board of several foundations, and his articles have appeared in a variety of publications, including *The Alternative, Dialogue* (U.S. Information Agency international magazine), *Human Events, Indianapolis News, Insight and Outlook, National Review, The New Guard, Santa Ana Register, Twin Circle* and the *UCLA Daily Bruin.* He has also contributed articles to the *Los Angeles Herald Examiner, Newsweek* and the *Washington Post.* A former political aide to Sen. James L. Buckley (Cons.-R., N.Y.), 1971–1973, Mr. Steinberg attended U.C.L.A. before receiving the B.A. in public affairs and economics from The George Washington University (Washington, D.C.) and the Master's in Business Administration (M.B.A.) from Pepperdine University (Malibu, Calif.).

Related Lexington Books

Alexander, Herbert E., *Financing the 1968 Election,* 376 pp., 1971
Alexander, Herbert E., *Financing the 1972 Election,* In Press
Hershey, Marjorie Randon, *The Making of Campaign Strategy,* 192 pp., 1974
Steinberg, Arnold, *Political Campaign Handbook: Media, Scheduling and Advance.* In Press